Cases in
Financial
Management

Cases in Financial Management

Second Edition

Joseph Sulock
University of North Carolina

John Dunkelberg
Wake Forest University

John Wiley & Sons, Inc.

New York • Chichester • Brisbane • Toronto • Singapore • Weinheim

ACQUISITIONS EDITOR   Whitney Blake
MARKETING MANAGER   Wendy Goldner
PRODUCTION EDITOR   Melanie Henick
DESIGNER   Harry Nolan
ASSISTANT MANUFACTURING MANAGER   Mark Cirillo

This book was set in 10/12 ITC Palatino by Carlisle Communications, Ltd. and printed and bound by Donnelley/Crawfordsville. The cover was printed by Lehigh Press Colortronics.

Recognizing the importance of preserving what has been written, it is a policy of John Wiley & Sons, Inc. to have books of enduring value published in the United States printed on acid-free paper, and we exert our best efforts to that end.

Library of Congress Cataloging in Publication Data:
Sulock, Joseph Michael.
Cases in financial management / Joseph Sulock, John Dunkelberg. -- 2nd ed.

p.   cm.
Includes bibliographical references.
1. Corporations--Finance--Case studies.   2. Business enterprises--Finance--Case studies.
I. Dunkelberg, John S.   II. Title.

658.15   dc20   96-29420
ISBN 0-471-11043-4 (pbk.; alk. paper)

Printed in the United States of America

10 9 8 7 6 5 4 3 2 1

PREFACE

This book contains fifty-seven cases divided among ten parts and was written with three criteria in mind. First, we wanted situations based on real firms, real products, real individuals and—most of all—real issues. Second, we wanted the cases to require the thoughtful application of financial concepts. Finally, we felt the cases should incorporate some of the complexities that are characteristic of real-life problems. Therefore, in order to develop reasonable solutions, students must first be able to apply financial theory. But they also must be sensitive to "real-world complications" surrounding the problems, such as any qualitative issues and the reliability of the information they are analyzing.

Case studies, therefore, provide an essential link between the classroom and the real world. Applying theory generates student excitement and develops the problem-solving skills that students need to become valuable members of any organization. In addition to reasoning out answers to questions and ultimately deciding upon solutions to cases, students must be able to communicate their recommendations effectively. Thus, working on cases develops the integrated thinking and communication skills required for success in the business world.

It is also possible to have students solve cases together in pairs or small groups, enabling them to practice oral communication and develop forms of co-operation that will also benefit them. Therefore, cases provide a transition between the academic setting in which students have learned their theory and the business setting in which they will be applying their knowledge.

A NOTE TO INSTRUCTORS

Some casebooks emphasize skill development where each case, in essence, is a separate problem set. At the other extreme are books that are completely unstructured and each case is virtually identical to a difficult real-life problem. This book is generally in the middle of the spectrum, though it does contain both a number of straightforward cases and a few others that approach the more involved Harvard ones. There is sufficient structure for students with one finance course to solve each "puzzle." Yet most of the cases incorporate a variety of issues, and students need to "fit all the pieces together" in order to devise sensible recommendations.

In our view the book is best used in either an undergraduate case course, or as a supplement in the second undergraduate or the first graduate corporate finance course. Still, a number of cases are relatively simple and resemble an extended problem set. In addition, the more involved cases can be "toned down" by having the students ignore some of the issues. Thus, it is possible to use the book as a supplement in the first undergraduate course. There is also a section called "Comprehensive Cases" for instructors who wish to test their students' ability to handle unstructured situations. Students typically require some guidance before undertaking such cases, and this section is preceded by a "note" that contains suggestions on how to approach unstructured problems. The *Instructor's Manual*, however, does provide a set of questions that can be used if desired.

As all instructors who use cases know, it is quite time-consuming to incorporate cases into a course. With this in mind, the *Instructor's Manual* contains a brief abstract of the case, including any subtopics covered, the difficulty of each case, and most important, a detailed set of answers.

FEATURES OF THE SECOND EDITION

There are 57 cases, up from the 50 in the first edition. Thirteen cases are completely new including ones on divestiture, bankruptcy, working capital policy and capital budgeting procedures. The old "Financial Analysis and Planning" section has been split into two parts, and the Comprehensive Section now contains nine cases (up from seven).

The narrative and at least some of the numbers to eighteen cases have been changed, and the narrative to five others has also been altered. Nearly all cases have been updated in terms of dates and economic events.

There is user-friendly software for 25 cases. Each of these cases contains a "software question" that extends the analysis in an unforced and natural way using sensitivity/scenario analysis. These questions are marked with an icon.

THE SOFTWARE

The software was developed by Joseph Sulock and Delvin Hawley (of the University of Mississippi). Twenty-five cases have software that is compatible with Windows-based versions of Lotus, Quattro Pro, and Excel.

The main objective of the software is to help students extend the case analysis. We accomplish this by developing sensitivity/scenario analysis templates. A user will be able to change the values of selected inputs and immediately see the impact on "outputs of interest." This type of analysis could easily change a recommendation that is based only on a single set of estimates.

One problem, though, is that students may need to be guided in the analysis. We provide this guidance by supplying for each case a software question that requires students to analyze specific scenarios.

Note that the use of these input/output spreadsheets is consistent with the main objective of the software. There is still a danger that students will not understand the financial concepts involved because it may appear to them that they are simply inputting values into a black box. The way the book is written, however, students can first work each case by hand with a minimum of number crunching. Then the software question is assigned and the software distributed to the students. This should eliminate the black box effect.

There are other uses of the software as well. For example, the templates could be used to help sharpen the students' spreadsheet skills. This as well as other possible uses of the software are explained in the preface to the IM.

ACKNOWLEDGMENTS

Much field work has been conducted to make the settings and issues in the cases realistic and relevant. We were fortunate that forty executives generously agreed to be interviewed. These include William Brown, Darrell Crouse, Jim Daniels, Dick Esperon, Ernest "Ted" Forbes, Mark Friedrick, Rob Geitner, Gordon Greenwood, Lindsay Harper, Doug Higgins, Jesse Karr, Mike Keeler, Carl Kessler, George Knopf, Charles Lillien, John McGeary, Lowell Pearlman, Phil Pressley, Jack Reinecke, Jeff Roberts, Terry Sanders, Charles Silver, William Stark, Steve Studebaker, Pat Thompson, Steve Vannucci, Gary Whalen, Robert Williams, and Vaughn Wilson.

Each edition of the Casebook benefited greatly from the comments and suggestions of a number of professors, and we would like to thank the following individuals:

Bruce L. Anderson, *Cornell University*
Thomas A. Bankston, *Angelo State University*
Ronald Copley, *University of North Carolina-Wilmington*
James Feller, *Middle Tennessee State University*
Andrew Fields, *University of Delaware*
Delvin Hawley, *University of Mississippi*
Hugh O. Hunter, *Eastern Washington University*
Riaz Hussain, *University of Scranton*
Jahan Janjigian, *Northeastern University*
Sayeed Kayvan, *Towson State University*
Fred Kittrell, *Middle Tennessee State University*
Leland A. Lahr, *Lawrence Technological University*
Dean R. Longmore, *Idaho State University*
Phil Malone, *University of Mississippi*

Nikos Milonas, *University of Massachusetts at Amherst*
Robert Phillips, *University of Richmond*
Philip R. Swenson, *Utah State University*
Clifford F. Thies, *University of Baltimore*
Emery A. Trahan, *Northeastern University*
Paul A. Vanderheiden, *University of Wisconsin-Eau Claire*
Michael C. Walker, *University of Cincinnati*
Richard A. Wall, *Canisius College*
J. D. Williams, *University of Akron*
K. Matthew Wong, *St. John's University*

A special thanks is given to the professional and courteous staff at Wiley, especially Finance Editor Whitney Blake. We also thank the production editor, Melanie Henick for her efficient supervision during the production stage. In addition, the manuscript benefited greatly from the thorough editing of Shelley Flannery.

A number of individuals graciously contributed cases to the book, and we acknowledge their help.

Tom Goho, *Wake Forest University* (GM-Europe and LaPosta)
Charles Moyer, *Wake Forest University* (Fabricare)

We are especially grateful to Robert Wuertz who wrote the AT&T, Everlast, and Slovo Wood Products cases, and reviewed numerous others.

Though considerable effort has gone into this book, we realize that any manuscript can be improved and we cheerfully welcome all suggestions.

This book is dedicated to our families and our students.

May 1996
Joseph M. Sulock
John S. Dunkelberg

CONTENTS

PART IX   Miscellaneous Topics   279

PART X   Comprehensive Cases   311

PART I

FINANCE FUNDAMENTALS

CASE 1

FINANCIAL PLANNING
TIME VALUE OF MONEY

Ambrose Studebaker received his Ph.D in history from a well-known Ivy League school at the age of 22. By the time he was 30, Studebaker was one of the most widely respected historians in the country and had published over 20 major articles and three influential books. His success at teaching has been equally impressive. Studebaker is well known among students for his quick wit, fine sense of humor, demanding but fair standards, and clear and interesting lectures. A few years ago he became "extremely dissatisfied" with textbooks dealing with the history of Western civilization and promptly wrote his own. Not surprisingly, the book is now the leading seller in the field.

His present (1996) income from his salary at the university, book royalties, and fees from guest lectures is fairly substantial. Being a frugal sort, Studebaker has accumulated a sizable portfolio of stocks, bonds, money market funds, and some fine art. He has never been especially conscious of money but, nonetheless, is desirous of acting in a prudent manner with his savings. Studebaker rarely sought any professional financial advice, yet it is hard to criticize his investment philosophy, which is based on the principles of diversification and buy-and-hold.

ROBERT MORTON

Robert Morton is president of R. G. D. Morton and Associates, a firm specializing in financial planning. Morton is licensed to sell insurance and securities and a few years ago obtained permission from the faculty welfare committee at Studebaker's university to solicit on campus. Morton had sent the faculty a memorandum "introducing a new financial product: equity transfer." (See Exhibit 1.) The basic idea was that individuals could borrow on the equity in their home and invest these funds plus any excess savings in a single-premium life insurance policy.

EXHIBIT 1
Morton's Explanation of Equity Transfer

The equity in your home is the difference between the property's market value and the balance on any mortgage. Over time the equity can increase dramatically as housing prices rise and the mortgage balance decreases. Unfortunately, homeowners have traditionally overlooked the tremendous potential in safely utilizing this equity. However, this large, dormant asset can be unlocked using a concept called equity transfer, which is nothing more than moving an asset from one coffer to another. This is done by investing excess equity within a vehicle that provides for the safe, tax-free accumulation of money. In addition, your family will be protected through the death benefit of the investment.

Studebaker knew that his home had appreciated in value and invited Morton to his office. They chatted for some 15 minutes, during which Morton talked briefly about the concept of equity transfer but mainly took information on Studebaker's personal and financial situation. Some of this information included the following:

1. Studebaker was interested in accumulating additional money for a possible early retirement in 20 years, or by 2016 at age 60. This money might also be used to defray the education expenses of his newborn child.
2. Studebaker had "an excess" of $30,000 in a money market mutual fund that he felt "virtually certain" he would not need.
3. The balance on his mortgage was $45,000, carried a 7 percent yearly rate with a yearly payment of $4,248, and had 20 years remaining.

Studebaker invited Morton to his home for a formal review of his situation not only out of curiosity as to what Morton's analysis would show, but also because of concern that he was not handling his financial affairs in a prudent manner. At this meeting Morton brought over 20 pages of illustrations, all very nicely bound. Morton first explained that Studebaker could "unlock $25,000 of equity" by obtaining a new mortgage. (See Exhibit 2.) This amount plus the excess $30,000 in the money market could be repositioned into a single-premium life insurance policy. According to Morton, $176,392 would be accumulated in 20 years, when Studebaker would reach age 60. "This," Morton triumphantly noted, "represents an annual return of 6 percent, which is above the 5 percent you are receiving now."

"Of course," Morton said with a smile, "there is a cost. No such thing as a free lunch, you know." He then explained that Studebaker's yearly mortgage would increase by $3,052 (from $4,248 to $7,300) but quickly added that the increase in the yearly earnings from the life insurance policy would far exceed this cost. (See Exhibit 3.) For example, after the first year the $55,000 would grow to

EXHIBIT 2
Morton's Calculation of the Amount of Studebaker's Equity That Could Be Transferred to Another Investment

Current market value of property	$100,000
Amount of new mortgage (75% of mkt. value)	75,000
Less balance on existing mortgage	45,000
Less closing costs on new mortgage	3,000
Less other costs	2,000
Total available equity	$25,000

EXHIBIT 3
Morton's Illustration of the Annual and Cumulative Cost to Studebaker of the Life Insurance Policy Compared to the Policy's Annual and Cumulative Accumulation Value

End of Year	Policy Payment	Accumulation Value	Increase in Accumulation Value	Annual Cost[a]	Cummulative Cost
0	$55,000				
1		$58,300	$3,300	$3,052	$3,052
2		$61,798	$3,498	$3,052	$6,104
3		$65,506	$3,708	$3,052	$9,156
4		$69,436	$3,930	$3,052	$12,208
5		$73,602	$4,166	$3,052	$15,260
6		$78,019	$4,416	$3,052	$18,312
7		$82,700	$4,681	$3,052	$21,364
8		$87,662	$4,962	$3,052	$24,416
9		$92,921	$5,260	$3,052	$27,468
10		$98,497	$5,575	$3,052	$30,520
11		$104,406	$5,910	$3,052	$33,572
12		$110,671	$6,264	$3,052	$36,624
13		$117,311	$6,640	$3,052	$39,676
14		$124,350	$7,039	$3,052	$42,728
15		$131,811	$7,461	$3,052	$45,780
16		$139,719	$7,909	$3,052	$48,832
17		$148,103	$8,383	$3,052	$51,884
18		$156,989	$8,886	$3,052	$54,936
19		$166,408	$9,419	$3,052	$57,988
20		$176,392	$9,984	$3,052	$61,040

[a]Calculated as the increase in Studebaker's yearly mortgage payment.

$58,300, an increase of $3,300. And during year 20 the amount invested in the life insurance would increase by $9,984, or over three times the yearly increase in Studebaker's mortgage payment.

FINANCIAL RAZZLE-DAZZLE

When Morton left, Studebaker leafed through the illustrations wondering what to do. On the one hand, he felt like all this was a bit of financial razzle-dazzle that he did not understand. On the other hand, he had the gnawing suspicion that something was not quite right with his present investment situation. He decided to call a colleague of his from the economics department, Phyllis Comer. They were frequent tennis partners, and Studebaker had much confidence in her.

Comer was eager to accommodate a friend and readily agreed to meet the next evening. She first queried Studebaker about his life insurance situation, and both concluded that it was quite satisfactory. As she examined the material Morton had left, she quickly saw a number of problems. First, the analysis completely ignored taxes. Second, the movement of Studebaker's equity into the life insurance policy would involve $5,000 of fees. Third, Studebaker would have to give up his 7 percent mortgage and take out a new mortgage at 9 percent. Finally, Comer noted that Studebaker would be paying for life insurance that he didn't need. That is, the life insurance provided an annual yield of 6 percent, but 7 percent could be earned on a long-term investment of similar risk. The difference, of course, pays for the insurance. "I am quite confident," summed up Comer, "that more money can be accumulated by simply investing the $30,000 and the yearly $3,052 (the increase in the annual mortgage payment) in some other long-term investment. You avoid the commission, you can keep your attractive 7 percent mortgage, and you'll earn a higher return."

"What you say makes perfect sense," Studebaker said glumly. "Why, then," he asked, referring to Exhibit 3, "does it *appear* that this is such a good deal? It looks to me that if I do what Morton recommends, all it would cost is the increase of $3,052 in my annual mortgage payment. And—or so it seems—the yearly earnings from the life insurance policy more than cover this increase. Am I missing something?"

"Economics," she responded, "teaches you to be alert for missed opportunities in addition to any out-of-pocket expenses. I like to think of these missed opportunities as hidden opportunity costs or hidden sacrifices." Comer then pointed out two subtle costs that the analysis ignored. First, by using the $3,052 a year to meet the increased mortgage payment, Studebaker gives up the opportunity to invest this money and earn interest. Second, by using the excess $30,000 in the money market to buy the life insurance policy, Studebaker loses the interest that this money could have earned.

"These numbers," she continued as her fingers pointed to the last two columns of Exhibit 3, "do not consider all this lost interest. The annual cost should consider not only the increase in your mortgage payment for that year but also the increase in the lost interest during the year. For example, with these adjustments the annual cost in year one is $5,152. This includes the extra $3,052 paid at the end of year one plus $2,100 of lost interest on the $30,000 assuming a 7 percent rate of interest. By year 20 this annual cost becomes $18,632. Notice that both of these amounts exceed the yearly increase in earnings from the life insurance investment. Thus, properly adjusted, this analysis indicates that the purchase of the single-premium life insurance policy is a bad deal."

Studebaker was obviously upset at his failure to detect these flaws, and Comer quickly added that Morton's proposal had uncovered two extremely important facts. First, Studebaker had an obvious need for some type of safe, long-term, tax-sheltered investment; and second, he had excess yearly income in addition to the money market funds that could be placed in such an investment.

QUESTIONS

Ignore taxes in all your answers.

1. Morton notes that the $55,000 invested in the single-premium life insurance policy would grow to $176,392 in 20 years for a return of 6 percent a year. Explain how this return was calculated.

2. In order to reposition the equity in his home, Studebaker would have to take out a 30-year, $75,000 mortgage at 9 percent. Explain how the yearly mortgage payments on this loan were obtained.

3. For the 9 percent mortgage in Exhibit 4, find the loan balance at the end of years 19 and 20.

4. Exhibit 3 indicates that $176,392 will be accumulated after 20 years in the life insurance policy. Is this really true? (*Hint:* If Studebaker were to make this investment, what would his debt position look like in year 20?)

5. (a) If the excess $30,000 were invested in a long-term asset yielding 8 percent a year, how much would be accumulated after 20 years?
   (b) Suppose Studebaker placed $3,052 a year into a long-term investment paying 8 percent a year. How much would be accumulated after 20 years (amounts invested at the end of each year)?

6. Repeat problem 5 but assume a 7 percent return can be earned.

7. Comer's criticisms implied that the single-premium life insurance policy is an unattractive investment for Studebaker. What do your previous answers suggest?

8. (a) Suppose Studebaker's goal is to accumulate $400,000 in 20 years. Assume the $30,000 is invested at 8 percent. How much will he have to save in equal amounts at the end of each of the next 20 years if he can earn 8 percent per year on any investments?
   (b) Repeat part (a) but assume he will not be able to save any money in years 13 to 20. This is, he will save an equal amount at the end of years 1 to 12 and nothing thereafter.

9. The yearly payment on the new 30-year, $75,000 mortgage is $7,300. This assumes one payment is made at the end of each of the next 30 years. Suppose that payments must be made at the end of each month. Would 12 of these monthly payments be equal to one of the yearly payments? Explain.

NOTE: No calulations are necessary here.

10. Exhibit 3 suggests that the annual cost of the life insurance policy is $3,052. With the adjustments mentioned in the case, Comer calculated the cost to be $5,152 in year 1 and $18,632 by year 20 assuming a 7 percent annual return. Explain how these were determined.

EXHIBIT 4
Amortization on Studebaker's Existing 7% Mortgage and the New 30-Year, 9% Mortgage*

| | ($45,000) 7% Mortgage | | |
End of Year	Balance	End of Year	Balance
1	$43,902	11	$27,675
2	42,728	12	25,364
3	41,471	13	22,892
4	40,126	14	20,247
5	38,688	15	17,416
6	37,148	16	14,388
7	35,501	17	11,147
8	33,738	18	7,679
9	31,852	19	3,970
10	29,834	20	0

(continued)

EXHIBIT 4
(Continued)

($75,000)
9% Mortgage (selected years)

End of Year	Balance	End of Year	Balance
1	$74,447	16	$56,839
2	73,848	17	54,654
3	73,194	18	52,273
4	72,482	19	_____
5	71,705	20	_____
•	•	•	•
•	•	•	•
•	•	•	•
•	•	•	•
•	•	•	•
•	•	•	•
12	63,916	28	12,841
13	62,369	29	6,697
14	60,682	30	0
15	58,843		

*The annual payment on the 7 percent mortgage is $4,248. The annual payment on the 9 percent mortgage is $7,300.

FINANCIAL PLANNING
TIME VALUE OF MONEY

In early March 1996, Ambrose Studebaker is discussing with his economist friend, Phyllis Comer, various ways to enable Studebaker to accumulate additional money in 20 years when Studebaker reaches age 60.

BACKGROUND

A local financial planner, R. G. D. Morton, had suggested that Studebaker, a nationally known historian, borrow the equity accumulated in his home and invest it plus $30,000 of excess cash in a single-premium life insurance policy. This appeared to be quite an attractive investment until Comer pointed out a number of problems with this strategy and said that more money could be accumulated in a variety of ways.

Studebaker, desirous of acting in a prudent manner with his savings, was obviously upset at his failure to detect the flaws in Morton's presentation. Comer noted, however, that Morton had uncovered two extremely important facts. First, Studebaker had an obvious need for some type of safe, long-term, tax-sheltered investment, and second, he had excess yearly income in addition to the money market funds that could be placed in such an investment. A review of Studebaker's situation confirmed the following.

First, Studebaker's life insurance situation was adequate.

Second, it was extremely unlikely that the $30,000 of "excess" cash in the money market fund would be needed.

Third, Studebaker, due to royalties from a best-selling college textbook, could afford to have his annual income reduced by 3,052 after-tax dollars.

And finally, any funds accumulated in 20 years would be used for a possible early retirement or to defray the education expenses of a newborn child.

THE CURRENT MEETING

Comer realizes that Studebaker is interested in specific investment suggestions but thinks it is best to begin by explaining the gain from the tax-free accumulation of interest. The excess $30,000 in the money market earns 5 percent per year compounded monthly, which converts to a 5.12 percent annualized return. Since interest is taxable as it is earned each year, however, this money is only growing at a 3.58 percent annual rate since Studebaker is in the 30 percent tax bracket. This means that 60,623 after-tax dollars will be accumulated after 20 years. If this money could grow tax free then there would be 81,438 before-tax dollars and 66,007 dollars after taxes at the end of the same period. This is an increase of nearly 10 percent. Comer then points out that some investments have even more advantages and gives Studebaker a handout on the various ways that investments could be taxed. (See Exhibit 1.)

Two Tax-Deferred Investments: The SPA and the TDA

The discussion next focuses on two investment vehicles for which Studebaker is eligible. One is a single-premium, tax-deferred annuity (SPA); the other is a tax-deferred annuity (TDA). The first investment requires Studebaker to invest after-tax dollars, and taxes on any accumulated interest are due only when funds are withdrawn. The TDA has even more advantages. An individual can invest before-tax dollars and the money grows tax-free. When the funds are withdrawn, taxes are due on the full accumulation value. This investment is available only to individuals employed at certain nonprofit institutions; it must be done as part of a payroll deduction; and there is a limit on the amount per year that can be invested. This limit is relatively generous and in Studebaker's case would be $12,000 per year.

Both the TDA and the SPA would pay a higher return than the money market. Comer then explains that there are numerous companies offering single-premium, tax-deferred annuities, and Studebaker is free to choose whichever one he wants. Comer does, however, highly recommend Mahac, Inc. Mahac pays a competitive return of 7 percent and imposes no penalty if the funds are withdrawn after two years. The options with the tax-deferred annuity are more limited, however. Comer reminds Studebaker that the money can be placed in a TDA only as part of a payroll deduction and only with a company that has obtained the approval of Studebaker's university.

Northern Annuities and Modern Investments

At present only two companies have university approval to offer their TDAs on campus. One firm, Northern Annuities, pays a 7 percent return and imposes no penalties on any withdrawals after one year. The other firm, Modern Investments, currently pays 8 percent but imposes a substantial penalty if the funds are withdrawn before the investor reaches age 55. Studebaker wonders if Modern Investments isn't the more appropriate company for his situation considering that "it offers the higher yield, and I shouldn't need this money prior to age 60, which suggests the withdrawal penalty is irrelevant." "The problem," Comer explains, "is that you may want to withdraw the money to invest somewhere else. Just because Modern Investments offers the higher return today doesn't mean it will in the future." Studebaker is quick to see the point. By imposing substantial withdrawal penalties, Modern Investments essentially locks an investor in until age 55 and could, if it wishes, reduce the yield below competitive rates. Fortunately there is a floor to any rate drop. Modern Investments does allow a penalty-free withdrawal if it pays, at any time, a rate below 5 percent per year. In addition, the firm guarantees the 8 percent rate for at least 10 years.

Three Investment Scenarios

Comer then says she will compare three possible strategies starting with the "as is" scenario. This involves leaving the $30,000 in the money market and investing Studebaker's excess 3,052 after-tax dollars each year in the money market. Though she is certain that this is not the way to go, Comer feels it will serve as a useful benchmark. The second strategy involves placing the $30,000 into an SPA and then putting Studebaker's excess yearly income into a TDA. The third is more subtle. This eventually involves putting everything into a TDA. The trick is how to move the $30,000 into the TDA. Comer recommends that Studebaker increase the yearly amount in the TDA to the legal maximum of $12,000. This, of course, would mean that Studebaker's remaining income would be insufficient to cover his yearly expenses. To cover this shortfall, therefore, Comer recommends using the funds in the money market until they run out and then reducing the amount placed in the TDA.

Studebaker next asks about the risks of each strategy. Comer says the default risk of all the investments is "infinitesimal" since all involve very safe investments and the companies are rated $A+$ by A. M. Best Company. The liquidity risk is the chance that Studebaker will need some, if not all, of this money but will not be able to get it without incurring a large penalty. Federal law allows penalty-free withdrawals on each investment after the owner reaches age 59½, though income taxes would have to be paid on any liquidated amounts that had previously gone untaxed. (The untaxed amount would be the accumulated interest with the SPA and the entire amount in a TDA.) Before this age the law allows withdrawals for any purpose on the SPA but with a 10 percent penalty in addition to the income taxes due. The TDA is more restrictive. Under present tax laws withdrawals before age 59½ are only allowed in the event of (1) death; (2) disability; (3) separation from service (as a professor); and (4) hardship. In all cases taxes would be due on any funds removed from the TDA, though the IRS does allow tax-free transfers from one TDA to another. Comer also pointed out that the IRS has not rigorously defined what constitutes a hardship. "In short," she says, "if you choose a TDA you are pretty much locked in until age 59½ the way the present tax laws read, unless you want to move funds from one TDA to another."

Before doing the analysis Comer decides that it is quite reasonable to assume that (1) any money placed in the SPA will earn 7 percent over the 20-year time horizon; (2) Northern Annuities (a TDA option) will also pay 7 percent; and (3) Modern Investments, the other TDA option, will pay 8 percent for the first 10 years (the guaranteed time) and 5 percent for the last 10. Under these conditions Comer would assume that any money placed with Modern Investments would grow at 8 percent during years 1 to 10 and 5 percent in years 11 to 15. Studebaker would then have reached age 55 and could move these funds without penalty to Northern Annuities. Thus, Studebaker's money would earn 7 percent during years 16 to 20.

QUESTIONS

For all questions assume the relevant tax rate is 30 percent and all annuities begin at the end of year 1.

1. (a) The $30,000 of excess liquidity is earning 5 percent compounded monthly in a money market fund. This is a 5.12 percent annualized return. How was this determined?

   (b) This annualized return of 5.12 percent results in an after-tax return of 3.58 percent since taxes on any interest must be paid each year. How was this determined?

2. Assume a 4 percent after-tax annual return will be earned in a money market fund. How much will be accumulated in 20 years if the $30,000 remains in the money market and $3,052 per year is placed in the same investment? (Note that you are analyzing the "as is" investment strategy.)

3. (a) If 30,000 after-tax dollars are invested at 7 percent in a single-premium tax-deferred annuity, how many after-tax dollars will be accumulated in 20 years?

   (b) Studebaker can afford to have his annual income reduced by 3,052 after-tax dollars. How much is this before taxes? If these before-tax dollars are invested each year at 7 percent, how many after-tax dollars will be accumulated in 20 years?

   (c) Redo part (b) assuming 8 percent is earned during years 1 to 10, 5 percent during years 11 to 15, and 7 percent in years 16 to 20.

4. (a) Studebaker is eligible to put 12,000 before-tax dollars each year into a tax-deferred annuity (TDA). In order to invest in a TDA, however, he must have his salary reduced, and the case indicates that he can afford a reduction in his spendable income of $3,052 each year without disrupting his lifestyle. One investment option is to increase the amount placed into a TDA each year to the legal maximum of $12,000 and move funds from the money market to cover the resulting shortfall in Studebaker's spend-

able income. How much money will he need to transfer each year from the money market?

(b) Assume Studebaker will earn a 4 percent after-tax annual return in the money market. For how many years can he contribute the maximum amount to the TDA and cover any shortfall in his spendable income with funds from the money market? (Round your answer to the next highest year.)

(c) How many after-tax dollars will be accumulated in 20 years if the legal maximum is placed in the TDA as long as possible and a 7-percent annual return is earned? (Keep in mind that Studebaker would reduce the annual amount invested in the TDA when the funds in the money market are exhausted.)

(d) Redo your answer to part (c) assuming 8 percent is earned during years 1 to 10, 5 percent during years 11 to 15, and 7 percent in years 16 to 20.

5. Based on your previous calculations and other information in the case, what do you recommend? Justify your answer.

⊡ SOFTWARE QUESTION

6. Studebaker has carefully analyzed how much he can afford to invest. He has decided that (1) he has $40,000 of "excess cash" and (2) his annual after-tax income could drop by $4,500 per year without any "lifestyle disruptions."

(a) Redo your answer to question 2 assuming that the before-tax money market rate is 5 percent per year and interest is compounded monthly.

(b) Redo your answers to questions 3 and 4 assuming that the SPA earns 7 percent per year, and the TDA pays 7.5 percent in years 1–10 and 6.5 percent in years 11–20.

EXHIBIT 1
Comer's Handout on the Effect of Taxes on the Amount Accumulated

For all three situations assume the investor:

1. Has 4,000 before-tax dollars to invest.
2. Is in the 40-percent tax bracket (combined federal and state).
3. Can earn a 10-percent annual return before taxes.
4. Will remain in the 40-percent bracket.

We will compare the amount of after-tax dollars accumulated in 10 years under different tax situations.

Situation One After-tax dollars are invested and taxes must be paid each year on any interest earned. Under our assumptions, $2,400 is invested and will grow at a rate of 6 percent per annum. No taxes will be due at the end of 10 years and the amount of after-tax dollars accumulated will equal

$$P_{10} = 2,400 \ (1.06)^{10} = \$4,298$$

Situation Two After-tax dollars are invested, but taxes on the interest can be deferred for 10 years. Under our assumptions, $2,400 is invested and will grow at a rate of 10 percent per annum. The amount in the investment after 10 years will be

$$P_{10} = 2,400 \ (1.1)^{10} = \$6,225$$

This is not, however, the amount of after-tax dollars available since the investor owes taxes on the accumulated interest of $3,825 ($6,225 − $2,400). The taxes due are $1,530 ($3,825 × .40). Thus, 4,695 after-tax dollars ($6,225 − $1,530) will be accumulated. This is a 9.2-percent increase over the first situation.

Situation Three Before-tax dollars are invested, and taxes on the interest can be deferred for 10 years. Thus, all taxes can be postponed for 10 years. Under our assumptions, $4,000 is invested and will grow at a rate of 10 percent per annum. The amount in the investment after ten years will be

$$P_{10} = 4,000 \ (1.1)^{10} = \$10,375$$

This does not, however, equal the after-tax dollars available since the investor owes taxes on this amount. The taxes due are $4,150 ($10,375 × .40). Thus, 6,225 after-tax dollars ($10,375 − $4,150) will be accumulated. This is an increase of 45 percent compared to the first situation and 33 percent compared to the second.

CAUTION: Free lunches are hard to find! Investments offering tax advantages frequently have restrictions and impose substantial penalties on early withdrawals.

CASE 3

HOME PRODUCTS
STOCK AND BOND VALUATION

In all textbooks, the valuation of stocks and bonds is simply stated as the present value of all the future cash flows expected from the security. The concept is logical, straightforward, and deceptively simple. The valuation of bonds is usually presented first, since the relatively certain cash flows are broken into an annuity and a payment of the par value at some specific date in the future. Preferred stock valuation follows bond valuation and the value of preferred stock is shown to be the present value of perpetual annuity. The cash flows from the constant-size dividend is fairly certain, and most preferred stock does not have a maturity date. Finally, common stock is presented but neither the future cash flows (from dividends) nor the final value is known with any degree of certainty. Generally students seem to understand the bond and preferred stock valuation techniques, but they tend to be very skeptical of the common stock valuation model. Using the discounted cash flow models on an actual company can help dispel some of the doubts, but more importantly it can indicate how the models explain price behavior.

HOME PRODUCTS, INC.

Home Products, Inc. (HPI) is a leading manufacturer of prescription and ethical drugs; speciality foods and candies; and proprietary drugs. Important product names include Advil, Anacin, Dimetapp, Norplant, and Robitussin. Total revenues in the last fiscal year were in excess of $9 billion.

Long-Term Debt

The company has a capital structure that is made up of 34 percent long-term debt, 3 percent preferred stock, and 63 percent common stock. One of the two largest domestic long-term debt issues is a 9⅛ percent coupon bond that is due in 26 years. This debenture is currently selling for $930. The bond is callable in seven years and if called will be redeemed at a premium of 104.4375. The other large publicly held bond is a 9 percent coupon bond that is due in nine years. This debenture is selling for $972.50. Both of these bonds are rated *A* by Moody's.

Preferred Stock

The preferred stock is a $2.75 cumulative preferred with a stated value of $30.50, but it is currently selling for $30. More than 5.5 million shares were issued in February 1979 in connection with the merger of FDS Holding Company into a subsidiary of HPI. The preferred stock has no voting rights unless the company is in arrears on six or more quarterly dividends, and then each shareholder is entitled to one-quarter vote per share. In the event of liquidation each share is entitled to $30.50 plus accrued dividends.

Common Stock

Returns from common stock come from the cash dividend payment and/or changes in the price of the stock. Investors receiving dividends can expect them to grow over time, but some stocks do not pay dividends, especially during their early growth years. As firms mature, they typically start paying dividends and then management is very reluctant to reduce the dividend. For the firms that do not pay dividends, the normal assumption is that the earnings are being retained by the firm to promote growth; thus, the stock price should grow at a higher rate than firms that have high payout ratios.

Two major factors that affect the price of stock are changes in the required rate of return, caused primarily by changes in the risk, and change in the growth rate of earnings, which in turn create changes in the growth rate of dividends.

The common stock of Home Products currently has over 95 million shares of $3.125 par value stock outstanding. A share of common stock presently sells for $40⅜ and pays a quarterly dividend of $0.385. A consensus estimate (Zack's and IBES) indicates that earnings and dividends are expected to grow at an annual rate of 9.7 percent for the next five years. The common shares have no preemptive rights. Stockholders of HPI have the opportunity to buy additional shares of common stock through a plan of automatic dividend reinvestment and optional cash purchase. This plan allows stockholders to have their dividends reinvested in shares of common stock, and they can purchase additional shares at the market price (with no commission) each month. Shareholders who participate in this plan are limited to a total of $1,000 per month that they can use to purchase additional shares.

QUESTIONS

1. Look at the 9⅛ percent coupon bond. What is its current yield, its yield-to-first call, and its yield-to-maturity?

2. Do you think this bond will be called? Why or why not?

3. What would be the value of the 9⅛ percent coupon bond if the time to maturity was 10 years rather than 26 years? Can you explain why your answer is correct?

4. What is the required rate of return for the preferred stock? How does this rate compare to the YTM for the HPI 9⅛ percent bond? Is this difference what you would have expected from a risk/return standpoint? Why or why not?

5. In the event of liquidation, HPI preferred stockholders are entitled to $30.50 plus accrued dividends. Does this mean that preferred stockholders will receive that amount?

6. What is the dividend yield and the expected capital gains yield for HPI common stock?

7. Given that HPI is selling for $40⅝, what is its required rate of return? (Use the constant growth valuation model.)

8. Assume that the risk-free rate is 7 percent and that the expected return of the market is 12 percent. According to the security market line valuation model, what is the required rate of return for HPI common stock if its beta is 1.10?

9. Using the constant growth valuation model, find the present value of HPI common stock. Would you buy or sell?

10. The constant growth model is used in textbooks as a conceptual model to explain changes in stock prices. Is the model also of value for the actual valuation of stocks?

HELPING HAND
ACCOUNTING FUNDAMENTALS

"I got real lucky when I was fired," William Pendleton was fond of telling his employees and business associates. Pendleton was an insurance salesman in Illinois nearly 70 years ago and was dismissed due to "insufficient sales." As a hobby, he loved to tinker around the house and he developed a local reputation as a person who knew how to "fix things." Pendleton decided to capitalize on this reputation and opened a hardware store, Helping Hand, based on the philosophy that customers need help in selecting the right tools, parts, and materials for the job at hand. The philosophy was sound and subsequently a number of other stores were opened in the Midwest.

When Pendleton died in 1965, the business was sold to the Stafford family and has remained in their control ever since. The family's main contribution was to expand the product line to include building materials, and over half of the company's sales are now made to contractors.

THE LETTER

Sharon Vincent is the current general manager of Helping Hand, and she recently received a letter from the present owner, Justin Stafford. Stafford is best described as a passive stockholder who pretty much leaves the operation of the firm to Vincent. From time to time, however, he is fond of bringing in consultants in order to evaluate the company's performance and to help Stafford develop pointed questions to ask management. Apparently as a result of a recent—but not exhaustive—study by one of these consultants, Stafford has raised a number of issues that he wants addressed. The three most important issues center on the firm's return on equity (ROE), debt policy, and what Stafford calls "a logical inconsistency" in Helping Hand's 1995 financial statements.

In the letter, dated February 9, 1996, Stafford wrote Vincent that he was "troubled by our consistently low ROE" and urged Vincent to "seek ways to bring this ratio at least up to industry standards." At the same time, he encouraged Vincent to minimize the firm's use of debt. Stafford notes that the sales of Helping Hand are quite sensitive to economic downturns, and he believes that the company will face intense competition from nationwide chains like Lowe's. Consequently he worries about "our ability to repay what we borrow, especially during a recession." Though he is aware that the company is not highly leveraged relative to industry standards, Stafford recommended that Vincent "strongly consider" (1) retiring all long-term debt as quickly as possible and (2) increasing the firm's liquidity position. Actually, Vincent is quite surprised at these two suggestions. Stafford is something of a "high roller" and he spends much of his time racing automobiles and playing bridge and poker for large stakes. Thus Vincent is a bit amused at Stafford's apparent fear of financial distress, given the chances he takes driving fast cars and his willingness to risk thousands of dollars on a single hand of poker. Still, she thinks that his points are well worth considering.

Stafford is also perplexed by Helping Hand's need for funds during 1995 and worries that the firm may be "chewing up cash unnecessarily." He notes that 1995 was highly profitable and yet he was asked to contribute $407,000 to support the company's operation. "It seems illogical," Stafford wrote, "for a profitable firm to have such a need for cash."

THE REACTION

As Vincent reflects on Stafford's letter, she decides that it is wise to develop a forecast for the coming year to see if any external funds will be needed. She realizes that part of the problem from Stafford's point of view is that he was unexpectedly—if not inappropriately—asked to contribute capital in 1995.

It is a good idea, therefore, to alert Stafford as soon as possible to any potential cash shortfall in 1996.

She estimates that sales in 1996 will total $24,707,000, a forecast that assumes no change in the firm's credit policy. About 15 months ago she decided that the company's credit terms and standards were "downright stingy" and certainly more conservative than those of the competition—especially the nationwide chains. It became quite clear that Helping Hand had to loosen its credit policy in order to remain competitive. "An absolutely essential defensive move," she argued at the time. The firm presently offers credit terms of 2/10, net 30 to qualified buyers. That is, Helping Hand offers a 2-percent discount to customers who pay within 10 days, and customers who pass up the discount are expected to pay in full within 30 days. Assuming no change in credit standards, Vincent expects that 60 percent of all sales will be on credit. She estimates that 50 percent of all credit sales will be paid on the tenth day, 40 percent on day 30, and 10 percent will pay late on day 40.

Vincent also thinks that inventory control can be tightened. She intends to purge slow-moving items and use purveyors with relatively short delivery times. These changes should increase inventory turnover, and she expects that cost of goods sold divided by inventory will rise to 3.

Vincent's forecast of accounts payable needs to consider the easier credit terms offered by many suppliers. Two years ago about 80 percent of the firm's purchases were on terms of net 30. That is, most suppliers offered no discount, and payment-in-full was expected by day 30. The remaining 20 percent were on terms of 2/10, net 30. Increased competition among hardware and lumber suppliers has resulted in more attractive credit terms. During the last year about half of Helping Hand's purchases were made on terms of 2/10, net 30. Vincent expects this to rise to 75 percent in 1996 with the remaining 25 percent on terms of net 30.

After she completes the 1996 forecast, Vincent intends to respond to Stafford's ROE and debt concerns. Her initial reaction, though, is that Stafford is much too cautious on the issue of debt financing. In fact, she really thinks that the firm is underleveraged and should increase its debt ratio to industry standards. She realizes, however, that such an increase is simply out of the question unless Stafford's position softens considerably.

As Vincent rereads Stafford's letter she is struck by the thought that "two perfectly sane and intelligent people can look at the same number, understand completely where it comes from, and yet disagree entirely on whether the number is 'good' or 'bad'." There is, of course, her difference with Stafford regarding the firm's debt ratio. And in the same letter Stafford also noted that the firm's current ratio (Current assets/Current liabilities) looked "suspiciously high." Yet a few weeks ago, the firm's banker complimented Vincent on Helping Hand's "extremely solid working capital position."

QUESTIONS

1. Stafford apparently thinks that it is a good idea to increase Helping Hand's liquidity position. Let's suppose that a firm increases its cash position. That is, assume that "cash" on a firm's balance sheet increases and there is no change in any other current asset nor in any current liability.

    (a) What will happen to the company's current ratio? Quick ratio?

    (b) What are the advantages of an increase in liquidity? What are the disadvantages?

2. "What's the problem?" Tim McClinton, a store manager, asked when Sharon Vincent casually mentioned to him that new capital might be required during the coming year. "I've seen our balance sheet," McClinton continued, "and we seem to be rolling in dough, at least judging from the impressive amount of retained earnings." Respond to McClinton's comments.

3. (a) Stafford thinks that it is "logically inconsistent" for a profitable firm to have cash problems. Is it "logically inconsistent?" Explain to Stafford how even a well-managed and highly profitable company can have cash flow difficulties.

   (b) Construct Helping Hand's 1995 sources and uses statement [no dividends were paid in 1995 and capital spending was 165.1(000)].

   (c) Many bankers use the format of Exhibit 3 to analyze a firm's cash flow situation. Use this format on Helping Hand for 1995.

   (d) Why did Helping Hand have a need for outside capital in 1995?

   (e) Does it appear that the firm's need for outside capital in 1995 was "to be expected," or does it appear that this need for cash was the result of suspect managerial practices? Use information in the case and any other financial statistics you think are appropriate to answer this question.

4. (a) The owner, Justin Stafford, is disturbed by the firm's consistently low return on equity (ROE). At the same time, he is reluctant to use much debt. Use the Dupont system to see if these views are complementary or competing. Defend your choice.

   (b) Compute Helping Hand's 1995 ROE. Use the Dupont system to help determine why the 1995 ROE differed from the industry median shown in Exhibit 4.

5. Vincent does not believe that Helping Hand is overleveraged at present. Part of her argument involves calculation of the firm's debt, times interest earned (TIE) and fixed charge coverage (FCC) ratios.

   (a) The debt ratio was 34 percent in 1995, well below the industry average of 57 percent shown in Exhibit 4. In addition, Vincent believes that the firm's debt ratio would be even lower if she adjusted for the fact that interest rates have risen since the long-term debt recorded on the balance sheet was incurred.

   Explain why a firm's debt ratio—other relevant factors the same—will be overstated during a period of rising interest rates if it is calculated from information on the balance sheet. (*Hint:* consider the difference between book value and market value.)

   (b) What are some other balance sheet items where a divergence may well exist between book and market value?

   (c) Vincent will compute the TIE as EBIT/INT. She doesn't like this ratio as a measure of the firm's ability to meet its financial expenses since it ignores contractual obligations such as leasing payments (LP) and debt due (DD). She prefers to compute the fixed charge coverage as follows.

$$FCC = EBIT/\,[INT \,+\, LP \,+\, DD/(1 \,-\, t)]$$

   Explain why only "debt due" is divided by $1 - t$, where t is the relevant tax rate.

6. Vincent expects that 60 percent of all 1996 sales will be on credit with terms of 2/10, net 30. She estimates that 50% of these credit sales will be paid on the tenth day, 40 percent on day 30 and 10 percent will pay late on day 40.

   (a) What will be the firm's 1996 average collection period on its credit sales?
   (b) Predict the 1996 level of receivables assuming sales of $24,707(000).

7. In part due to price discounts from suppliers, cost of goods sold is expected to be 65 percent of sales in 1996. Purchases are predicted to equal 70 percent of CGS. Seventy-five percent of these purchases will be made on terms of 2/10, net 30, and Vincent fully intends to take the discount and pay on day 10. The remaining 25 percent will be made on terms of net 30.

   (a) What will be the firm's 1996 average payment period?
   (b) Predict the 1996 level of accounts payable.

8. Assuming no change in notes payable or long-term debt, consider the following equation for estimating "funds needed."

   $$FN_t = \Delta A - \Delta L - RE_t$$

where FN_t = funds needed in period t
   ΔA = change in assets from period $t - 1$ to period t
   ΔL = change in accounts payable and accruals from period $t - 1$ to period t
   RE_t = retained earnings during period t (net income less dividends)

   (a) If FN were negative, what would that mean?
   (b) Estimate FN in 1996 for Helping Hand assuming no dividends and using predicted sales of $24,707(000). Keep in mind that Vincent expects (1) accruals to equal 4 percent of sales; (2) net fixed assets in 1996 will total $870.6(000); (3) net profit margin (i.e., NI/Sales) to be .022; (4) cash to equal 2 percent of sales; and (5) CGS/inventory to equal 3.

9. (a) If offered credit terms of 2/10, net 30, Vincent thinks it is a good idea to take the discount. Do you agree? Explain.
   (b) Is it reasonable to think, as Vincent does, that using suppliers with shorter delivery time will increase inventory turnover? Explain.

10. Vincent observed in the case that "two perfectly sane and intelligent people can look at the same number, understand completely where it comes from, and yet disagree entirely on whether the number is 'good' or 'bad.'"

   (a) Explain why the banker thought Helping Hand's current ratio was "impressive," while Stafford was decidedly unimpressed.
   (b) Consider the reactions of two individuals to the rising average collection period of their firm. The sales manager is quite pleased at the increase while the credit manager is quite concerned. Explain these different reactions.
   (c) Consider two stockholders who have identical subjective probability distributions about the future earning prospects of the company. That is, they both

feel the same way about the firm's probable earnings. Yet one stockholder favors using additional debt financing while the other thinks that using more debt is simply too risky. Explain why this disagreement has occurred.

11. Many of the issues Stafford raised were based on comparing Helping Hand's financial statistics to the industry numbers shown in Exhibit 4. And part of Vincent's response will be based on the same type of comparison.

    (a) Discuss the limitations of such a comparative financial analysis.

    (b) In view of these limitations, why are such industry comparisons so frequently made?

12. Consider the debt disagreement between Vincent, who is the CEO, and Stafford, the owner. Who do you think is "right?" Defend your position.

SOFTWARE QUESTION

13. Sharon Vincent thinks it is a good idea to discuss with Justin Stafford the firm's cash outlook for 1996. She knows that Stafford believes that he was unexpectedly asked to contribute funds in 1995 and she wants to avoid, if possible, any "financial surprises" in 1996.

    Given the information available to her at present, the estimate developed in question 8(b) represents her best-guess or most-likely estimate of the company's 1996 cash situation.

    There are, however, a number of scenarios that she wants to investigate before her meeting with Stafford (set the other inputs at their base-case values).

	S-1	S-2	S-3	Base
1996 Sales	$25,340.00	$24,707.00	$25,340.00	$24,707.00
NI/Sales	.02	.022	.02	.022
Cash/Sales	.02	.022	.022	.02
CGS/Inventory	3.00	2.80	2.80	3.00
ACP (credit sales)	25.00	23.00	27.00	21.00

The first scenario is based on Vincent's suspicion that the firm's credit standards are still too restrictive. If she decides to loosen these standards, she expects an increase in sales and the average collection period (ACP), as well as a decrease in the net profit margin (NI/Sales) in part due to an increase in the bad debt percentage.

The next scenario considers the possibility that the firm's working capital management may not be as efficient as Vincent would like. The last set of assumptions is the most pessimistic and is a combination of the first two scenarios. It considers the possibility of sloppy working capital procedures at the same time of relaxed credit standards. (For convenience, her base-case estimates are also shown.)

Perform this scenario analysis.
(a) How important is working capital management to Helping Hand's 1996 cash situation?
(b) What, if any, are the implications for Vincent's meeting with Stafford?

EXHIBIT 1
Helping Hand's Income Statements: 1993–1995 ($000s)

	1993	1994	1995
Sales	$20,816.1	$21,152.4	$23,366.7
Cost of goods sold	13,946.8	14,383.7	15,562.2
Gross margin	6,869.3	6,768.7	7,804.5
Operating expenses	5,932.6	5,986.2	6,846.5
Depreciation	138.8	141.2	145.2
Earnings before interest and taxes (EBIT)	797.8	641.3	812.9
Interest	108.8	105.7	107.0
Earnings before taxes	689.1	535.6	705.9
Taxes	275.6	214.2	282.4
Net income	$413.4	$321.3	$423.5

EXHIBIT 2
Helping Hands Balance Sheets: 1993–1995 ($000s)

	1993	1994	1995
Assets			
Cash	$624.5	$519.7	$461.4
Accounts receivable	289.0	387.9	766.0
Inventory	4,649.0	4,875.7	5,518.5
Current assets	5,562.5	5,783.3	6,745.9
Net fixed assets	694.0	705.9	725.8
Total assets	$6,256.5	$6,489.2	$7,471.7
Liabilities and Equity			
Short-term bank loans	$325.8	$307.7	$380.1
Accounts payable	697.4	743.2	652.7
Accruals	832.6	767.6	958.0
Current liabilities	1,855.8	1,818.5	1,990.8
Term loans	633.5	582.2	561.6
Common stock	543.0	543.0	950.3
Retained earnings	3,224.2	3,545.5	3,969.0
Total liabilities and equity	$6,256.5	$6,489.2	$7,471.7

EXHIBIT 3
Cash Flow Analysis of Helping Hand: 1993–1994 ($000s)

	1993	1994
Net income	$413.4	$321.3
Depreciation	138.8	141.2
Cash flow operations	552.2	462.5
–Change adjusted working capital	203.6	344.8
–Capital spending	159.5	153.0
–Dividends	0	0
Cash flow	$189.1	($35.3)

Adjusted Working Capital			
	1992	1993	1994
Accounts receivable		$ 289.1	$ 387.9
Inventory		4,649.0	4,875.8
–Accounts payable		697.4	743.2
–Accruals		832.6	767.6
Adjusted working capital	3,204.4	3,408.1	3,752.9
Change adjusted working capital		$ 203.7	$ 344.8

EXHIBIT 4
Selected Ratios for Hardware Stores: 1993–1995

	Median[a]	Lower/Upper Quartiles[b]
Current	2.1	1.5/3.1
Quick	0.5	0.3/1.0
Debt (%)	57	38/74
Times interest earned	2.6	1.1/5.5
Average collection period[c]	18	10/34
Inventory turnover (CGS)	2.9	1.8/3.9
Return on equity (%)	11.9	1.7/18.2
Return on total assets (%)	5.1	0.7/7.3
Total asset turnover	3.0	1.7/3.6
Net profit margin	1.7	0.7/2.6

[a]The median is the middle value of the industry statistic. For example, half the industry firms had a current ratio above 2.1 and half had a current ratio below 2.1.

[b]The left or lower number shows the cutoff for the bottom 25 percent. The right or higher number shows the cutoff for the top 25 percent. For example, 25 percent of the industry firms had a current ratio below 1.5, and 25 percent had a current ratio above 3.1. By implication, 50 percent of these ratios fell between 1.5 and 3.1.

[c]Calculated as [Receivables/(Sales/360)].

DOVER INTERNATIONAL
ECONOMIC FUNDAMENTALS

Carol Downing is CEO of Dover International, a firm whose annual sales in the most recent year, 1996, exceeded $900 million. The company produces a wide range of business equipment including copiers, automatic teller machines, vaults, and office equipment such as desks and filing cabinets. Downing is a firm believer in creating an environment of open communication; she encourages Dover executives to "express themselves" and believes that all suggestions—even her own—need to be critically analyzed if correct decisions are to be reached.

A few years ago, for example, there was widespread industry concern at a time when Dover was considering a major expansion that American office equipment suppliers would lose market share to Japanese competitors. Downing, after carefully listening to the arguments on both sides, decided that this fear was unfounded and gave her approval to the costly expansion. She was especially swayed by the observation that Japanese firms would find it difficult to compete with American companies such as Dover which have a larger network of direct sales and service.

History has shown that her decision was the correct one. She is quick to point out, though, that she was greatly aided by many insightful comments received during the evaluation process.

Consistent with her philosophy of open communication, Downing periodically likes to have luncheon retreats with three to six Dover executives. Topics range from the very heavy (Should we grow by acquisition?) to the very light (How can the office Christmas party be improved?).

Today's retreat involves three issues of varying importance: an offer by a present customer to buy 4,000 copiers at a reduced price; the excess demand that exists for one of Dover's office products; and a proposal to use an outside vendor to supply a component used in the production of automatic teller machines.

THE COPIER PROBLEM

The firm recently has received an offer from a very large petroleum corporation to purchase 4,000 copiers at $1,200 a unit, which is 20 percent under the usual price of $1,500. On one hand, the offer is quite welcome. Dover's copier operation is the only area of the firm that experienced a loss during the last three months. Copier sales are down and significant excess capacity exists in this part of the firm's operation. In fact, Dover could fill the petroleum company's order with no strain on its production facilities. The company's chief accountant, Timothy Wiles, is "the other hand." Wiles is adamant that accepting the offer is a "losing proposition." He cites as evidence the most recent income statement of the copier operation. (See Exhibit 1.) He notes that unit sales price has been $1,500, and the information in Exhibit 1 indicates that unit or average cost is $1,585. Wiles' argument is that to sell these copiers at a price of $1,200 will only "put the copier operation even more in the red" since this price is well below the operation's average cost.

Mark Thatcher is a finance officer and is skeptical of Wiles' argument. Thatcher believes that what is needed is an estimate of the marginal or incremental cost incurred if 4,000 additional copiers are produced. He is not convinced that Wiles' numbers capture such costs.

AN EXCESS-DEMAND PROBLEM

Production of the firm's executive desk cannot keep up with demand. Operating at capacity, Dover can manufacture about 18,000 desks per year, and orders on an annual basis total 20,000. Thus, capacity is 10 percent less than the amount demanded. Management is confident that demand will remain strong. Service-sector employment, which includes a relatively large proportion of office workers, is expected to increase. In addition, overseas demand for the product is strong and growing.

Management is considering two options for dealing with the excess demand: raise price or increase capacity without changing unit price. Don Rountree, a marketing executive, has put together some numbers on the impact of a price increase. He estimates that a 20 percent price increase will lower orders by 10 percent, thus eliminating the excess demand.

When asked where he got the estimate, Rountree explains it is based on the firm's experience during 1994. The price of the desk was increased by 10 percent, yet unit sales were only down 2 percent from the previous year. "This information," Rountree continues, "suggests that every 10 percent increase in our price causes a mere 2 percent decrease in unit sales." In order to be conservative and because he realizes that this is only one year's information, Rountree decided to assume that every 10 percent increase would cause a drop of 5 percent in unit sales. This estimate, therefore, indicates that a 20 percent price increase will lower the amount demanded by 10 percent; that is, the yearly quantity demanded is predicted to drop from 20,000 to 18,000.

Margaret Williamson, one of the firm's economists, is skeptical of this evidence and thinks that the drop in unit sales will be "much more" than these numbers suggest. She points out that customers are quite price conscious and that reasonable substitutes for the desk are made by other firms. She also notes that 1994 was a very strong year for the economy and especially the office furniture industry. "Plus," she continues, "in 1994 nearly all competitors raised prices because of substantially higher material costs. What we're analyzing here is a price hike while our competitors keep theirs constant."

Thatcher agrees with Williamson and thinks that it makes more sense to expand capacity. He has worked up a set of numbers on such an expansion assuming a 10-year time period, the firm's typical planning horizon for a project of this type. Thatcher claims that the present value of the yearly cash flows is $14 million, or nearly 100 percent more than the up-front cost of $7.6 million. These numbers, therefore, suggests that Dover would make a rather large economic profit from an expansion.

Williamson finds these numbers "interesting" but questions Thatcher's unit sales projections. Thatcher defends these forecasts by noting that he's assuming no changes in unit price or existing demand. "There's no pie-in-the-sky here," he claims. "Marketing feels that the demand increase for the desks is quite permanent. And, besides, all the information we have indicates that our competitors are operating at or near capacity also."

A "MAKE OR BUY" DECISION

Plant 2 is used primarily to manufacture automatic teller machines (ATMs). The plant typically purchases most of the required parts and manufactures the remainder in-house. One part currently done in-house is a component of the ATM's keyboard, and 200 of these are used each month. A vendor has offered to sell Dover this component for $40 a unit. The production engineer estimates that it costs $53.56 a unit to produce the component in-house. (See Exhibit 2.) Thus, his numbers imply a savings of $13.56 per unit if a vendor is used, for a total savings of $2,712 per month or $32,544 per year.

Wiles is quick to note that the analysis suggests that two workers may be laid off if the vendor is used. He argues that it is "simply not good business" to do so no matter what the numbers show. First, it would go against the company philosophy of promoting a team atmosphere. Second, it would reduce the range of skills at the plant and could also create significant morale problems since the workers are a rather tightly knit group. "In any event," he points out, "even if the vendor is used I'll bet that we could reemploy the workers somewhere else, especially if we choose to expand desk production."

QUESTIONS

1. (a) Explain how the firm's accountant used the information in Exhibit 1 to determine that the average or unit cost of a copier is $1,585.

   (b) Evaluate his argument that it does not make sense to sell 4,000 copiers to the petroleum company since the offer price of $1,200 is below the unit cost of $1,585.

2. (a) Calculate the additional revenue to Dover of accepting the copier offer.

   (b) Given the significant excess capacity in the copier operation and using the information in Exhibit 1, estimate the additional cost of producing 4,000 more copiers. Defend your estimate.

3. (a) Based on your previous answers, is it a good idea to sell the copiers to the petroleum company? Explain briefly.

   (b) Suppose the copier operation is producing at capacity. How, if at all, would this affect your answer to 3(a)? Explain.

4. (a) What is a demand curve? What are some factors that influence demand but are assumed to be constant for a demand curve?

   (b) What is the price elasticity of demand?

   (c) Rountree estimates that a 20 percent increase in the price of the executive desk will cause a drop of 10 percent in unit sales. What price elasticity of demand is he assuming? Is this price elasticity realistic? Explain.

   (d) What are the implications of your answer to part (c) for the firm?

5. (a) What are economic profits?

   (b) Under what circumstances, if any, can a firm expect to make economic profits?

6. The firm's economist is quite skeptical of the cost/revenue estimates associated with the option to expand the capacity of the executive desk. Why? (*Hint:* If the present value of all revenues exceeds the present value of all costs, then the project has a positive net present value and the firm expects to make an economic profit.)

7. Last year Dover spent $40,000 to install an access road to a potential plant site. This plant site may well be used if management decides to expand production of the executive desk. How relevant is this $40,000 to any decision that management must make?

8. (a) Assume that management would lay off the two individuals who make the ATM component in-house if an outside vendor is used. How, if at all, should the items in Exhibit 2 be adjusted to get the incremental savings of using a vendor? Be as specific as possible for each item. And keep in mind that you only want to consider those costs that will change if the part is purchased from a vendor.

(b) Based on your answer to part (a) and other information in the case, would you recommend that a vendor be used? Explain.

EXHIBIT 1
Income Statement of the Copier Operation

Sales[a]	$15,000,000
CGS[b]	9,000,000
Gross profit	6,000,000
FOC[c]	5,500,000
Depreciation	600,000
EBIT	(100,000)
Interest	750,000
Earnings before taxes	(850,000)

[a]10,000 copiers at $1,500 a unit.

[b]Cost of goods sold. Includes direct labor and material costs. $900 per copier.

[c]Fixed operating costs. Doesn't include depreciation. Does include items such as supervisory salaries, marketing expenses, secretarial support, property taxes, and corporate fees.

EXHIBIT 2
Estimated Monthly Cost of Producing the ATM Component In-House

1. Direct labor	$4,000
2. Indirect labor	600
3. Pension + welfare	552
4. Payroll taxes	460
5. Utilities	700
6. Material costs	400
7. Repairs & maintenance	700
8. Space	400
9. General factory	800
10. Depreciation	2,100
	$10,712
Unit Cost	$53.56 = 10,712/200

Description of the above items:
1. Two workers at $2,000 per month.
2. 15 percent of Item 1. Mainly the component's share of supervisory salaries.
3. 12 percent of Items 1 plus 2. This includes the firm's contribution to the employee's pension fund, plus health and disability insurance.
4. 10 percent of Items 1 plus 2. This is mainly for social security and unemployment insurance.
5. The component's share of electricity, heat, water, etc.
6. Parts and supplies directly related to the production of the ATM component.
7. Maintenance and repair on the equipment used by the two workers.
8. The component's share of the factory space occupied by the two workers.
9. The component's share of items like property taxes, corporate fees, secretarial support, etc.
10. Based on historical cost of the equipment.

PART II

FINANCIAL ANALYSIS

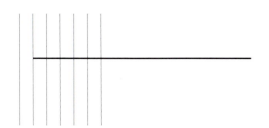

HOLLY FASHIONS
RATIO ANALYSIS

Billion-dollar apparel companies such as Calvin Klein and Liz Claiborne are un-usual in the garment industry, which consists primarily of much smaller apparel makers. One such firm is Holly Fashions (HF), located in Cherry Hill, New Jersey. HF was started 14 years ago by William Hamilton and John White, who between them had over 25 years of experience with a major garment manufac-turer. And the partnership initially blended very well. Hamilton, reserved and introspective, is extremely creative with a real flair for merchandising and trend spotting. Mainly as a result of his genius, the HF label is synonymous with qual-ity and "in" fashions. White, outgoing and forceful, has contributed important merchandising and marketing ideas, but has mainly assumed the duties of the firm's chief operating officer.

Hamilton has had little interest in the financial aspects of the company, much preferring to work on designing new fashions and the development of market-ing strategies. A few months ago, however, he decided that he had better be-come more involved with the company's financials.

His motivation is twofold. First, he is considering the sale of his 50 percent in-terest in HF. Though he enjoys the creative side of the business, he is tired of the cash crunches that the firm has experienced in recent years. Periodically, the re-tailers HF deals with have encountered financial problems and have strung out their payments, which often caused a mad scramble for cash at HF. And if Hamilton decides to sell, he knows that he is likely to be involved in some stress-ful negotiations surrounding the company's value. Though he would hire a con-sultant to aid him in any negotiations, he decides it is a good idea to educate himself about HF's financials.

Another reason that Hamilton is interested in the firm's financials is so he can better judge the managerial competence of White. When HF was small Hamilton thought White did a fine job, but now he wonders whether White is capable of running a firm as large as HF. Actually, if Hamilton were convinced that White is a competent manager, he would not consider selling out since he genuinely enjoys being an owner of an apparel firm. But he thinks the apparel industry will face even tougher times in the next few years, and wonders if White is talented enough to successfully meet these challenges.

BORROWING CONCERNS

White's personality is such that he makes virtually all major operating and financial decisions. An important example of this was his decision three years ago to retire all long-term debt, a move triggered by White's fear that HF's business risk was increasing. He cited the difficulties of seemingly rock-solid retailers like Bloomingdale's and Campeau to support his claim. White is also concerned that firms the size of HF have had difficulty maintaining stable bank relationships. Due to increasingly strict federal regulations, some banks have called in loans at the slightest technicality, and most are scrutinizing new business loans very carefully. Consequently White views bank debt financing as "unreliable" and thinks that loan officers are capable of "chewing up my time."

Hamilton isn't sure what to make of these arguments, but he is concerned that this debt avoidance has significantly reduced HF's financial flexibility because it means that all projects will have to be equity financed. In fact, over the past five years there have been no dividends because all earnings have been reinvested. And two years ago each of the partners had to contribute $15,000 of capital in order to meet the company's cash needs. Another infusion of capital may be necessary since the firm's present cash position is low by historical standards. (See Exhibit 2.)

More importantly, however, Hamilton feels that the company is not benefiting from the leverage effect of debt financing, and that this hurts the profitability of the firm to the two owners.

WORKING CAPITAL CONCERNS

Hamilton suspects that HF's inventory is "excessive" and that "capital is unnecessarily tied up in inventory." White's position is that a large inventory is necessary to provide speedy delivery to customers. He argues that "our customers expect quick service and a large inventory helps us to provide it."

Hamilton is skeptical of this argument and wonders if there isn't a more efficient way of providing quicker service. He knows that a consultant recommended that HF "very seriously" consider building a state-of-the-art distribution center. The proposed facility would allow HF to reduce inventory and also handle big orders from retailers such as Kmart and Wal-Mart. White rejected the suggestion arguing that the estimated $5-million to $8-million cost is excessive.

Hamilton also questions White's credit standards and collection procedures. Hamilton thinks that White has been quite generous in granting payment extensions to customers, and at one point nearly 40 percent of the company's receivables were more than 90 days overdue. Further, White would continue to accept and ship orders to these retailers even when it was clear that their ability to pay was marginal. White's position is that he doesn't want to lose sales and that the rough times these retailers face are only temporary.

Hamilton also wonders about the wisdom of passing up trade discounts. HF is frequently offered terms of 1/10, net 30. That is, the company receives a 1-percent discount if a bill is paid in ten days and in any event full payment is expected within 30 days. White rarely takes these discounts because he "wants to hold onto our cash as long as possible." He also notes that "the discount isn't especially generous and 99 percent of the bill must still be paid."

FINAL THOUGHTS

Despite all of Hamilton's concerns, however, the relationship between the two partners has been relatively smooth over the years. And Hamilton admits that he may be unduly critical of White's management decisions. "After all," he concedes, "the man seems to have reasons for what he does, and we have been in the black every year since we started, which is an impressive record, really, for a firm in our business."

Further, Hamilton has discussed with two consultants the possibility of selling his half of the firm. Since HF is not publicly traded, the market value of the company's stock must be estimated. These consultants believe that HF is worth between $55 and $65 per share, figures that "seem quite good" to Hamilton.

QUESTIONS

1. Calculate the firm's 1996 ratios listed in Exhibit 3.

2. Part of Hamilton's evaluation will consist of comparing the firm's ratios to the industry numbers shown in Exhibit 3.

   (a) Discuss the limitations of such a comparative financial analysis.

   (b) In view of these limitations, why are such industry comparisons so frequently made?

3. Hamilton thinks that the profitability of the firm to the owners has been hurt by White's reluctance to use much interest-bearing debt. Is this a reasonable position? Explain.

4. The case mentions that White rarely takes trade discounts, which are typically 1/10, net 30. Does this seem like a wise financial move? Explain.

5. Calculate the company's market-to-book (MV/BV) ratio. (There are 5,000 shares of common stock.)

6. Hamilton's position is that White has not competently managed the firm. Defend this position using your previous answers and other information in the case.

7. White's position is that he has effectively managed the firm. Defend this position using your previous answers and other information in the case.

8. Play the role of an arbitrator. Is it possible based on an examination of the firm's ratios and other information in the case to assess White's managerial competence? Defend your position.

9 (a) Are the ratios you calculated based on market or book values? Explain.

    (b) Would you prefer ratios based on market or book values? Explain.

EXHIBIT 1
Holly Fashions' Income Statements: 1993–1996 (000s)

	1993	1994	1995	1996
Sales	$985.0	$1,040.0	$1,236.0	$1,305.0
Cost of goods	748.6	774.8	928.2	978.8
Gross margin	236.4	265.2	307.8	326.3
Administrative	169.4	202.8	236.1	249.3
Depreciation	10.8	11.4	13.6	14.4
EBIT	56.1	51.0	58.1	62.6
Interest	7.0	6.0	5.0	4.0
EBT	49.1	45.0	53.1	58.6
Taxes	19.7	18.0	21.2	23.5
Net income	$29.5	$27.0	$31.9	$35.2

EXHIBIT 2
Balance Sheets of the Holly Fashions Company: 1993–1996 (000s)

	1993	1994	1995	1996
ASSETS				
Cash	$40.4	$51.9	$38.6	$10.6
Receivables	153.2	158.9	175.1	224.8
Inventory	117.0	121.1	193.4	191.9
Other current	5.9	6.2	7.4	7.8
Current assets	316.5	338.0	414.5	435.1
Gross fixed	44.8	58.9	78.1	96.4
Accumulated depreciation	(12.0)	(23.4)	(37.0)	(51.4)
Net fixed	32.8	35.5	41.1	45.0
Total assets	$349.3	$373.5	$455.5	$480.1

(continued)

EXHIBIT 2
(Continued)

	1993	1994	1995	1996
LIABILITIES & NET WORTH				
Accounts payable	$53.8	$54.7	$86.2	$84.2
Debt due	10.0	10.0	10.0	10.0
Accruals	19.7	26.0	24.7	26.1
Current liabilities	83.5	90.7	120.9	120.3
Long-term debt	60.0	50.0	40.0	30.0
Common stock	150.0	150.0	180.0	180.0
Retained earnings	55.8	82.8	114.6	149.8
Total L&NW	$349.3	$373.5	$455.5	$480.1

EXHIBIT 3
Financial Ratios for the Holly Fashions Company: 1993–1996

	1993	1994	1995	(Present) 1996	Industry Average 1993–1996*
Liquidity Ratios					
Current	3.8	3.7	3.4		2.6 1.7 1.3
Quick	2.4	2.4	1.8		1.6 .8 .6
Leverage Ratios					
Debt(%)	41.1	37.7	35.3		41 57 71
Times interest earned	8.0	8.5	11.6		7.4 3.9 1.3
Activity Ratios					
Inventory Turn- over (CGS)	6.4	6.4	4.8		8.1 6.0 3.5
Fixed Asset Turnover	30.0	29.3	30.1		40 25 12
Total Asset Turnover	2.8	2.8	2.7		3.5 2.8 2.0

(continued)

EXHIBIT 3
(Contined)

	1993	1994	1995	(Present) 1996	Industry Average 1993–1996*
Average Collection Period	56	55	51		41 50 68
Days Purchases Outstanding**	25	22	31		18 25 32
Profitability Ratios Gross Margin (%)	24.0	25.5	24.9		28 26 24
Net Profit Margin (%)	3.0	2.6	2.6		4.2 3.1 1.2
Return on Equity (%)	14.3	11.6	10.8		27.3 19.5 7.8
Return on Total Assets (%)	8.4	7.2	7.0		11.8 8.7 3.4
Operating Margin*** (%)	6.8	6.0	6.1		9.9 7.2 3.1

*The three numbers for each ratio are computed in the following way. Ratios for all firms in the industry are arranged in what is considered a strongest-to-weakest order. The middle number represents the median ratio; that is, half the firms in the industry had ratios better than the median ratio and half had ratios that were worse. The top number represents the upper quartile figure, meaning 25 percent of the firms had ratios better than this. The lower number represents the lowest quartile, that is, 25 percent of the firms had ratios worse than this.

**This shows the average length of time that trade debt is outstanding. Also called the average payment period. Calculated as $A/P \div (CGS/360)$.

***Calculated as $(EBIT + Dep)/Sales$.

DUNHAM COSMETICS FINANCIAL EVALUATION

For the last 26 years, Dunham Cosmetics has obtained virtually all of its business loans from the Graham County Bank (GCB). For the most part, Dunham has been a valued customer, though in 1980 Dunham fell behind in its debt payments when a new line of toiletries was a complete disaster. After this the bank monitored Dunham's financial situation extremely closely, requiring monthly financial statements. As the company's financial situation improved, the bank went to quarterly and—eight years ago, in 1987—yearly evaluations. This was a sign that GCB felt the company was a good credit risk, and in recent years Dunham has had little difficulty obtaining bank financing. In fact, Dunham will seek a $675,000 loan in the near future. It is in the second year of its Equipment Improvement Program and will use the funds to modernize the factory and much of the equipment. The completion of this program is considered vital to the current and future health of the company.

Jean Reardon was promoted to corporate banker with GCB four months ago and is the officer in charge of Dunham's account, replacing an officer who apparently was considered too lenient in corporate loan decisions. Reardon has known of Dunham's intended loan request for three weeks, and her initial reaction was that approval of the loan would be highly probable. Fortunately she never expressed this opinion to Lionel Jensen, Dunham's general manager. She realizes circumstances do change, and it would be very embarrassing to turn down a loan request from a longtime client after hinting such a loan would be "likely." There are a number of factors indicating Dunham will have borrowing difficulties, and she calls a meeting with Jensen to discuss the company's debt situation.

JENSEN AND REARDON MEET

Reardon reminds Jensen that the Federal Reserve is tightening credit in order to eliminate inflationary pressures in the economy. This means that loans will become harder to obtain and the bank will be looking at each loan request much more carefully. Even more serious, the bank has just finished its yearly financial evaluation, and Reardon emphasizes to Jensen that, in her opinion, Dunham's financial position is "poor and seems to be getting worse." She also points out as tactfully as possible that Dunham is violating its loan agreements. For example, one provision stipulates the current ratio can't fall below 1.85.

A final issue concerns the terms of the company's loans. Jensen tells Reardon that "I am considering whether to restructure the company's debt" and "might request" that the bank take all of Dunham's debt and amortize it over five years. "Of course, this may be unnecessary," he is quick to add. Reardon explains to Jensen that in light of Dunham's difficulties the loan committee would much prefer that any debt be repaid as quickly as possible. This means that (1) the loan committee would prefer not to restructure the debt; and (2) the new loan request, assuming it is even granted, would likely be in the form of a note payable. However, Reardon does tell Jensen that the bank is willing to "work with you to develop a financial plan satisfactory to all parties." Reardon then suggests they meet again in the near future to discuss the situation further.

A few minutes after Jensen leaves, Reardon wonders if she wasn't a bit too "hardline," especially regarding Jensen's request to restructure Dunham's existing debt. She knows that the officer previously in charge of the firm's account had raised no red flags with Jensen at last year's annual meeting. This is surprising given the company's "off" year in 1994. Prudent banking dictates that an officer express concern over a deterioration in a firm's position and seriously investigate the reasons for any poor performance.

And there are possible legal considerations. Suppose that the bank either calls the loan or refuses to allow Dunham to restructure. If, as a result, Dunham ends up in serious financial difficulties, then it is possible that GCB could be held legally liable for these problems because of the failure to adequately warn Dunham a year ago.

Everything considered, Reardon thinks it may well be in the bank's interest to allow Dunham to restructure its existing debt. The new loan request is another matter, however. Although approval of the loan is not out of the question, Dunham will need a very solid and convincing business plan to stand any chance.

Back at his office, Jensen reflects on the meeting with Reardon and the firm's situation. He is annoyed that he had not anticipated the bank's evaluation but feels there is a positive side to the situation. "Perhaps this will give our board the kick in the pants it needs," he thinks. Jensen knows Dunham is in difficulty and has a number of measures he wants implemented. Unfortunately, the board feels the company's problems are largely the result of a poor cosmetics market; the members believe there is little to do but wait for the "inevitable recovery."

Jensen agrees that part of Dunham's problem has been the soft market that has existed for the past two years. However, industry experts agree this decline is over, and there are indications that demand is on the rise. Jensen himself believes a safe prediction is for sales to increase by 10 percent in 1996.

JENSEN'S RECOMMENDATIONS

He also feels there are a number of changes Dunham can make. When the company realized that demand would be down, it hoped to increase sales with more liberal credit and through a larger inventory that would increase customer selection. Jensen opposed those measures at the time on the grounds that "they have never worked in the past, and we have a competitive, even generous credit policy." At present Dunham has an especially large level of inventory and a very high amount of receivables. Jensen believes receivables should be reduced to 60 days of sales in 1996 and the inventory turnover (sales/inventory) ratio could be raised to 5.4, the industry average. In addition he has a number of suggestions for reducing Dunham's costs. He believes the company can increase its gross profit margin to 31 percent and reduce selling and administrative expenses to 21.5 percent of sales.

"One reason for our lousy current ratio is we've gradually taken longer and longer to pay our bills! I've gotten more than one nasty letter in the last year! I'm going to suggest we get payables to 9 percent of sales, which would be competitive with other firms."

Jensen has also been critical of how the company has obtained external funding for the last few years. Virtually all such money has been supplied by GCB, and Jensen has secretly felt that the bank has been "extremely generous" in honoring Dunham's loan requests. Personally he believes the firm should have used more equity by eliminating dividend payments and selling more stock. In fact, in 1993 he had recommended that the firm lower its payout ratio from 50 to 20 percent of net income. The proposal received little support then and consequently Jensen hesitates now to propose a reduction in dividends. He decides to make any financial forecast assuming the payout ratio remains at 50 percent.

Though Jensen doesn't really think GCB will grant the $675,000 loan request, he believes that Dunham should not accept the money even if it is offered. "But maybe I am wrong," he admits. "I will work up a financial forecast based on these changes and see what the numbers look like."

Jensen will present his suggestions at the meeting he has called in 72 hours, and believes "they'll be implemented considering the situation with the bank." Jensen knows that the board wants the $675,000 loan, and if Dunham doesn't show the bank a solid plan, it will not only have no chance to obtain the $675,000, but the bank could foreclose on the existing loans. "And maybe, just maybe," he sighs, "if the bank likes our plan we won't be required to submit a monthly review. I really hate those!"

QUESTIONS

1. Calculate Dunham's 1995 financial ratios. (See Exhibits 1, 2, and 3).

2. Does a trend analysis indicate Dunham's position has been deteriorating? (See Exhibit 3.)

3. Is the bank justifiably concerned? Justify your answer.

4. Nineteen ninety-four was a "down" year for Dunham. Do you think that GCB had a responsibility to express concern in 1994, especially since the current ratio was close to 1.85, the number that could trigger a call of the loan? Explain.

5. Suppose Dunham had followed Jensen's 1993 recommendation to lower its payout ratio. Recalculate the firm's debt and current ratios for 1995 assuming that the payout ratio was 20 percent from 1993 to 1995. (Assume that the extra money was used to reduce the firm's notes payable.)

6. (a) Jensen discussed Dunham's situation with Paula Robinson, an accounting friend. Robinson said that, in her opinion, Dunham has "too little long-term capital, especially considering your receivables and inventory needs." Why is it frequently appropriate to use a long-term capital source like bonds or equity to finance items like inventory and receivables that appear on a balance sheet as short-term assets?

   (b) What advantages are there to using short-term debt to finance long-term assets? What are the disadvantages?

7. (a) Project Dunham's income and balance sheet for 1996 (see Exhibit 4) assuming the bank grants Dunham a $675K note payable at 12 percent and no existing interest-bearing debt is retired. (Dividends will be 50 percent of net income.) Cash will be the residual or balancing item in the forecast.

   (b) Estimate the firm's 1996 minimum cash balance assuming that on average during 1993 to 1995 its cash situation was normal.

   (c) Use any excess cash at the end of 1996 to retire notes payable.

8. (a) Will the bank be impressed by Jensen's changes? Explain.

   (b) What other options does Dunham have, assuming the bank denies the loan request? Critically evaluate each of these options.

🖫 SOFTWARE QUESTION

9. Dunham Cosmetics presently has $4,466,000 of interest-bearing debt. Nearly all of the debt is due in the next three years.

   Jean Reardon thinks that it is a good idea to allow Dunham to restructure its debt and spread the payments over at least five years. She reasons that Dunham is unlikely to generate sufficient cash to pay the annual debt due the way the loans are presently structured. This could create problems for Dunham and the bank, and she wants to avoid, if possible, any "collection hassle."

She also is considering a new loan of up to $325,000 which is about half of the $675,000 that Lionel Jensen requested.

Reardon is convinced that (1) any loan would be adequately secured and (2) Jensen has a solid business plan, though she believes it may take him longer than he expects to fully implement it. Before she approves any loan, however, she would require Dunham to reduce its payout ratio, perhaps even have Dunham eliminate dividends entirely.

NOTE 1: Dunham's payout ratio is presently .50, that is, half of net income is paid out as dividends.

NOTE 2: Dunham needs $675,000 of financing. If the new loan is granted, this provides Dunham with $325,000 of the needed financing, and it would raise the remainder by selling new stock. If only the existing debt were restructured, that is, no new loan is granted, then all of the $675,000 would be financed with equity. Thus, any new loan amount reduces dollar-for-dollar the amount of new equity that Dunham must raise.

Reardon decides to evaluate Dunham's ability to pay off a new five-year $325,000 loan in the following scenarios, and assuming equal amounts of principal are due each year. The interest rate would be 12 percent. She also decides to evaluate payout ratios of .50, .25, and 0 for each scenario.

NOTE 3: This loan would total $4,791,000, which equals the $4,466,000 of existing interest-bearing debt plus the additional $325,000. Principal due each year is $958,200.

S-1 is Reardon's best-guess (most-likely) scenario. Reardon labels S-2 "conservative" and S-3 "pessimistic."

1996 Estimates	S-1	S-2	S-3
Sales growth	.10	.10	.08
Gross margin	.30	.29	.29
ACP	60.00	65.00	65.00
Sales/Inv.	5.40	5.40	5.10
1997–2000 Estimates			
Sales growth	.05	.05	.03
Gross margin	.31	.30	.30
ACP	55.00	60.00	65.00
Sales/Inv.	5.70	5.40	5.40

For all scenarios she will assume in every year that administrative expenses and payables are 21.5 percent and 9 percent of sales, respectively. Reardon will also assume that capital spending will be $900(000) in 1996, $200(000) in 1997, increasing by the sales growth rate after that. Finally, the minimum cash balance each year is $1,127(000).

Perform the appropriate analysis.

(a) Does it appear that allowing Dunham to restructure its $4,466,000 of existing (old) debt is a good idea? Explain.

(b) Would you grant Dunham an additional $325,000? Explain.

NOTE: Make sure when you address part (b) that (1) the "new equity" input is set at $350 for 1996 and 0 in 1997–2000, and (2) "net new debt" is set at $325.

EXHIBIT 1
Income Statements (000s)

	1993	1994	Present year 1995
Sales	$25,264	$25,769	$26,671
Cost of goods	17,180	17,508	18,793
Gross profit	8,084	8,261	7,878
Administrative expenses	5,254	5,516	6,068
Depreciation	302	393	479
EBIT	2,528	2,352	1,331
Interest	296	451	578
Earnings before taxes	2,232	1,901	753
Taxes (50%)	1,116	951	377
Net income	1,116	950	376
Common stock dividends	558	475	188
Retained earnings	558	475	188

EXHIBIT 2
Balance Sheets (000s)

	1993	1994	Present Year 1995
Assets			
Cash & marketable securities	$ 1,264	$ 1,237	$ 879
Receivables	3,789	5,204	5,920
Inventory	4,042	5,102	6,133
Current assets	9,095	11,543	12,932
Gross fixed assets	3,024	4,123	5,337
Accumulated depreciation	(1,129)	(1,521)	(2,001)
Net fixed assets	1,895	2,601	3,336
Total assets	10,990	14,144	16,268
Liabilities and Equity			
Notes payable	$ 1,111	$ 1,804	$ 2,400
Accounts payable	2,021	3,126	3,866
Accruals	656	1,010	1,334
Current liabilities	3,788	5,940	7,600
Term loans	1,254	1,781	2,066
Common stock	4,050	4,050	4,050
Retained earnings	1,898	2,373	2,552
Total liabilities and equity	10,990	14,144	16,268

EXHIBIT 3
Financial Ratios for Dunham Cosmetics

	1993	1994	1995	Industry Average 1993–1995
Liquidity				
Current	2.40	1.94		1.95
Quick	1.33	1.08		1.00
Leverage				
Debt (%)	46.00	55.00		53.00
Times interest earned	8.54	5.20		5.00
Activity				
Inventory turnover (sales)	6.25	5.10		5.40
Fixed asset turnover	13.33	9.91		10.00
Total asset turnover	2.30	1.82		2.10
Average collection period (days)	54.00	72.70		51.00
Profitability				
Gross profit margin (%)	32.00	32.00		30.50
Net profit (%)	4.40	3.70		3.00
Return on total assets (%)	10.10	6.70		6.30
Return on equity (%)	18.70	14.80		13.30

EXHIBIT 4

*1996 Income Statement
of Dunham Cosmetics (000s)*

Sales	
Cost of goods	_____
Gross profit	
Administrative expenses	
Depreciation	568
EBIT	
Interest	_____
Earnings before taxes	
Taxes	_____
Net income	==============

*1996 Balance Sheet
(000s)*

Assets	
Cash & marketable securities	
Receivables	
Inventory	_____
Current assets	
Gross fixed assets	6,214
Accumulated depreciation	(2,569)
Net fixed assets	_____
Total assets	==============
Liabilities and Equity	
Notes payable	
Accounts payable	
Accruals	1,366
Current liabilities	
Bonds	2,066
Common stock	4,050
Retained earnings	_____
Total liabilities and equity	

C A S E 8

SPARTAN ROOFING LOAN EVALUATION

"The Spartan Roofing Company makes excellent products!" So concluded a laudatory independent report commissioned by a bank in 1996.

THE SPARTAN ROOFING COMPANY

The Spartan Roofing Company was established in 1951 as a sole proprietorship in Ohio. The company is an innovative manufacturer of aluminum roofing products. Its standard products include the safeguard gravel stop system, the reglet and expansion joint system, and a wide variety of roofing panel systems. The safeguard system, which is patented, is designed to correct three major problems encountered by the roofing industry—water leakage of joints, tar drippage on the exterior of the finished building, and shrinkage.

The company's products are designed to favor both building owner and contractor. The building owner benefits because of design technology that ensures Spartan's materials will last many years with little maintenance. The contractor benefits because the materials are simple to install. As a result the firm's products are extremely popular with the building industry, and many architects and engineers specify Spartan materials by brand name. Market studies support this claim and also indicate that Spartan could increase its market share substantially, given that the company has only a 5-percent share at present. Not surprisingly the firm is very strong in technical expertise; the engineering department is an important component of the business, and the development of new products is very much encouraged. Consequently, the company has been granted over eight patents in the last 20 years.

While Spartan's technical expertise is unquestioned, the firm is a bit suspect in financial matters. Periodically it has had difficulties with such matters as inventory control and pricing. Historically, however, when the firm has experienced serious problems in an area it has been able to show improvement by the following year. All things considered, there is little doubt that Spartan has compiled an impressive track record over the last 20 years. In fact, when one bank evaluated Spartan in 1991 it concluded that "this is one of the best-run companies we have ever encountered in its size-sales category."

In 1985, the firm relocated to Tennessee at the suggestion of Lawrence Wilson, the firm's CEO and son of the founder. The company's bank has been First City since the move South, but Tennessee National Bank (TNB) has aggressively sought Spartan's business. Since 1985 TNB has called on Wilson on more than 30 occasions and has made six different financing proposals. Wilson was always reluctant to switch, though he almost left First City for TNB in November 1993 because he was upset at First City for a reason never clear to TNB.

JOHN PATTILLA

In December 1994 John Pattilla of TNB had written a 12-page memorandum recommending that the bank make a specific financing proposal to Spartan. Pattilla's analysis was quite thorough and included projections of the firm's situation using a "best guess" or "most likely" and "worst case" set of assumptions. (See Exhibit 1 for excerpts from his 1994 report, Exhibit 2 for his net income projections, Exhibit 3 for his balance sheet projections, and Exhibit 4 for his "worst case" cash flow estimates.)

Pattilla had a few conversations with Wilson to get information for the projections. The final estimates, however, reflect Pattilla's assessment of the situation, and Wilson has never seen these numbers. Pattilla had recommended that TNB extend the company up to $700,000 in loans. The money would be used to finance Spartan's working capital and fixed-asset needs for anticipated strong sales growth from an expanding economy and the introduction of a number of new products. The company was especially excited about its new macrocarbide product line. Macrocarbide is known for its unusually long life and is therefore very useful in the roofing industry.

It is now early 1996 and Pattilla has to decide whether TNB should make another proposal to Lawrence Wilson. As Pattilla leans back in his chair, he leafs through information on Spartan, and a number of items catch his eye. He smiles as he notices the nearly 40-percent increase in sales for 1995, an increase he predicted almost to the penny. Pattilla realizes, however, that Spartan must have benefited enormously from the economic upturn, since the sales of its new products have not gone as well as expected. Especially disappointing were the sales of Spartan's macrocarbide product line. It appears to Pattilla that the sales growth is due more to an external factor outside the company's control—the economy—than to internal factors under its control. He also notes that Wilson tapped the firm's line of credit with First City for over $500,000, a result not at all consistent with his 1994 projections. Pattilla knows that any proposal would involve a buy-out of First City, and TNB's offer should be at least the amount of Spartan's credit line with First City, or about $750,000. Pattilla had concluded his

1994 report by noting that "this represents an excellent opportunity for TNB." But now, nearly 14 months after he made that recommendation, Pattilla wonders if he will reach the same conclusions as he begins his evaluation of Spartan's financial records.

QUESTIONS

1. (a) Complete the 1995 pro forma balance sheet listed in Exhibit 3.

   (b) Complete the "worst case" cash flow projection for 1997 listed in Exhibit 4.

2. Do you agree that TNB should have actively sought Spartan's business at the end of 1994? Fully support your answer. (*Note:* When this recommendation was made, Pattilla only had financial information on the first three quarters of 1994. He did possess, however, a projection for the last quarter that was virtually identical to what actually occurred.)

3. Calculate the ratios listed in Exhibit 9 for the Spartan Roofing Company for 1995.

4. Evaluate the Spartan Roofing Company's situation at the present time (early 1996). What difficulties, if any, does your evaluation indicate?

5. Note that in 1995 Spartan's cash flow from operations (net income plus depreciation) was its highest during the 1992–1995 period. Yet its need for external funds, reflected in the large increase in its short-term bank loans, was also the greatest over the same period. Resolve this apparent paradox.

6. Use the format of Exhibit 4.

   (a) Prepare what you think is a "best guess" ("most likely") cash flow forecast for 1996. State your assumptions clearly. Do assume, however, that capital expense will be $120(000) and depreciation remains at $80(000). Defend the assumptions of your forecast.

   (b) Prepare what you think is a "worst case" cash flow forecast for 1996. Clearly state your assumptions. Do assume, however, that there is no change in sales from the 1995 level, depreciation remains at $80(000), and that the firm will postpone all expansion projects and incur only replacement capital expenses of $50(000). Defend the assumptions of your forecast.

7. Do a liquidation analysis on the firm for the end of 1995. That is, estimate its liquidation value and compare it to the amount of its debt obligations. It is customary in a situation like this for Pattilla to make the following, perhaps conservative, assumptions: (1) all cash on the balance sheet is used for liquidation expenses; and (2) receivables can be converted into cash at 60 percent of book value, inventory at 30 percent, and net fixed assets at 25 percent.

8. Based on your previous answers and information in the case, do you recommend that TNB seek Spartan's business at the present time (early 1996) and offer a $750,000 buy-out of First City? Fully support your recommendation. (*Note:* Do not consider any smaller loan amount, and assume the offer would involve a six-year term loan with the principal paid in equal amounts each year.)

9. What additional information would help you make a more informed decision in question 8?

💾 SOFTWARE QUESTION

10. *Attention instructors:* Questions 6 and 8 should probably not be assigned if this question is used.

   John Pattilla of Tennessee National Bank has to decide whether to seek Spartan's business. He is considering a $750,000 loan, which would enable Spartan to buy out First City, Spartan's present bank. The principal would be payable in equal amounts each year for the next six years (1996–2001).
   After some thought, Pattilla decides to analyze Spartan's cash flow in the following scenarios (1997 capital spending is $50(000) in all scenarios).

	S-1	S-2	S-1A	S-2A
Annual sales growth	.05	.02	.05	.02
Net income/sales	.024	.018	.028	.022
Average collection period	60.00	65.00	55.00	60.00
Sales/inventory	8.00	7.00	8.00	7.00
(AP & accruals)/sales	.10	.10	.10	.10
Capital spending (1996)	120.00	80.00	120.00	80.00

NOTE: AP refers to accounts payable.

S-1 and S-2 represent Pattilla's best-guess (most-likely) and worst-case forecasts, respectively, assuming no additional concrete information about Spartan Roofing.

   S-1A and S-2A are based on a recent conversation that Pattilla had with Lawrence Wilson, the owner. Wilson claimed that he is going to "implement sounder credit policies," and "eliminate some production inefficiencies."
   Pattilla has not had time to carefully examine these claims, and wonders if these changes "would make any difference, anyway, assuming Wilson is right."
   Perform the appropriate analysis. What would you recommend to Pattilla? Defend your advice.

EXHIBIT 1
Excerpts from John Pattilla's 1994 Report on the Spartan Roofing Company

- "The company expects, and I agree, that sales growth will be 37 percent, 20 percent, and 20 percent over the next three years. This will result partly from the economic growth of the overall economy but mainly from the sales generated by its new macrocarbide products."

- "Lawrence Wilson is exceptionally strong in the technical aspects of the business and is very much involved in new product development. He has a B.S. and an M.S. in chemical engineering from MIT. On the other hand, being a technical sort, his financial expertise is somewhat limited. Nonetheless, Wilson's track record over the last 10 years speaks for itself, and we have had no reason to question his integrity."

- "One area of concern is the quality of the accounts receivable, given that the majority of the customers are contractors. It should be noted, however, that the majority of the contractors have been doing business with Spartan for a number of years and the company is familiar with their financial condition. In fact, its bad debt expense has never exceeded 0.6 percent in any of the last 10 years, a solid statistic considering the customer base."

- "The main reason for the company's poor earnings in 1994 was the large expenses incurred by a former salesman of the company. Lawrence hired a salesman who was very expensive but did not produce. As a result, selling expenses increased sharply in 1994."

- "From 1992 to 1994, the period I analyzed most intensively, Spartan generated sufficient cash flow from operations to meet its capital expenditure needs and its debt service. Adjusted working capital was a net source of funds for the company which partly reflects the attention given to the management of working capital. The result of all this was a large positive cash flow (see Exhibit 8) which Spartan used to repay a number of relatively expensive term loans. Whether this was a wise financial move is debatable."

- "Due to the working capital requirements of the large expected sales growth and the fixed-asset needs of the company, the company will not be in a position to begin repaying any of the principal on the debt until 1997."

- "Even my 'worst case' cash flow forecast indicates that Spartan will have sufficient funds to repay sizeable chunks of any new debt beginning in 1997." (See Exhibit 4.)

(continued)

EXHIBIT 1
(Continued)

- "I recommend we finance Spartan's working capital and fixed asset needs. This will require up to $700,000. I also recommend that we do not amortize any of the loans for two years. The loans would be secured by the accounts receivable, inventory, and equipment of the company, and would be personally guaranteed by Lawrence."
- "I believe this to be an attractive opportunity for us, but it does involve several elements of risk. The company's sales and earnings are quite sensitive to overall economic conditions and the construction industry in particular. In addition, the nature of the customer base (contractors) is suspect. On the other hand, given the company's track record, it appears that they have effectively managed these risks."

EXHIBIT 2
Net Income Projections for the Spartan Roofing Company: 1995–1997 (000s)
(Developed by John Pattilla for TNB in 1994)

	1995		1996		1997	
	B.G.[a]	W.C.[b]	B.G.	W.C.	B.G.	W.C.
Sales	$5,400	5,000	$6,500	5,300	$7,800	4,900
Net income	$ 135	75	$ 162	80	$ 195	74

[a]B.G. is the "best guess" ("most likely") forecast and assumes sales will increase by 37 percent in 1995, 20 percent in 1996, and 20 percent in 1997. Net income is assumed to be 2.5 percent of sales.

[b]W.C. is a "worst case" forecast that assumes net income will be 1.5 percent of sales.

EXHIBIT 3
Pro Forma Balance Sheets for the Spartan Roofing Company: 1995–1997 (000s)
(Developed by John Pattilla for TNB in 1994)

	1995		1996		1997	
	B.G.[a]	W.C.[b]	B.G.	W.C.	B.G.	W.C.
Assets						
Cash	$ 40	$ 40	$ 50	$ 50	$ 60	$ 40
Receivables		833	993	883	1,193	816
Inventory		694	776	736	931	680
Current assets	$1,510	$1,567	$1,819	$1,669	$2,184	$1,536
Gross fixed assets	929	929	1,309	1,309	1,339	1,339

(continued)

EXHIBIT 3
(Continued)

	1995		1996		1997	
	B.G.[a]	W.C.[b]	B.G.	W.C.	B.G.	W.C.
(Depreciation)	(537)	(537)	(657)	(657)	(787)	(787)
Net fixed assets	392	392	652	652	552	552
Total assets	$1,902	$1,959	$2,471	$2,321	$2,736	$2,088
Liabilities and Equity						
Short-term debt due	$ 169	$ 326	$ 198	$ 308	$ 166	$ 66
Accounts payable		194	252	206	303	190
Accruals		300	390	318	468	294
Current liabilities		$ 820	$ 840	$ 832	$ 937	$ 550
Term loans	155	155	425	425	400	400
Common stock	50	50	50	50	50	50
Retained earnings	994	934	1,156	1,014	1,351	1,088
Total liabilities and equity	$1,902	$1,959	$2,471	$2,321	$2,738	$2,088

[a]B.G. refers to a "best guess" ("most likely") forecast that incorporates these assumptions: (1) receivables will be 55 days of sales; (2) inventory turnover will be 8.4 (43 days of sales); (3) accounts payable will be 3.9 percent of sales (round your estimate down); (4) accruals will be 6 percent of sales; and (5) capital expenditures will be $90 in 1995, $380 in 1996, and $30 in 1997.

[b]W.C. refers to a "worst case" forecast that incorporates these assumptions: (1) receivables will be 60 days of sales; and (2) inventory turnover will be 7.2 (50 days of sales). Assumptions 3 to 5 in the "best guess" situation remain unchanged.

EXHIBIT 4
Worst Case* Cash Flow Projections for the Spartan Roofing Company: 1995–1997 (000s)
(Developed by John Pattilla in 1994)

	1995	1996	1997
Net income	$ 75	$ 80	$ 74
Depreciation	80	120	130
Cash flow operations	$155	$200	$204
−Adjusted working capital needs	332	62	
−Capital expense	90	380	30
−Dividends	0	0	0
Cash flow	($267)	($242)	$257

(continued)

EXHIBIT 4
(Continued)

Adjusted Working Capital

	1994	1995	1996	1997
Accounts receivable		$ 833	$ 883	
Inventory		694	736	
−Accounts payable		194	206	
−Accruals		300	318	
Adjusted working capital	$701	$1,033	$1,095	
Change adjusted working capital		332	62	

*This assumes (1) net income will be 1.5 percent of sales; (2) receivables will be 60 days of sales; (3) inventory turnover will be 7.2 or 50 days of sales; and (4) accounts payable will be 3.9 percent of sales and accruals 6 percent. (See Exhibits 2 and 3 for projected net income and pro forma balance sheets.)

EXHIBIT 5
Income Statements and Bad Debt Expense for the Spartan Roofing Company: 1992–1995 (000s)

	1992	1993	1994	1995
Sales	$3,978	$3,902	$3,946	$5,399
Cost of goods	2,884	2,872	2,959	4,173
Gross profit	$1,094	$1,030	$ 987	$1,226
Administrative & selling expenses	815	762	837	904
Depreciation	53	61	55	80
EBIT	$ 226	$ 207	$ 95	$ 242
Interest	66	44	20	80
Earnings before taxes	$ 160	$ 163	$ 75	$ 162
Taxes (40%)	64	65	30	65
Net income	$ 96	$ 98	$ 45	$ 97
Bad debt expense	0.1%	0.6%	0.4%	0.9%

EXHIBIT 6
Normalized Income Statements for the Spartan Roofing Company: 1992–1995

	1992	1993	1994	1995
Sales	100	100	100	100
Cost of goods	72.5	73.6	75	77.3
Gross profit	27.5	26.4	25	22.7
Administrative & selling expenses	20.5	19.5	21.2	16.7
Depreciation	1.3	1.6	1.4	1.5
EBIT	5.7	5.3	2.4	4.5
Interest	1.7	1.1	0.5	1.5
Earnings before taxes	4.0	4.2	1.9	3.0
Taxes (40%)	1.6	1.7	0.8	1.2
Net income	2.4	2.5	1.1	1.8

EXHIBIT 7
Balance Sheets for the Spartan Roofing Company: 1992–1995 (000)

	1992	1993	1994	1995
Assets				
Cash	$ 85	$ 120	$ 21	$ 43
Receivables	707	785	580	1,124
Inventory	476	446	428	773
Current assets	$1,268	$1,351	$1,029	$1,940
Gross fixed assets	669	698	757	914
(Accumulated depreciation)	(251)	(312)	(367)	(447)
Net fixed assets	418	386	390	467
Total assets	$1,686	$1,737	$1,419	$2,407
Liabilities and Equity				
Notes payable—banks	$ 180	$ 220	$ 162	$ 700
Accounts payable	148	157	150	306
Accruals	218	277	157	310
Current liabilities	$ 546	$ 654	$ 469	$1,316
Term loans	374	219	41	85
Common stock	50	50	50	50
Retained earnings	716	814	859	956
Total liabilities and equity	$1,686	$1,737	$1,419	$2,407

EXHIBIT 8
Spartan's Cash Flow 1992–1994 (000s)

	1992	1993	1994
Net income	$ 96	$ 98	$ 45
Depreciation	53	61	55
Cash flow operations	$149	$159	$100
−Adjusted working capital needs	(80)	(20)	(96)
−Capital expenditures	40	29	59
−Dividends	0	0	0
Cash flow	$189	$150	$137

		Adjusted Working Capital		
	1991	1992	1993	1994
Accounts receivable		$707	$785	$580
Inventory		476	446	428
−Accounts payable		148	157	150
−Accruals		218	277	157
Adjusted working capital	$897	$817	$797	$701
Change adjusted working capital		(80)	(20)	(96)

EXHIBIT 9
Financial Ratios for the Spartan Roofing Company: 1992–1995

	1992	1993	1994	1995	Industry Average[a] 1992–1995
Liquidity Ratios					
Current	2.32	2.07	2.19		2.4 1.6 1.2
Quick	1.45	1.38	1.28		1.5 1.0 0.7
Leverage Ratios					
Debt (%)	55	50	36		38 55 71
Times interest earned	3.42	4.7	4.75		11 5 2
Activity Ratios					
Inventory turnover (sales)	8.4	8.7	9.2		13.6 9.7 6.5
Fixed asset turnover	9.52	10.1	10.1		16.4 9.8 5.5
Total asset turnover	2.36	2.25	2.78		2.9 2.3 1.7
Average collection period	64	72	53		37 49 61
Profitability Ratios					
Gross margin (%)	28	26	25		32 26 23
Net profit margin (%)	2.4	2.5	1.1		3.6 2.4 1.6
Return on net worth (%)	12.5	11.3	4.9		25 13 9
Return on total assets (%)	5.7	5.6	3.2		10.4 5.8 2.7

[a]The three numbers for each ratio are computed in the following way. Ratios for all firms in the industry are arranged in what is considered a strongest-to-weakest order. The middle number represents the median ratio; that is, half the firms in the industry had ratios better than the median ratio and half had ratios that were worse. The top number represents the upper quartile figure, meaning 25 percent of the firms had ratios better than this. The lower number represents the lowest quartile; that is, 25 percent of the firms had ratios worse than this.

PALMETTO SOUPS
BREAK-EVEN
ANALYSIS

Palmetto Soups is a household name in much of the Southeast and Southwest. It wasn't always so.

Thirty years ago Robert Rivera founded Palmetto Soups when numerous "informal and unscientific" taste tests convinced him that his recipes generated soups that were different and flavorful. Only six years out of college, Rivera literally had to pester grocery stores to sell his soups. The first three years were difficult as few stores were willing to give shelf space to the products of a firm owned by someone not quite thirty years of age. Yet the soups were good and grocers who did carry Palmetto products quickly noticed that customers began asking for Palmetto by name. Sales and profits grew rapidly and, in fact, in the last few years earnings per share have increased at a rate well above companies of similar size. And the future looks bright also. The company's market area is experiencing an economic boom, and sales are projected to increase in real terms (i.e., adjusted for inflation) for at least the next three years.

COST REDUCTION

Earlier this year (1995), Palmetto's board of directors approved a switch to a highly capital-intensive method of production. This change will be made in part to accommodate the anticipated sales growth but mainly to lower unit costs. At present raw materials and direct labor are 77 percent of sales, which is the industry average. By 1997, these inputs are expected to be roughly 45 percent of sales—primarily due to substantial labor savings—and the gross margin should be 52 percent, which would be the highest in the industry. The year 1996, however, will be a transition year. That is, it will take time to fully implement the new production techniques. Management believes that raw materials and direct labor will be 60 percent of sales. Since variable selling expense is predicted to be 3 percent of sales, the 1996 gross margin is estimated to be 37 percent. Of course, the change will increase the firm's overhead costs. Administrative and other fixed expenses are predicted to reach $3 million and $1 million, respectively, in 1996 due in part to the necessity of hiring a number of experienced technicians. Depreciation in 1996 will be $3.75 million. Production is confident that these cost estimates are quite reasonable and also believes that the projected future level of sales will not strain the firm's capacity. For example, in 1996 the company will operate at roughly 57 percent of its production capability.

Everyone in the company believes the change will be very profitable in the long run, but there is a heated debate over the financing of the project. The company's investment banking firm, Smith, Peabody and Associates, believes that all money could easily be borrowed considering Palmetto's "extremely strong net working capital position, very competitive debt ratio, and low business risk."

FINANCING CONTROVERSY

Rivera, the company president, wants to use this debt alternative. First, he feels the risk is minimal since the demand for the company's product is quite stable. "After all," he argues, "we've never been more than 10 percent off in any of our sales forecasts." Second, sales and profits are both expected to increase for at least the next three years. Next year's (1996) sales, for example, are predicted to increase 10 percent, though half of this is pure inflation. Rivera simply finds it hard to believe that the money to pay the debt won't be there. Third, equity financing will bring in outsiders to the business, and he is very proud of the fact that all the firm's stock is owned by the Rivera family. Finally, since he strongly believes that the company's profits will "take off," Rivera is loathe to "divide up the pie into more slices," which could be the result if additional stock were issued. As he puts it, "The possibility of sharing what I've worked so hard to develop bothers me a great deal."

Theodore Tipps, a financial officer, has a very different view. He worries that the huge interest expense associated with the debt may embarrass the company. Specifically, his concern is that net operating income in 1996, the transition year, will be insufficient to pay the firm's interest, which he estimates would increase by $1.4 million if debt is used. Tipps agrees with Rivera about Palmetto's future prospects but cautiously points out that "too much debt could mean we won't be around to enjoy the fruits of our investments. And there is another problem: the *threat* of bankruptcy needs to be considered. Adverse rumors could cause key employees to leave, make it difficult to deal with our suppliers, and might even cost us sales. It is, therefore, not just a question of whether we can pay the debt, but whether we can do so without disrupting the operation of the firm." Tipps also suggests lengthening the term of the loan in order to lower the yearly payment, assuming the firm decides to borrow. Rivera is reluctant to do this because (1) it would raise the interest rate; and (2) he wants to repay any debt as soon as possible.

Though Tipps feels strongly that the firm's borrowing should be completely financed from Palmetto's yearly operations, he admits that in a pinch assets could be liquidated. But he initially told Rivera that he would be reluctant to do this because "we need all our assets to adequately support our future sales projections." When pressed by Rivera, though, Tipps conceded that Palmetto's working capital position is too conservative; also, if sales were below projection, less working capital would be needed.

As they part, Rivera feels that Tipps has made a number of good points but wonders if he isn't overreacting and thinking too conservatively. However, Rivera has a great deal of respect for Tipps's financial savvy and is taking the objections very seriously.

QUESTIONS

1. Project the 1996 income statement assuming the firm uses debt. (Assume sales will increase by 10 percent.)

2. Compute the company's EBT break-even sales volume and DOL for 1996. Express the break-even sales volume as a percent of sales. (In 1995, this break-even sales volume was $14,750,000, and 57.8 percent of sales. The firm's DOL was 2.)

3. If sales are 10 percent below the 1996 estimate, predict the firm's net operating income (EBIT). Would it be sufficient to cover the interest due?

4. After reviewing the answers to 1 to 3, Rivera says, "What we're really after is the level of sales that generates sufficient cash flow to pay the principal and interest due on our debt. What is that sales amount?" (Principal due will be $1,900,000 in 1996 if the company borrows.) Use

$$S^* = \frac{(FC - Dep) + Prin}{1 - V/S}$$

5. The correct use of the break-even formulas in questions 2 and 4 rests on certain assumptions. What are they? Do these assumptions appear to hold for Palmetto? Explain.

6. Based on your answers to 1 to 5 and information provided in the case, would you recommend the use of debt to finance the new production methods? Explain.

7. What additional information would you like to have to make a more informed decision?

8. One of Rivera's arguments for using debt is that Palmetto expects increases in both sales and profits in the coming years. Apparently, he believes that the larger expected profits will generate sufficient cash to pay any debt due. Is there a fallacy in this reasoning? That is, is it possible that larger profits resulting from higher sales could actually be associated with less *cash* available for debt service? Explain.

Perform the appropriate analysis. How do the results effect your answer to question 6?

SOFTWARE QUESTION

9. Robert Rivera, the company president and major stockholder, feels pretty good at this point about the decision to borrow all the funds needed to finance the new production techniques. Still, he is taking very seriously the objections of Theodore Tipps, a financial officer. Rivera doesn't want to be bothered with any cash flow problems, especially over the next few years during the production changes. He decides to "think pessimistically" regarding the future, and analyze the firm's ability to meet the debt due under adverse circumstances.

The scenarios Rivera will investigate are shown below, and the debt due is $1,900(000) in both 1996 and 1997. Interest expense will be $1,400(000) in 1996 and $1,210(000) in 1997.

	Scenario			
	Base-case 1996/1997	Conservative 1996/1997	Pessimistic 1996/1997	Very Pessimistic 1996/1997
Sales growth	.10/.05	.05/.05	.05/.02	.02/.00
Gross margin	.37/.52	.36/.49	.35/.47	.34/.44
Overhead*	4000/4200	4200/4400	4400/4800	4600/5000

*Overhead represents fixed cash operating costs, and is expressed in thousands of dollars.

NOTE: The large increase in the gross margin from 1996 to 1997 in all scenarios is a result of the implementation of the new production techniques.

Perform the appropriate analysis. How do the results affect your answer to question 6?

EXHIBIT 1
Income Statement (000s)

	1995 (Present)	1996
Sales	$25,500	
Cost of goods sold	20,400	
Gross profit	5,100	
Administrative	1,275	
Depreciation	850	
Other fixed	425	
EBIT	2,550	
Interest	400	
Earnings before taxes	2,150	
Taxes (40%)	860	
Net income	$1,290	

FRIENDS BREAK-EVEN ANALYSIS

Friends is a charitable organization that sponsors group activities and provides adult companionship for troubled youths from single-parent families. Friends screens, trains, motivates, and supervises the adult volunteers, who are paired with children referred by local agencies and by parents concerned with their children's future. The organization provides a service that can augment any professional help a child may be receiving. But its main role is one of prevention by providing a meaningful adult relationship for a child before the child becomes a severe parental or societal problem. Friends is a nationwide organization that began in 1911 in Cincinnati, Ohio, and there are over 200 local agencies throughout the country with the parent office, Friends Central, in New York. Friends Central provides support in establishing and administering local programs, but each agency is responsible for raising its own funding.

The Culver City branch in Forsyth County, Virginia, was started only six months ago and has an operating budget for the current year of $60,000. The budget is modest by most standards but will be hard to achieve given the newness of the organization and the nationwide recession that has hit Culver City especially hard. About 30 percent of the necessary funds will come from the United Appeal, and the remainder from a government grant, some fund-raising events, and donations.

THE IMPORTANCE OF THE DANCE

The final event planned is a dance that the organization hopes will raise $8,000, which is the projected yearly deficit. Although eliminating the shortfall is an important objective, there are other reasons why the dance needs to be successful. The Forsyth County United Appeal has made it clear that it wants local agencies to establish their own fund-raising events. There even is talk that the United Appeal will implement a financing scheme in which it matches every dollar in profit generated by an organization. Friends Central also encourages its local agencies to develop their own fiscal base. A number of studies have found that agencies that rely heavily on outside monies tend to stagnate, in part due to the restrictions that often accompany such monies. Nationwide, United Appeal has been known to oversee quite strictly the running of organizations that it funds heavily. It is precisely this type of rigidity that Friends Central wants to avoid by encouraging local units to raise a large proportion of their budget on their own. And although the Forsyth County United Appeal has in the past adopted a policy of minimum intervention, one can never be sure when this philosophy might change. Finally, a successful event would raise the status of Culver City's Friends organization. Friends Central would raise the agency's classification from an agency-in-formation to a provisional agency, which would enable more children to be served.

Tickets for the dance will be sold at $50 per couple, and the sale of drinks should net $10 per couple. The dance will be held at the Mountain Lodge, which has a ballroom seating 300 couples. Bob Lyttle, a manager at the lodge and a member of Friends' board of directors, has arranged for the owners to donate the ballroom. Hors d'oeuvres will be provided at a cost to Friends of $5.00 per couple, and $500 will cover labor and miscellaneous expenses. The only other expense is the cost of the band, whose selection is generating some controversy among the dance organizers. The choice is between the Flames and the Charms. Both play the same type of music, a mixture of old-time rock and roll and beach music. The Flames, however, will cost $6,000, the Charms only $3,000.

SOME ARGUMENTS FOR EACH BAND

Supporters of the Flames believe that this band will increase ticket sales, and they cite the band's 15 years' experience and recognition among the 30–45-year age group, the target population of the dance. These individuals also believe that a long view is appropriate. "We can't just look at one year," they argue, "but we also have to consider the impact of our decision on future dances. The Flames will set the tone for the event and increase its future popularity. This is especially relevant if the United Appeal implements its matching scheme on any money raised by a charity from an event such as the dance." Finally, they point out that if the Flames were selected it would be a "big deal" for Culver City and the dance would receive more publicity, thus benefiting the Friends organization. They cite this as an intangible factor that should not be ignored.

Supporters of the Charms agree that the Flames are the better band but question whether the Flames will generate enough extra sales to make up for the increased cost. Both sides feel 200 tickets will likely be sold even if the Charms are selected, but there is some concern that the dance tickets will not sell as well as expected. "After all," says Bill Frady, an accountant by profession, "there is a recession out there. The $50 ticket price may be a bit steep for this town, especially in view of the economy. Let's be realistic and admit we may not be able to sell 200 tickets. The Flames increase the overhead and Friends can't afford to take a loss on this dance. Eliminating the deficit has to be our number one priority. There is just no slack in our budget, and any shortfall may well have to come out of the salaries of the staff, which would not only be unfair but would also be bad business. In short, we simply do not have the luxury to worry about the future. Let's get by this year and then concern ourselves with future dances."

Supporters of the Charms do admit that any additional publicity from using the Flames would benefit Friends. They are not convinced, however, that the Flames would be best for the organization in the long run. Lyttle points out that two local philanthropists "have their eye on our agency." He believes that these individuals would "bail us out" in the event of a shortfall. "But," he cautions, "they would be much less likely to support us in the future." Lyttle is convinced that if Friends can stand on its own this year, these philanthropists will be generous in coming years since "they admire agencies that try to be self-supporting." He agrees with Frady that the Charms make more sense, though he believes that Frady is too pessimistic about ticket sales. He wonders, however, whether the price should be lowered to $40 per couple. "Perhaps," he speculates, "we can more than gain on volume what we would lose on the unit price."

After much discussion all agree it is highly probable that 200 tickets can be sold even if the Charms are used and that 150 is the absolute lower limit. It is also estimated that lowering the price to $40 will increase sales by 20 to 40 tickets.

QUESTIONS

For questions 1 to 4 assume the price of a ticket is $50.

1. (a) Calculate the break-even ticket sales for each band.
   (b) Express your answer as a percentage of the estimated ticket sales.

2. (a) Assume the Charms are selected. Develop a table showing the profits on the dance at the following ticket levels: 150, 200, 250, and 300 (sellout).
   (b) Repeat part (a) assuming the Flames are selected.

3. How many extra tickets must be sold to compensate for the higher cost of the Flames?

4. If the dance is to raise $8,000, how many tickets must be sold if the Flames are used? The Charms?

5. Evaluate the proposal to lower the price of a ticket to $40. What implications, if any, does it have for the band choice?

6. Based on your previous answers and other information provided in the case, which band would you pick? Why?

7. The break-even and profit formulas you used are based on certain assumptions. What are they? Are they likely to hold for this situation? Explain.

8. Suppose the dance organizers were sure that 270 tickets could be sold at a price of $50 regardless of the band used. How would this affect the choice?

9. How would knowledge of the demand curve for each band be helpful for determining which group to use and what price to charge?

PART III

FINANCIAL PLANNING

TIPTON ICE CREAM
FINANCIAL
FORECASTING

George Tipton began the Tipton Ice Cream Company nearly five decades ago. He patented a soft ice cream and right from the outset paid special attention to quality. "We only make one product, but we make it in many flavors and we make it well," Tipton was fond of saying. The company was an immediate success and sales quickly reached seven figures.

DEBT AVERSION

The firm expects strong growth in the coming year (1996) and Brenda Hood, Tipton's chief financial officer, hopes she can make a strong case for borrowing to finance the company's expansion. She realizes, however, that she is likely to face stiff opposition from the Tipton family. George Tipton, perhaps unduly influenced by the Great Depression of the 1930s, detested borrowing money and his motto was "Never a lender nor borrower be." For nearly 25 years all the company's stock was owned by the Tipton family, but due to expansion new shares have been sold during the last 15 years to individuals outside the family. By 1995 the Tipton family owns 60 percent of all shares, and although the family has not been very active in running the firm, it does insist on one family tradition: "Never a lender nor borrower be." To this day Tipton has never owed anything beyond its accounts payable and accruals.

Hood knows this is an extreme case of debt aversion and the policy has hurt the owners' profits. For example, historically Tipton has been slightly above the industry average in return on total assets but consistently below in return on owner's equity. At each annual meeting she has tried unsuccessfully to convince the Tipton clan to use more debt. And each year Hood heard a chorus of "Never a lender. . . ." But perhaps this year would be different.

She recalls two sessions on financial management that she held for the nonfinancial executives of Tipton. Some members of the Tipton family had attended these sessions. She explained that when sales increase, then inventory, cash, and accounts receivable must also increase. Further, if the firm's existing operating capacity was insufficient to support the increased sales, additional fixed assets would be required. She had also stressed the need for pro forma statements to determine the magnitude of the funds needed. It was the first time members of the Tipton family had received any formal financial exposure, and she recalls they seemed interested and attentive.

At the previous annual meetings Hood had avoided using any technical financial analysis to make her case for borrowing. But now she thinks, "Why not?"

FORECASTING ASSUMPTIONS

She decides to estimate (1) the amount of funds Tipton will have to obtain in 1996; (2) the 1996 income statement assuming all of the financing is done through borrowing; and (3) another income statement assuming all new stock is issued. To help in the estimates Hood enlists Frank Davis, a recent MBA. Davis reminds her that 1996 is expected to be a big year for the company; sales are predicted to increase by 25 percent. Due to the strong demand, marketing feels any cost increases can easily be passed on. Consequently, the gross margin should exceed the current level of 21 percent. Hood notes that the sales-to-inventory ratio will be lowered to 6.5, and that purchases should total $101,481,000. This suggests cost of goods for 1996 would be $93,750,000.

"What about administrative and selling expenses?" Hood asks Davis. He informs her that management salaries would have to rise sharply because these salaries had increased very slightly over the past three years. Davis believes a 20 percent increase in administrative and selling expenses is reasonable.

Fixed assets are likely to change sharply in the coming year. Currently, Tipton is operating virtually near capacity, demand is expected to remain high, and thus extra capacity will be needed. In addition, some major improvements to existing equipment will have to be made in order for the company to remain competitive. The planning for these changes has been anticipated for some time, and though all of these changes do not have to be made in 1996, it is clear that the company cannot grow beyond 1996 without them. In any event, it is urgent that the financing question be resolved as soon as possible. A reasonable estimate is that Tipton will purchase $5 million of new plant and equipment in 1996.

"During the past year we've been a bit slow in paying our suppliers," Hood remarks. "We definitely will have to pay more promptly or we're going to have some annoyed creditors; plus we'll pick up cash discounts by paying earlier. See if you can come up with an estimate of our payables using past information."

Hood and Davis also feel that over the last few years factors (other than sales) affecting accruals and receivables have been relatively constant. For example, the company has not altered its credit policy in the last three years. Nor can they think of any reason why these items should change significantly in the coming year. "Of course, an *exact* relationship between each of these and sales is unlikely to exist," Hood cautions. "We can expect some yearly random fluctuation. And keep in mind the 'big/little' mix will be changing since we'll be selling to smaller food chains. This has implications for our receivables since these firms are relatively slow to pay. This shouldn't be a major factor, Frank, but it is something you should be aware of when you make your estimate."

Hood and Davis think the cash management of the firm has been a "bit sloppy" over the past few years, and both agree the company could make do with a lower level of liquidity. Davis suggests he assume a level of 2 percent of sales, which is the approximate industry average, and Hood agrees. "What about dividends?" Davis asks Hood. "Our payout ratio is usually around 50 percent. However, if we borrow all the extra money, let's work backwards on the dividends; that is, out of net income subtract the amount of the retained earnings we would obtain if we used all-equity financing."

FORECASTING RESTRICTIONS

There are two final problems. While Hood believes the company should use more debt, she recognizes that the final decision rests with the Tipton family. Given their debt aversion it is important that any projections not appear too debt-heavy. She also wonders how much flexibility she would have to use short-term debt, assuming the decision to borrow is made. Hood, therefore, instructs Davis to work within the following constraints when doing the forecast. As working hypotheses she wants Tipton's debt ratio to remain below 0.5, and the current and quick ratios must not fall below 2 and 1, respectively. In other words, the financial projection cannot violate any one of these restrictions. "Given these limitations, see how much flexibility we have in raising any funds needed," Hood tells Davis.

QUESTIONS

1. Project the 1996 income statement assuming no borrowing.

2. Project Tipton's 1996 balance sheet assuming no borrowing.

3. Explain how the $93.75 million cost-of-goods estimate for 1996 was obtained.

4. How much money will Tipton need to raise in 1996?

5. (a) How much of this money can Tipton borrow long term without violating the constraints imposed by Hood?

(b) How much of this money can be raised using notes payable without violating these constraints?

6. Redo the 1996 income statement assuming all of the funds needed are borrowed as long-term bonds at 8 percent. (Keep retained earnings at the same level as in question 1.)

7. Will the Tipton family own less than 50 percent of the firm's stock if no funds are borrowed? (Assume shares are sold to nonfamily members at $11.50 per share, which nets $10.50 after brokerage fees.)

8. Calculate the dividend per share and earnings per share if the expansion is

   (a) Financed by new equity.
   (b) Financed by borrowing.

9. Use the percent of sales method to forecast the amount of financing. Why does this estimate differ from your answer in question 4?

10. (a) When making a financial forecast, which one of the items that must be estimated is the most important? Why?

    (b) Which item do you think is typically the most difficult to forecast?

11. (a) What are some ratios you would calculate to help determine the risk of using debt?

    (b) Play the role of a consultant. Industry averages for all categories of ratios are given in Exhibit 3. Based on your previous answers, the ratios calculated in part (a), and these industry averages, would you endorse the debt financing if you were a member of the Tipton family? Explain.

SOFTWARE QUESTION

12. Hood is generally quite comfortable with the assumptions of her forecast. Still, she recognizes that her estimates could be wrong and she decides to analyze the following scenarios.

	S-1	S-2	S-3	S-4
1996 sales	$115,000.00	$125,000.00	$125,000.00	$130,000.00
CGS/sales	.76	.75	.75	.77
Cash/sales	.023	.028	.025	.02
ACP	38.00	36.00	39.00	38.00
AP/sales	.07	.06	.063	.063
Sales/inv.	6.30	6.50	6.30	6.10

NOTE: AP refers to accounts payable.

The first two scenarios, S-1 and S-2, represent the estimates of the firm's marketing director and sales manager, respectively, people whose judgment Hood respects.

The third scenario considers the possibility that the firm's working capital management won't be as efficient as Hood expects. The final set of estimates assumes that sales exceed Hood's original projection.

Analyze each scenario assuming first that all needed funds are raised by equity, and then assume all needed funds are raised by selling bonds, that is, "long-term debt." How, if at all, do the results affect your answer to question 11(b)? (Keep all other estimates at their base-case values.)

EXHIBIT 1
Selected Financial Information for Previous Three Years (000s)

	1993	1994	1995
Sales	$88,500	$96,000	$100,000
Receivables	$ 7,432	$ 8,533	$ 8,000
Average collection period (days)	30.2	32	28.8
Accounts payable	$ 5,700	$ 6,000	$ 9,500
Accruals	$ 2,400	$ 1,800	$ 3,000

EXHIBIT 2
Balance Sheets (000s)

	1995	Equity 1996	Debt 1996
Assets			
Cash & marketable securities	$ 3,000		
Accounts receivable	8,000		
Inventory	11,500	_____	_____
Current assets	22,500		
Gross fixed assets	24,000		
Accumulated depreciation	(4,000)	$(4,600)	$(4,600)
Net fixed assets	20,000	_____	_____
Total assets	$42,500	_____	_____
Liabilities and Equity			
Notes payable	$ 0		
Accounts payable	9,500		
Accruals	3,000	_____	_____
Current liabilities	12,500		
Bonds	0		
Common stock	20,000		
($10 par)			
Retained earnings	10,000	_____	_____
Total liabilities and equity	$42,500	_____	_____

(continued)

EXHIBIT 2
(continued)
Income Statements (000s)

	1995	Equity 1996	Debt 1997
Net sales	$100,000		
Cost of goods	79,000	_____	_____
Gross profit	21,000	_____	_____
Administrative & selling expenses	10,000		
Depreciation	600	$600	$600
Miscellaneous	200	220	220
EBIT	10,200		
Interest	0	_____	_____
Earnings before taxes	10,200		
Taxes (50%)	5,100	_____	_____
Net income	5,100		
Dividends	2,550		
To retained earnings	2,550		

EXHIBIT 3
Industry Averages

Current	1.8
Quick	0.8
Debt (%)	50.0
Times interest earned	6.0
Inventory turnover (sales)	6.0
Average collection period (days)	26.0
Total asset turnover	2.1
Gross profit margin (%)	18.0
Return on total assets (%)	8.5
Net profit on sales (%)	3.9
Return on net worth (%)	17.0

CASE 12

TOPEKA ADHESIVES (I)
FINANCIAL FORECASTING

Karen and Elizabeth Whatley are twins. Their mother teaches Physics at a midwestern university and their father runs a successful engineering firm. Not surprisingly, they are quite gifted at math and science, and they've displayed these talents in numerous ways over the years. For example, they have won a number of state science fairs, achieved near-perfect math SAT scores, and graduated Summa Cum Laude with Chemistry degrees from California Institute of Technology. After graduating college they took jobs with a major chemical company, though their long-term goal was to open their own firm. The Whatleys completed a number of evening courses to increase their business skills. In their spare time the sisters loved to experiment and developed two relatively low-cost adhesives: a glue and a tape.

They fulfilled a dream seven years ago when—with modest capital but contracts with a number of regional building supply stores— they formed Topeka Adhesives. The firm's products were top-notch and the company finished in the black its very first year, although the sisters were not entirely comfortable with the financial side of the business.

A MARKETING DECISION

About 12 months ago the partners concluded that Topeka's products were "underappreciated" and that "sales could—and should—be substantially higher." They fired an unproductive salesperson and, more importantly, made a key marketing decision. The twins decided to reduce Topeka's advertising in trade journals and use the money saved to attend more trade shows. They reasoned that trade shows are a relatively inexpensive way to display the company's products and are an opportunity to meet major corporate buyers face to face. That is precisely what happened. The firm's exhibits were impressive, and the Whatleys made important contacts with some industrial users and even one national retailer, Spears. The sisters are in the process of negotiating a number of large contracts for the coming year (1996) and product inquiries are markedly higher.

As a result of all this, Topeka's sales growth is expected to increase sharply in the next three years, and sales are estimated to more than double by the end of 1998. The Whatleys predict sales of $1,933,100 in 1996, $2,609,700 in 1997, and $3,131,600 in 1998. On one hand, the twins are extremely pleased with the forecast because it is evidence of what they have long believed: The company manufactures quality products at a reasonable price. The downside is that such large growth will undoubtedly require external financing and could cause managerial difficulties.

While the partners will explore a number of financing alternatives, they recognize that the first step is to estimate the external funds needed for the 1996–1998 period. After all, before they decide on a financing option, they want a reasonable projection of what needs to be raised. And it is even possible that most of the expected growth can be internally financed.

FORECASTING CONSIDERATIONS

In order to develop the forecast the partners decided to meet with Fred Lanzi, the firm's accountant, and Karl Shatner, Topeka's general manager. All agree that the sales projections are "quite reasonable" in view of the activity resulting from the trade shows and may even be a bit low. They also decide to concentrate on the 1996 forecast at the initial meeting.

A few months ago Shatner began implementing a number of cost-cutting measures that are expected to generate a 32 percent gross margin each year of the forecast. Due to economies of scale administrative expenses are expected to increase less than proportionately with sales, and the group estimates a 20 percent increase in 1996. The relevant tax rate is 40 percent.

Lanzi pointed out that the financial forecast needs to consider the tighter credit terms offered by many of the firm's suppliers. Company records show that two years ago about 80 percent of Topeka's purchases were on terms of 2/10, net 30. That is, most suppliers offered a 2 percent discount to customers who paid within ten days but, in any event, full payment was expected by day thirty. Roughly 20 percent of the purchases were on terms of net 30. "We, of course," noted Lanzi, "always took the discount when it was offered."

Company records also show that during the past year only about half of the firm's suppliers offered the above discount. Lanzi strongly believes that even fewer vendors will offer a discount in the future, and thinks that it is wise to assume—and the Whatley's concur—that only a third of all future purchases will be made on terms of 2/10, net 30. In addition, he recommends that Shatner's gross margin estimate be reduced to 31 percent, in part because of fewer trade discounts. After some discussion, Shatner agrees that Lanzi's points "are well made and my estimate of gross margin is probably a bit high."

The discussion then turns to working capital management. Inventory control has been a problem for Topeka at times. Elizabeth Whatley believes that inventory turnover (CGS/inventory) can be increased to 7.7 mainly by using suppliers with shorter delivery time. Karen Whatley, however, is skeptical. She thinks that it is unrealistic to think that the firm's inventory management can be improved and believes that some type of estimate based on historical inventory patterns is appropriate. Despite her objections, however, the group decides to use Elizabeth's estimate.

It is clear that the firm's historical experience with its accounts receivable will be of little help in predicting future receivables. In the past, Topeka has offered terms of net 30; 1/10, net 30; and 2/10, net 30. Quite frankly, which one Topeka offered depended on the bargaining power and importance of the customer. And many of Topeka's new clients are quite large firms who have insisted on a longer payment period.

For the purpose of this forecast, the Whatleys decide to assume that they will offer credit terms of net 30 and net 45. They estimate that 40 percent of all sales will be on terms of net 30, and that 80 percent of this group will pay on time, though taking the full 30 days. The 20 percent who pay late are expected to take an extra 10 days, or 40 days in all.

Sixty percent of all sales are estimated to be made on terms of net 45. The Whatleys believe that these customers will tend to be "more reliable and stable" and, thus, expect that 90 percent of these sales will be paid on time, that is, on day 45. The 10 percent who will be late are predicted to take an extra ten days.

The Whatleys expect that "virtually all" sales will be collected and they estimate that bad debt expense will be "insignificant" and can be ignored.

The group also thinks that cash should be 3 percent of sales, "other current" assets will be .6 percent of sales, and accruals are best estimated using past information.

The firm's predicted 1996 spending on plant, land, and equipment is $175,000. These expenditures partly reflect the replacement of existing equipment but mainly result from the new facilities necessary to accommodate the growth in sales.

FINANCIAL ISSUES

Topeka will pay no dividends during 1996. The firm has one loan outstanding and the amount due is $20,000 each year. Assuming no additional borrowing, annual interest expense will decline since the loan's balance also declines and the rate is fixed. Still, it is likely that some if not most of any new funds would be borrowed. For the time being, however, the forecasters decide to ignore the possibility of any new debt except for the assumption that interest expense will remain constant over the forecasting period.

Lanzi says he has enough information to develop an estimate for 1996 and then, as the meeting is about to break up, Karen Whatley raises an issue that she'd like to discuss at a future time. "We frequently negotiate credit terms with customers," she notes. "And we often give in to the customer, especially if we sense we risk losing a sale. I'm interested in knowing when—if ever—we should be more hardcore about our credit terms. We've never really looked carefully at this question, you know."

QUESTIONS

1. When Jim Davidson, a company foreman, heard that Topeka may need external funds he was quite puzzled. "I've seen the most recent balance sheet. And we seem to be rolling in dough, judging from the impressive amount of retained earnings." Respond to Davidson's comment.

2. Develop a pro forma income statement for 1996. You may assume that depreciation equals the 1995 amount plus one-sixth of 1996 capital spending. The relevant tax rate is 40 percent.

3. (a) What will be Topeka's 1996 average collection period?
   (b) Predict the 1996 level of receivables. Assume a 360-day year.

4. Estimate purchases in 1996. (*Hint:* Cost of goods equals purchases plus beginning inventory minus ending inventory.)

5. (a) What will be the firm's 1996 average payment period?
   (b) Predict the 1996 level of payables. Assume a 360-day year.

6. (a) Develop the 1996 pro forma balance sheet.
   (b) What is your estimate of funds needed in 1996?
   (c) Suppose that Elizabeth Whatley is correct and that Topeka's inventory management is unlikely to improve. Develop an estimate of inventory using the "historical information" in Exhibit 1 and Exhibit 2. How does this affect the estimate of funds needed in 6(b)?

7. Use the percent of sales method to estimate funds needed in 1996 using the 1995 percentages.

8. Would you expect your answers in 6(b) and 7 to be similar? Explain.

9. When offered terms of 2/10, net 30, the firm has always taken the discount. Does this make financial sense?

10. As the case states, Topeka frequently negotiates credit terms with customers, and the Whatleys are interested in knowing when it is worthwhile to lengthen the credit period rather than lose a sale. A common situation is the request by a customer who places orders of $100,000 a year with Topeka for terms of net 45 when Topeka only wants to allow net 30.

Is it a wise financial move for Topeka to grant the extra 15 days rather than lose the sale? Does your answer depend on whether Topeka has "significant excess capacity?" Explain. (You may assume that Topeka will lose the sale if it does not grant terms of net 45.)

EXHIBIT 1
Income Statements of Topeka Adhesives: 1993–1995 (000s)

	1993	1994	1995
Sales	$1,347.0	$1,448.0	$1,546.5
Cost of goods	956.4	1,010.7	1,076.4
Gross margin	390.6	437.3	470.1
Administrative	323.3	350.4	368.1
Depreciation	29.6	31.9	34.0
EBIT	37.7	55.0	68.0
Interest	14.0	12.0	10.0
EBT	23.7	43.0	58.0
Taxes	9.5	17.2	23.2
Net income	$14.2	$25.8	$34.8

EXHIBIT 2
Balance Sheets of Topeka Adhesives: 1993–1995 (0000s)

	1993	1994	1995
Assets			
Cash	$47.6	$56.6	$47.0
Receivables	97.3	88.5	110.8
Inventory	134.7	138.5	149.5
Other current	8.1	8.7	9.3
Current assets	287.7	292.2	316.6
Gross fixed assets	194.3	232.1	266.1
Accumulated depreciation	(59.6)	(91.5)	(125.5)
Net fixed assets	134.7	140.6	140.6
Total assets	$422.4	$432.8	$457.2
Liabilities and equity			
Accounts payable	$39.8	39.5	$48.3
Debt due	20.0	20.0	20.0
Accruals	28.3	33.3	34.0
Current liabilities	88.1	92.8	102.4
Long-term debt	120.0	100.0	80.0
Common stock	110.0	110.0	110.0
Retained earnings	104.2	130.0	164.9
Total liabilities and equity	$422.4	$432.8	$457.2

TOPEKA ADHESIVES (II)
FINANCIAL FORECASTING

Karen and Elizabeth Whatley are twins and the owners of Topeka Adhesives, a company they started seven years ago. The technical expertise of the firm is unsurpassed, and Topeka has developed a number of adhesives like tapes and glues that are popular with industrial users as well as home supply and hardware stores.

About twelve months ago the partners concluded that Topeka's products were "underappreciated" and that "sales could—and should—be substantially higher." They fired an unproductive salesperson and, more importantly, made a key marketing decision. They decided to reduce advertising in trade journals and increase the funds spent on attending trade shows. The marketing change worked. The firm's exhibits were impressive, and the Whatleys made important contacts with some major industrial users and even one large retailer, Spears. The sisters are in the process of negotiating a number of large contracts for the coming year (1996) and product inquiries are markedly higher.

As a result of all this, Topeka's sales are expected to increase sharply in the next three years, more than doubling by the end of 1998. The partners estimate sales of $1,933,100 in 1996, $2,609,700 in 1997, and $3,131,600 in 1998. On one hand the twins are extremely pleased with the forecast because it is evidence of what they have long believed: The company manufactures quality products at a reasonable price. The downside is that such large growth will undoubtedly require external financing and could cause managerial difficulties.

FORECASTING CONSIDERATIONS

The partners have met with Fred Lanzi, Topeka's accountant, and Karl Shatner, the firm's general manager, in order to compile a forecast for 1996–1998 and to discuss the financing options. The table below shows the 1996 pro forma balance sheet resulting from the meetings, and indicates that $226,100 needs to be raised.

Topeka's 1996 Pro Forma Balance Sheet (000s)

Assets		Liabilities & Equity	
Current assets	$485.2	Payables & accruals	$141.1
Net fixed assets	267.5	Debt due	20.0
		Long-term debt	60.0
Total assets	$752.7	Equity	305.5
		Funds needed	226.1
		Total liabilities & equity	$752.7

The partners need to develop forecasts for 1997 and 1998, though they are confident that 1996 will be the year of the "largest need" for external funds.

The Whatleys do not intend to declare any dividends and expect the net profit margin (NI/sales) to equal 3.5 percent. The net profit margin estimate is a bit conservative since it considers the possibility that new funds may be borrowed, which would increase interest expense. They also believe that there will be little if any economies of scale in working capital requirements, and consequently it is reasonable to assume that current assets will increase proportionately with sales in 1997 and 1998, as will accruals and accounts payable, that is, "spontaneous liabilities."

Net fixed assets are expected to increase by $140,000 in 1997 and $50,000 in 1998. Topeka has one loan outstanding and the amount due each year is $20,000.

FINANCING DIFFERENCES

It is no surprise, since the Whatleys are twins, that they are similar in many ways. For example, both are gifted at math and science, they enjoy hiking and horseback riding in their spare time, and they rarely disagree about even the most important business decisions. Yet it is clear that they have very different views about how the expected growth should be financed.

Karen Whatley wants to borrow all the necessary funds for a number of reasons. First, she argues that "we have very limited capital of our own." This implies that any equity beyond retained earnings will have to be raised from new investors. She is loathe to do this because she has been told that during the past twelve months privately held companies with sales under ten million have sold at four to six times EBDIT (earnings before depreciation, interest, and taxes). During the five previous years the multiple was seven to ten. In short, Karen is convinced that any new shares of stock would be sold at relatively low prices.

In addition, she really believes that "profits are going to explode" and she doesn't like the idea of "sharing them with outsiders." Further, Karen wants to borrow as much short-term debt as possible in part because of its relatively low interest rate. And she realizes that much of the external financing will be used to expand receivables and inventory. She considers these to be short-term assets and believes that it is appropriate to finance them using a short-term debt instrument.

The possibility of borrowing makes Elizabeth a bit uneasy. Frankly, she doesn't believe that her sister thinks enough about the consequences of a "downside disaster." Elizabeth doesn't want to worry about "cash crunches," that is, the possibilty that in bad times the firm may have to scramble to raise the funds necessary to meet debt payments.

Elizabeth agrees with Karen that this is not a good time to sell new equity. Still, she is not convinced that new equity could not be raised at an acceptable price. True, it appears that it is a buyer's market for small firms. Yet Topeka has an extremely strong customer and product base, and unusual growth prospects. Thus, Elizabeth reasons, an equity interest in Topeka might well be sold at a "very attractive price."

She does admit, though, that borrowing at least some of the necessary funds is a good idea. Still, she is not willing to concede that she and her sister will be unable to supply additional capital. For example, the Whatleys own land that could be sold to raise needed funds.

After further input from Lanzi and Shatner, the twins decide on two things. First, the forecast needs to be completed to see "what the numbers look like." Second, the forecast should consider "prudent liquidity and debt ratios." And the decision about what constitutes a "prudent" ratio was made for them. Topeka's bank, Kansas City Federal, said it would "strongly consider" a loan request but that any loan agreement would likely contain the following provisions: Topeka's current ratio must exceed 2 and its debt-to-equity ratio, that is, total debt divided by equity (at book values), can't fall below 1. These are numbers that Elizabeth is comfortable with, so the forecast will be made incorporating these constraints.

MANAGERIAL CONTROL

The partners are convinced that one reason Topeka has been and is successful is because they've been involved in all phases of the business: production, research, marketing, finance, and so on. The sisters believe they can "keep on top" of the business through 1998. They are concerned, though, that "large growth" beyond that time may cause them to lose managerial effectiveness, and think it may be a good idea to limit sales growth beyond 1998. "I wonder," muses Karen, "whether we should cap our growth after 1998 at the amount we can internally finance?"

QUESTIONS

1. Use the format of the table in the case and develop Topeka's 1997 and 1998 pro forma balance sheets.

2. How much of the funds needed in 1996–1998 can be borrowed each year without violating the debt-to-equity constraint given in the case?

3. How much of the funds needed in 1996–1998 can be borrowed each year as short-term debt without violating the current ratio constraint given in the case?

4. Carefully evaluate Karen Whatley's arguments for using short-term debt.

5. How do you recommend the partners procede? Defend your advice.

6. Consider the following formula for estimating the maximum annual sales growth rate, g, that can be financed out of retained earnings.

$$g = ROA*b/ (1 - D/A - ROA*b)$$

where b = retained earnings ratio, ROA = $[NI/S]*[S/TA]$ and ROA = return on assets, NI/S = net profit margin, S/TA = total asset turnover, and D/A = total debt-asset ratio.

(a) The Whatleys are interested in estimating the maximum annual sales growth after 1998 that can be financed out of retained earnings. Estimate this assuming the Whatleys maintain a D/A ratio of .5, pay no dividends, and use the 1998 total asset turnover and net profit margin.

(b) There is some possibility that the Whatleys will decide not to use any additional interest-bearing debt after 1998. Reestimate your answer to part (a) assuming that this occurs. Continue to assume no dividends, and use the 1998 total asset turnover and net profit margin. (*Hint*: The D/A ratio in the above formula should now only consider the debt that will "spontaneously" increase with sales.)

7. The partners are worried that "large growth" after 1998 may reduce their ability to effectively manage Topeka. Is it reasonable to believe that the sales growth rate that can be internally financed is also the growth rate that the Whatleys can effectively manage? Defend your position.

SOFTWARE QUESTION

8. The Whatleys have worked hard at firming up the estimates of the financial forecast. Shown below is the set of estimates that they feel most comfortable about, and they call it the Base-case Scenario.

Karen has convinced Elizabeth that selling new equity is not a good idea, and both sisters would like to raise any needed funds by borrowing and/or using their own capital. They feel they could raise $200,000 of equity over the next three years (1996–98).

Elizabeth is also concerned about the debt-equity constraint and would like it to be set at .75 instead of 1. Neither sister has difficulty using the current ratio constraint of 2.

The other scenario shown below reflects a "pessimistic" set of estimates from a funds-needed standpoint. That is, if this scenario materializes, then the Whatleys will undoubtedly need more cash than if the Base-case Scenario occurs. Though they agree that the Pessimistic Scenario is unlikely, no one, of course, knows exactly what the future will bring.

	Base-case Scenario	Pessimistic Scenario
1996 sales	$2,000(000)	$2,100(000)
1997 sales growth	.30	.35
1998 sales growth	.25	.30
CA/sales	.26	.285
SL/sales	.07	.07
NI/sales	.035	.03
Debt due	$20(000)	$20(000)
1997 P&E	$200(000)	$200(000)
1998 P&E	$75(000)	$75(000)

NOTE: SL refers to spontaneous liabilities. P&E refers to plant and equipment (fixed-asset purchases).

(a) Estimate funds needed for the next three years (1996–98) under the Base-case Scenario. If the debt-equity constraint is 1, will the Whatleys' capital of $200,000 cover the firm's equity needs? What if the constraint is .75?

(b) Estimate funds needed for the next three years under the Pessimistic Scenario. If the debt-equity constraint is 1, will the Whatleys' capital of $200,000 cover the firm's equity needs? What if the constraint is .75?

(c) Based on the results in (a) and (b), how reasonable is it to impose a debt-equity constraint of .75? Defend your position.

T R I A D   C A M P E R S
C A S H   B U D G E T / C A S H FLOW

After graduating from college in 1980 with a degree in mechanical engineering, Tim Cook worked for four years with a well-known recreational vehicle (RV) company in Iowa. As a hobby, he started building camping trailers for outdoor and camping enthusiasts who wanted many of the conveniences that the RVs contained without the costs. He soon realized that there was a big demand for high-quality campers and decided to go into building campers full-time. Tim's business grew rapidly to where this year Triad Campers, as his business is known, will produce almost 4,000 campers for dealers throughout a six-state area.

EARLY YEARS

From the beginning, Tim, who had a background in engineering and production, emphasized the building of quality trailers as efficiently as possible. In this endeavor he was very successful, and he developed a reputation for producing high-quality trailers at a reasonable cost. From a financial standpoint, the business was successful. The trailers were custom built on a cost-plus basis and, since the trailers had already been sold and were simply being customized, the dealers paid Tim on the delivery of the completed product.

After three years of building only custom-built trailers, Tim realized that he was building only 11 basic models that had very minor variations within the basic model. He also believed that the manufacturing process could be much more efficient if he would build on a semi-assembly line setup. He visited several similar operations in other parts of the United States and then decided that he could build trailers at a much lower cost than at present. He also believed that the sales potential in the four-state area he was presently serving offered him room to easily expand his output. The bottleneck in sales was due to the fact that most consumers were not willing to wait while a trailer was built for them but purchased whatever was available that was close to what they really desired. Tim's goal was to produce a quality trailer at a price that would be about 20 percent less than his existing custom-built price.

With this goal in mind, Triad Campers built a plant that would ultimately be capable of manufacturing 1,000 trailers per month and would employ 40 people. This was a rather ambitious undertaking for an operation that employed 10 people and was building 20 trailers per month. Tim believed that the production setup would allow him to expand production efficiently and add employees gradually.

NEW PLANT

Since moving into the new plant and getting the bugs out of the new production operation, Triad Campers has started building trailers for inventory, selling to dealers from that inventory, and customizing the standard model when requested by the dealer. The terms of sale were changed to 2/10, net 90. Tim believed that these terms would encourage dealers to stock his trailers in larger numbers than if the terms required payment sooner. He also hoped that the discount would encourage several dealers to take the discount and pay by the tenth day. Tim was partly correct in that dealers did order more trailers than they had in the past, and he was able to sell to a growing group of new dealers, but he found that only about 10 percent of his sales were paid for in 10 days, and most of those were from dealers who requested special custom work.

As sales grew, Tim realized that he had asked for several increases in his line of credit at the bank, but this fact had not concerned him, since his accountant kept telling him that his business was very profitable. Tim would have remained unconcerned with the situation; he assumed that a growing business required more cash, until his banker, Will Brawley, had told him he was technically bankrupt. When Tim asked Will to explain the company's financial status, Will replied that Triad had a big and growing cash flow problem that could increase to the point that Triad might not have the cash it needed to pay its suppliers and other creditors. This situation would occur if Triad Campers realized an increase in the time dealers took to pay him or if his lenders would not increase his lines of credit.

Tim was amazed and a little worried that he could be profitable yet face the very real prospect of going bankrupt. He had always assumed that if he had an efficient operation, produced high-quality trailers, and watched his costs, that there would not be any financial problems. What Will was telling him was that as his business grew, he was increasing the possibility of financial distress and that more growth would only increase the financial pressure on his firm. The bottom line was that as Triad Campers sold more trailers each month his financial situation grew worse, not better, even though he was running a very profitable operation.

To help Tim understand what he was talking about, Will asked Tim to provide him with the information that would allow him to develop both a pro forma profit-and-loss statement and a cash flow budget for the next three months. These two statements would be based on Tim's forecast of sales as $204,000,

$223,000, and $240,000 in July, August, and September, respectively. The profit-and-loss-statement for the last three months (April–June) is shown in Exhibit 1. Tim estimates that the cost of sales will stay very close to 62 percent of sales and that the general & administrative expense will average 8.8 percent over the next three months. Depreciation and interest expenses will remain unchanged over the next three months and taxes (federal and state) will average 38 percent.

Triad Campers never had a cash budget, but Tim's accountant had set up an excellent system for keeping the records of collections and payments. From these Tim learned that about 10 percent of sales are paid for in the month of purchase and 75 percent of the sales are paid about 90 days after the sale. Another 12 percent are paid within 120 days and 3 percent are written off as uncollectible. That last number surprised Tim, who knew that a few dealers had not paid due to disagreements over damaged trailers and that a few dealers had gone out of business, declared bankruptcy, or were seeking court protection from creditors under chapter 11 of the bankruptcy laws.

To determine the cash outflow, Tim learned that purchases were about 32 percent of each month's sales and that salaries were $4,200 per month. Wages averaged 19.5 percent of sales, direct factory was 4.9 percent of sales, and administration expenses, which were $11,000 in June, were rising $500 per month. Selling expenses were constant at 7.8 percent of sales, and Tim's accountant told him that he had a lease payment of $19,000 in July and an expected tax payment of $19,800 in September. Tim had tried to maintain a minimum cash balance of $15,000, and by the end of June the firm had borrowed $57,000 on its $60,000 line of credit from the bank. (March sales had been $112,255.)

QUESTIONS

1. Calculate the cash flow budget and a pro forma profit and loss statement for Triad Campers for the coming July–September quarter.

2. How much increase in his line of credit will Tim need for the July–September quarter? If the increase is not granted, what can Tim Cook do?

3. If sales are 20 percent greater than the July–September forecast, what will be the dollar effect on the cash flow and the profit and loss statements?

4. If sales are 30 percent less than the July–September forecast, what will be the dollar effect on the cash flow and the profit and loss statements?

5. In an attempt to encourage dealers to pay sooner, Tim offered terms of 2/10, net 90. Do you find it surprising that only 10 percent of his customers took advantage of the discount and paid within 10 days? Defend your answer.

6. Tim apparently thought that high profits guaranteed adequate cash to pay any bills as they came due. Explain to Tim the difference between profit and cash flow. In particular, explain how even a profitable, highly efficient firm can experience "cash crunches" and have a need for outside capital.

7. Do you think that a cash budget is a more important financial tool for a small firm like Tim's or a very large firm like General Motors? Defend your position.

SOFTWARE QUESTION

8. Tim thinks there is a chance of an economic slowdown in the region where he sells most of his recreational trailers. Consequently, he realizes that his sales estimates may be too high and dealers may take longer to pay him. He also thinks that it is wise to increase Triad's minimum cash balance to $20,000.

   (a) Evaluate Triad's July–September cash flow situation assuming (1) sales are .90 of the original estimates, (2) the minimum cash balance is $20,000, (3) 97 percent of all sales eventually pay, and (4) 5 percent of the sales are collected in the month of the sale, with the remainder paid as follows.

Month After Sale	% Collected
First	5
Third	60
Fourth	20
Fifth	7

   What increase, if any, will Tim require in his line of credit (LOC) in order to "survive" the July–September period?

   (b) Suppose Tim learns that he will not be able to get an increase in his LOC. What must sales be, as a proportion of the original estimates, in order to avoid a "cash crunch" in July–September assuming no change in his LOC? (Keep all other inputs at their values in part (a).)

EXHIBIT 1
Triad Campers Profit and Loss Statement

	April	May	June
Net sales	$148,700	$165,800	$183,600
Cost of sales	92,194	102,796	113,832
Gross profit	$56,506	$63,004	$69,768
General & administrative expenses	13,383	14,622	16,224
Depreciation	14,430	14,430	14,430
Interest	7,917	7,917	7,917
Income before taxes	$20,776	$26,035	$31,197
Taxes	7,895	9,893	11,855
Net income	$12,881	$16,142	$19,342

DEERPARK
CASH BUDGETING

"My instincts tell me that we could have cash flow problems sometime in the next six months, Patrick Harding the manager of Deerpark, a West Virginia resort, says to Lambert Purcell, the assistant manager. "I need to know now what we're dealing with and I think I'd better redo the forecast."

CASH FLOW CONCERNS

Three months ago Harding had prepared a cash flow forecast for the period October 1995 to May 1996. November through March is generally a slow period for the resort, and it is not unusual for the lodge to run cash deficits during most, if not all, of these months. However, the cash surplus generated during the peak period, from August through October, is typically sufficient to meet the shortfall. This is precisely what Harding had predicted would occur when he had made the cash budget projection in July. But now, in early October, he is having second thoughts about the forecast.

Three factors concern Harding. First, the renovations planned for January need to be more extensive than originally thought. Harding had estimated the cost to be $420,000, but it appears $500,000 of work is necessary. Second, the resort's long-time sales manager left unexpectedly in August and her replacement does not seem to be as effective in obtaining convention business. Third, a recession has hit much of the area and Deerpark's sales are definitely sensitive to the state of the regional economy. All this suggests Harding's sales forecasts, which he had labeled "conservative" in July, are too high. "I can see indications of this now," he tells Purcell. "Revenue is off 10 percent for September and October, and our advance bookings for the rest of the year are also down. I'm sure we won't hit the levels we predicted." Harding has always been an advocate of cash budget forecasts and constantly revises an estimate in light of new information. There is no doubt a new projection is necessary.

THE ALTERNATIVES

"What will you do in the event of a cash shortfall?" Purcell asks. Harding explains the options available. The resort could postpone or reduce the renovations, delay accounts payable, ask the owners for additional money, arrange a loan with the resort's bank, or use some combination of these options.

There are problems with most of these alternatives, however. If the renovations are not made in January, sales will likely suffer in future months; the resort is showing signs of wear, and it is important to alter the hotel's decor periodically. And, of course, the renovations are best made during an off-peak month like January. Further, the owners at a recent meeting had made it clear that it would be "extremely difficult, if not impossible" for them to raise capital at this time. Nor is the prospect of a loan an appealing option. Relations with the bank have been strained since the resort nearly went bankrupt a few years ago, before Harding's arrival as manager. The bank, assuming it would grant a loan, is likely to impose severe restrictions on the operation of the resort. That would be interference that neither Harding nor the owners would welcome. Harding's most attractive option is to delay accounts payable with the other alternatives used if needed. He intends to call a meeting of all Deerpark's purveyors and explain the situation.

His strategy is to be completely open with the purveyors about Deerpark's financial plight and ask for a deferment of some, if not all, payments until April. In return he will promise to pay COD when business picks up. "They just might agree to this," he tells Purcell. "We've been a good customer, and it is in their interest to help us out. After all, it's not like we're in danger of bankruptcy. Reservations for next April through September are extremely strong, and we should be rolling in cash by early summer. In any event, we've got to do another forecast. I must know how bad the situation is. Do I ask them to postpone 50 percent of what we purchase, 75 percent, 100 percent? I'm not even sure a complete deferment will be enough."

Harding then asks Purcell to prepare a cash budget for October through March. He hands Purcell a revised estimate of sales (see Exhibit 1) and reminds Purcell that sales in September were $448,000.

Typically, 70 percent of the resort's sales are paid in cash and 30 percent are paid using the resort's Deerpark Charge and collected in the month following the sale. Deerpark also incurs the following monthly expenses: mortgage, $50,000; utilities and maintenance, $70,000; and lease, rental, and miscellaneous expenses, $25,000. Property taxes of $107,000 are due in February, income taxes of $5,000 are due in December and March, and the renovations will be paid for in January. Exhibit 2 shows the resort's estimated payroll and purveyor expenses. Half of the purveyor expenses are paid one month after they are incurred and half in two months. Deerpark's required minimum cash balance at its bank is $100,000, and the current balance is $550,000.

QUESTIONS

1. Should the resort's depreciation expense of $30,000 per month be considered in your cash budget? Explain.

2. Prepare a cash budget for the period October through March.

3. Is there any advantage to extending the forecast through April and May? Explain.

4. Let's assume Deerpark's cash flow would not be sufficient to cover any shortfall occurring during the October-through-March period. What amount of payables must be deferred to get the resort through this period?

5. Harding in essence will be asking the firm's vendors for a loan. From Deerpark's point of view, the size of the loan is your answer to question 4. From the suppliers' point of view, however, the size of their investment in the loan is actually less than that amount. Explain why. (*Hint:* The price charged will reflect the suppliers' costs plus profit, and costs are the sum of fixed and variable costs).

6. Do Deerpark's purveyors have an incentive to cooperate? Explain.

7. If the purveyors are unable or unwilling to cooperate, how do you think Harding should proceed?

8. Which do you think is more likely to revise a cash budget: a firm like Deerpark or an electric utility? Explain.

9. What do you think is the most important variable in a cash budget forecast? Why?

10. Do you think that a cash budget is a more important financial tool for a small firm like Deerpark or a large firm like Exxon? Explain.

🖫 SOFTWARE QUESTION

11. Patrick Harding, the resort's manager, is convinced that the estimates used to develop the October–March cash budget are as accurate as he can make them. Thus, he intends to ask the resort's purveyors for an extension of $285,700.

    He intends to pay COD (cash on delivery) effective April and will use any surplus monthly cash to repay the purveyors.

    The purveyors have indicated in preliminary conversations that they are willing to cooperate. In order to help their planning, however, they would like Harding to estimate how much of the $285,700 will be paid in April, how much in May, etc.

Harding was going to do this anyway, and has compiled the following sales estimates.

Month	Sales ($000)
April	500
May	550
June	560
July	570
August	615
September	650

Past experience, though, indicates that actual sales could be as low as .90 of these estimates or as high as 1.1.

He also expects purveyor expenses to equal between .24 and .28 of sales, with a best-guess (most likely) estimate of .26.

Past experience indicates that .70 of sales are paid in the month the sale is made, and .30 in the first month after the sale. Harding thinks, however, that come April the hotel's collection procedures may be relaxed a bit. He believes the historical .70/.30 proportions are slightly optimistic. His best-guess estimate is that .60 will be paid in the month of the sale, .30 in the following month, and .10 two months after the sale. A pessimistic scenario is proportions of .50/.40/.10.

Harding decides to develop a cash budget for April–September for the following scenarios in order to get an idea of how quickly he can repay the $285,700.

	SCENARIO		
	(Base-Case) Most Likely	Optimistic	Worst-Case
Sales, proportion of base-case estimate	1.0	1.1	.9
Proportion Collected			
in month t = 0	.6	.6	.5
in month t + 1	.3	.4	.4
in month t + 2	.1	.0	.1
Purveyor expenses/sales	.26	.24	.28

NOTE: All scenarios assume the purveyors are paid COD come April. The existing credit terms involve paying half one month after an expense is incurred and half in two months. For all scenarios, set "payroll expenses" at .28.

Perform the appropriate analysis. When do these results suggest that the purveyors will be repaid? Do these results suggest that Harding will need more than the $285,700 originally estimated?

EXHIBIT 1
Sales Forecast: October–March

Month	Sales (000s)
October 1995	$609.5
November	370.3
December	257.4
January 1996	178.2
February	202.4
March	288.2

Note: September sales were $448(000).

EXHIBIT 2
Forecast of Payroll and Purveyor Expenses

Month	Payroll (000s)	Purveyor (000s)
October 1995	163.3	103.5
November	120.7	96.6
December	112.2	50.6
January 1996	82.5	57.2
February	85.8	82.5
March	99.0	105.6

Note: Purveyor expenses were $140(000) in August and $120(000) in September.

PART IV

WORKING CAPITAL MANAGEMENT

REED'S CLOTHIER, INC.
WORKING CAPITAL POLICY

Jim Reed, II had just left a rather unpleasant meeting with his banker, Harold Holmes of First Virginia National Bank. Jim had banked with First Virginia for almost 30 years and his father, who had established Reed's Clothier in 1934, had only banked with First Virginia. Holmes, however, had just informed Jim that the bank would not extend their line of credit any further. In addition, the overdue note payable for $130,000 must be paid within 30 days. Jim could not believe that Holmes had the temerity to tell him he needed to drastically reduce the store's inventory and to strongly suggest an inventory reduction sale. Since its founding, Reed has only held the industry's traditional semiannual sales—in January and July. Although Jim was piqued by this young banker's demand, the note was over 45 days past due, and Jim did not know how he could make any more than a token payment on the note within the next 30 days.

BACKGROUND

Reed's Clothier was founded in 1934 by Jim Reed shortly after he had completed his military tour. He had hoped to make a career of the military but during the early 1930s the U.S. Army was reduced in size, and there seemed little chance that this trend would change in the near future. Jim Reed had loved the community near his beloved military school, and he decided to open a men's clothing shop that would cater to the numerous Virginia Military Institute (VMI) graduates who lived in and around Lexington, Virginia.

During the first six years, the store barely made enough money to provide a living income for Jim and his family. But he could see that sales were growing each year and that his primary customer base of ex-VMI graduates was growing.

Shortly after 1940, he hired his first additional salesman, Leon Hearn, a 1909 graduate of VMI who had just retired from the army after 30 years of service. After World War II, the business continued to grow and by 1976 annual sales had grown to $800,000. Jim decided to retire in 1976 and turned the company over to his son, Jim Reed II, who had graduated from VMI in 1960 and served eight years in the U.S. Army, including a tour in Vietnam, where he had been wounded. Since 1968, the younger Reed had worked in his father's store.

In 1976, Reed's occupied the first floor of a three-story building in the heart of downtown Lexington. Reed's used the second floor of the building as the store's office and as a warehouse. The third floor, with an outside entrance and elevator access, was rented to the law firm of Bundy, Hawk, and Harrington. In 1981, Jim decided to expand the retail floor space by refurbishing the second floor as a retail shop and using the third floor as a warehouse and office. The first floor was then also modernized and the store had a very contemporary look and an $880,00 long-term mortgage debt.

Jim Reed II had slowly increased the amount of inventory in the store with the belief that many sales were lost because an item was not in the store when a customer requested it. Sales did grow steadily each year, topping $2 million in 1994, which bolstered Jim's belief that the increase in sales was directly related to the increase in inventory. In fact, sales had doubled in the last 10 years, but inventory had tripled over that same period of time.

CURRENT SITUATION

The increase in purchases and the interest and principal payments on the mortgage had seriously eroded Reed's positive cash flow in the past three years. The cash crunch had been met through a combination of slowly increasing the line of credit at the bank and, during the last year, not taking the cash discounts offered by the store's suppliers. Reed's purchased about 80 percent of its purchases on terms of 3/10, net 60 and until this year had always taken the cash discount, but its accounts were now almost 40 days past due, and the suppliers were demanding payment with the threat of ceasing deliveries until payment was made. This threat had pushed Jim into going to see his banker with the idea of increasing his line of credit another $100,000.

In the past, Jim had only dealt with his VMI classmate at First Virginia National Bank, Bob Roberts, and after talking about the good old days at the military school, an increase in the line of credit had always been granted without Bob ever looking at Reed's financial statements. Today, however, had been a different story. Two months ago, Roberts had been promoted to a public relations job with the bank and Jim had been introduced to Holmes, who had asked to see an up-to-date set of financial statements at their first meeting. In today's meeting Holmes had talked about cash flow problems and even mentioned the possibility of financial distress. There had been no easy talk about the past or how great and valued a customer Reed was, only talk about how they could get Reed's on a strong financial footing.

Holmes had strongly suggested that Jim request the help of a consultant who could help him establish a better inventory system. In addition, the condition for continuing the present line of credit was payment of the overdue note payable within 30 days. Holmes also suggested that Jim reduce his inventories and accounts receivables to the industry averages. (See Exhibits 1 and 2 for income statement and balance sheet information for the last full fiscal year. Both statements have common-size columns for Reed's and the industry.) Jim had argued that reducing inventory would reduce his sales and make it even harder to become current on his accounts. Holmes had countered this argument by saying that he thought his sales would be reduced less than 5 percent annually, and that by not reducing the inventory through an inventory reduction sale, Reed's would not be able to raise the cash required to meet its financial obligations.

Finally, Holmes suggested that accounts receivable be reduced by aggressively collecting its past-due accounts. (See Exhibit 3.) This was a particularly sore point with Jim, for he knew he had allowed his collections efforts to lapse in his efforts to increase sales. Jim was afraid that if he aggressively attempted to collect his past-due accounts, these customers might become angry and take their business elsewhere. Reed's sold about 75 percent of its sales on terms of net 30, which were the same terms offered by all its major competitors. As he slowly walked the two blocks between the bank and his store, Reed finally realized that his store was in serious financial trouble and wondered what he needed to do to regain control.

QUESTIONS

1. Calculate a few ratios and compare Reed's results with industry averages. (Some industry averages are shown in Exhibit 4.) What do these ratios indicate?

2. Why does Holmes want Reed's to have an inventory reduction sale, and what does he think will be accomplished by it?

3. Jim Reed had adopted a very loose working capital policy with higher current assets than industry averages. If he merely tightens his working capital policy to the averages, should this affect his sales?

4. Assuming that Reed's can improve its operations to be in line with the industry averages, construct a 1995 pro forma income statement. Assume that net sales will be reduced 5 percent to $1,938,000 but that depreciation and amortization will not change but remain at $32,000.

5. What type of inventory control system would you suggest to Jim Reed?

6. What type of accounts receivable control would you suggest to Jim Reed?

7. Is the increase in sales related to the increase in inventory? (See Exhibit 5.)

8. What is Reed's cost of not taking the suppliers' discounts?

EXHIBIT 1
Reed's Clothiers Income Statement (in 000s)

		Common Size	
		Reed's	Industry
Net Sales	$2,035	100%	100%
Cost of goods	1,428	70.2	67.0
Gross profit	$607	29.8	33.0
General & administrative expenses	374	18.4	18.2
Depreciation & amortization	32	1.6	0.9
Interest expense	63	3.1	1.2
Earnings before taxes	138	6.7	12.7
Income Taxes	53	2.6	4.9
Net income	$85	4.1%	7.8%

EXHIBIT 2
Reed's Clothiers Balance Sheet (in 000s)

		Common Size	
		Reed's	Industry
Cash	$17	1.0%	1.5%
Inventories	491	30.9	20.0
Accounts receivable	413	26.0	20.1
Total current assets	$921	57.9	41.6
Fixed assets	670	42.1	58.4
Total assets	$1,591	100.0%	100.0%
Accounts payable	$205	12.9%	9.3%
Notes payable	234	14.7	6.4
Other current liabilities	18	1.1	0.2
Total current liabilities	$457	28.7	15.9
Long-term debt	604	38.0	30.4
Total liabilities	$1,061	66.7	46.3
Stockholders' equity	530	33.3	53.7
Total liabilities and stockholders' equity	$1,591	100.0%	100.0%

EXHIBIT 3
Reed's Clothiers Aging Schedule

Days Past Due	Amount (000s)	Percent
0–29	132	32.0
30–59	90	21.8
60–89	89	21.5
Over 90	102	24.7
	$413	100.0

EXHIBIT 4
Reed's Clothiers Selected Ratios*

Liquidity Ratios	Industry
Current ratio	2.7
Quick ratio	1.6
Receivables turnover	7.7
Average collection period	47.4
Efficiency Ratios	
Total asset turnover	1.9
Inventory turnover	7.0
Payable turnover	15.1
Profitability Ratios	
Gross profit margin	33.0
Net profit margin	7.8
Return on common equity	25.9

*Since many ratios may have different meanings the following definitions were used in the above calculations:

Receivable turnover = sales/accounts receivable

Average collection period = 365/receivable turnover

Total asset turnover = cost of sales/total assets

Inventory turnover = cost of sales/inventories

Payable turnover = cost of sales/ accounts payable

EXHIBIT 5
Reed's Clothiers

Year	Inventories	Net Sales
1991	$378	1,812
1992	411	1,886
1993	452	1,954
1994	491	2,035

HORTON BUILDING SUPPLIES
WORKING CAPITAL

Millsbaugh County is located a few miles south of Kansas City, Kansas and Kansas City, Missouri and has a population of over 175,000. Population growth has been about 2 percent annually for the last decade, but there are signs that the area will grow sharply in the next five years or so. Attracted by relatively low taxes, a skilled labor pool, and low-cost industrial sites, numerous businesses have begun to relocate to Millsbaugh and more are expected to follow.

The economy is diverse and there is no single dominant industry or employer. Roughly 70 percent of employment is in service, retail, wholesale, and financial, and the remainder is in manufacturing.

HORTON BUILDING SUPPLIES

The Kansas-Nebraska Act in 1854 opened the territories of Kansas and Nebraska to homesteaders. Thomas Horton, I, a land-owning farmer in Indiana, was aware of the opportunities being presented in these territories and moved to Millsbaugh in 1858. After the Civil War he started the Horton House, a stage-coach stop on the Santa Fe Trail. The railroad came to the area in 1871 and the Horton House ceased operations. An enterprising sort, Thomas I quickly saw that the railroad meant economic growth for the area and he established the Horton Lumber Company in 1874. The firm began as a retail lumberyard selling to townspeople and local contractors. Over time, however, it has gradually expanded into numerous other products like paint, hardware lines, and even finished and semifinished lumber items like deck flooring and fencing. In short, the company is a rather "all-purpose" building supplies company and the name was changed to Horton Building Supplies (HBS) twenty years ago to reflect this.

HBS has been continuously run by five generations of Hortons and at present nearly every important position is occupied by a family member. For example,

Thomas V is president, Abigail Horton is treasurer, and Jackson Horton is director of marketing. And there is little doubt that HBS has been and is efficiently managed. Amazingly, the company has been "in the black" every year despite the fact that sales are fairly sensitive to the state of the economy and at times Millsbaugh County has experienced an unemployment rate of over 20 percent.

WORKING CAPITAL FINANCING

The company's sales are seasonal and during the colder months building activity slows down. If the winter is mild, some building projects continue, but large new projects are not usually started until early spring. The low point of the year is January, and from that time on, sales build. HBS has a small, year-round labor force and employs seasonal labor during peak business periods.

Management is well aware of the "ebb and flow" of the firm's working capital, caused by the seasonality of the business. Historically HBS has kept an unusually large amount of cash, and when receivables and inventory have increased, they have been primarily financed by drawing down the cash balance. Thus the company's cash balance is inversely related to the seasonality of the business. That is, the firm's cash position increases during off-peak months and decreases during peak times.

Management is taking a critical look at this strategy, however. Millsbaugh County is expected to grow sharply in the next three to five years and HBS wants to expand its operation. Abigail Horton realizes that such an expansion requires financing and she thinks that HBS may have difficulty in internally raising the needed funds. Her position is that the firm's traditional method of financing its seasonal working capital is "unnecessarily tying up capital" and the company's large cash balance is a "luxury that will have to stop." She argues that it is more appropriate to use short-term financing to finance the seasonal variation in receivables and inventory.

FAMILY REACTION

Thomas V thinks that this suggestion is well worth pursuing. He realizes that HBS's large cash position is tying up long-term sources of capital like equity and long-term debt. Thus, using seasonal borrowing would free up capital for the expansion.

Jackson Horton is not convinced, though, and thinks that the company's financing methods "have worked just fine." In addition, he doesn't like the idea that more debt will increase interest expense and may involve "hassling with a bank."

Jane Horton, the company's sales manager, isn't opposed to using debt to finance working capital and, in fact, would like all working capital financed with short-term borrowing. She argues that all the firm's receivables and inventory are short-term assets and thus it is appropriate to finance them using a short-term debt instrument. In addition, she notes that short-term debt is usually cheaper than long-term debt.

KANSAS CITY NATIONAL BANK

Kansas City National Bank (KCNB) has dealt with HBS for nearly three decades. HBS has never established much of a relationship with the bank except for an occasional term loan, mainly because it has relied heavily on equity as a source of financing. KCNB, on the other hand, has been willing—even eager—to develop a closer relationship with HBS, in part because the bank considers HBS to be a stable and well-run company. Thus when Robert Miller, an account executive at KCNB, received a call from Thomas V he was more than willing to cooperate. Thomas V wants Miller to help analyze the working capital position of HBS and both agree that Miller's objectives are to (1) estimate the firm's temporary and permanent working capital and (2) determine if the bank is willing to extend HBS a line of credit sufficient to finance the firm's temporary working capital.

NOTE: "Working Capital" is defined here as receivables plus inventory minus accounts payable.

Kansas City National suggests that a company's seasonal working capital be estimated as follows. First, working capital is calculated at the "low" point of operation, which for most firms is December. This calculation gives an estimate of the firm's permanent working capital for the year. Next, working capital is computed at the company's peak time. The difference in the two working capital figures provides an estimate of the company's seasonal working capital needs for the year.

Exhibits 1 and 2 show HBS's income statements and balance sheets for the last four years. A local CPA firm, Goldsmith and Starne, has audited HBS's statements for years according to generally accepted accounting principles and has always issued unqualified opinions. Goldsmith and Starne's work is well known and respected and they perform tax preparation and audits for several of the largest locally owned businesses. Exhibits 3 and 4 show quarterly income statements and balance sheets for the most recent year. These were prepared internally by Abigail Horton, and Miller thinks that they are quite reliable except, perhaps, the inventory estimate, since HBS performs only one annual inventory audit.

Miller would prefer monthly statements but realizes that they would be difficult and time consuming to prepare.

QUESTIONS

1. (a) A firm's "cash cycle" is measured by the inventory period (IP) plus the Average Collection Period (ACP) minus the Average Payment Period (APP);

where

$$IP = DAYS/(CGS/inventory)$$
$$ACP = DAYS/(Sales/receivables)$$
$$APP = DAYS/(CGS/accounts\ payable)$$

where "DAYS" is the amount of time in the fiscal period: "30" for one month, "90" for one quarter, and "360" for one year.

The cash cycle for HBS was 188.7 days for the first quarter of 1995, 115.7 for the second, and 100.3 for the third. Calculate HBS's cash cycle for the fourth quarter.

(b) Explain the meaning of your estimate.

2. What is HBS's working capital in each quarter of 1995?

NOTE: "working capital" is defined here as receivables plus inventory minus accounts payable.

3. (a) Estimate the firm's seasonal working capital.
   (b) Estimate its permanent working capital.

4. Which firm is more likely to have a longer cash cycle: a retailer like HBS or a firm providing a service like insurance? Explain.

5. Do you think a firm is more likely to receive a loan to cover its working capital needs if increases in working capital result from increases in receivables or increases in inventory? Explain.

6. Suppose you know that HBS's cash cycle will permanently decrease after 1995 because it will tighten its collection procedures, which will reduce its average collection period. How will this policy change affect your estimates in question 3? Explain.

7. Evaluate Jane Horton's arguments for financing all the company's working capital needs using short-term debt.

8. (a) HBS has financed seasonal changes in working capital by maintaining a large cash balance that it "taps" when working capital increases. Most financial analysts would describe this as a "conservative" method of financing seasonal working capital requirements. What are the advantages and disadvantages of such an approach?
   (b) Based on financial theory and the information in the exhibits, argue for or against the following statement: "HBS is too conservative in its financing of seasonal increases in working capital and could probably reduce the level of cash it holds by at least $250,000."

9. What is the "matching principle" of financing working capital? What are the advantages and disadvantages of using this approach?

10. How do you recommend that HBS finance its working capital? Defend your recommendation.

11. (a) Suppose that HBS asks Robert Miller to approve a short-term loan of $450,000 to help finance seasonal increases in working capital. Based on information in the case and the exhibits and your previous answers, would you advise Miller to grant the loan? Explain.

   (b) What additional information would you like to make a more informed decision?

12. Is HBS's seasonal working capital the result of higher sales, a lengthened cash cycle, or both? Explain.

13. Why would Miller like monthly financial information instead of quarterly financial statements?

EXHIBIT 1
Income Statements of Horton Building Supplies: 1992–1995 (000s)

	1992	1993	1994	1995
Sales	$5,795.4	$5,749.6	$6,961.9	$7,981.6
CGS	4,071.5	4,099.0	5,135.2	5,850.5
Gross profit	1,724.0	1,650.6	1,826.7	2,131.1
Administrative	1,192.1	1,201.3	1,324.1	1,467.2
Lease	14	15.1	15.6	14.8
Depreciation	127.5	126.5	153.2	175.6
EBIT	390.4	307.7	333.8	473.5
Interest	55.0	15.9	10.4	17.1
EBT	335.4	291.9	323.3	456.4
Taxes	134.1	116.8	129.3	182.6
Net income	$201.2	$175.1	$194.0	$273.8

EXHIBIT 2
Balance Sheets of Horton Building Supplies: 1992–1995 (000s)

Assets	1992	1993	1994	1995
Cash	$917.0	$926.2	$1,065.1	$1,256.8
Receivables	962.9	1,082.1	1,283.8	1,338.8
Inventory	1,100.4	1,149.9	1,256.3	1,302.1
Other current	34.7	34.4	41.8	47.9
Current assets	3,015.0	3,192.6	3,647.0	3,945.6
Gross fixed assets	1,764.3	1,931.2	1,973.4	2,085.3
(Acc. depreciation)	(968.3)	(1,094.8)	(1,248.0)	(1,423.6)
Net fixed assets	796.0	836.4	725.4	661.7
Total assets	$3,811.0	$4,029.0	$4,372.4	$4,607.3

(continued)

EXHIBIT 2
(Continued)

Liabilities & equity	1992	1993	1994	1995
Accounts payable	$148.6	$256.8	$306.3	$304.4
Accruals	102.7	91.7	124.7	157.7
Notes payable	0.0	0.0	0.0	0.0
LT debt due	50.0	50.0	50.0	50.0
Current liabilities	301.3	398.5	481.0	512.1
Long-term debt	208.5	154.2	221.0	151.0
Common stock	1,000.0	1,000.0	1,000.0	1,000.0
Retained earnings	2,301.2	2,476.3	2,670.4	2,944.2
Total lia. + equity	$3,811.0	$4,029.0	$4,372.4	$4,607.3

EXHIBIT 3
1995 Quarterly Income Statements of Horton Building Supplies (000s)

	3/31	6/30	9/30	12/31
Sales	$1,119.1	$2,530.9	$2,787.7	$1,543.9
CGS	843.6	1,837.6	2,019.2	1,149.9
Gross profit	275.5	693.3	768.5	394.0
Administrative	256.8	421.8	440.2	348.5
Lease	3.7	3.7	3.7	3.7
Depreciation	24.6	55.7	61.3	34.0
EBIT	(9.6)	212.1	263.3	7.8
Interest	4.3	4.3	4.3	4.3
EBT	(13.9)	207.8	259.0	3.5
Taxes	(5.6)	83.1	103.6	1.4
Net income	($8.3)	$124.7	$155.4	($2.1)

EXHIBIT 4
1995 Quarterly Balance Sheets of Horton Building Supplies (000s)

Assets	3/31	6/30	9/30	12/31
Cash	$1,210.2	$415.3	$820.0	$1,256.8
Receivables	1,003.2	2,213.6	1742.3	1,338.8
Inventory	1,610.3	1,668.9	1467.2	1,302.1
Other current	47.1	47.6	47.8	47.9
Current assets	3,870.8	4,345.4	4,077.3	3,945.6
Gross fixed assets	1,972.7	2,030.6	2,086.2	2,085.3
(Acc. depreciation)	(1,272.6)	(1,328.3)	(1,389.6)	(1,423.6)
Net fixed assets	700.1	702.3	696.6	661.7
Total assets	$4,570.9	$5,047.7	$4,773.9	$4,607.3

Liabilities & equity	3/31	6/30	9/30	12/31
Accounts payable	$597.9	$913.3	$478.7	$304.4
Accruals	110.0	146.7	152.2	157.7
Notes payable	0.0	0.0	0.0	0.0
LT debt due	50.0	50.0	50.0	50.0
Current liabilities	757.9	1,110.1	680.9	512.1
Long-term debt	151.0	151.0	151.0	151.0
Common stock	1,000.0	1,000.0	1,000.0	1,000.0
Retained earnings	2,662.0	2,786.7	2,942.1	2,944.2
Total lia. + equity	$4,570.9	$5,047.7	$4,773.9	$4,607.3

EXHIBIT 5
Selected Ratios of Horton Building Supplies

	1992	1993	1994	1995	Industry Average
Current	10.0	8.0	7.6	7.7	1.8
Quick	6.4	5.1	5.0	5.2	.9
Debt (%)	13.4	13.7	16.1	14.4	55.4
ACP (Days)	59.8	67.8	66.4	60.4	45
TAT*	1.5	1.4	1.6	1.7	2.5

*Total Asset Turnover = Sales/TA

EXHIBIT 6
Normalized Balance Sheet for the Building Supplies Industry

Assets

Cash	6.7
Receivables	27.2
Inventory	38.2
Other Current	1.9
Current assets	74.0
Net Fixed Assets	26.0
Total assets	100.0

Liabilities & Equity

Accounts payable	18.5
Accruals	9.1
Long-term debt due	3.1
Notes Payable	10.8
Current liabilities	41.5
Long-term debt	13.9
Equity	44.6
Total liabilities & equity	100.0

BOWEN BUILT, INC.
INVENTORY— ECONOMIC ORDER QUANTITY

Tim Bowen started building recreational trailers in 1978 as a custom manufacturer for a local distributor of recreational vehicles. His first trailer, built with the help of one other worker, took over one month to assemble. From this very slow beginning, Tim's firm has grown to where this year Bowen Built, as his company is now known, will manufacture almost 4,000 custom-built trailers for dealers throughout a four-state region.

As sales have grown, Tim, who has a background in engineering, has had to learn a lot about the financial side of managing a business. His first big surprise was learning about the difference between being profitable from an income statement standpoint yet being constantly short of cash. As Bowen Built was growing rapidly, his accountant kept telling him how profitable his business was, but his banker kept saying that he was technically bankrupt. (A firm is technically bankrupt when it is unable to pay its bills on time.) This crisis occurred after Tim, who was profitable in his first three years of operation, decided to expand from a 10-person and 20-trailer per month operation to a semiautomated assembly line plant that would eventually employ 40 people and manufacture 1,000 trailers per month.

During his first three years of operation, Tim built only to dealer's orders and was paid when delivery was made. Since he charged on a cost-plus basis, there was never any cash flow problem. When Tim moved to a new plant and started producing a set number of models for inventory, he sold to dealers on terms of 2/10, net 90. Sales grew very fast, but less than 10 percent of the dealers took the discount, resulting in a serious cash flow problem.

Bowen Built survived that first cash flow crunch through the help of a very understanding banker, but Tim decided that he needed an office manager for the business and additional business education for himself. Although he was a graduate mechanical engineer, he enrolled in a local technical college, taking some basic business courses at night. With this background, Tim felt like he understood what his new office manager, banker, and accountant were talking about. In addition, he took an active interest in making the business run as efficiently in its financial aspects as he had previously worked to make the business operationally efficient. Certainly Tim's first interest was in producing quality trailers, and this effort had paid off in an increasing demand for his product.

At present Bowen Built produces 11 different trailer models for sale to a network of dealers throughout a four-state area. Manufacturing is done over a 50-week period, with the two weeks at the end of December used for major maintenance projects and vacation. Sales last year totaled $24 million, and Tim has been able to maintain a steady production output in a business that has the majority of its sales over a six-month period from mid-spring to mid-fall. Sales growth, however, seems to have peaked last year, and Tim expects only a 10 percent increase for the present season. Although Tim has worked hard to have an efficient operation, with the decrease in the growth of sales, he looked again at ways to improve efficiency and profitability.

Inventory

As the business grew, Tim realized that he had maintained a huge ($2.4 million) parts inventory that was about 30 percent larger than similar-sized manufacturing firms, and he wondered if there was not some way to reduce this inventory and, thereby, its cost. The office manager, Perry Roth, had instituted a just-in-time system for the 19 most expensive items, all of which cost more than $100 each. All parts costing less than $20 were ordered according to a two-bin system that held the parts in two bins with additional inventory ordered when one bin was empty. The inventory with an individual cost of $20–$100 was the focus of Perry Roth's current concerns. These items had a total inventory value of almost $800,000.

Most of these relatively inexpensive items have been ordered according to a reorder point (RP) calculation that can be stated mathematically as:

$$RP = (\text{lead time} \times \text{weekly usage}) + \text{safety stock}$$

The safety stock has been set very generously at a two-week supply and, as a result, it is rare for a part to be out of stock.

Perry decided to study in detail a single item, brake pumps, to help him learn more about the potential savings in the ordering and inventory of the $20–$100 items. Brake pumps, like most of the parts in this price range, are used in the manufacturing process at a relatively constant rate. Thus if the savings from a change in ordering technique could be determined for the brake pumps, then most of the other parts could be ordered on the same system.

At present brake pumps are purchased from Precision Engineering for $30 per pump. Bowen uses 12,000 of these pumps (3 per trailer) per year, and the standard shipping unit is 100 pumps; that is, pumps are normally shipped in units of 100 unless the purchaser pays a special handling fee of $300 per order. Through analyzing the time it takes to process an order, Perry has determined that the average cost to process an order, from order to payment after receipt of the order, is $60. Perry has also determined that the carrying cost of inventory (including the cost of funds, obsolescence, breakage, insurance, storage, taxes, etc.) is about 20 percent. At present the pumps are ordered 500 at a time at almost two-week intervals.

Last week Kentech Manufacturing, Inc., extended a tentative offer to sell an identical pump to Bowens for $29 per pump on orders of 1,000 or more and $28.50 for orders of 2,000 or more pumps. With all this information, Perry decides to determine what, if anything, can be done to improve the inventory costs at Bowen.

QUESTIONS

1. Determine the economic order quantity (EOQ) for brake pumps if they are ordered from Precision Engineering.

2. Determine the EOQ cost if the pump can be purchased from Kentech Manufacturing.

3. Should Bowen use Kentech if he is offered the quantity discounts?

4. What order quantity would Bowen have?

5. What are the implied assumptions of the EOQ model? Do these assumptions appear reasonable in this case?

6. What factors besides EOQ should be used in the determination of a supplier?

7. Determine the reorder point if safety stock is reduced from two weeks to one week and the lead time is two weeks. What is the yearly savings from the reduction in safety stock?

8. In this case, Perry has based the carrying cost on the average cost of short-term capital to the firm plus the loss due to obsolescence, breakage, insurance, and storage. Do you think that this figure includes all of the carrying costs?

9. Assume that the actual carrying cost is 30 percent. Would this affect the EOQ? The choice of supplier?

10. Explain how a growing firm could be profitable but have a cash flow problem.

11. Do you think a firm should separate parts inventory into different groups according to their dollar value?

STANLEY PRODUCTS CREDIT POLICY

Twenty-nine-years old and already the inventor of two patented products, Morgan Stanley has unquestioned technical expertise. Stanley grew up in his dad's sealant business and four years ago, in 1992, decided to start Stanley Products (SP), his own company. A chemistry major, Stanley thoroughly enjoys the research and development side of the business, which he pursues mainly on weekends. It is literally true that SP is Stanley's vocation and avocation. And he has developed a number of products for commercial and home use. He is especially proud of Quick Jel, an adhesive with improved qualities, and NoRust, an unusually effective and easy-to-use rust treatment in aerosol form.

SP has something of a regional reputation, and sales reached nearly $1 million in the most recent fiscal year. At the suggestion of a colleague, Faith Allen, Stanley set up exhibits at a number of trade shows. He was at first reluctant to take the time from the day-to-day operation of the business to do so, but Allen persuasively argued that this was a relatively inexpensive way to gain exposure. Good advice, it appears, judging by the expected sales for the next three years. (See Exhibit 2.)

Based on advance orders and the unusually large number of product inquiries, Stanley believes that sales will increase by over 40 percent next year (1997) and will more than double in three years. These forecasts flatter Stanley's scientific side because they imply that users recognize the technical superiority of SP's products. His business side is more cautious, however. Such large growth will undoubtedly require external financing, and Stanley is unsure how best to raise any needed funds, especially since his ability to supply capital is quite limited.

BANK FINANCING

Stanley's first reaction is to approach First National, SP's bank. No formal request has been made, but conversations with Tina McClellan, a loan officer, indicate that the best rate Stanley can expect is 13 percent, somewhat higher than Stanley expected. She cautioned, however, that SP might not be able to obtain any loan whatsoever. The main problems, McClellan explained, are the soft economy and regulators who are forcing banks to be stricter. Tighter credit standards are simply an inevitable consequence of all this, with the result that a sort of two-tiered loan structure develops. Larger, more stable businesses are on one tier. Because they are considered to be more creditworthy, they get the loans. And they get a reasonable rate because they generate transaction revenue well over five figures per year. Small businesses, like SP, are the second tier. Lenders will require of them greater loan documentation, more collateral, and higher rates. And in many cases small firms will be denied any loan at all. McClellan urged Stanley to make any request "very well justified" and suggested he shop around and look at other banks.

OTHER OPTIONS

Discouraged by this conversation, Stanley met with Tim Roberts, a lifelong friend and Stanley's informal business adviser. Over lunch they listed other options that Stanley might pursue.

1. Pass up trade discounts and use suppliers with the longest pay period. Most of SP's purveyors offer 2/10, net 30. That is, SP receives a 2 percent cash discount if it pays within 10 days and is allowed 30 days if it passes up the discount. A few suppliers offer 1/10, net 20 and, in some cases, SP receives 2/10, 45. Stanley would, of course, be careful not to take so long to pay as to endanger his credit standing.
2. Offer more enticing credit terms in order to shorten the firm's average collection period. SP currently offers net 30, and would consider 3/10, net 30.
3. Limit growth to what can be internally financed.
4. Take in a partner.
5. Reduce the firm's inventory and fixed-asset requirements.

Stanley quickly dismisses the fifth possibility. He is quite capable at the production side of the business and feels that there is little slack in these items. Though Stanley finds the limit-growth and partner options distasteful, he can see advantages to each. By capping annual growth, it is more likely that the firm will not get out of control. He is painfully aware of one area company that went under a few years ago because of (according to the corporate grapevine) too much growth too fast.

Taking in a partner represents the flip side of the preceding option. Stanley believes that, with some searching, he could find an individual who would not only supply capital but also would be willing to assume managerial responsibilities. Such a person—properly selected—would allow Stanley to concentrate on the technical side of the company that he enjoys so much.

Roberts thinks the first two options are worth pursuing and proceeds to state their case. "Look at it this way," he muses. "Think of your purveyors as minibanks, each capable of providing you a bit of credit. True, no single one of these minibanks provides much financing, but put them all together and I bet you'll end up with a sizeable amount, especially if you can locate more suppliers willing to let you take 45 days to pay. And think of your receivables as miniloans you make. If these loans are paid earlier, that means more cash for you. Put all this together and, who knows, perhaps you can tell your bank to take a hike—politely, of course." And Roberts has a suggestion regarding SP's credit standards. He is a bit alarmed at the firm's bad debt expense, which is 1.3 percent of sales. "It's clear you need to stiffen credit standards since your bad debt percentage seems pretty darn high for a firm in your line of business."

STANLEY'S REACTION

Impressed with Roberts's arguments, Stanley decides to pursue these options first. After some thought he decides to consider altering SP's credit terms from net 30 to 3/10, 30; that is, he would offer a 3 percent discount to customers who pay within 10 days, and 30 days of credit would be offered to customers who pass up the discount. At the same time he would also tighten SP's credit standards, as Roberts suggested.

Stanley believes that 60 percent of sales will involve the 3 percent discount, and these buyers will take the full 10 days to pay. He also thinks that 30 percent of the sales will be paid on day 30 and 10 percent will be late on day 50. Further, bad debt expense, including collection costs, is predicted to be 0.7 percent of sales.

The proposed changes in SP's credit terms and standards should affect sales in two ways. On one hand, the cash discount will attract new customers. On the other hand, the tighter credit standards will result in SP losing some customers. Stanley believes, however, that the sales-enhancing effect will dominate, and he predicts an increase of 5 percent in sales. (*Note:* The forecasts in Exhibit 2 are based on the existing credit policy.)

Variable cost is predicted to remain at 75 percent of sales. The percent of sales method can be used to determine inventory requirements, and the appropriate after-tax cost of capital (required return) is 12 percent for any funds tied up in receivables and inventory. Plant and equipment needs will remain unaffected by the relatively modest sales changes that might result from the credit changes.

As Stanley ponders these issues, a number of points cross his mind. He notices that there are really two separate questions to answer: Is it a good idea to alter the terms of credit? Is it a good idea to tighten credit standards? For the time being, he decides to evaluate them together but thinks it makes more sense to evaluate each one separately. And he also wonders about the reaction of SP's competitors to the price discount. While SP's present credit terms are more typical of what goes on in the industry, cash discounts are not unheard of. Stanley realizes that his sales projections implicitly assume little reaction from SP's competitors, which he thinks is "very likely but not certain." In any event, Stanley doesn't expect any widespread reaction and believes that in the worst case there will be no change in predicted sales.

QUESTIONS

1. Evaluate Roberts's assertion that "it's clear you need to stiffen credit standards since your bad debt percentage seems (quite) high for a firm in your line of business." (You may assume for the sake of argument that SP's bad debt percentage is in fact quite high.)

2. (a) Assuming no change in its receivables or payables policies and no dividends are paid, use the percent-of-sales method to estimate SP's external financing requirements, EFR, for year $t + 1$. Use

$$EFR = N(\Delta S) - bmS_{t+1}$$

where

$N = A/S - L/S$ and L refer to spontaneous liabilities.

ΔS = change in annual sales

b = retained earnings ratio

m = net profit margin = NI/Sales

S_{t+1} = sales in year $t + 1$

(b) Estimate the maximum yearly sales growth, g, that SP can internally finance. Continue to assume no change in its receivables or payables policies and no dividends are paid. Use

$$g = \frac{mb}{N - mb}$$

(c) If Stanley chooses to limit growth to the amount that can be internally financed, predict SP's annual sales over the next three years.

3. Determine the cost to SP of forgoing the cash discount assuming credit terms of:

(a) 1/10, net 20

(b) 2/10, net 30

(c) 3/10, net 45

4. (a) Estimate SP's days sales outstanding, that is, its average collection period (*ACP*), assuming the proposed credit changes are made.

   (b) Complete Exhibit 3.

5. Complete Exhibit 4.

6. Redo Exhibits 3 and 4 assuming the credit changes do not affect sales.

7. As Stanley noted, there are two changes: easier credit terms and stricter credit standards.

   (a) Which change is more likely to trigger a reaction from SP's competitors? Explain.

   (b) In judging the reaction of Stanley's competitors to the price discount, how relevant is the following information about the average collection period in the industry? The median ACP is 44 days, and 25 percent of the industry firms have ACPs of less than 33 days.

8. Keep in mind that Stanley's main problem is how to finance the anticipated sales growth. Based on your previous answers and other information in the case, how do you think Stanley should proceed? Fully support your answer.

SOFTWARE QUESTION

9. Morgan Stanley decided to sell an interest in Stanley Products to Judith Leffe in order to obtain capital to finance the company's growth.

Leffe and Stanley decide to carefully examine the firm's credit policy. They agree that Stanley's initial set of estimates can and should be firmed up before a final decision is reached. They also agree that Stanley collectively evaluated two potentially divisible changes. That is, he simultaneously evaluated a tightening of credit standards and a change in credit terms from net 30 to 3/10, net 30.

They decide to first evaluate the change in credit terms, assuming no change in credit standards. After some discussion, Leffe and Stanley can't agree on a final set of estimates.

They think it is a good idea to evaluate the changes in credit terms for the scenarios listed below to see if any differences affect the decision.

S-1 and S-2 represent scenarios that Stanley is having trouble deciding between. S-3 is Leffe's best-guess (most-likely) scenario and S-4 was developed by a mutual friend, Tim Roberts, who is familiar with the company. (Set the "sales discount" to .03 in all scenarios.)

	S-1	S-2	S-3	S-4
Sales	$1,500	$1,460	$1,520	$1,450
VC/sales	.76	.75	.77	.76
Inventory/sales	.13	.12	.10	.12
ACP	15	20	25	25
Required return	.12	.13	.14	.11
Proportion taking the discount	.65	.60	.50	.60
Bad debt proportion	.009	.01	.011	.013

(a) Perform the appropriate analysis. Based on these results, how do you recommend that Leffe and Stanley proceed? Defend your advice.

(b) Suppose that Roberts, who developed S-4, decides that the sales estimate in S-1 is appropriate, though he "stands behind" all the other estimates he made. Does this affect your answer to (a)? Explain.

EXHIBIT 1
Stanley Products Present 1996 (t = 0)
Income Statement and Balance Sheet ($000s)

Income Statement

Sales	$987.0
Bad debt expense	12.8[a]
Net sales	974.2
Variable cost	740.3
Fixed cost	176.7
Earnings before taxes	57.2
Taxes (40%)	22.9
Net income	$ 34.3

[a]Includes collection costs

Balance Sheet

Assets		Liabilities and Equity	
Cash	$ 29.6	Debt due	$ 9.9
Inventory	123.4	Accounts payable	45.6
Receivables	109.7	Accruals	39.7
Currents assets	262.7	Current liabilities	95.2
Net fixed assets	98.7	Long-term debt	65.4
Total assets	$361.4	Equity	200.8
		Total liabilities and equity	$361.4

EXHIBIT 2
Projected Annual Sales ($000s)

	Year		
$t = 0$ 1996	$t + 1$ 1997	$t + 2$ 1998	$t + 3$ 1999
$987.0	$1,400.2	$1,778.3	$2,294.1

These forecasts assume no change in SP's credit policy.

EXHIBIT 3
Worksheet to Calculate Incremental Asset Requirements and Capital Cost of Credit Changes for 1997 (Year $t + 1$) ($000s)

	No Credit Changes	With Changes	Difference
Investment in receivables	$116.7	————	————
Inventory needed	175.1		
Total	291.8		
Capital cost	35.0		

EXHIBIT 4
Worksheet to Evaluate the Credit Changes for 1997 (Year $t + 1$) ($000s)

	No Credit Changes	With Changes	Difference
Sales	$1,400.2		
Bad debt expense	18.2		
Discounts taken	0	————	————
Net sales	1,382.0		
Variable cost	1,050.2		
Fixed cost	252.0	————	————
Earnings before taxes	79.8		
Taxes (40%)	31.9	————	————
Net income	47.9		
Capital Cost	35.0	————	————
Gain (loss)	$12.9		

PART V

CAPITAL BUDGETING

FORT GREENWOLD CAPITAL BUDGETING

The public image of business in the latter part of the nineteenth century was hardly flattering.

The adventures of so-called "Robber Barons" constantly made the headlines and their exploits matched those of their contemporaries in the Wild West. For example, J. P. Morgan hired an army of toughs to literally battle for a section of railroad near Binghamton, New York. And business leaders often expressed their contempt for the public interest, exemplified by such infamous comments as W. H. Vanderbilt's "the public be damned" and J. P. Morgan's "I owe the public nothing." Recent research suggests that these individuals were probably not the villains they were portrayed to be, though it is undeniable that they wielded enormous power.

It was precisely during the era of these powerful business leaders that Harold Cole founded Fort Greenwold (FG), a firm that is currently one of the largest producers of paper and pulp with annual sales of $3.5 billion. Cole located his first plant in a rural town in New England, partly to create jobs for the many unemployed workers in the area. "Having a heart does not mean you can't make a buck," Harold was fond of saying. The firm has always been active in the affairs of the community and donates generously to local civic and charitable organizations. It also takes special pride in promoting a family atmosphere among its employees. Personnel experts believe that these policies are largely responsible for the enviable productivity record of FG's workers.

For its first 80 years FG had an impressive record of growth in earnings and sales. But as the company grew, the willingness of top-level management to decentralize and delegate authority did not. The company stagnated until the appointment of Andy Kurzer as chairman eight years ago in 1988. Kurzer was shocked at the "nickel-and-dime stuff" that reached corporate headquarters, and he moved quickly to decentralize authority. One major change involved the company's capital budgeting procedures. FG actually had no formal mechanism for capital projects. Kurzer changed this and set up a six-person expenditures committee (EC) that would decide projects costing more than $200,000. Smaller expenditures would be decided at the regional and local levels.

At present (1996) the EC is considering two alternatives for achieving a much-needed increase in the firm's production capacity. One option involves modernizing an existing mill in Lees Point, North Carolina. If the plant is not renovated in the near future, production would drop to 600 tons per day and the yearly cash flow would be $11,422,320. (See Exhibit 1 for more complete information). The other alternative is to build a new mill at Midtown, North Carolina, which is 15 miles from Lees Point.

Barbara Wadkins, a member of the EC, was responsible for estimating the cost and yearly cash flows from building the new paper mill at Midtown. She calculated the cost to be $618.8 million net of any tax considerations and including working capital, and estimated the yearly after-tax cash flow to be $107,728,000. Exhibit 2 presents the information used to determine these figures. All committee members agree that these numbers are "quite reasonable."

CONTROVERSY

The figures on modernizing the existing facility at Lees Point are more controversial, however. Information on this project was originally sent by the management of the Lees Point plant and is also presented in Exhibit 2. The controversy centers on the estimated tonnage per day of the plant and its per-unit variable cost. Wadkins politely pointed out that it would be "extremely difficult for an old facility like the one at Lees Point to achieve output of 1,600 tons per day." In contrast to Wadkins's mild reaction was Kurzer's angry response. "You can forget it! I'll be the NBA's MVP before *that* plant puts out *that* tonnage!"

Everyone on the EC knew what the problem was. Management is from Lees Point and is worried that a new facility will reduce jobs. "I don't know why I got so angry. I should expect an estimate like this," said Kurzer. After much discussion the committee unanimously agreed that 1,200 tons per day was much more accurate and, if anything, a bit optimistic. It was also decided that a per-unit variable cost of $282.1 per ton was appropriate instead of the original figure of $263.9 per ton. With these changes the yearly cash flow after taxes was estimated to be $40,634,680; this was considerably lower than the projection of $61,863,160 based on the figures sent by Lees Point management.

MORE CONTROVERSY

Both projects are assumed to last 20 years. This is a relatively long time horizon for a capital budgeting project, but the company feels a paper mill is unlikely to become technologically obsolete since paper production techniques have changed very little in the last century. At least one EC member, however, thinks that a 20-year period is too long for the "modernize-the-old" option. Past experience, he argues, indicates that revitalizing an existing facility will rarely extend its life that much, and 15 years seems more probable. If so, he wonders if "we aren't being extremely charitable to the Lees Point plant. By my calculations, assuming a 20-year time horizon for this project adds $40,634,680 times 5 or $203,173,400 to the total yearly cash flows. That's some largesse!" The rest of the committee concedes that 20 years may be a bit long, but decides to retain this time period as a working hypothesis.

EMPLOYEE CONCERNS

Some EC members are worried about the impact on employee morale if the factory is relocated. "Apparently," says Wadkins, "there is considerable opposition to closing down the old factory, judging from the inaccurate figures we received." It is noted, however, that the move will "most certainly" not cost anyone a job, but will, in fact, create new positions, including some relatively high-paying managerial ones. Nonetheless, it was obvious that the proposed relocation would impose costs on the employees. Many would either have to relocate to Midtown or face a 30-mile round trip daily commute. Wadkins wondered if it "was fair and appropriate" to ask the employees to bear such costs, especially in light of the remarkable loyalty the Lees Point employees had shown to the company. She notes that a large proportion of the employees have worked for FG for more than 10 years.

"One thing is clear," remarks a subdued Kurzer. "If we choose to relocate the plant, it is important that it does not appear to be some type of ivory-tower decision that would be inconsistent with the management philosophy we've promoted all these years. Barbara, I am sensitive to the issues you bring up. Employee morale and employee loyalty are very important considerations. Maybe we could work something out—you know, like some type of moving allowance." Kurzer also reminded the committee that Midtown was the closest suitable site to Lees Point should the company move.

QUESTIONS

1. (a) Calculate the NPV of modernizing the existing paper mill.
   (b) Calculate the NPV of building a new paper mill.
2. (a) Calculate the IRR of each investment.
   (b) Calculate the payback of each.
3. (a) Do the NPV and IRR methods give the same accept/reject signals?
   (b) Explain why the NPV and IRR methods can give divergent signals when evaluating mutually exclusive alternatives.

4. Suppose that the appropriate life of a modernized factory is 15 instead of 20 years. Evaluate the argument that "assuming a 20-year time horizon for this project adds $40,634,680 times 5 or $203,173,400 to the yearly cash flows."

5. Based on your calculations in the previous questions and information in the case, what decision do you recommend? Justify your choice.

6. (a) Building a new mill requires $464.1 million more than modernizing the old mill but will generate an extra $67,093,320 in yearly cash flow. Calculate the IRR on this incremental expenditure. Compare your answer to the 12 percent required return.

   (b) Based on your answer in part (a), suggest a decision rule for the IRR in evaluating mutually exclusive alternatives with different initial costs.

7. Use the information in Exhibit 2 to explain how the yearly cash flow estimate was obtained for:

   (a) Modernizing the old mill.
   (b) Building a new mill.

8. Suppose depreciation is over 5 years instead of 20 years:

   (a) How would the NPV and IRR of each project be affected? Explain briefly.
   (b) Which of the two projects will have the larger NPV change? Why?

9. How low can average annual production go before each proposal is unacceptable?

10. (a) Is it appropriate to use the same discount rate to evaluate both proposals? Explain your position.

    (b) How, if at all, does your answer to 10(a) affect your choice in question 5?

⊟ SOFTWARE QUESTION

11. *Attention Instructors:* Question 10 probably should not be assigned if this question is used.

    (a). There is some concern about the interest rates used to evaluate each project. Top management thinks that the 12 percent rate used may be somewhat low. In addition, a number of managers persuasively argued that the rate used to evaluate the new facility should be a bit higher than the rate for the renovation. They argued that the new facility is of higher risk since it involves a larger sales increase. After much discussion, management decides to evaluate the projects in the following scenarios (keep all other values at their base-case estimates).

Interest Rates

Scenario	Build New	Renovate (Lees Pt.)
#1	.1225	.12
#2	.1250	.12
#3	.1275	.12
#4	.1300	.12
#5	.1325	.13
#6	.1350	.13
#7	.1375	.13
#8	.1400	.13

Calculate the NPVs for each project in each scenario.

(b) There is also some concern about the price per ton. The base-case esti-mates assumed a price of $455 per ton, but a number of managers feel that a price of $425–$435 is more reasonable.

    i. Calculate the NPV of each project using a price of $435.

    ii. Now assume a price of $425.

(In part (b) make sure that all other values, including the discount rate, are at their base-case values.)

(c) Management initially assumed a unit variable cost of $282.1 for the ren-ovation project and $227.5 for the build-new alternative. Management feels quite good about the $55 differential, but questions the specific es-timate for each project.

    i. Calculate NPVs if unit variable cost is $272 and $217, respectively.

    ii. Now assume $292 and $237.

(Set all other values at their base-case estimates.)

(d) Some managers believe that the output estimate of 2,200 tons per day for the build-new alternative is a "bit high." Recalculate the NPV assuming 2,100 tons per day, with other values at their base-case estimates.

(e) Do the results of (a)–(d) affect your project choice in question 5? Explain.

EXHIBIT 1
Figures on Lees Point Facility without Renovation

Plant life (years)	20
Price per ton ($)[a]	455
Tonnage per day	600
Variable cost/ton ($)	345.8
Fixed operating cost per year ($)	4,550,000
Depreciation per year	Negligible
After-tax yearly cash flow ($)	11,422,320

[a]Plant usage would be 360 days per year..

EXHIBIT 2
Information on Renovation and New Facility

	New Facility	(Original) Old Facility	(Revised) Old Facility
After-tax cost ($)[a]	618,800,000	154,700,000	154,700,000
Tax rate (%)	40	40	40
Project length (years)	20	20	20
Price per ton ($)	455	455	455
Tonnage per day[b]	2,200	1,600	1,200
Variable cost per ton ($)	227.50	263.9	282.1
Fixed operating cost per year ($)[c]	52,200,000	19,860,000	19,860,000
Fixed operating cost per ton ($)[c]	65.91	34.48	45.97
Depreciation method	SL	SL	SL
Depreciation life (years)	20	20	20
Depreciation per year ($)	30,940,000	7,735,000	7,735,000
Depreciation per ton ($)	39.07	13.43	17.91
After-tax yearly cash flow ($)	107,728,000	61,863,160	40,634,580
Required return (%)	12	12	12
Recapture of working capital	Negligible	Negligible	Negligible

[a]Net of tax considerations and including all working capital requirements.

[b]Each facility will be used 360 days per year.

[c]Includes depreciation.

C A S E 2 1

FRANKLIN LUMBER
CAPITAL BUDGETING PROCEDURES

Pete Parker, the owner and CEO of Franklin Lumber, is being quite frank with Courtney Jones, a recent hire. "As I told you at our interview, I'm hiring you despite your MBA. I haven't had good experiences with MBA's. They tend to be too technical, lack communication skills, and view problems as mere academic exercises. But you seem to be different. Your recommendations cited your sensitivity to real-world complexities and I've been impressed with your communication and people skills. I think you can help us."

Jones received her MBA four weeks ago from a southern university with a strong regional and a bit of a national reputation. She received a number of "big city" job offers but turned them down to accept a position with Franklin Lumber, a firm based in Lenoir, North Carolina. The company has four plants in the southeast, and primarily manufactures lumber that is used to produce various types of furniture such as desks and doors.

Jones took the job because she wanted a position with a small firm where she "could make a difference," the company is located very near her family, and the compensation is surprisingly attractive. She is also impressed with Parker. Though a bit gruff, he seems sharp, fair, direct, and willing to give her much job freedom and responsibility. In fact, her first assignment is of some importance and consists of two parts. Parker wants Jones to (1) perform a financial evaluation on two new machines that he is considering and (2) "critique" the company's capital budgeting policies.

PLYWOOD PRESSES

The plywood division is an important component of the firm's business and nearly two entire plants are devoted to the production of plywood panels. In brief, the production process involves gluing a thin layer of wood to each side of a particle board that forms the core of the plywood. The plywood is then cut into panels of various sizes suitable for the manufacturing of furniture.

The plywood division is operating very close to capacity and Parker is seriously considering the purchase of an additional plywood press in order to expand the division's production capability. He has narrowed the choice to two models: the Nakoi, which is made in Japan, and the American-manufactured Dakota.

The Nakoi costs $750,000 and the Dakota $1,300,000, both figures including installation. The Dakota has three advantages over the Nakoi. First, because it is a bit faster its daily production rate is higher, and Parker is confident he could sell the extra output. Second, labor costs will be lower since it is easier to operate. Finally, the Dakota should hold its value better because it is a more state-of-the-art press. Still, the Dakota is nearly twice as expensive and Parker isn't sure, these advantages are worth the extra cost.

Exhibit 1 shows information on each machine. For the purpose of analysis, straight-line depreciation will be used over the seven-year time horizon of the project. The relevant tax rate is 40 percent.

The purchase of either machine will cause a modest increase in inventory and receivables. Parker thinks that these increases will be almost completely offset by changes in accounts payable and accruals. Thus, on balance, working capital requirements for both machines will be negligible and can be ignored in any evaluation.

PARKER'S FAPG

Parker then explains his capital budgeting practices, which he calls his fixed asset purchase guidelines (FAPG). The first step is to make sure that a proposal fits with the company's mission. Parker is "simply not interested in projects outside the lumber industry." He is quick to add that nearly all proposals fall within the industry though occasionally one "seems far-out." As an example, Parker recalls a suggestion that the firm buy a local convenience store. "No way I'd do this. After all, I have enough headaches with the lumber industry. One industry is about all I can handle."

For relatively small investments the company relies exclusively on the payback method. There is no set guideline but Parker admits that he wants to see "at least a two-year payback, three years tops." And he defines a "small investment" as a project less than $10,000 and "maybe as much as $15,000." Examples include the replacement of relatively inexpensive equipment and the installation of energy-saving devices.

Parker uses somewhat different techniques for more expensive proposals, such as a plant modernization, an expansion, or the purchase of a new plywood press. The payback is still used in part because Parker uses it as a measure of risk, and in part because it is simple to calculate and easy to understand.

He also wants a measure of the project's expected return and—based on the suggestion of a friend with a strong accounting background—the firm calculates the investment's average accounting rate of return (AARR). The AARR is determined by dividing the project's average annual net income by its average book value. An example of the AARR is presented in Exhibit 2.

In order to be acceptable, a relatively large investment must pass two tests. First, the AARR must exceed the firm's target book return. This book return is currently 20 percent, the figure that Parker uses to evaluate the performance of the firm's plant managers.

In addition, the project must have an "acceptable payback." Parker explains, "I use my judgment about what is an 'acceptable' payback. There are no strict guidelines." He admits, though, that he doesn't like to see a project's payback exceed five years.

FORECASTING ACCURACY

In Parker's view the most important part of a capital budgeting decision is the accuracy of the forecasts, and he goes to great lengths to make this clear to the firm's executives. He constantly reminds them that "forecasters need to be 'honest seekers of truth' if the company is to be the best it can be."

He monitors the company's forecasting efforts in two ways. First, if a project's payback looks "suspiciously low," he personally investigates the forecast. Second, from time to time Parker has hired outside consultants to compare the actual cash flows of a project with those predicted. And if a set of estimates looks "severely optimistic," then Parker will question the forecasters, perhaps intensively. As he puts it, "I had better receive satisfactory answers to my questions." Executives who Parker thinks are negligent or allowing personal bias to cloud their judgment face a severe reprimand and even dismissal in one extreme case.

Parker is aware that many companies are plagued by overly optimistic forecasts, and he is proud of the fact that a postaudit indicated that this has not been true for Franklin. In fact, there appears to be a tendency for the forecasts to be too conservative. That is, the postaudit showed that on average the predicted cash flows were less than the actual cash flows.

REFLECTIONS

Back at her apartment that evening Jones reflected on her meeting with Parker. She sees "both good and not so good" with Parker's capital budgeting procedures. Perhaps the biggest negative is the lack of any discounted cash flow technique. It is clear to Jones, however, that Parker recognizes that the 20 percent target return is a book and not a market rate. It also appears that Parker is willing to consider "capital budgeting techniques based on market returns," as he puts it. Conversations with Parker suggest that a 15 percent market return would be acceptable. That is, Jones thinks that Parker would undertake a project if he felt that the expected return exceeded 15 percent per year.

Jones is pleased at the responsibility of the assignment and is eager to "make a difference." At the same time, however, she is a bit apprehensive. Jones realizes that Parker will take her report very seriously, and knows that her recommendations must not only be correct, but must also be clearly justified and explained.

QUESTIONS

1. Calculate the annual cash flows of the Dakota (the Nakoi's cash flow is $265,820 per year, not including its after-tax terminal value).

2. Calculate the Dakota's

   (a) payback period
   (b) average accounting rate of return (AARR)
   (c) IRR
   (d) NPV
   (e) profitability index (PI)

NOTE: The table below shows these figures for the Nakoi.

Financial Statistics for the Nakoi

Payback	2.8 years
AARR	42.3%
IRR	30.4%
NPV	$384,000
PI	1.51

3. Rank the plywood presses by the five techniques listed in Question 2.

4. Do the techniques rank the projects the same? If not, why do the rankings differ?

5. Parker's two primary capital budgeting methods are the payback and the average accounting rate of return.

   (a) What are the disadvantages of the payback? What, if any, are its advantages?
   (b) What are the disadvantages of the AARR? What, if any, are its advantages?

6. Jones intends to discuss with Parker the net present value and internal rate of return methods. She wants to be well prepared for the meeting and feels that Parker is quite likely to want the following questions addressed.

   (a) How do you interpret an NPV? an IRR?
   (b) What are the accept/reject criteria for each?

(c) What are the advantages of the NPV? What, if any, are its disadvantages?

(d) What are the advantages of the IRR? What, if any, are the disadvantages?

(e) Does it really matter which method is used to evaluate a project? Defend your answer.

7. What are the advantages of the profitability index? What, if any, are the disadvantages?

8. Parker apparently spends much time and effort trying to obtain accurate cash flow forecasts. Is Parker's concern about and attention to these estimates justified? Explain.

9. Any capital budgeting decision involves estimating future cash flows. Financial theory suggests that we want these estimates to be "unbiased." That is, we want forecasts that are just as likely to be above as below the actual cash flow. Thus, given numerous "unbiased" estimates, *on average* the cash flow forecasts will equal the actual cash flows.

(a) It does not appear that Franklin's executives generate "unbiased" forecasts since a postaudit concluded that "on average the predicted cash flows were less than the actual cash flows." Are you surprised by the result of the postaudit? Explain.

(b) Suppose that a firm's estimates are consistently too low, i.e on average the predicted cash flows are below the actual cash flows. What difficulties, if any, would this create?

10. (a) What do you like about Parker's capital budgeting procedures and why?

(b) What do you dislike and why?

11. What suggestions would you give Parker regarding his capital budgeting procedures? Make sure that each suggestion is appropriately justified.

12. Which, if any, of the two presses do you recommend that Parker buy? Defend your position.

SOFTWARE QUESTION

13. (a) Courtney Jones immediately realized that her evaluation would have to be redone. Pete Parker, the firm's owner and CEO, has revised the information Jones used to evaluate the plywood presses. He now thinks that it is more appropriate to assume:

1. The selling (market) price of plywood increases by 4 percent per year.

2. Cash costs also increase by 4 percent per year.

3. Material costs will run 72 percent of sales.

4. The appropriate discount rate is 17 percent.

5. Other estimates are at their original values.

Evaluate the equipment with these changes.

(b) Parker feels quite good about all his estimates in (a) except for the growth rates in selling (market) price and cash costs.

Evaluate the machines in the following scenarios, and keep all other estimates at the values used in (a).

1. Both grow at 3 percent per year.

2. Both grow at 4 percent per year (actually done in part (a)).

3. Both grow at 5 percent per year.

(c) Parker also thinks there is some possibility that cash costs will increase faster than unit selling price.

Evaluate the machines in the following scenarios, and keep all other estimates at the values used in part (a).

1. Selling price grows at 3 percent per year, cash costs at 4 percent.

2. Selling price grows at 4 percent per year, cash costs at 5 percent.

3. Selling price grows at 3 percent per year, cash costs at 5 percent.

(d) Based on your answers to (b) and (c), does it appear that Parker should be concerned about the growth rates he is using? Explain.

EXHIBIT 1
Information on the Plywood Presses

	Nakoi	Dakota
Output per day (square feet)	6,000	7,000
Days used each year	240	240
Market price per square foot of plywood	$1.80	$1.80
Raw materials (% of sales)	70	70
Annual labor cost	$276,000	$245,000
Annual maintenance cost	$52,000	$60,000
Annual overhead(cash)	$78,000	$60,000
Year 7 after-tax market value	$75,000	$390,000

EXHIBIT 2
Example of the Average Accounting Rate of Return

The example assumes that a project's initial cost is depreciated over the life of the project on a straight line basis.

	Year				
	0	1	2	3	4
Initial project cost	$8				
Accumulated depreciation	$0	2	4	6	8
Book value	$8	6	4	2	0
Net Income	NA	1	2	2	1

Average Book Value = $4
Average Net Income = $1.50
AARR = 1.50/4 = .375 = 37.5%

AMERICAN GRAIN COMPANY
EQUIPMENT REPLACEMENT

Most corporations have standard procedures for the submission of capital budgeting requests. These requests include a detailed enumeration of all costs involved. Capital budgeting is normally done on an annual basis and the requests from the various operating units are compiled to determine the total amount of the capital requests for the year. Each project and its estimated future cash flows are analyzed by a capital budgeting committee, and in many cases the operating unit managers must justify the rationale behind the estimates.

American Grain Company (AGC) is a multinational firm with total revenues in excess of $5 billion per year. The firm is made up of four major divisions and each division must submit its annual capital budgeting requests to AGC headquarters in Minneapolis by May 15. Michael Paschall is the plant manager at AGC's pet food plant in Louisville. The plant produces both wet and dry food for a wide variety of pets, from tropical fish to greyhounds. Michael's job includes determining the capital needs of the plant and preparing the capital request. At this time he is preparing a capital request for a new pellet mill system that will increase his plant's productivity.

PRODUCTION OF DRY PET FOOD

At the Louisville plant, the dry pet food pellets are produced through an extrusion process. The process begins with the grinding of all grains into a meal; the different grains are then mixed with other ingredients, including vitamins, in 3-ton mixers. Each 3-ton mix is called a batch. The process is not unlike what an individual would do when making a batch of pancake mix or bread dough. Each batch is then moved through a system of conveyors and elevators into a holding bin above pellet mills.

In the Louisville plant there are four pellet mills, each driven by a 120-horsepower electric motor and rated at a capacity of 10 tons per hour. The mixed ingredients are fed by a conveyor into the top of the pellet mill where steam is added to the dry mix as a binder. The wet mixture is then forced through a fixed die. The die is a round steel drum about 3 feet in diameter and about 3 inches thick. (A die looks like a car tire in size and shape.) The die contains hundreds of holes all the same diameter. Three rotating rollers roll around the inside surface of the die, forcing the ingredients through the holes. On the outside of the die a rotating knife cuts the extruded pellets off at various lengths depending on the type of pet food being produced.

These hot pellets are then conveyed to a cooler, which cools and drys the pellets. The drying process is needed before the pet food is bagged to reduce the moisture; if the pellets had a high moisture content before being placed in a paper bag or a cardboard box, they would "sweat" and then mildew in the container. After drying, the pellets are held in a bin above the bagging and sewing line. The bagging and sewing operation is highly automated: a measured amount of the pellets is dumped into a paper bag and the bag is sewed shut. The bags are then moved on conveyors to the warehouse, where they are stacked on pallets ready for shipping to grocery and other retail stores' distribution centers.

Currently the four pellet mills are producing an average of 400 tons of pellets per 12-hour day. The plant has two full shifts, but the pellet line runs only 12 hours. The mill, which is rated at 10 tons per hour, is producing only 8.3 tons per hour. The reason for this seeming inefficiency is that a cleaning-out process is required after each type of feed is run through the dies. the cleaning process is needed to push the last of the previous batch out through the dies before the new batch is started. The length of each run is constrained by the amount of available floor space in the warehouse and an estimate on the amount of orders that will be received. (A run is the number of batches of a single type of pet food that is produced before stopping and switching to another type of pet food.) The best way to achieve greater production efficiency is to have longer runs and/or produce more pellets per mill. For this reason, Michael has been looking at a new pellet mill that is produced by the California Pellet Mill Company.

CALIFORNIA PELLET MILL

California Pellet Mill Company, a major manufacturer of pellet mills, has introduced a new pellet mill that is rated at 10.6 tons per hour. Based on the current production efficiency, the actual production rate would be 8.82 tons per hour. The new pellet mills will cost $120,000 each, including installation. If four new mills are purchased, a one-time $15,000 improvement in the steam line to the mills will be required. The new pellet mills would be depreciated over a five-year period according to the Modified Acceleration Cost Recovery System

(MACRS) that was created by the Tax Reform Act of 1986. (Depreciation rates are given in Exhibit 1.) The four old machines have been fully depreciated but could be sold as junk for $10,000 each. If the four new mills are purchased there would also be a net increase in working capital of $12,000.

THE CAPITAL BUDGETING PROCESS AT AGC

Among other capital projects, the plant capital budgeting committee thinks that the purchase of the new pellet mills should be given a high priority. Paschall knows that he must present any capital budgeting requests before the divisional capital budgeting committee. Each year he is given certain guidelines for the preparation of capital requests. Among these guidelines are the specific instructions for preparing the capital budget requests. It was noted in this year's instructions that the cost of capital for plant production is 16 percent and the company has a combined state and federal tax rate of 38 percent for its Kentucky plants.

The Louisville plant operates five days a week and 50 weeks a year (10 holidays) with the pellet line averaging 12 hours of operation per day. The average sales price per ton of pet food is $280. The raw materials cost $152 per ton, and operating costs—including all overhead, selling, and administrative expenses—are $108 per ton. Both sales and costs are expected to increase 6 percent per year over the seven-year economic life of these mills. At the end of their economic life the mills are expected to have a salvage value of $10,000 each.

QUESTIONS

1. Determine the initial net cash outflow for this project.

2. Determine the net cash flows (years 1 to 7) if the new pellet mills are purchased.

3. Calculate the NPV for the pellet mill project.

4. Calculate the IRR for the pellet mill project.

5. What is the payback for the pellet mill project?

6. Should AGC invest in the new pellet mills?

7. For what reasons besides those presented in this case might this project be unacceptable?

8. How would you respond if a member of the divisional budget committee made the comment at the end of your presentation that he was against the project because it only made a profit of $35,000?

🖬 SOFTWARE QUESTION

9. Michael Paschall knows that any capital budgeting proposal will be carefully examined at divisional headquarters in Kansas City. In order to give him a better idea about what estimates are most important to the project, Paschall will investigate how the following changes impact the NPV and IRR.

1. An increase (from the base-case estimate of .16) in the discount rate to .18, and a decrease to .14; other variables at their base-case values.

2. An increase (from the base-case estimate of 8.82) in hourly production to 9.44 tons per hour, and a decrease to 8.2 (return the discount rate to the base-case estimate of .16).

3. An increase in annual sales growth to .07, and a decrease to .05; other variables at their base-case values.

4. An increase in the growth of annual operating costs to .07, and a decrease to .05; other variables at their base-case values.

5. An increase in the growth of annual material costs to .07, and a decrease to .05; again keeping other estimates at their base-case values.

6.(a) Annual growth of .05 in sales, material, and operating costs.
  (b) Annual growth of .04 in sales, material, and operating costs.
  (c) Annual growth of .03 in sales, material, and operating costs.
  (d) No annual growth in sales, material, or operating costs (Paschall calls this the "no-growth scenario").

NOTE: For each part of question 6, keep the discount rate and the hourly production rate at their base-case estimates of .16 and 8.82, respectively.
Based on the results of the above changes, what estimates are most crucial to the project? Looked at from a different angle, where do you recommend Paschall concentrate his forecasting efforts? Defend your answer.

EXHIBIT 1
Depreciation Rates for MACRS Property

Recovery Year	3-Year	5-Year
1	33.33%	20.00%
2	44.45	32.00
3	14.81	19.20
4	7.42	11.52
5		11.52
6		5.76

DELAWARE PIPE
MAKE OR BUY

"If we do decide to produce the 10- and 12-in. pipe internally, it could solve our overstaffing problem," Phillip Walker, owner of Delaware Pipe, remarked to Helen Riggins, the plant manager. "I'm reluctant to lay anyone off or even cut back hours. It's not good business and it's not the right thing to do if it can be at all avoided."

THE FIRM

Phillip Walker had no intentions of starting his own firm in 1966. Since graduating from college in 1958 he had worked for ATV Pipe, a company based in Wilmington, Delaware. In January 1966 the company decided to relocate to New York state, and Walker went also. Walker and his wife were quite unhappy in New York, mainly because they felt so distant from their relatives, nearly all of whom were located around Wilmington. In May of 1966 he decided to move back to Wilmington and start his own pipe company—quite a bold decision, really, for a man with three children and a fourth on the way.

Walker felt he understood the manufacturing side of the piping business "inside and out." He recognized, however, that in order to be successful he needed marketing and financial expertise, and he worked very hard to strengthen himself in these areas. By his own admission Walker made "many mistakes" during the first 18 months, but nonetheless, the business surged ahead. By the third year it was clear not only that the company would be successful, but that it had the potential to prosper.

And prosper it has. Delaware Pipe (DP) operates on 14 acres and employs 31 people. In fiscal year 1995 sales totaled nearly $25 million despite a regional recession and the highly competitive nature of the piping business.

Walker attributes his success to two factors: service and dedication to quality. While many firms are concerned with the quantity of pipe they produce, right from the start Walker was dedicated to manufacturing the best quality of pipe possible. "If we achieve quality the quantity will take care of itself," he often tells his employees. The company also provides exceptional service. DP keeps an unusually large volume and selection of inventory at all times and maintains a relatively large fleet of trucks. As a result the company can fill an order quite quickly. Such fast delivery means that distributors DP sells to—many of whom are nationally known wholesalers of building materials—are able to keep their inventory low.

A PROBLEM OF SIZE

The bulk of the firm's sales comes from PVC pipe, which is mainly used in residential and commercial plumbing and government sewer systems. This pipe comes in many different sizes, and sales depend in part on customers viewing the firm as a "full-line producer." That is, a salesman is more likely to win an account if a distributor is convinced that the manufacturer can promptly deliver various sizes of pipe as needed. This typically means that a producer can quickly fill orders for the most commonly used sizes of PVC pipe; that is, pipe with diameters of 3 in., 6 in., and 8 in.

Sometimes, however, a distributor is interested in 10-in. and 12-in. pipe as well. DP has never produced these sizes internally because Walker felt that annual sales volume was too low to justify the start-up cost. If a customer does request such pipe, DP will typically buy it from a competitor who does manufacture the desired sizes. Walker has never carefully analyzed whether this is a good policy, and he thinks now is the time to do so, especially given the firm's staffing situation.

As he sees it, there are two main advantages to producing the 10-in. and 12-in. pipe internally. First, DP avoids the expense of buying the pipe from another firm. DP pays 45 cents per pound for this pipe plus another 2 cents per pound in distribution costs to get the pipe to DP's customers. Unit selling price is 56 cents per pound. A second advantage is that the company's staffing problem would be helped.

Though dollar sales have increased slightly in the last two years, the increases have not kept up with inflation. Walker realized six months ago that the firm is overstaffed by two employees. The orders simply aren't there to keep all the production workers busy full time. He thinks this could continue, given not only the state of the economy but also the increase in industry competition.

In its entire 29-year history, the firm has never been forced to even cut any worker's hours, let alone lay someone off. And Walker has decided that he won't start now.

WALKER'S ESTIMATES

Walker can't be certain, of course, what future sales of the 10-in. and 12-in. pipe will be. He finds it helpful to think in terms of scenarios, and he has devised a set of estimates shown in Exhibit 1. These estimates are based on Walker's judgment and they reflect the firm's experience with these sizes of pipe.

In addition, two salespeople complained that accounts are lost when some distributors learn that DP does not produce 10-in. and 12-in. pipe internally. Apparently these distributors do not view DP as a "full-line producer" and are concerned that DP would not be able to fill an order as quickly as they would like. As a result the entire account is lost and not just the orders for 10-in. and 12-in. pipe. Thus, these salesmen argue, if DP produces the 10-in. and 12-in. internally, then new customers and new sales will result.

Walker is unsure what to make of this "new sales" argument. If the sales personnel are correct, then DP will more than double the figures shown in Exhibit 1 by producing the 10-in. and 12-in. pipe in-house. Looked at from a different angle, the salesmen claim that new sales will exceed Walker's estimates, which consider only orders by existing customers. Though he can believe that new sales will be obtained, Walker finds it hard to believe that the volume is near what the salespeople claim. His first reaction is that new orders would total at least 20 and probably 50 percent of the amounts shown in Exhibit 1.

For the time being, however, Walker decides to ignore the possibility of new sales. He wants time to investigate the claims of the sales personnel who, he believes, have a strong incentive to inflate this benefit of in-house production.

The most inexpensive equipment that is capable of producing the quality that Walker desires costs $1 million and can generate 3 million pounds of pipe per year. For the purpose of analysis Walker will assume straight line depreciation over the eight-year life of the project. The value of the equipment after eight years is a bit of a problem. Walker expects that it will be worth $225,000 after taxes, though he admits it could be as low as $150,000.

THE ACCOUNTANT'S ESTIMATES

The firm's accountant, Bob Cooper, has developed a set of numbers that, in his view, "strongly indicates" in-house production is a "losing proposition." (See Exhibit 2). Cooper estimates it will cost 54.64 cents per pound to produce the 10-in. and 12-in. pipe internally. He notes that DP can purchase the same pipe for 45 cents per pound from another manufacturer and incurs another 2 cents per pound to get the pipe to DP's customers. Thus, Cooper argues, internal production results in a 7.64 cent per pound loss, or $126,060 per year assuming 1.65 million pounds of pipe.

As Walker scans these figures he smiles as he notices that Cooper used Walker's sales estimates and annual sales probabilities. He wonders, though, how accurate the accountant's numbers really are. For one thing, the estimates are based on the "most likely" sales figure and do not consider the other sales possibilities. In addition, Walker questions the appropriateness of including depreciation, given that it is a noncash item. For these and other reasons he decides to rethink the figures the accountant has compiled.

Walker is comfortable with a number of the items listed in Exhibit 2. He believes it is quite reasonable, for example, to assume material costs will be 33 cents per pound. And, yes, the project would use two laborers and will require plant space and supervisory personnel. Yet the firm has significant excess space and the equipment could be operated in an unoccupied area of the factory. In addition, Walker believes that the firm's plant manager could easily supervise the project without affecting her efficiency in other areas.

Walker then reflects further on his staffing situation. Although it may not be good business, he is quite comfortable with his decision not to terminate any employees. Walker realizes that at most he will be overstaffed for three years, since two workers are scheduled to retire at that time. And there is the possibility that sales will increase sufficiently over the next three years so that all the staff would be fully utilized. If this did happen, of course, new workers would have to be hired (but no new supervisors) if the project were implemented. Walker estimates there is only a 20 percent chance that this would happen in any year. Looked at from a different angle, there is an 80 percent chance in each of the next three years that the two laborers used in the project could not be productively employed somewhere else in the firm.

QUESTIONS

1. The accountant's estimates in Exhibit 2 use the "most likely" sales projection in Exhibit 1 for each year. Is this appropriate? Explain.

2. (a) What is the opportunity cost (sacrifice) of using two workers to produce the 10-in. and 12-in. pipe internally?

   (b) How, if at all, should the items in Exhibit 2 be adjusted to get the incremental cash flows of the project? Be as specific as possible for each item using financial theory, information provided in the case, and the sales projections in Exhibit 1. And keep in mind that you only want to consider those items that will change if the project is implemented.

   (c) Calculate the project's annual incremental cash flows. (The project life is eight years and the relevant tax rate is 40 percent.)

3. What is the project's NPV? (Don't forget the after-tax salvage value of the equipment. The appropriate after-tax discount rate is 10 percent.)

4. Recall that Walker is unclear what the market value of the equipment will be after eight years. He thinks it could be as low as $150,000 after taxes. How important is this issue to the project? Be specific in terms of any impact.

5. (a) Recall that Walker is quite skeptical of the salesmen's estimate of the new sales as a result of internal production of the 10-in. and 12-in. pipe. Is there any basis for this skepticism, especially given that the salesmen are much closer to the situation than Walker? Defend your answer.

   (b) Walker does think that in-house production of the 10-in. and 12-in. pipe will generate new customers and new sales. To help him in the evaluation

Walker is interested in the minimum annual increase in new sales necessary to make the project worthwhile. What is this figure assuming equal annual sales? [You may assume that (1) only material and distribution costs will vary with increased production; (2) no additional equipment is needed; (3) unit selling price is 56 cents per pound; (4) the relevant after-tax discount rate is. 12 percent; and (5) the appropriate tax rate is 40 percent.]

(c) Does it make sense to use a higher discount rate in question 5(b) than in question 3? Explain.

6. Based on your previous answers and other information in the case, what do you recommend? Fully support your answer.

7. The case raises the issue about when, if ever, it is appropriate in the face of insufficient sales to terminate an otherwise competent employee.

(a) Assume you are the manager (but not the owner) of a firm. When, if ever, is it *inappropriate* to do so? You may use any ethical and social arguments that you deem relevant as well as any "good business" arguments.

(b) Repeat part (a) assuming that you are the owner of the firm.

SOFTWARE QUESTION

8. Phillip Walker, the owner of Delaware Pipe (DP), has spent some time sharpening the estimates. He decides that he was a bit optimistic in his projection of annual sales of 10-in. and 12-in. pipe. Walker now thinks that annual sales in each of the three scenarios in Exhibit 1 will be 100(000) pounds less (no change in the probabilities). He also believes that unit material cost will run $.32 per pound and the after-tax market value of the equipment in eight years will be $200(00).

(a) Evaluate the project with these changes. Continue to assume that the appropriate discount rate is .10, unit vendor cost is $.45 per pound, and unit selling price is $.56 per pound. Ignore any possible increase in sales of 3-in., 6-in., and 8-in. pipe (i.e., set "New Sales" = 0).

(b) Walker projects that 400(000) pounds per year is the "bare minimum" increase in unit sales of 3-in., 6-in., and 8-in. pipe that DP will achieve if the firm produces the 10-in. and 12-in. pipe in-house. Evaluate the project using this sales assumption. Continue to use the other estimates in part (a).

(c) i. Walker used a .10 discount rate on "Normal Sales." That is, he used a .10 discount rate to find the present value of the annual savings from producing the 10-in. and 12-in. pipe in-house. He thinks this may be a bit low and he really should use .11 and perhaps even .12. How does this "interest rate concern" affect the project? Continue to use the other estimates in part (b).

    ii. Walker used a .12 discount rate on "New Sales." That is, he used a .12 discount rate to find the present value of the annual cash flows caused by any increase in the unit sales of 3-in., 6-in. and 8-in. pipe. He believes this should be .13 and maybe even as high as .15. How important is this "interest rate concern" to the project? Return the "Normal Sales" discount rate to .10.

    iii. If Walker has enough time to more precisely estimate only one of these interest rates, which one do you recommend that he concentrate on? Why?

(d) The vendor who currently sells DP the 10-in. and 12-in. pipe says that "I can sell you this pipe at $.44 per pound and maybe even $.42 per pound." Evaluate the project at these vendor costs. Use a discount rate of .11 for "Normal Sales" and .13 for "New Sales," and retain all other assumptions used in part (b).

(e) All things considered, do you recommend in-house production of the 10-in. and 12-in. pipe? Defend your advice.

EXHIBIT 1

Walker's Estimate of the Probability Distribution of Annual Sales of 10-in. and 12-in. Pipe, Years 1–8 (In Thousands of Pounds).*

Annual Sales	Probability
1,350 lbs.	.10
1,650	.60
2,250	.30

*These estimates do not consider the possibility that in-house production may generate new customers and new sales (see case).

EXHIBIT 2
Accountant's Estimate of Annual Cost of Producing 10-in. and 12-in. Pipe In-House

1.	Raw materials	$544,500
2.	Distribution cost	33,000
3.	Direct labor	40,000
4.	Indirect labor	8,000
5.	Pension and welfare	6,720
6.	Payroll taxes	4,800
7.	Utilities	8,000
8.	Repairs and maintenance	7,000
9.	Space	6,600
10.	General factory	18,000
11.	Depreciation	125,000
12.	Lost interest	100,000
		$901,620

Unit cost 54.64 cents = 901,620/1,650,000

Description of the above items:

1. 33 cents per pound times 1.65 million pounds per year.

2. 2 cents per pound times 1.65 million pounds per year.

3. Two workers at $20,000 per year each.

4. 20 percent of item 3. This is mainly the project's share of supervisory salaries.

5. 14 percent of items 3 plus 4. This includes the firm's contribution to the employee's pension fund, plus health and disability insurance.

6. 10 percent of items 3 plus 4. This is mainly for social security and unemployment insurance.

7. The project' share of electricity, heat, water, etc.

8. Maintenance and repair on the equipment.

9. The project's share of the factory space occupied by the equipment and the two workers.

10. The project's share of items like property taxes, corporate fees, secretarial support, etc.

11. Based on the cost of the equipment: $1 million/8.

12. Lost interest on the $1 million used to purchase the equipment: $.10 \times \$1$ million where .10 is the project's after-tax discount rate.

CLEAR LAKE BAKERY CAPITAL BUDGETING

Mike Ulig, a fourth generation member of a family-owned bakery in Clear Lake, is thinking about ways to automate more of his baking operation to both accommodate the increase in demand for the cookies and reduce the labor costs of his operation. Labor, in this resort community, has become much harder to find and, as a result, is much more expensive. Mike, a Business major in college, has worked at the bakery since he was about twelve years old with the exception of about two years after college when he worked for a construction firm. Mike is evaluating three projects: an automated mixer, a continuous baking oven, and a semiautomated packing unit.

BACKGROUND

Clear Lake Bakery was founded in 1892 by a first-generation German family, Claus and Sonja Ulig, that had moved to the resort community looking for work. During the summer months, work had been easy to find in the construction business as the town grew to accommodate the tourists who were coming in increasing numbers to the lake for a vacation. During the winter months, however, there was not much construction work and the Uligs started a small bakery business from their own home, baking German pastries. The business grew until the Uligs bought a small piece of property in the downtown area and opened the town's first and (still today) only bakery. Currently the bakery serves the Clear Lake community, which has a year-round population of about 15,000 people, with fresh baked goods, plus the bakery has a large and growing mail-order business, shipping cookies all over the United States and to several foreign countries.

The mail-order business is due to the popularity of their sugar cookie, which has a very long shelf life and will stay fresh and tasty for almost one year. The cookie business fits nicely with the huge increase in demand for fresh pastries that occurs with the influx of vacationers in the summer. The high demand for cookies occurs during the Easter, Thanksgiving, and Christmas seasons, giving the bakery time to build up an inventory of cookies before the peak demand. For example, during the peak Christmas period, as many as four UPS trucks per day will be filled with cookies. The company prides itself on shipping any order that arrives before 3 o'clock on that same day. During the off-season, any order that arrives by 5 P.M. will be shipped that same day. The bakery has about 100 full-time employees.

The shares of Clear Lake Bakery are traded over the counter and currently have a market price of $27 per share. This year the company paid a dividend of $1.215 per share. Earnings and dividends have been growing at a constant rate of 8 percent annually for the past ten years and are expected to continue to maintain this growth into the foreseeable future. The firm has one bond outstanding, a mortgage bond with an 8 percent coupon, which pays interest semiannually, with ten years until it matures. This bond is currently selling at a discount and is quoted at 87 1/2 ($875). The marginal tax rate for Clear Lake Bakery is 35 percent. A partial balance sheet is given in Exhibit 1.

Production Process

Although the fresh bakery business has stabilized over the past five years, Clear Lake Bakery has seen a tremendous increase in the demand for its cookies, most of which are mail orders. The method of making cookies is known to almost every one and making cookies at Clear Lake Bakery is not much different from baking cookies at home; just the scale is different. But Clear Lake Bakery uses a secret recipe that has been handed down through the generations. Today, only two family members know the recipe.

First the ingredients are mixed in a large stainless-steel bowl and then the dough is cooled in a large walk-in cooler. Next, the dough is rolled out on a marble counter, with a rolling pin, and then the cookie is cut out with a cookie cutter. The cookie is then place on a baking tray and the trays are placed in a rolling bin that holds twenty trays. The bins are then rolled into a gas-fired oven that accommodates two bins. The cookies are baked at 360 degrees for twenty minutes and then rolled into a cooling area. The cookies are allowed to cool over a twenty-four-hour period to room temperature. The final step in the process is to wrap the cookies and place them in one-pound tins or half-pound tubes.

As part of the planning for the coming year, Mike is evaluating three pieces of equipment: an automated mixer, a continuous baking oven, and a semiautomated baking unit. He plans to consider each a separate project to be evaluated on its own merit, that is, each is an independent project. Taking into consideration his expected earnings and his borrowing capacity, Mike thinks he can commit up to $1,000,000 to capital projects this year.

Automated Mixer

To replace an old mixer, Mike is considering a new automated mixer that will increase the amount of cookie dough that can be mixed by 500 pounds per day. The new mixer will cost $240,000 installed. The older mixer has been fully depreciated and has no market value, but it will be retained as a backup or for extra capacity if needed. The new mixer is expected to increase revenues by $62,500 per year and to decrease expenses by $22,500 per year. Both revenues and expenses are expected to increase 5 percent each year. The new mixer will be depreciated on a three-year MACRS, which assumes that the half-year convention applies, to a salvage value of zero. The anticipated salvage value at the end of the five-year economic life of the mixer is also zero. Mike expects to replace the mixer at the end of five years. The increased production of cookies can be easily stored in an unused portion of the warehouse. With the installation of the new equipment, Mike has determined that the value of the average increase in cookies stored in the warehouse will be about $16,000, accounts receivable will increase $4,000, and accounts payable will increase about $6,000. These figures should increase with the installation of the mixer.

Baking Oven

Mike is also evaluating a continuous baking oven. The new oven would cost $685,000, which includes the cost of the equipment, shipping, and installation. The installation costs include some minor changes in the current production layout to accommodate the most efficient use of the continuous oven. Clear Lake Bakery currently uses six large upright ovens that are loaded from the front end with two large roll-in racks that contain twenty cookie trays each. A continuous oven would allow the cookie trays to be placed directly on a roller belt that feeds directly to the oven. The oven would replace the six roll-in ovens that are currently being used. Although there would be no increase in capacity, Mike has calculated that the new oven would result in a savings in operating expenses of $105,000 per year. The oven would be depreciated on a seven-year MACRS schedule to a value of zero, although Mike believes he can sell the oven for $30,000 in 10 years. He also expects that these expenses would have increased at least 5 percent per year over the ten-year economic life of the oven.

Semiautomated Packing Unit

The final project that Mike is considering is a semiautomated packing unit that would cost $390,000 including installation. The new packing unit would be depreciated on a seven-year MACRS schedule. The economic life of the packer is ten years, at which time the unit would have no market value. Currently Clear Lake Bakery has a wrapping machine which was purchased four years ago for $90,000 and was being depreciated on a seven-year MACRS schedule. The wrapper has a current market value of $20,000. The packing unit will result in a savings in operating expenses of $90,000 per year. These expenses are expected to increase 5 percent per year over the ten-year economic life of the unit.

QUESTIONS

1. Calculate the yield-to-maturity for the mortgage bond.

2. Estimate CLB's cost of equity.

3. What is the firm's overall cost of capital?

4. Find the net cash flows for the automated mixer.

5. Calculate the net present value for the automated mixer project.

6. What is the internal rate of return for the mixer?

7. Determine the net present value of the continuous oven.

8. Determine the net present value of the semiautomated packing unit.

9. Which capital projects should Mike undertake this year?

EXHIBIT 1
Clear Lake Bakery
Balance Sheet as of Dec. 31

Current liabilities	$1,000,000
Mortgage bond	5,143,000
Common stock (500,000 shares outstanding)	500,000
Contributed capital in excess of par	2,000,000
Retained earnings	8,640,210
Total liabilities & common equity	$17,283,210

EXHIBIT 2
Depreciation Rates for MACRS Property

Year	3-Year	7-Year
1	33.33%	14.29%
2	44.45	24.49
3	14.81	17.49
4	7.41	12.49
5		8.93
6		8.92
7		8.93
8		4.46

THE PINNACLE CORPORATION
CAPITAL BUDGETING

The Pinnacle Corporation manufactures golf balls, clubs, and accessories like golf gloves, bags, shirts, and shoes. In an industry where image is quite important, the Pinnacle label is synonymous with excellence. Pinnacle was the first company to build a mechanical golfer, which dramatically improved the reliability of golf ball and equipment testing. Pinnacle introduced the Surlyn (hard-covered) golf ball and in the early 1970s developed a radically different dimple design, called the icosahedron pattern. It has also been a leader in metal equipment and in designing more "forgiving" clubs for the average player. In recent years Pinnacle entered the accessories market, partly to be known as a "full-service" golf manufacturer and partly to be in a position to capitalize on expected growth in this area.

The firm is organized by product line and has separate ball, equipment, and accessories divisions. Sales during the most recent fiscal year (1995) were $391 million, broken down by division as follows: ball, $213 million; equipment, $157 million; and accessories, $21 million. Thus, the first two areas account for nearly 95 percent of revenue and represent the divisions most consistent with the firm's strategic policy, since Pinnacle sees itself primarily as developing and manufacturing "tools" to assist golfers in their quest for lower scores. Although it is unfair to say that Pinnacle entered the accessories market as an afterthought, it is appropriate to say that top management doesn't believe the firm has any particular advantage in this area. In fact, until three years ago, the accessories unit was not a separate division but simply a part of the equipment division. Top management felt, however, that this arrangement did not allow accessories to be properly represented in capital budgeting discussions and decisions.

The accessories that Pinnacle has marketed, though, have been consistent with the firm's reputation. This has been due mainly to the efforts of George Carrington, an energetic and flamboyant divisional manager with ten years' experience in the clothing industry. Carrington took the Pinnacle position even though the change was merely a lateral move in terms of salary and represented a bit of a loss in prestige, since the budget he controls at Pinnacle is much less than the one he had at his former company. Still, Carrington wanted to be closer to the game he loves and felt that he was associating with the industry leader.

THE PROBLEM

Pinnacle is currently involved in deciding its capital budget for the coming year, and there are proposals from each division that are especially important to the long-term prospects of the firm. What is common to them all is the belief that the industry is and will continue to be in a golf boom. It is likely, therefore, that the demand for balls, equipment, and accessories will increase in "real" terms, that is, adjusted for inflation, for at least the next four to five years.

One difficulty is that top management, for a number of reasons, doesn't think that more than one major project can be successfully implemented. First, annual sales growth of 10 percent is expected even without any new projects. Second, a major commitment to R + D has recently been made to stay ahead in the race for new products. Finally, the industry is facing a skilled labor shortage, and quality technicians and managers are hard to find. Top management, which is fiercely protective of the Pinnacle image, believes that if more than one major project is implemented, none will be done right. In fact, the corporate grapevine indicates that Elizabeth Robinson, the CEO, is not likely to approve any significant capital budgeting request from the accessories division unless it looks "extremely attractive." Robinson's thinking is that Pinnacle should capitalize on its relative strengths, which she thinks are in balls and equipment.

DIVISIONAL CONSIDERATIONS

By varying the cover, core construction, and to a certain extent dimple design, manufacturers can develop balls with somewhat different flight characteristics and feel. For example, a soft (balata) cover combined with a wound, liquid center results in a ball that is relatively easy to hook or slice; it tends to fly higher and gives more "feel" on the finesse shots. A hard (Surlyn) cover with a solid two-piece interior is more difficult to hook or slice, tends to fly lower, and is more durable.

Pinnacle produces six balls for the varied abilities and whims of golfers. The company recently developed a new ball, the Medallion LS, with a new cover of Lithium Surlyn, which combines some of the advantages of balata and Surlyn. A Lithium Surlyn-covered ball will fly a bit higher and farther than a Surlyn-covered one, though it is not as durable. In terms of the six balls Pinnacle currently produces, the Medallion LS is closest to the ProFlite LD. Although management doesn't feel that the LS would have much of an effect on the sales of the other five balls, it does believe that the LS would hurt sales of the ProFlite LD. Still, Pinnacle thinks that the LS represents a step forward in ball technology and should sell at a premium over existing balls.

Twelve months ago the firm began manufacturing its Precision line of clubs, which are machine-made from cast iron. Four factors account for their success. First, they have the largest "sweet spot" of any club produced. This means that the ball can be contacted considerably off center and still produce a respectable shot. This characteristic has made Precision clubs especially popular with below-average golfers. Second, the shaft is extremely lightweight, which helps get shots up in the air more easily. Third, though the clubs are machine-made, they don't have an "assembly-line" look. Finally, a set sells for $600, about 10 percent under competitive brands. Pinnacle can produce 40,000 sets a year, but annual demand is running at about 65,000 sets. And management feels this demand will continue. Exhibit 1 shows future sales projections assuming no change in the current price of $600.

The accessories division is proposing that the production of bags, gloves, shirts, and shoes be expanded. Though no real shortage exists for these items at the present time, divisional managers are convinced that sales have been hurt by the relatively low-key approach Pinnacle has taken in marketing these products. Carrington strongly feels that additional promotion, coupled with the projected golf boom, will cause the sales of accessories to more than double in three years and make an expansion of his division "highly attractive." He also argues that this project would result in Pinnacle achieving greater diversification in terms of product sales. Exhibit 2 shows the yearly incremental sales and cash flow estimates that Carrington has submitted to top management.

THE OPTIONS

The expansion of the accessories division is considered a major project and, for reasons stated, would rule out the Keep Old option of the ball project and the Expand alternative of the equipment project. (These are also considered major projects and are described later.)

Pinnacle is considering three options with regard to the golf ball decision. One alternative is simply to continue as is and not introduce the Medallion LS. The second option, called Pull Old, involves producing the LS and taking the ProFlite LD off the market. A third possibility, Keep Old, is to produce both the LS and LD.

Everyone involved finds the As Is option distasteful because the LS would not be introduced at all, and it is probably only a few years before a competitor develops a similar ball. Thus, if this option is chosen, Pinnacle would have lost the opportunity to be the first to produce this new ball, a failure that could hurt its image as an industry pacesetter.

If the ProFlite LD were discontinued (i.e., if Pull Old were selected), the firm's existing manufacturing facilities would have to be redesigned and additional equipment would be required. Still, some increase in production facilities would be needed but not enough to preclude any necessary expansion of the equipment or accessories divisions. However, if Keep Old is selected, then the firm would lack sufficient managerial and technical expertise for any other major expansion.

Here is information compiled by the ball division and considered relevant to the analysis.

1. The relevant time horizon is six years.
2. Cost of goods sold will run 60 cents per ball for both the Medallion LS and the ProFlite LD.
3. (a) The ProFlite LD will be sold for $1 apiece. Division managers believe—and top management agrees—the Medallion LS is a "cut above" most balls. The LS, therefore, should sell at a premium until competitors develop a similar ball. A reasonable estimate is that the LS can be sold for $1.10 a unit in years 1–3 and $1 during years 4–6.
   (b) Annual unit sales of various LS/LD combinations are shown in Exhibit 3. These estimates assume the above prices.
4. Working capital requirements are $0.10 per ball.
5. The appropriate tax rate is 40 percent.
6. Exhibit 4 shows yearly marketing, administrative, and miscellaneous fixed cash expenses for the As Is, Keep Old, and Pull Old options.
7. (a) The Pull Old alternative will require $4.8 million to redesign and expand existing manufacturing facilities and for the purchase of additional equipment.
   (b) The Keep Old option will require $15.9 million for new equipment and to expand the firm's manufacturing capacity.

NOTE: For purposes of analysis, the expenditures in number 7 are assumed to occur "up front," that is, at time $t = 0$, and will be depreciated on a straight-line basis over six years, the relevant time horizon of each option.

8. The Keep Old and Pull Old options will require additional land whose market values are $200(000) and $25(000), respectively. (For tax purposes these amounts are *not* depreciable.)
9. The after-tax terminal value of Pull Old is $480(000) and Keep Old is $3,180(000). As Is has a negligible terminal value and can be ignored. These estimates do *not* consider the recapture of any working capital.

Management is considering two alternatives regarding the equipment decision. One possibility, called Price Increase, is simply to raise the price of its Precision clubs in order to eliminate or at least reduce any excess demand. Management thinks that price can be raised from $600 to at least $650 a set without reducing sales below the present capacity of 40,000 per year. The other option, called Expand, involves leaving the price unchanged and building additional facilities to accommodate the expected demand. If Expand is chosen, then the firm would not pursue either the accessories project or the Keep Old alternative of the ball project. The equipment division has made cash flow estimates of Price Increase and Expand. Exhibit 5(a) shows the yearly incremental cash flow estimates for Price Increase assuming a $50 increase in the price of a set of Precision clubs and annual sales of 40,000 sets per year. Exhibit 5(b) gives these estimates for Expand, assuming no change in unit price and the yearly sales shown in Exhibit 1.

Management does not believe that projects in each division have the same degree of market risk. Equipment sales are considered to be relatively vulnerable to economic downturns because of their high unit price and because consumers can easily postpone their purchase and use their old equipment a little longer. Ball sales are of the lowest risk since they are a necessity for players. Management uses a required return (cost of capital) of 11 percent for projects of the ball division, 12 percent for accessories, and 14 percent for equipment projects.

MANAGEMENT OPINION

And there is no shortage of opinions among Pinnacle's executives about what should be done. Here is a sample of those views.

- Paul McKinney, chemist and head of Pinnacle's research and development department. He favors introducing the new ball since "all the tests show that it really works," but he has no strong opinion about whether the old ball should be discontinued.

- Lyle Snead, ex-touring pro and a member of the firm's advisory board. He doesn't have much faith in McKinney's scientific tests but has played the new ball and believes it works. Thinks it will sell.

- Jane Sherry, director of communications. Wants either golf ball or equipment production to expand. She believes that any equipment price increase would give the firm "bad press" but could be avoided simply by expanding manufacturing facilities. And not to introduce the LS "makes little sense if Pinnacle values its reputation as an industry pacesetter."

- Warner Covington, senior vice president. Covington is sympathetic to Sherry's position and notes that "some type of expansion will never be cheaper." He points out that the firm has $1 million of excess working capital and owns the land necessary for any expansion. "Thus," observes Covington, "if we expand now we save $1 million of working capital and the land costs us nothing."

- Deborah Dresnik, chief of production. Dresnik is very concerned about the managerial and technical bottlenecks of the firm. She wonders (1) if doing *any* major expansion now would mean foregoing some profitable investment project in the future; and (2) if the accessories proposal represents too much of a shift in the firm's strategic policy. Notes that the Precision clubs are a "proven winner."

- Elizabeth Robinson, CEO. She thinks Dresnik has made some good points. Her gut reaction is to increase the price of the Precision equipment and discontinue production of the ProFlite LD, replacing it with the Medallion LS, because these options leave room for possible future investments.

- John Knudson, marketing director. He's the only senior manager sympathetic to the accessories expansion. He thinks that quality golf shirts and shoes would be "extremely popular," and he favors some option that allows this expansion. He notes that while the accessories division accounts for 5 percent of the firm's sales, it receives less than 2 percent of the advertising and marketing budget. Knudson, therefore, is very sympathetic to the theory that the sales of accessories have been hampered by a lack of promotion.

QUESTIONS

1. (a) What is a firm's strategic policy? How, if at all, does it influence a firm's choice of capital budgeting projects?
   (b) What is an "unbiased" cash flow forecast? Do you find it surprising that studies have found that the actual cash flows of "sales projects" tend to be well *below* the predicted amounts? Defend your answer.

2. Management uses an 11 percent required return (cost of capital) for projects of the Ball Division, 12 percent for Accessories', and 14 percent for Equipment's projects.
   Some of Pinnacle's plant managers feel that it is "unfair" to use three different rates. They argue that "we are all part of one firm so all projects should use the same rate." How would you respond to this objection?

3. The yearly cash flow estimates of the Price Increase option (see Exhibit 5a) on the equipment decision ignore any possible working capital requirements. That is, these estimates assume that no additional working capital is necessary. Is this a reasonable assumption to make? Defend your answer.

NOTE: "Working capital" is defined here as A/R + INV − A/P − Accruals.

4. Assuming a discount rate of 12 percent, the NPV of the proposal of the Accessories Division is $6,043(000) (see Exhibit 2 for the yearly cash flow estimates). Write out the equation used to determine this NPV.

5. Assuming a discount rate of 14 percent, the NPV of the Price Increase option of the Equipment Division is $4,666(000) (see Exhibit 5a for the cash flow estimates).
   Calculate the NPV of the Expand Option using a rate of 14 percent (See Exhibit 5b).

6. The Equipment Division really has another option, which is literally to "Do Nothing."

(a) It is not necessary to do an NPV to determine that Price Increase is superior to Do Nothing. Why?

(b) What, then, is the advantage of doing an NPV on Price Increase?

7. (a) Complete the table below, which shows the incremental yearly cash flows ($000s) of the Pull Old option of the Ball Division (use the As Is position as the base from which to calculate these incremental amounts).

(b) Calculate the NPV of this project using a discount rate of 11 percent.

				Year			
	$t = 0$	$t + 1$	$t + 2$	$t + 3$	$t + 4$	$t + 5$	$t + 6$
	1996	1997	1998	1999	2000	2001	2002
Inc. CF	(4825)	1900	2600	2600		1100	2280

8. (a) Calculate the yearly incremental cash flows of the Keep Old alternative of the Ball Division using "As Is" as the base position.

(b) Calculate the NPV using a discount rate of 11 percent.

9. Given the managerial and technical bottlenecks that Pinnacle faces, and its apparent desire for "orderly growth," list the firm's capital budgeting "choice set." That is, list the ball/equipment/accessories options open to management.

10. If a project's predicted NPV > 0, the implication is that the firm expects to make an economic profit from the project.

(a) What are economic profits?

(b) Under what circumstances, if any, can a firm expect to earn economic profits?

11. Play the role of a consultant. Based on your previous answers and other information in the case, how do you think management should proceed? Fully support your position.

SOFTWARE QUESTION

12. (a) Pinnacle's top executives still think that it is prudent to do only one "major" project, though it appears that no other major projects are likely in the foreseeable future. They have also carefully examined the estimates of each proposal and concluded that the following assumptions are appropriate.

1. Annual unit golf ball sales should remain as originally projected (see Exhibit 3).

2. The price of the old ball (the ProFlite LD) will be $1 in years 1–3, $.95 in years 4 and 5, and $.90 in year 6.

3. The price of the new ball (the Medallion LS) will be $1.10 in year 1, $1.05 in years 2 and 3, and $1 in years 4–6.

4. Cost of goods sold will be $.60 per unit each year for the old ball and $.63 for the new ball.

5. The annual cash flow projections of Price Increase should be raised by 10 percent (see Exhibit 5a).

6. The annual cash flows of the Expand (equipment) option remain as originally projected (see Exhibit 5b).

7. The annual cash flow projections of the Accessories Division for years 1996 ($t+1$) – 2001 ($t+6$) should be reduced by 20 percent (see Exhibit 2).

8. The appropriate discount rates are 10 percent for Keep Old, 11 percent for Pull Old, 10 percent for Price Increase, 13 percent for Expand (equipment), and 11 percent for Accessories.

Analyze this scenario. What do you recommend based on these results? Explain.

(b) Note that the above scenario uses a slightly lower discount rate on Keep Old than Pull Old. The thinking is that Pull Old is a bit riskier since it involves removing from the market a "known product." A number of Pinnacle's managers, however, think this interest rate differential is inappropriate. They believe that the same discount rate should be used on Keep Old and Pull Old, either 10 percent or 11 percent. How does all this affect your recommendation in part (a)? Explain. (Keep all other inputs at the values in part (a).)

EXHIBIT 1
Projected Unit Sales of Precision Clubs (000s)*

t + 1	t + 2	t + 3	t + 4	t + 5	t + 6
1997	1998	1999	2000	2001	2002
65	70	75	75	75	75

*These projections assume no change in the current price of $600 per set. The firm is presently producing at capacity of 40(000) sets per year.

EXHIBIT 2
Projected Yearly Incremental Sales and After-Tax Cash Flows of the Accessories Division Project ($000s)

	t = 0	t + 1	t + 2	t + 3	t + 4	t + 5	t + 6
	1996	1997	1998	1999	2000	2001	2002
Incremental Sales	—	$13,000	18,000	25,000	30,000	30,000	30,000
Incremental cash flow	($12,300)	1,600	2,700	4,300	5,600	5,600	9,800

EXHIBIT 3
Projected Unit Golf Ball Sales, Various Scenarios (Millions)*

	t + 1	t + 2	t + 3	t + 4	t + 5	t + 6
	1997	1998	1999	2000	2001	2002
As Is	40	40	40	40	40	40
Pull Old	47	47	47	47	47	47
Keep Old	65	65	65	65	65	65

Description of Each Scenario

As Is   Only the old ball, the ProFlite LD, is sold. The new ball, the Medallion LS, is not introduced.

Pull Old   The new ball is introduced and the old ball is discontinued.

Keep Old   Both the new and the old balls are produced and sold. Annual unit sales are distributed as follows: 35 (million) due to the new; 30 (million) due to the old.

*These forecasts assume the old ball (ProFlite LD) sells for $1 a unit, and the new ball (Medallion LS) for $1.10 during years 1–3 and $1 in years 4–6.

EXHIBIT 4
Selected Cost Estimates of the Ball Division ($000s)

Marketing						
	t + 1	t + 2	t + 3	t + 4	t + 5	t + 6
	1997	1998	1999	2000	2001	2002
As Is	$1,600	1,600	1,600	1,600	1,600	1,600
Pull Old	$4,200	4,200	4,200	2,000	2,000	2,000
Keep Old	$4,700	4,700	4,700	2,700	2,700	2,700

Administrative						
	t + 1	t + 2	t + 3	t + 4	t + 5	t + 6
As Is	$3,800	3,800	3,800	3,800	3,800	3,800
Pull Old	$4,400	4,400	4,400	4,400	4,400	4,400
Keep Old	$5,200	5,200	5,200	5,200	5,200	5,200

Miscellaneous Fixed (Cash)						
	t + 1	t + 2	t + 3	t + 4	t + 5	t + 6
As Is	$4,000	4,000	4,000	4,000	4,000	4,000
Pull Old	$4,500	4,500	4,500	4,500	4,500	4,500
Keep Old	$5,500	5,500	5,500	5,500	5,500	5,500

EXHIBIT 5 (a)

Projected Yearly Incremental After-Tax Cash Flows of the Price Increase Option of the Equipment Project ($000s)

$t = 0$	$t + 1$	$t + 2$	$t + 3$	$t + 4$	$t + 5$	$t + 6$
1996	1997	1998	1999	2000	2001	2002
0	$1,200	1,200	1,200	1,200	1,200	1,200

NOTE: These forecasts assume the price of a set of clubs is raised $50 to $650 a set, 40,000 sets per year are sold, and the relevant tax rate is 40 percent.

EXHIBIT 5 (b)

Yearly Incremental After-Tax Cash Flow Estimates of the Equipment Project's Expand Option ($000s)

$t = 0$	$t + 1$	$t + 2$	$t + 3$	$t + 4$	$t + 5$	$t + 6$
($11,600)	3,100	3,400	4,200	4,200	4,200	9,000

NOTE: These estimates assume no change in the present price of $600 per set and are based on the yearly sales shown in Exhibit 1.

COOPER LABORATORIES
CAPITAL BUDGETING: MULTIPLE OPTIONS

"I think the time is right to push Sonica," Susan Tarver, a general manager with Cooper Laboratories, remarked at a recent company meeting. "Hospitals are becoming much more cost conscious and the political pressure to contain costs is clearly building. Sonica might save a hospital big bucks. I'm eager to see what the numbers look like."

HEALTH CARE

Third-party payments exist if the expenses of a product or service are paid by someone other than the provider or user. In the health care industry the role of third parties—either the government or private insurance companies—has increased sharply in the last forty years. In 1955, for example, about 30 percent of all expenses were paid by third parties while in 1995 it is nearly 80 percent. And for many years third parties would reimburse hospitals on the basis of the "reasonable" cost of providing a medical service. Not surprisingly, hospitals were neither especially cost conscious nor interested in techniques that would lower costs. In fact, management consulting firms found that most hospitals didn't even know what their costs were, let alone how to reduce them. This began changing about ten years ago when health insurers implemented a payment system based on what they think a specific medical service might cost. Hospitals are not able to collect more than this, but if they reduce expenses they will be able to keep the difference as profit. The incentive to trim costs is obvious.

There is also political pressure to contain costs. Many politicians have made health care reform a major issue, and most industry analysts expect legislation that not only provides more health care protection but also attempts to reduce the rate of inflation in the medical industry.

SONICA

Cooper Laboratories is a major producer of medical equipment and drugs, and has been a leader in the development of ultrasonic medical equipment. And Cooper's management feels that the time is right to push its Sonica machine. This machine is based on ultrasonic technology and is used in gallbladder surgery, where it will reduce a 30-minute operation to a mere 5 minutes and lower the cost of the operation from $1,200 to about $200. At present Cooper sells only 40 Sonica machines a year, a total that reflects the lack of any substantial marketing effort by the company and the unwillingness of hospitals to pay Sonica's $200,000 price. Management estimates, however, that sales will reach 170 by year 3 given the increased cost-consciousness of hospitals. (See Exhibit 1 for complete sales projections.) These estimates assume that the relevant market consists of hospitals that perform at least 100 gallbladder operations a year. Thus, the implicit assumption is that hospitals doing fewer than 100 operations annually will find it unprofitable to purchase Sonica.

There are three options regarding Sonica under consideration, all of which assume the effective life of the machine is seven years; two of the options involve no increase in the firm's production capacity, which is 50 machines per year.

Option 1. The "As Is" alternative. No increase in capacity or price change. Yearly production would be raised to the present limit of 50.

Option 2. The "Price Increase" alternative. No increase in capacity. Yearly production would be raised to the present limit of 50 and price would be increased.

Option 3. The "Expand" alternative. No change in price but an expansion of capacity to accommodate the expected growth in demand.

Given the future sales projections, Option 1 would generate substantial excess demand since the price of Sonica would remain at $200,000. Option 2—suggested by one of Cooper's economists—is designed to eliminate, or at least reduce, the potential excess demand by raising price. One problem with this alternative is that any substantial price increase could easily be viewed by hospitals as price-gouging and could hurt Cooper's ability to sell its other products to these hospitals. In addition, two other firms make equipment that is similar, though not identical, to Sonica. These possible substitutes limit the amount of any price increase. After considerable discussion management decided that a 5 percent increase in price in year 1 is reasonable, followed by $5,000 increases for the next two years, and no changes after that. A few executives, though, are adamantly opposed to these price changes for the reasons previously stated.

Option 3 involves no change in price but requires an expansion of the company's Sonica factory to accommodate the expected increases in sales. It would take six months and $7.5 million to expand the existing facility, and capacity would rise to about 210 machines a year. (Any smaller expansion is architecturally unsound.) This figure includes all equipment except three machines that would be leased for a total of $60,000 a year. (You may assume an eight-payment lease with the first payment due immediately.) For purposes of analysis any depreciation is assumed to be straight line over five years. The building and equipment are assumed to have a negligible salvage value at the end of the project in seven years.

OPERATING COST CONSIDERATIONS

With the existing plant and equipment, the unit variable cost (including sales commissions) of producing Sonica would be $125,000. If the addition is built, however, Cooper would achieve greater efficiency in production. Whereas unit variable cost would remain at $125,000 in year 1, it would fall to $118,000 in year 2 and $115,000 in year 3. At this point all economies of scale would be exhausted, and unit variable costs are anticipated to remain at $115,000. Maintenance and all supervisory labor are presently $310,000 a year. Exhibit 2 details this expense for each alternative. Other fixed expenses during the past year were $245,000, and management is confident that no increase will be necessary unless the facilities are expanded. (See Exhibit 3.) The figures in Exhibit 3 allow for an increase in the technical personnel necessary to service the Sonica machine, since Cooper's policy is to provide free maintenance and repair on equipment of this sort for five years.

NOTE: The "other" category does not include marketing expenses, computer use, or depreciation. It also does not include $150,000 of administrative salaries, which is the subject of some controversy that will be discussed later.

Any increase in sales, of course, will require additional net working capital (see Exhibit 4), which should be recovered at the end of the project.

The previous figures are noncontroversial, but there is concern about how the following items should be handled. One is the cost of computer use, another is treatment of part of the administrative expense, and a third is the cost of the land necessary for the plant expansion. (*Note:* These items are relevant only for the expansion alternative.) Cooper owns a $400,000 computer that at present has a significant amount of excess capacity. Without any new Sonica facilities the computer would be replaced in six years. With the new facilities, the capacity on the computer would be reached after five years. Thus, given the seven-year time horizon of the Sonica project, choosing Option 3 would tax the computer system for the last two years of the project.

Cooper is also in the process of reorganizing one of its divisions. The reorganization will be completed in about one year and result in the lay-off of administrative personnel, saving Cooper about $150,000 annually. These individuals, however, would be shifted in six months to the Sonica project if Option 3,

"Expand," is selected. If this reassignment occurs it is likely that no new personnel would be hired. This means that the workload of employees in the division vacated by this staff would increase for the last six months of the first year until the division's reorganization was complete.

The land necessary to expand is adjacent to the factory and is presently used as a company parking lot. It has negligible market value, and no one has any idea what it would be used for except as a parking area for Cooper employees. With the expansion these employees would be forced to park in lots a bit more inconvenient but containing a substantial amount of unused space. Consequently—as far as anyone can determine—the only real sacrifice with the use of the land is the inconvenience imposed on some of the company's employees.

MARKETING CONCERNS

Part of the success of Sonica depends on convincing surgeons that the machine performs as advertised. This should not be a big obstacle, though, since the equipment already has an excellent reputation among the medical community. Nonetheless, if Cooper chooses the expansion option, it wants to promote the technical merits of the equipment—especially during the first year—by advertising heavily in trade journals, at medical conventions, and by developing quality brochures for use by its sales representatives. Marketing expenses under "Expand" would be $860,000 in year 1, $265,000 in year 2, and $90,000 in years 3 to 7. The firm currently spends only about $20,000 annually on such promotion, and no increases are planned if the "As Is" option is selected. If Cooper decides to raise Sonica's price while not expanding capacity (i.e., if it chooses Option 2), these expenses will rise to $60,000 per year.

There is little doubt, however, that Sonica's success depends mainly on the ability of its sales representatives to convince the hospitals' accountants and administrators that the equipment makes financial sense. Management, therefore, wants to focus on the profitability of the machine from a hospital's point of view. Many hospitals Cooper deals with perform about 100 gallbladder operations a year, and the use of the high-frequency equipment would reduce the cost of this operation from $1,200 to $200. The machine would have a useful life of five years with no predicted salvage value and could be depreciated over five years. Management consultants in the medical field believe the appropriate after-tax cost of capital is 12 percent.

Delores Putnam, a company sales representative, has raised a point she wants addressed. Cooper deals with hospitals that perform as few as 30 gallbladder operations a year. Putnam wants to know the minimum number of operations a hospital must perform a year to make the purchase of Sonica profitable. "We certainly don't want to waste our time on hospitals that are too small to use the equipment," she remarked at a recent meeting. "And, who knows, perhaps even 100 operations a year is too little."

QUESTIONS

1. Assume the appropriate cost of capital (required return) is 16 percent and the relevant tax rate is 40 percent.

   (a) Calculate the relevant incremental cash flows for the "As Is" alternative (Option 1).
   (b) Calculate the NPV.
   (c) Complete the table below showing the incremental cash flows ($000s) of the "Price Increase" alternative.

$t + 1$	$t + 2$	$t + 3$ to $t + 6$	$t + 7$
1996	1997	1998–2001	2002
$366		$906	$1,146

   NOTE: The NPV of this option is $3,163.9(000).

2. The case discusses three options, but there is also a fourth, which is literally to "Do Nothing"; that is, keep production at 40 machines a year.

   (a) It is not really necessary to do a discounted cash flow analysis on the "As Is" option to determine that it is superior to "Do Nothing." Explain why.
   (b) It is also not necessary to do a discounted cash flow analysis on the "Price Increase" alternative to see that it is superior to "As Is." This implies, given part (a), that "Price Increase" is better than "Do Nothing." Explain why.
   (c) Given parts (a) and (b), what is the point of doing the NPVs in question 1? That is, can you see any advantage in calculating NPVs even though it seems obvious without this information that "Price Increase" is superior to both "Do Nothing" and "As Is"? Explain.

3. What cost, if any, should be charged to "Expand" (Option 3) for computer use, land, and the administrative personnel targeted for a lay-off? (Assume that the price of the relevant computer system remains constant over time.) Explain.

4. Assume the appropriate cost of capital (required return) is 16 percent and the relevant tax rate is 40 percent.

   (a) Develop a table summarizing for each year the incremental amount for "Expand" of the following items: variable cost, marketing, and net working capital.
   (b) Complete the table below showing the incremental cash flows ($000s) for the "Expand" option.
   (c) Calculate the NPV of this option.

$t = 0$	$t + 1$	$t + 2$	$t + 3$	$t + 4$	$t + 5$	$t + 6$	$t + 7$
1995	1996	1997	1998	1999	2000	2001	2002
($7,536)		$1,557	$4,695	$5,895	$5,895		

5. Calculate the NPV of Sonica from the hospital's point of view. (The relevant tax rate is 40 percent.)

6. What is the minimum yearly after-tax cash flow the machine must generate to make it profitable for a hospital to purchase it? What is the minimum number of gallbladder operations necessary to generate this cash flow?

7. Based on your previous calculations and other information in the case, which alternative do you recommend? Fully justify your choice.

8. Note that Cooper uses a 16 percent required rate of return to evaluate the Sonica investment, and the hospitals that may use Sonica are assumed to use 12 percent. Does this make financial sense in view of the fact that the same piece of equipment is being evaluated? Explain.

SOFTWARE QUESTION

9. Harold Henning is the company executive in charge of preparing the capital expenditure analysis for the Sonica project. He is quite sensitive to top management's opinion that (1) most capital budgeting requests are based on an optimistic set of assumptions and (2) the requests invariably do not consider the impact of different assumptions on a project's profitability.

As Henning reviews the base-case set of estimates, he is convinced that the projections for the "As Is" and "Price Increase" options are noncontroversial. Henning also thinks that the assumptions of the "Expand" alternative are "sane and reasonable." He knows, though, that top management is likely to carefully scrutinize this option given its relatively large up-front cost. Henning decides that it is a good idea to investigate how different assumptions affect "Expand's" profitability, and compiles the following scenarios (unit variable cost and sales are in thousands).

Scenarios

Unit Variable Cost	S-1	S-2	S-3	S-4	S-5	S-6
Year 1	$125	$125	$125	$125	$125	$125
Year 2	118	122	125	118	122	115
Years 3–7	115	120	125	115	120	112
Unit Sales						
Year 1	55	50	55	50	50	60
Year 2	120	110	120	100	100	140
Years 3–7	170	160	170	140	140	200
AR/sales	.20	.15	.13	.13	.15	.13
Inv/sales	.12	.12	.10	.10	.12	.10

NOTE: AR is Accounts Receivable.

Scenario 1 (S-1) assumes that much easier credit terms will be needed to achieve projected sales, and receivables are over 50 percent more than originally estimated. It also assumes inventory requirements will be 20 percent higher than estimated. Unit variable cost and sales are at their base-case estimates.

S-2 considers the possibilities that (1) economies of scale will not be as large as expected, (2) unit sales will be about 8 percent less than projected, and (3) working capital requirements will be somewhat larger than originally forecast. Henning describes this scenario as "quite conservative, but not pessimistic."

S-3 assumes no economies of scale, with other values at their base-case estimates.

S-4 assumes unit sales are roughly 15 percent below their base-case estimates, a possibility that Henning feels is "very unlikely and pessimistic." Other values are at their base-case projections.

S-5 is a combination of S-2 and S-4 and is considered to be "very pessimistic."

S-6 assumes the project is a "winner," with sales exceeding expectations and unit variable cost below the original estimate.

Perform the appropriate analysis.

(a) Based on your results, would you advise management to carefully examine the variable cost, unit sales, or working capital estimates? Explain.

(b) How, if at all, do these results affect your original recommendation? Defend your position.

EXHIBIT 1
Projected Unit Sales of Sonica[*]

	$t = 0$ 1995	$t + 1$ 1996	$t + 2$ 1997	$t + 3$ 1998	$t + 4$ 1999	$t + 5$ 2000	$t + 6$ 2001	$t + 7$ 2002
Q	40	55	120	170	170	170	170	170

[*]These estimates assume price remains at $200,000 and the relevant market consists of hospitals performing at least 100 gallbladder operations a year. (Present capacity is 50 machines per year.)

EXHIBIT 2
Maintenance and Supervisory Labor ($000s)

	Year						
	1996 $t+1$	1997 $t+2$	1998 $t+3$	1999 $t+4$	2000 $t+5$	2001 $t+6$	2002 $t+7$
Option 1 (as is)	$510	$510	$510	$510	$510	$510	$510
Option 2 (price increase)	510	510	510	510	510	510	510
Option 3 (expand)	810	1,400	1,400	1,400	1,400	1,400	1,400

NOTE: At present these costs are $310(000).

EXHIBIT 3
Other Fixed Expenses ($000s)

	Year						
	1996 $t+1$	1997 $t+2$	1998 $t+3$	1999 $t+4$	2000 $t+5$	2001 $t+6$	2002 $t+7$
Option 1 (as is)	$245	$245	$245	$245	$245	$245	$245
Option 2 (price increase)	245	245	245	245	245	245	245
Option 3 (expand)	945	1,345	1,500	1,500	1,500	1,500	1,500

NOTE: At present these expenses are $245(000).

EXHIBIT 4
Current Assets and Spontaneous Liabilities as Percentage of Sales

Current Assets		Spontaneous Liabilities	
Cash	2	Accounts payable	9
Receivables	13	Accruals	4
Inventory	10		

LINCOLN SPORTS EQUIPMENT CAPITAL BUDGETING

"This could be about the riskiest project we have ever considered," Sam Ledford *remarked at a company staff meeting. Ledford is the president and largest stockholder of Lincoln Sports Equipment, a firm based in* Springdale, Illinois.

Lincoln is a family-owned business with annual sales of over $20 million. It manufactures a variety of sports equipment, including footballs and athletic shoes. The company is best known, however, for a batting glove that is made of spandex and English leather, and is contoured to fit around a bat.

A NEW PRODUCT

Brian Fitzpatrick is the firm's chief financial officer and has a passion for baseball. Fitzpatrick plays for two teams in over-35 baseball leagues and loves to tinker with equipment. He has designed a number of products with limited appeal, including a fluorescent baseball and a portable batting cage. A few months ago, however, Fitzpatrick developed a new baseball cleat that seems to have the potential to be a big hit, although the design is hardly revolutionary.

Metal-spiked cleats have been banned in most nonprofessional leagues since the mid-1980s. They are considered too dangerous since the metal spikes would frequently puncture and gash athletes, and caused twisted ankles and knees when they lodged into the ground when a player's body turned.

Manufacturers responded to the ban by developing cleats made with rows of plastic spikes. Fitzpatrick's idea was to put two circular ridges of plastic cleats around the soles of the shoes. He showed the cleats to Lynn Baber, the firm's marketing director, who immediately felt that Fitzpatrick had "hit on something." Baber had five-dozen pairs made and distributed them to three local high school teams. The response was quite enthusiastic. Players noted the exceptional grip of the cleats and their ability to dig into the ground, yet the feet could turn easily. As one player put it, "the stop-and-go bite was terrific."

Impressed with the idea and the results of this nonscientific survey, management decided to carefully investigate the possibility of mass producing the new cleat and discontinuing production of the firm's existing spike (see Exhibit 1 for projections on the existing cleat).

THE RISKS

The sports equipment industry is quite competitive and risky and contains such giants as Adidas, Nike, and Spalding. It is not necessarily the best product that has the largest sales, since marketing is so important. An exceptional product with poor marketing can end up being no product at all.

It can be quite difficult for a firm the size of Lincoln to successfully compete with the industry titans. At times, for example, the company's salespeople have had trouble getting shelf space at sporting goods outlets. And though the shoe is patented, this is no guarantee that competitors won't be able to produce and market a similar style cleat.

Further, the shoe may not be well received. It is one thing for the cleat to be successful in a limited, local area. It is quite another thing for it to be sufficiently well received to justify mass production. In addition, it is clear that the product is not completely debugged. For example, there were complaints that the cleats had a tendency to suddenly snap off.

Still, information obtained during the first year of the project will be quite helpful in assessing the future acceptability of the cleat. Management would spend these first twelve months perfecting and market testing the shoe. The consensus is that there is a 75 percent chance that the market testing will be successful. If so, management expects what it calls the Full Production Scenario, and annual sales estimates are shown in Exhibit 2. In addition, a successful market test is likely to benefit the firm in a hard to quantify way. If the new cleat becomes sufficiently well known, then the firm's credibilty with sporting-goods stores should increase, thus making it easier to sell other products like gloves and balls. If the first year's testing is not successful, then—assuming the project is continued—management anticipates the Limited Production Scenario.

Lincoln would sell the new cleat for $28 a pair, $8 more than the price of the existing spike. Cost of goods sold is predicted to be 64 percent of expected dollar sales for the Full Production Scenario and 67 percent for the Limited Production Scenario. The difference arises because larger production results in the use of more efficient equipment and quantity discounts on raw materials. Exhibit 3 shows yearly administrative, marketing, and miscellaneous cash expenses.

Most managers feel that the cost estimates are quite reasonable. There are reasons to believe, though, that the sales forecasts for each scenario are too low.

Ledford is notorious for making conservative sales estimates for "big-ticket projects," and he considers this to be one. He is fond of noting that there are two types of mistakes that can be made. "We can fail to do a worthwhile project or we can undertake a project we shouldn't."

Ledford's attitude is that it is better to make the first type of error and, consequently, he tends to be something of a "pessimistic forecaster." These sales estimates reflect his views, and many of the company's executives think they should be raised by at least 10 percent.

IMPLEMENTATION COSTS

The first year's testing is estimated to cost $125,000 after taxes. After that, in 1997 ([:t+1:]), management will decide whether to discontinue the old spike and produce only the new one. The fixed asset cost of manufacturing the new cleat depends on which scenario is expected. The consensus is that if all the necessary assets were purchased, then this cost would be $890,000 with the Full Production Scenario and $480,000 with the Limited Production Scenario.

However, the old cleat would be discontinued, which would free up space and equipment that could be utilized in the production of the new cleat. This would save about $90,000 of startup costs. Some of Lincoln's executives, therefore, argue that the relevant incremental fixed asset costs are only $800,000 and $390,000, respectively.

Other managers disagree, however, and believe that it is inappropriate to make the $90,000 reduction in the startup cost of each scenario. Phyllis Betts, a production manager, expressed their view. "This reduction assumes that the space and equipment can only be used to produce cleats. But the company could use the fixed assets of the old spike in other ways," she argued. "For example, the ball department is short of area and I estimate that if they used these assets along with another $15,000 worth of equipment, then they could generate an extra $28,000 after taxes each year for at least the next seven years."

Baber thinks that though the ball department may well need facilities, the issue is "irrelevant." She argues that Lincoln is going to produce *some* cleat since the firm needs such a shoe in its product portfolio if it is to be viewed as a "full product" supplier by customers. Therefore, the space and equipment will be used to produce either the old or new spike. Ledford agrees with this reasoning and feels that "letting the ball department use these facilities is not an issue."

Betts is disappointed with these responses because she believes that the old cleat is a "loser," and the facilities it occupies can be put to a better use. She decides not to pursue the issue, however, when she hears Ledford's firm position on the matter.

There is general agreement, though, that it is reasonable to assume that the after-tax terminal value of the project will equal 30 percent of the incremental cost of the fixed assets.

NOTE: This estimate does not consider the recapture of any working capital.

For purposes of analysis, depreciation is assumed to be straight line over six years on the incremental fixed asset cost. The relevant tax rate is 40 percent.

WORKING CAPITAL CONSIDERATIONS

Lincoln offers credit terms of net 30 and net 45. And, frankly, which one Lincoln offers depends on the bargaining power of the customer. Management believes that 70 percent will receive net 30 and the rest will receive net 45. Management expects that 80 percent of the "net 30" group will pay on time (on day 30), and the remaining 20 percent will pay 10 days late. They also expect that all of the "net 45" customers will pay on time.

Inventory is expected to run 15 percent of dollar sales, and purchases 80 percent of cost of goods sold. Lincoln typically receives credit terms of net 30 and, in fact, the firm's average payment period is 30 days. Accruals are predicted to be 2.2 percent of dollar sales.

DISCOUNT RATE CONTROVERSY

The firm uses a 12 percent required return for projects of average risk for the company. A number of managers believe that the hurdle rate for the project should be substantially higher. They argue that "This project is as risky as any the firm has ever done," and the discount rate should be raised 7 percentage points to reflect this risk. In addition, they note that the company's degree of operating leverage (DOL) is increasing, and the 12 percent hurdle rate does not consider this change. In their judgement, the required return should be raised another percentage point. Thus, both adjustments considered, this group believes a 20 percent rate is appropriate.

Other managers, however, are not convinced that the 8 percent adjustment is appropriate. Yes, the one point for the DOL change is appropriate. And, yes, there is substantial risk, but much of the risk will be resolved by the market research. That is, after a year the firm will have an excellent idea about whether the Full Production or Limited Production scenario will materialize. At that point, the project should be only a bit riskier than typical. These managers believe that only a two percentage point increase is justified. This group, therefore, argues that a 15 percent hurdle rate is appropriate.

A few executives wonder if the project's risk could not be substantially reduced by leasing the necessary space and equipment, making sure that any lease has a cancellation clause. They argue that "such an arrangement would allow us to simply walk away from the project if it looks like a failure."

QUESTIONS

1. Management has used a 12 percent discount rate to evaluate projects of average risk. The case presents two reasons why this rate is too low. Critically evaluate each of these reasons. What hurdle rate do you recommend?

2. Based on information in the case, does it appear that expanding the ball department will add value to the firm? Explain.

3. Evaluate the argument that leasing the necessary equipment will reduce the business risk of the project to the firm.

4. Use the following format to estimate the annual net working capital requirements of the Full Production Scenario.

	$t+1$ 1997	$t+2$ 1998	$t+3$ 1999	$t+4$ 2000	$t+5$ 2001	$t+6$ 2002	$t+7$ 2003
Receivables							
Inventory							
−A/Payable							
−Accruals							
Net Working Capital	$49.0						

NOTE: The 1997 amount is working capital with the old spike ($000s). Assume a 360-day year.

5. (a) Consider the fixed asset cost of the Limited Production and Full Production scenarios. Some managers believe that these costs are $890,000 and $480,000, respectively, which are the amounts that would have to be spent if all the necessary assets are purchased. Others argue that these costs should be reduced by $90,000, which is the amount of space and equipment that would be saved if production of the existing cleat is discontinued.

Based on information in the case, which set of estimates is most appropriate? Explain.

(b) Estimate the cash flows in years 1998 ([:t+2:]) through 2003 ([:t+7:]) for the Full Production Scenario. Keep in mind that only the change in net working capital is relevant when calculating these cash flows, and the relevant tax rate is 40 percent.

NOTE: The table below shows the annual cash flows (in $000s) of the Limited Production Scenario from 1998–2003. The amounts are based on information in the case and Exhibits 2 and 3. The year-7 amount includes the recapture of working capital plus the after-tax market value of the fixed assets.

	$t+2$ 1998	$t+3$ 1999	$t+4$ 2000	$t+5$ 2001	$t+6$ 2002	$t+7$ 2003
Cash Flow	(28.6)	17.8	82.6	108.2	108.2	330.0

6. Sam Ledford, Lincoln's president and largest stockholder, is willing to make the mistake of not doing worthwhile projects as long as he avoids undertaking projects that he shouldn't. Is this likely to be a value-maximizing approach to capital budgeting decisions? Explain.

7. Calculate the NPV of the project and make a recommendation. Defend your position.

SOFTWARE QUESTION

8. A number of executives have convinced Sam Ledford, the company's president, that his forecasts tend to be too conservative for "big ticket items." He also realizes that the original estimates did not consider inflation. Ledford decides to analyze the "spike project" in three different scenarios in order to get an idea of the variability of the NPV.

   In conjunction with two other managers, Ledford has developed the following scenarios.

Pessimistic Scenario

1. Unit sales for the Full Production and Limited Production scenarios at .90 of the original estimates shown in Exhibit 2.
2. Unit sales of the old cleat at 1.3 times the estimates shown in Exhibit 1.
3. The probability is .60 that the market tests will be successful.
4. Cost of goods sold at .66 of dollar sales in Full Production, .68 for Limited Production, and .70 for the old cleat.
5. The selling price of the new cleat will be $28, increasing at 2 percent per year.
  The appropriate discount rate is 20 percent.

Best-Guess (Most-Likely) Scenario

1. Unit sales for the Full Production and Limited Production scenarios at 1.1 of the original estimates shown in Exhibit 2.
2. Unit sales of the old cleat at 1.2 times the estimates shown in Exhibit 1.
3. The probability is .75 that the market tests will be successful.
4. Cost of goods sold at .64 of dollar sales in Full Production, .66 for Limited Production, and .70 for the old cleat.
5. The selling price of the new cleat will be $28, increasing at 4 percent per year.
6. The appropriate discount rate is 15 percent.

Optimistic Scenario

1. Unit sales for the Full Production and Limited Production scenarios at 1.2 of the original estimates shown in Exhibit 2.

2. Unit sales of the old cleat at 1.1 times the estimates shown in Exhibit 1.

3. The probability is .80 that the market tests will be successful.

4. Cost of goods sold at .64 of dollar sales in Full Prodction, .66 for Limited Production, and .70 for the old cleat.

5. The selling price of the new cleat will be $28, increasing at 6 percent per year.

6. The appropriate discount rate is 15 percent.

NOTE: For all scenarios the after-tax cost of the market test ("testing costs") is $125(000), the average collection period (ACP) is 35.9, inventory is 15 percent of sales, the incremental fixed-asset costs (P&E) is $800(000) with Full Production and $390(000) for Limited Production, and the after-tax terminal value of the fixed assets is 30 percent of their "up-front" cost.

(a) Perform he appropriate analysis. Based on your results, what do you recommend? Defend your recommendation.

(b) It is now 1997, that is, you are in year [:t+1:]. The company decided to perform the market tests which, unfortunately, were not successful.

Do you recommend Limited production given the test results? Use the appropriate spreadsheet outputs from each scenario to form your recommendation.

EXHIBIT 1
Annual Projections on the Existing Cleat: $t + 1$ to $t + 7$ 1997–2003

Unit sales	$13,000
Unit selling price	$20
Dollar sales	$260,000
Cost of goods sold	$182,000
Administrative costs	$30,000
Marketing	$5,000
Miscellaneous fixed (cash)	$15,000
Depreciation	Negligible
After-tax cash flow	$16,800

EXHIBIT 2
Annual Unit Sales Estimates for Each Scenario*

	Scenario	
Year	Limited Production	Full Production
1998 (t + 2)	20,000	70,000
1999	25,000	80,000
2000–2003	30,000	110,000

*Assumes the existing spike is discontinued.

EXHIBIT 3
Selected Cost Estimates for Each Scenario

	Full Production		
	$t+2$ 1998	$t+3$ 1999	$t+4$ to $t+7$ 2000-2003
Administrative	$156,800	$179,200	$246,400
Marketing	$137,200	$112,000	$ 77,000
Miscellaneous fixed (cash)	$ 70,600	$ 78,400	$ 80,100

	Limited Production		
	$t+2$	$t+3$	$t+4$ to $t+7$
Administrative	$ 84,000	$105,000	$100,800
Marketing	$ 30,000	$ 30,000	$ 25,000
Miscellaneous fixed (cash)	$ 39,200	$ 49,000	$ 50,400

THE VANDERMEER COMPANY
RISK CLASSES

Kenneth Vandermeer, president of the Vandermeer Company, is fretting about the long-term investment decisions of the firm. "It's not like they've been bad, but I feel like we could be making better decisions," he tells his son Carlton. "And I worry that we're going to get burned by a project. Competition is fierce and a new product could easily flop. Look, let's face it, we've been lucky that we haven't had any real losers. What do you think, anyway?"

THE FIRM

Nearly 100 years ago, Commodore George Vandermeer built a home in the mountains of North Carolina that many considered the greatest architectural achievement of the nineteenth century. The house was built with such "necessities" as an indoor swimming pool, bowling alley, and fitness center, and was surrounded by 20,000 acres. Eventually the property passed to the commodore's great-grandson, Kenneth, who realized he was unable to adequately care for it and decided to open the estate to the public. The home became an immediate hit as a tourist attraction, and the Vandermeer Mansion became synonymous with quality, especially in the western part of North Carolina.

Kenneth capitalized on this reputation by forming the Vandermeer Company, which manufactured and distributed a number of dairy products, including ice cream and cheese. Their quality was consistent with the Vandermeer name and sales grew rapidly. The company gradually expanded into other areas such as wine and liquors. Geographically, the firm has been most successful in North Carolina, southern Georgia, and eastern Tennessee, but its management is always eager to penetrate new markets.

CAPITAL BUDGETING DIFFICULTIES

Carlton agrees with his father that the company's long-term investment policies can be improved and, in fact, he has been thinking about the problem for some time. Although he has no hard evidence, he thinks the firm "ends up doing projects it shouldn't and not doing ones it should." Carlton has a number of suggestions he wants to present at one of the weekly managers' meetings. First, he feels the quality of the information used in the capital budgeting process needs to be improved. "Part of the problem is you, Dad. The way it is now, virtually every project needs your say-so. The company is much too big for that now. Delegate someone else to look after the smaller stuff and you concentrate on the more important. . ." At that point Kenneth Vandermeer cut off his son's remark and said he agreed and would "take care of it."

Carlton then suggested that another problem was the use of a single hurdle rate for all projects. He felt it made more sense to adjust the rate to reflect the riskiness of each proposal. The elder Vandermeer thought this sounded "promising but potentially confusing." Both decided that Carlton should put together a proposal incorporating this suggestion. The father was adamant, however, that any procedure be "understandable" to top management. "Keep in mind," he told his son, "that any recommendation—no matter how sound theoretically—is useless if we don't feel comfortable with it.

CARLTON'S RESEARCH

As a first step Carlton wanted to reestimate the required return for the firm's typical project. Carlton wondered about the accuracy of the 10 percent discount rate currently being used. He recalled a study that found stocks returned about 6 percent per year more than the before-tax yield on the bonds of the same firm. Carlton knew, though, that the study involved companies whose stockholders held well-diversified portfolios. This was not the case with the Vandermeer Company, since nearly all the family wealth was invested in the firm. He decided that an additional premium of 4 percent was necessary to compensate for this lack of diversification. Scanning a recent *Wall Street Journal,* he noticed that the yield on long-term government bonds was 7.5 percent. The yield to maturity on the bonds of the Vandermeer Company is 9 percent; the rate on the firm's short-term debt (i.e., notes payable) is 8 percent, and the relevant tax rate is 30 percent.

Next he requested audits on a number of projects implemented in the last five years. Unfortunately the company did little follow-up regarding its long-term investments, and there were no formal attempts to compare actual costs and revenues with those that had been projected. However, he was eventually able to obtain data that he considered "imprecise but considerably better than nothing." After spending numerous hours analyzing this information and consulting with company executives, he developed four classifications of projects with various risk ratings. (See Exhibit 2.) And while the relative risk of each category was subjectively determined, there is little doubt that Carlton's analysis was extremely thorough. He attempted to consider, for example, the sensitivity of the returns on different types of projects to such factors as the state of the economy, interest rates, the entry of new competition, and even changes in local labor markets.

Carlton also feels that a worst-case analysis should become standard operating procedure in the top two risk classes. He wants to propose that such projects must pass two tests to be approved. First, the IRR must exceed the risk-adjusted required return; and second, the estimated loss in the worst case should be no greater than 20 percent of the project cost. When he asked the opinion of a number of managers on the second requirement, most complained that it seemed too arbitrary and was biased against market expansion projects. A few, however, thought the criterion was quite sound and would help the company avoid disastrous investments.

CAN IT DIFFERENTIATE?

One manager raised a point she wanted addressed. In her opinion most of the company's capital budget is spent on investments in which the riskiness of the projected cash flow increases the further into the future the estimate lies. That is, for most projects it is easier to estimate the cash flow for year 1 than, say, year 3. Examples include expanding a product in a market where the firm is well known or replacing a piece of equipment with a newer model that does essentially the same task. But there are situations where the riskiest years are the early ones. An example is one in which the firm enters a growing market where it is not well known. "In this case," she notes, "we are pretty confident that we will be successful, and the real uncertainty is how long it takes." Another example could involve equipment replacement decisions regarding technology with which the firm is relatively unfamiliar. The later cash flow projections are relatively more certain as the firm gains experience with the equipment. She wonders if the risk technique Carlton wants to implement can differentiate between these two types of risk situations, and if it can't, how much difference can it make.

As Carlton prepares to do the analysis, he recognizes that a number of good questions have been raised, and he isn't sure what the answers are. "Maybe I can't completely debug our capital budgeting procedure," he admits to no one in particular, "but it seems to me that the relevant issue is not whether I can devise a theoretically perfect system, but whether I can devise one that is an improvement over what is used now."

QUESTIONS

1. The case suggests that Carlton Vandermeer developed Exhibit 2 after analyzing the total risk of projects. That is, he appears to have considered both systematic and unsystematic risk in his study. Does this seem correct? Does it

make any difference that all of the firm's stock is owned by the Vandermeer family and that it represents virtually their entire wealth? Explain.

2. Calculate the required return (or cost of capital) for the firm's typical project. You may assume the current capital structure is optimal. Use book values in your calculations and estimate the required return on equity using the risk-premium approach.

3. (a) Determine the risk premiums for the four classifications of projects shown in Exhibit 2.
   (b) Determine the risk-adjusted discount (hurdle) rates.

4. What do you think is the most difficult step in developing risk premiums for various risk classes? Explain.

5. (a) Evaluate Carlton's suggestion to use a worst-case analysis on projects in the top two risk classes.
   (b) Does the risk-adjusted discount rate method Carlton is considering differentiate projects whose cash flow estimates are more uncertain in later years from those in which the cash flow estimates are more uncertain in the earlier years? Explain.

6. Carlton feels that the company "does projects it shouldn't and doesn't do ones it should." How might the use of a single hurdle rate for all projects contribute to this problem?

7. Evaluate the possibility of using the certainty equivalent method for risk evaluation in a situation in which the firm's general manager owns nearly all the stock, the remainder held by other family members.

8. Based on your previous answers and other information in the case, how—if at all—should the Vandermeer Company incorporate risk evaluation into its capital budgeting process? Fully support your position.

EXHIBIT 1
The Vandermeer Company's Current Balance Sheet ($000s)

Assets		Liabilities and Equity	
Cash	$ 546	Notes payable	$ 824
Receivables	5,437	Accounts payable	4,065
Inventory	2,969	Accruals	995
Current assets	$ 8,952	Current liabilities	$ 5,884
Net fixed assets	4,364	Term loans	2,373
Total assets	$13,316	Retained earnings	3,760
		Common stock	1,300
		Total liabilities and equity	$13,316

EXHIBIT 2
Carlton's Suggested Risk Classes

Risk Class	Description of Project	Relative Risk
A	Below average risk. Routine replacement of equipment, etc. Cost-reduction-type projects.	0.6
B	Average risk. Continuation of existing products within established market areas.	1.0
C	Above-average risk. Development of new products within established market areas.	1.8
D	Very risky. Expansion of existing products outside established market areas.	3

MONTERREY PLASTICS
PROBABILITY DISTRIBUTIONS

Monterrey Plastics, a Mexican affiliate of a Fortune 500 company, was considering building a plant to manufacture polyvinyl chloride (PVC), a plastic with many established uses such as pipe and bottles. Monterrey's general manager, Elliot Mendelson, felt the idea was worth pursuing. First, the Mexican market for PVC was relatively untapped and growing. Second, distribution costs would be low since the plant's location at San Tamica was near Monterrey's suppliers and potential buyers. Third, the project should meet with the approval of the Mexican government since one-half of the financing would come from influential Mexican investors and the plant would use a significant amount of local labor. Fourth, the technical risk of the project was minimal since the proposed plant would be almost a duplicate of an existing unit. Finally, PVC is considered to be a fundamental material and is unlikely to become technologically obsolete in the foreseeable future.

AN EARLIER MEETING

Mendelson had assembled six of Monterrey's most capable executives to help with the financial evaluation. At a meeting a few weeks ago, the group had agreed on a number of points crucial to the project. The consensus was that the initial after-tax cost to the firm, including working capital and net of any tax considerations, would be $150 million. The relevant time period is 10 years and the appropriate tax rate is 40 percent. The terminal value of the project is considered negligible and thus would be ignored. Finally, to implement the project, the group felt it needed to satisfy three criteria: the expected IRR should exceed 16 percent; the project should have a 95 percent chance of generating at least a simple payback; and it should have a 70 percent chance of producing an IRR above the risk-free rate of 8 percent.

At one point there was considerable discussion about the appropriate hurdle rate to use. Monterrey Plastics typically uses 13 percent as the required return for its average-risk investments. There was concern, however, that the project entailed some political risk. A few of Monterrey's managers felt there was a chance that the Mexican government would prove "uncooperative" and impose some type of price controls. The consensus was that it was possible but very unlikely that the Mexican authorities would react this way, especially in view of the large amount of Mexican involvement. Moreover, given the low technical and obsolescence risks, it was not clear that the project was really above average in risk. Nonetheless, Mendelson chose the 16 percent figure mainly to placate the vocal minority in support of a higher hurdle rate. Mendelson also recommended increasing the proportion of Mexican managers. He felt this would reduce the probability (which was already small) of any adverse government reaction and would make Monterrey more flexible and quick in response to market change and customer relationships.

Though a number of points surrounding the project had been settled, Mendelson knew there were still other key estimates that had to be made. These included market share, selling price, unit variable cost, and fixed operating costs. Mendelson directed the group to divide into two teams and independently develop subjective probability estimates of each of these variables, considering any interdependencies where appropriate. "We can't take the judgment out of the decision," he told the group, "but we can *think* about the issues. That's why I want your estimates of these probabilities. When we get consensus information we'll feed it into the computer, run a simulation, and develop an expected IRR and a probability distribution on the possible IRRs."

THE TEAMS

Team *A* was headed by Harry Stuyvesant. Stuyvesant is a well-respected Monterrey executive with a fine track record, and he has a good feel for the Mexican environment that the company operates in. It is well known, however, that he vehemently opposed the San Tamica site, instead favoring a location near the Quama River because he felt labor there would be relatively cheap. He was overruled by Mendelson, who thought that any wage advantage of the Quama site would be offset by higher distribution costs.

Team *B* was headed by Ivan Comeshey, who has been with Monterrey five years, a relatively short period of time. But his business acumen is considered top-notch, and in fact it was he who first suggested the PVC plant and encouraged the use of Mexican investors to finance the project.

When Mendelson received the teams' reports, he ran a simulation on each model to develop the IRR probability distributions. (See Exhibit 2.) As he examined the models, he noted that there was some disagreement surrounding the project's fixed operating costs and market share. The differences were not significant and Mendelson, after some reflection, developed his own estimates. The real problems were selling price and unit variable cost, since the two teams had developed quite different estimates. (Exhibit 1 shows these figures for 1997, year 1.) Mendelson decided to call a meeting, partly to present his revisions on the project's fixed operating costs and market share but mainly to address the price and variable-cost issues.

At the meeting, Mendelson's revisions were noncontroversial and the group unanimously agreed to incorporate them into the final model. The remaining part of the agenda, however, generated considerable discussion. Stuyvesant said his team felt that an economic downturn, predicted for next year by a number of economists, would likely depress the price of PVC. "And keep in mind we could sell as much as 120,000 tons annually. That is not a negligible market share. This amount of tonnage could easily cause the price to drop and, perhaps, to decrease sharply. Our price estimates also consider the possibility of controls by the Mexican government. As for costs, it is true the current per-unit variable cost of producing PVC is $530 per ton. But there's evidence that the Mexican labor market is tightening, and Monterrey may well have to pay premium wages to get the workers it needs."

Comeshey pointed out that the current price of PVC was $1,140 per ton and that Stuyvesant's estimates suggested a 30 percent drop was possible. Historically the price had never fallen by more than 10 percent over any three-year period. "Our group agrees that 120,000 tons might cause some drop in price, but a 30 percent decrease seems out of the question. It is true that there is not much historical evidence on PVC prices in the Mexican market. But our experience in similar areas, plus our own marketing studies, simply do not support Harry's estimates—unless you take an *extremely* pessimistic view. And while there's some possibility of a recession, this is not the consensus forecast among economists. I do feel, though, that Harry's point on the Mexican labor market is well taken. Monterrey's labor costs could easily be more than our team considered."

Mendelson then brought up another issue. Though the models assumed the yearly cash flows are dependent, he realized the probability estimates of each team implicitly assumed that yearly price and unit variable cost were independent, and he wondered if this assumption was reasonable. "In parts of a recession, for example, isn't it true that we will face higher per-unit variable costs at the same time we experience a soft market for PVC?"

Mendelson then said he would "consider carefully" the issues that had been raised and would develop his own estimates based on the arguments he had heard. The entire model would be reviewed—he hoped for the last time—in 72 hours. Although Mendelson was pleased that the discussions had been conducted in a straightforward and congenial manner, he secretly wished that another meeting would be unnecessary.

PROCEDURAL QUESTIONS

After the meeting Stuyvesant and Mendelson chatted briefly about Monterrey's capital budgeting procedures. Stuyvesant wondered about the theoretical advisability of assessing risk using probability distributions and questioned the company's ad hoc procedure for determining the hurdle rate for the Mexican project. He noted that most of the stockholders of Monterrey's parent company hold well-diversified portfolios and any investment made by Monterrey would constitute a relatively small portion of their financial holdings. Mendelson responded that he does not see why the composition of the portfolios of the stockholders is relevant to Monterrey's capital budgeting policies. He is not eager to alter the firm's investment procedures, especially in light of a recent study, done in conjunction with a respected consulting firm, that concluded Monterrey's choice of capital budgeting projects has been quite good. Nonetheless, Mendelson admits that he is always looking for ways to refine the company's financial techniques and would welcome any suggestions.

QUESTIONS

1. (a) Calculate the expected IRR, that is, E(IRR), for the probability distributions of each team.
   (b) Calculate the standard deviation of these IRRs, that is, σ_{IRR}, for Team B. (The standard deviation is 6.15 percent for Team A.)

2. Assume a normal distribution. Using Team B's IRR probability distribution:
   (a) Calculate the chance that the IRR will exceed 16 percent.
   (b) Calculate the chance it will exceed the risk-free rate of 8 percent.
   (c) Calculate the chance the project will generate at least a simple payback (you want to solve for the probability that the IRR≥0).

3. Repeat question 2 for Team A.

4. (a) List each possible risk associated with the project.
   (b) Which of these would be considered systematic (nondiversifiable) risk and which unsystematic (diversifiable) risk?

5. Both teams assume that price and per-unit variable cost are independent in any year. How might Mendelson determine the reasonableness of this assumption?

6. (a) Which set of probability estimates seems more accurate? Defend your choice.
   (b) Ignoring any dependency problems, how do you think Mendelson should proceed?

7. Play the role of a consultant. Critically evaluate the capital budgeting technique used for the Mexican project. In particular evaluate (1) the use of probability distributions to assess risk; (2) Mendelson's charge that the project hurdle rate was somewhat arbitrarily chosen; and (3) the criteria that the project must meet to be acceptable. What recommendations, if any, do you have for Monterrey's capital budgeting procedures? (Do you see a possible agency problem?)

EXHIBIT 1
Price and Unit Variable Cost Probability Estimates of Each Team for 1997
(Year 1)

1. Team A (Stuyvesant)

Price/Ton

Outcome	Probability
$1,200	.25
1,000	.50
800	.25

Variable Cost/Ton

Outcome	Probability
$ 650	.25
590	.50
530	.25

2. Team B (Comeshey)

Price/Ton

Outcome	Probability
$1,200	.10
1,150	.25
1,100	.40
1,050	.15
1,000	.10

Variable Cost/Ton

Outcome	Probability
$580	.10
560	.20
540	.40
520	.20
500	.10

EXHIBIT 2
The IRR Probability Distributions Derived from Simulations Using Models of Each Team

Team A (Stuyvesant)

IRR Range (%)	Probability (%)
18–24	20
12–18	30
6–12	30
0–6	20

Team B (Comeshey)

IRR Range (%)	Probability (%)
33–39	5
27–33	15
21–27	30
15–21	30
9–15	15
3–9	5

PART VI

CAPITAL STRUCTURE/ COST OF CAPITAL

TAYLOR BRANDS
COST OF CAPITAL OR REQUIRED RATE OF RETURN

The management of Taylor Brands has a philosophy of "better to be safe than sorry" when selecting a discount rate. At present the firm uses a 30 percent rate, which many company executives feel is unreasonably high and results in the following difficulties. First, some projects considered to be worthwhile and important are rejected because their expected return is close to, but still below, the 30 percent minimum. Second, managers have a tendency to be overly optimistic in their cash flow projections in order to get their pet projects accepted. Third, there is the feeling that the rate is at best arbitrarily determined and at worst something that Trevor Unruh—Taylor's general manager—has "pulled out of a hat."

ROBERT WEST

Robert West is one of Taylor's more innovative and thoughtful executives. A few years ago he correctly perceived that a successful firm in the food wholesalers industry—Taylor's main industry—would have to expand into nonfood items. After extensive study, West recommended that Taylor add such products as light hardware and paper plates to the variety of goods it sells to grocery stores. This strategy worked remarkably well. Taylor's customers benefited because they dealt with fewer vendors and invoices. Taylor gained customers (many were referrals) and also reduced its unit cost by making more efficient use of its trucking capacity.

West has developed an interest in the financial side of the business. During the past year he attended two seminars on cost-of-capital estimation, using his personal leave time and at his own expense. He has been eager to apply this newly acquired knowledge, and after a number of discussions Unruh told West to "determine Taylor's cost of capital and make a formal report on your findings." It seemed to West that this was a major coup since Unruh paid little attention to the financial side of the business. He was told privately, however, that Unruh is "really unimpressed and bored with the entire idea; he assigned you this project because he knew that *you* were eager to do it, and Unruh admires your initiative." West was told quite bluntly that "nothing will come of your efforts."

Initially deflated, West became determined to do a thorough evaluation, and he felt sure that he could convince Unruh of the importance of obtaining an accurate cost of capital. "At the very least," West thought, "a formal investigation of our cost of capital will eliminate the perception that it is arbitrarily determined."

In preparation for making the estimate West reviewed his notes from one of the seminars he had attended. (See Exhibit 1.) He recalled the instructor emphasizing that estimating the required return on equity was especially delicate; and although the instructor gave two models for measuring this return, he emphasized there was "no substitute for good judgment."

FINANCIAL INFORMATION

West also collected some financial information that he felt was relevant to the analysis. He knows the company has recently obtained a bank note at 7 percent and that the company's bonds were originally issued at 7 percent but are currently selling at a discount with a yield to maturity of about 8 percent.

Taylor's EPS has grown quite impressively in the last five years (see Exhibit 3), but West knows Unruh encouraged a relatively constant dividend per share over this period since he preferred to reinvest much of the company's earnings. West doesn't believe this will continue since Unruh is under pressure from major stockholders to bring dividend growth in line with earnings growth. Nor is it likely that past EPS growth can be maintained. First, during this period the industry itself had unusual prosperity. Second, some of this past growth was a result of the firm's movement into nonfood items, and these opportunities are virtually exhausted. Third, many corporate insiders felt Taylor had been a bit lucky.

West decides it is reasonable to suppose that Taylor will implement a 70 percent payout ratio; after all, it makes no sense to retain a large proportion of earnings when investment opportunities are not as plentiful as in the past. He also feels that the company will achieve an average return of 12 percent on any retained earnings. Though these figures on payout and return are something of "guesstimates," West was able to find support for these numbers among Taylor's managers.

Most financial analysts consider the industry to be of average risk, and in fact, beta estimates for Taylor range from .8 to 1.2. West decides, however, that these estimates are a bit high, because the firm is in the process of altering production techniques that will reduce the company's degree of operating leverage.

And there is another difficulty. At present Taylor has no preferred stock in its capital structure. But West knows that there are plans to issue some in the next few months, though the price and dividend per share have not yet been determined. However, he does have some information on the preferred stock of three of Taylor's competitors. (See Exhibit 6.) These companies are much larger than Taylor and are considered less risky because they have a more diversified product line and customer base and enjoy a lower degree of operating leverage (even after the change in Taylor's production techniques). He is also aware that the yield difference on the preferred stock of firms in roughly the same industry is 75 to 100 basis points.

"I've got quite a bit of info," West thought. "I hope I can put it all together to make a report that will impress Unruh."

QUESTIONS

1. West intends to adjust Taylor's beta estimates slightly downward in view of the fact that the firm's degree of operating leverage is decreasing. Does such an adjustment seem appropriate? Explain.

2. The required return on equity (cost of equity), K_e, can be estimated in a number of ways.

   (a) Estimate K_e using a risk premium approach.
   (b) Use the dividend valuation model to estimate K_e.
   (c) In your view, what is K_e? Justify your choice.

3. Estimate Taylor's cost of capital or required rate of return. (You may use book values in your calculations. Assume the existing capital structure is optimal and ignore preferred stock. The relevant tax rate is 40 percent.)

4. Preferred stock is a riskier investment than a bond. Yet companies have been known to issue preferred stock at a lower yield than they issue bonds. How can this be, assuming investors are rational?

5. (a) Estimate the cost of preferred stock (required return of preferred stock).
   (b) Redo question 3 including preferred stock as a financing source, and assume the target weights are as follows: notes, 5 percent; bonds, 40 percent; preferred, 5 percent; equity, 50 percent.

6. What additional information would you like in order to make more informed estimates about the cost of equity and the cost of preferred stock?

7. (a) What would you guess is the market value of the firm's notes payable? Explain.
   (b) Taylor has one long-term debt security outstanding with a coupon rate of 7 percent. It is a debenture issue maturing in 10 years, and interest is paid semiannually. Determine the debenture's current market value assuming that all principal will be paid in 10 years. Assume also that the bond's semiannual required return is 4 percent.

(c) The MV/BV ratio is 1.15. Calculate the market value of Taylor's stock.

(d) Estimate Taylor's cost of capital or required return assuming that these market values are consistent with the financing weights desired by management. (You may ignore preferred stock.)

8. (a) Argue for using market values to determine a firm's required return (cost of capital).

(b) Argue for using book values.

9. (a) Apparently the 30 percent hurdle rate used by Taylor exceeds its actual cost of capital or required rate of return. Let us suppose a company errs in the other direction and chooses a hurdle rate considerably less than its actual cost of capital. What difficulties could this cause?

(b) West believes that Taylor's high cost of capital encourages managers to develop overly optimistic cash flow forecasts. Is a more accurate cost-of-capital estimate likely to reduce this bias, as he apparently thinks? Explain your answer.

10. (a) Suppose that West will present a summary of his findings to senior management. Would you recommend that he present his estimate of Taylor's required return (cost of capital) as XX percent, XX.X percent, or XX.XX percent? That is, how—if at all—would you suggest the estimate be rounded off? (Keep in mind that he is likely to be questioned thoroughly by Unruh, who appears skeptical of West's efforts.)

(b) Would you recommend that West use market or book values in his presentation? Defend your recommendation.

EXHIBIT 1
Excerpts from West's Notes on the Cost of Capital Seminars

1. The instructor said the cost of capital is really the *required rate of return* or hurdle rate that should be used to evaluate capital budgeting projects of average risk for the company. (Indeed, he much prefers the term "required rate of return" to the more common but potentially misleading "cost of capital.")

2. The cost of capital is a weighted average of the required return on each financing source. Theoretical accuracy requires these weights be obtained at the market values of debt, equity, and (if applicable) preferred stock. The instructor said, however, that most firms use book values because (1) it is easier, and (2) market values tend to vary widely.

3. The instructor recommended that all debt that does not require an *explicit* return be excluded when calculating the weights described in part 2. (Usually this means excluding accounts payable and accruals.)

(continued)

EXHIBIT 1
(Continued)

4. The required return on each financing source should be based on current market conditions.
5. The instructor recommended that flotation costs be ignored. While theoretically incorrect this omission simplifies the calculations and does not significantly alter the estimate.

EXHIBIT 2
Historical Estimates of Yearly Returns on Various Investments: 1926–1992

Investment	(Arithmetic Average) Average Yearly Return (%)
Common stocks	12.1
Small capitalization stocks	17.1
Long-term government bonds	4.9
Long-term corporate bonds	5.5

Source: R. G. Ibbotson and R. A. Sinquefield, *Stocks, Bonds, Bills, and Inflation: 1993 Yearbook* (Chicago: Ibbotsen Associates, 1993).

EXHIBIT 3
EPS and DPS Information on Taylor

Year	EPS	Change (%)	DPS	Change (%)
1991	$0.73	—	$0.40	—
1992	0.82	12.3	0.40	0
1993	1.14	39.0	0.40	0
1994	1.85	62.3	0.41	2.5
1995	2.35	27.0	0.43	4.9
1996 (present)	2.83	20.4	0.45	4.7

EXHIBIT 4
Financial Information Compiled by West

Treasury bill rate	5.5%
Long-term government bond rate	7%
Long-term corporate bond rate	8%
Current annual yield on Taylor's long-term debt	8%
Current dividend on Taylor's stock	$0.45
Price range of Taylor's stock, previous year	28–36
Rate on recent short-term loan (note)	7%
Taylor's tax rate	40%

EXHIBIT 5
Taylor's Financial Structure at Book Values ($000s)

Accounts payable	45,000
Notes payable	16,000
Accruals and other current liabilities	8,000
Bonds	89,000
Common stock	58,000
Retained earnings	72,000
Total liabilities and equity	288,000

EXHIBIT 6
Preferred Stock Information on Taylor's Competitors

Firm	Original Price of Preferred	Current Price of Preferred	Dividend
Super Foods	$50	$40	$3.00
Easton	$41	$31	$2.25
Westgate	$46	$45	$3.00

W O N D E R   B A R S
C O S T   O F   C A P I T A L   O R   R E Q U I R E D   R E T U R N

All rational investors want to invest in securities (or projects) that are expected to yield a return greater than their cost of capital. For the chief financial officer (CFO) of a company, the procedure for determining where to invest is a three-step process. The first step is finding the expected return on the securities (or projects) in which the firm may be interested. The second step is the determination of the firm's cost of capital. The final step is selecting those securities (or projects) whose expected return is greater than the firm's cost of capital. In reality neither of the first two steps precedes the other as the CFO may calculate the firm's cost of capital on an annual, a semiannual, or even a quarterly basis, depending on changes in the capital markets. The calculated cost of capital may then be compared to the expected returns of the various securities and capital projects available.

HISTORY OF WONDER BARS

Wonder Bars (WB) was founded in 1896 by Earle Greymore as a manufacturer of quality chocolate candy. As with most food companies established in the United States in that period, WB started as a modest manufacturer of a single product that was sold locally. Later, if successful, those firms expanded their sales efforts to state, regional, national, and sometimes even to international areas.

Wonder Bars was one of the successful companies. Greymore's first product was a chocolate bar that sold for two cents. The bar, known as the Wonder Bar, soon became famous for its quality and fine taste. Greymore expanded production to meet the rising demand for the Wonder Bar, but growth never exceeded cash available to pay for the expansion. Two of the basic tenets on which Greymore founded and ran WB were to make a quality chocolate bar and not to go into debt. These tenets were considered almost sacrosanct, and Greymore believed they were the reasons for his success while many other food companies failed.

By 1936, when Greymore turned the reins of his company over to his son, John, WB had grown into a respected and well-known $2.5-million regional chocolate firm. It had survived the Great Depression, according to Earle Greymore, because the firm still produced a quality product and, above all, had no debt. John Greymore followed the principles laid down by his father, and in the next 30 years WB grew to a national firm with $125 million in sales. Although WB had purchased a confectionery candy firm, over 90 percent of the sales were from chocolate candy. Significantly only 5 percent of the firm's capital structure was in long-term debt, the debt needed to purchase the confectionery candy firm.

In 1967, when John's son Earl became president of WB, the family still owned all the stock of the firm and the board of directors was made up entirely of family members. However, in 1971 the company was forced into going public because of two circumstances. The first was the need to raise cash to pay estate taxes following the death of John Greymore. The second came from the increasing awareness that the firm needed to modernize its plants to compete with other food companies, which were slowly taking market share from WB with better quality candy products and higher profits from their automated, modern equipment.

By the early 1980s the firm had completed its modernization, improving the quality of its products and reducing operating expenses. However, the firm was totally dependent on the chocolate and confectionery business and its managers were beginning to realize that diversification into other lines of the food business might be necessary for WB to survive in the increasingly competitive business environment. In addition, some family members were beginning to question the financial practices of the firm and the effects those practices had on the stock price. They noticed that throughout the 1970s, many of the old-line family food businesses were purchased by larger, publicly held firms run by managers who were not majority shareholders of the firm. More importantly they noticed that the returns on the shares sold seemed much higher than the returns they were receiving from their stock.

During the early 1980s, WB did expand into the pasta business through the purchase of three family-owned firms and by 1989 had an 18 percent market share of the $1 billion U.S. pasta business. Salem financed the purchase of these businesses through two bond issues. Long-term debt, however, was never more than 20 percent of total assets.

Sam Wendover

Sam Wendover, the chief financial officer (CFO) of WB, was hired in 1988 with specific instructions to improve the return on the financial resources of the firm. Wendover's background included four years as the cash manager of a large corporation with sales in excess of $9 billion. He was a graduate of an MBA program that is nationally known for its emphasis on financial management.

Wendover saw the job as CFO of WB as an outstanding opportunity to affect the financial decision making of a firm in transition from family ownership to one that was becoming a multibillion dollar, publicly held firm.

This Monday morning, Wendover had just walked into his office at 7:40 to find a note stuck on his computer's video monitor to call Earl Greymore, the CEO of Wonder Bars. The posting of the note was unusual in that most intra-office memos were sent via the electronic mail system, by then very few of WB's top executive managers ever used their computers for this or any other purpose. Greymore, however, was making a real effort to bring WB into the modern era, insisting that the computers be installed and that all managers below the level of the executive officers take in-house training on how to use them. He also had many of the top executives attend financial seminars sponsored by the Wharton School. Wendover had suggested the seminars to Greymore as a vehicle to help these executives understand some of the changes he thought were necessary to improve Wonder Bars' financial performance.

Wendover called Greymore, who asked him to come up to his office. In the next 30 minutes Wendover learned that WB was considering the purchase of Sonzoni Foods, a pasta producer with annual sales in excess of $100 million, for $85 million. Before a decision could be made, Greymore wanted the answers to three financial questions from Wendover. First, what was the expected return from this proposed purchase? Second, what was Wonder Bars' cost of capital? Finally, what was Wendover's recommendation on how the purchase could be financed?

Financial Information

Wendover reviewed the WB financial data. (See Exhibits 1 and 2.) The average outstanding balance of short-term, interest-bearing debt in 1994 was $76,132,000 and the weighted average interest rate was 8.2 percent. Domestic borrowing under lines of credit and commercial paper was used to fund seasonal working capital requirements and provide interim financing for business acquisitions. Maximum short-term borrowings at any month were $372,400,000.

WB had two long-term, AA+ rated bonds outstanding. The first was an 8.25 percent sinking fund debenture due in 12 years. This debenture is traded on the New York Stock Exchange and closed Friday at 91⅜. Of the original $150 million issue, $133 million is still outstanding. The second issue was for $100 million and had a coupon interest rate of 9.375 percent. The entire issue was sold in 1990 in a private placement to two life insurance companies, and the issue will mature in 2020. Wendover then called WB's investment banker and learned that the banker was highly confident that Wonder Bars could issue up to $100 million of new debt at the current return on WB's outstanding long-term debt.

Like many other family-controlled but publicly held businesses, WB has two classes of common stock: Common Stock and Class B stock. The Common Stock has one vote per share and the Class B stock (held or controlled by family members) has 10 votes per share. However, the Common Stock, voting separately as a class, is entitled to elect one-sixth of the board of directors. With respect to dividend rights, the common stock is entitled to cash dividends that are 10 percent higher than those declared and paid on the Class B Stock. There are a total of 75 million shares of common stock and 10 million of Class B Stock outstanding. The current price of both the common stock and Class B Stock is $35 and its beta is 0.95. The common stock and Class B Stock generally vote together without regard to class on matters submitted to stockholders.

The growth rate of net income, earnings per share, dividends, and common stock prices are given in Exhibit 3 and have averaged about 14 percent a year over the last five years. Some of this growth rate is the result of an aggressive repurchase of the firm's common stock. Over the past three years the firm has repurchased over 5 million common stock shares. Finally, Wendover looked up the capitalization ratio for other firms in the food industry. (See Exhibit 4.) As he expected, WB had a much lower debt ratio than almost all other companies in the industry group.

Sam Wendover wrote down the additional information that he thought he needed before starting to work. The current Treasury Bill rate was 5.0 percent and the return on the S&P 500 has averaged 12 percent over the past 10 years. Salem's current combined federal and state income tax rate is 40 percent. The beta for Sonzoni Food was 0.90, almost the same as Wonder Bars.

QUESTIONS

1. What is WB's capital structure?

2. What is WB's before-tax cost of long-term debt?

3. What is the firm's cost of equity?

4. Calculate the cost of capital for WB.

5. If Wonder Bar uses book value rather than market value to determine its capital structure, what is the impact of the cost of capital on its budgeting decisions?

6. Which is superior, using the book value or the market value of the firm's capital in the determination of the cost of capital? Why?

7. Wendover apparently believes that WB's cost of capital can be used as the hurdle rate for the required return to evaluate the acquisition of Sonzoni Foods. Under what conditions, if any, is this appropriate?

8. How can the firm raise $85 million for the acquisition without changing the present capital structure?

9. Assuming an expected net income in 1995 of $182 million, how would you suggest that the firm finance the acquisition?

EXHIBIT 1
Wonder Bars Income Statement ($ Millions)

	1994	1993	1992
Net sales	$2,168.0	$1,863.8	$1,635.5
Operating income	263.8	246.1	216.2
Interest expense	27.7	22.4	8.1
Pretax income	236.1	223.7	208.1
Taxes	91.6	99.6	100.9
Income from continuing operations	144.5	124.1	107.2
Discontinued operations			
Income	16.0	24.1	25.6
Gain on disposal	53.4	—	—
Net income	$ 213.9	$ 148.2	$ 132.8
Earnings per share			
Continuing operations	$ 1.60	$ 1.38	$ 1.15
Discontinued operations	2.37	1.64	1.42

EXHIBIT 2
Wonder Bars Balance Sheet Comparison ($ Millions)

	1994	1993
Assets		
Cash	$ 70.1	$ 7.8
Accounts receivable	166.8	121.5
Inventory	308.8	263.2
Other current assets	73.4	329.5
Total current assets	619.1	722.0
Net property, plant equipment	736.0	564.5
Other assets	409.6	257.9
Total assets	$1,746.7	$1,544.4
Liabilities stockholders' equity		
Accounts payable	$ 128.8	$ 108.0
Short-term debt	54.9	29.7
Other current liabilities	161.7	119.1
Total current liabilities	345.4	256.8
Long-term debt	233.0	280.9
Other long-term liabilities	48.0	43.2
Deferred income taxes	132.4	131.1
Stockholders' equity	1,005.9	832.4
Total liabilities stockholders' equity	$1,764.7	$1,544.4

EXHIBIT 3
Wonder Bars 5-year Financial Summary

Year	Net Income	EPS[a]	DPS	Stock Price
1994	$213.9	$1.60	$0.67	36⅜
1993	189.2	1.44	0.60	31⅝
1992	171.8	1.28	0.52	28½
1991	151.3	1.15	0.48	25
1990	130.9	1.02	0.43	22¼
5-Year Growth rate	12.3%	12.0%	12.0%	13.0%

[a]Primary earnings per share.

EXHIBIT 4
Ratio of Long-Term Debt to Total Assets: Industry Group Analysis

Dreyer's Grand	65%
Borden	42
Hudson Foods	42
Flowers Industries	33
IGA Average	32
Gerber Products	31
Campbell Soup	26
Kellogg Company	24
Wonder Bars	22
Hershey Foods	18
Smucker (J.M.)	3
Tootsie Roll Industries	0

FULTEX
LONG-TERM
FINANCING

The memo was unexpected and emotionally written.

R. Craig Harrof is a board member of the Fultex Corporation and a general manager with Titus Electronics. Harrof recently sent a memo to Elizabeth Bethea, the chief financial officer of Fultex. Harrof wrote that he "strongly believes that Fultex is highly overleveraged" and that "it is not in the best interests of our stockholders to borrow in order to fund the $81 million expansion." These concerns are based on a comparison of the firm's current, quick, debt, debt/equity (D/E), times interest earned, and fixed charge coverage ratios to the industry average. (See Exhibit 3.) Harrof is especially concerned about the D/E ratio, which is the ratio of long-term debt to equity. The firm's D/E is more than double the industry standard, a situation he finds "alarming." And Harrof has taken great care to compile the industry standards. For comparison, he selected seven companies, affectionately called the Magnificent Seven, which are roughly similar to Fultex in terms of sales and asset size. "The facts speak for themselves: We're much too debt-heavy at present. There's no point in considering the use of debt to raise this $81 million."

FULTEX

Fultex is a medium-sized producer of athletic uniforms, sportswear, sleepwear, and a variety of fabrics. Fultex has a well-deserved reputation for running a fully modernized operation with a commitment to maintaining state-of-the-art production facilities. And it has always paid considerable attention to cost management. For example, more than a decade ago Fultex became the first apparel company to install a fully integrated information system, which resulted in a faster, more accurate distribution of company data. This commitment to production and cost management has paid off. Fultex is the envy of the industry, combining as it does low cost with product quality and service dependability.

The firm is the dominant supplier of athletic uniforms to teams in nearly all sports and has a well-developed distributing and marketing network in this area. Management correctly estimated a few years ago, however, that the team uniform business was maturing, and it made the decision to expand into the retail market. The main strategy was to capitalize on Fultex's reputation for quality and styling and to develop its own brands of leisure apparel such as sweatshirts and jogging suits. The company began promoting these brands on the retail level through sporting goods dealers, many of whom were already selling Fultex's athletic uniforms. The move into the retail business has been quite successful, and management has decided to increase sales to department stores and to design additional clothing lines to appeal to a wider range of the consumer market.

A few weeks ago Fultex's board of directors unanimously voted to approve the acquisition of $81 million of external funds that will be used to expand manufacturing facilities and to develop a new R+D plant. The R+D factory is another of Fultex's steps to improve efficiency and will enable the firm to test production systems. Top management considers this project absolutely essential for Fultex to succeed in increasing its market share, though it is not expected to improve the firm's profitability in the near future.

REACTION TO HARROF'S MEMO

The financing of the needed $81 million has generated some controversy, and Bethea is discussing Harrof's memo with William Gibbs, a vice president. Bethea concedes that Harrof has raised some interesting points. She is far from convinced, however, that the company is debt heavy. Harrof's figures are indisputable but, she believes, they ignore the capacity of the firm to incur debt. "First," she remarks to Gibbs, "I suspect we're more profitable than the typical firm. I also suspect our business risk is low compared to these companies. For example, we're well diversified in terms of markets and product line for a firm our size. An important issue is the overall risk that our stockholders are exposed to, which is determined by our business risk as well as our financial risk. Harrof is looking at only one side of the issue. And don't forget the customer loyalty we've worked so hard to develop. This makes us less vulnerable than our competitors to economic downturns."

THE VIEWS OF THE LARGEST STOCKHOLDER

Bethea then shared with Gibbs the details of a recent meeting with Anthony Barro. Barro, a billionaire, is Fultex's major stockholder and owns 4 million shares (36 percent of the firm's stock). He is eager to maintain effective control of the company, which he believes can be accomplished with at least 30 percent of the shares. Barro understands that Fultex needs external funds and told Bethea that, due to other business ventures, his financial situation was such that he could only commit up to $25 million of equity any time during the next three years. In addition, Barro believes that the market does not fully appreciate Fultex's future prospects and cites the 1995 drop in the price-earnings (P–E) ratio as evidence. He acknowledges, however, that Fultex's current P–E ratio is relatively high by historical standards. (See Exhibit 2.) In addition, Barro feels that the Federal Reserve will do "almost anything" to avoid a recession. In his view there is a real danger that inflation will escalate sharply. This would cause an increase in inflationary expectations that, in turn, would cause interest rates to rise. In short, he feels that interest rates are currently very attractive. All things considered, Barro would prefer that Fultex issue debt to raise the needed funds. However—and he leaves this up to Bethea to determine—if the bond option seems too risky or if there are other mitigating factors, Barro would support the stock option.

Bethea was a bit surprised at Barro's interpretation of the Federal Reserve's priorities. Fultex is a client of Wharton Econometrics, a well-respected macroeconomic forecasting firm, and Bethea faithfully reads such prominent financial publications as the *Wall Street Journal* and the *Economist*. Most economists feel that the Fed is very much concerned with containing inflation, even at the risk of precipitating a recession, and some even feel that an economic downturn is quite likely in the next 12 to 24 months. She has noticed, however, that no economic forecaster believes that any recession will be as severe as the ones in 1974 to 1975 and 1982. Bethea realizes, though, that economic forecasting is an inexact science and majority opinions can easily be wrong.

THE FINANCING OPTIONS

There are three financing possibilities Fultex is considering to raise the needed $81 million.

Stock Option. This involves the sale of new common stock at $32 per share. The firm would net $30 after the $2 per share flotation cost.

Bond Option. The bonds would be 15-year debentures bearing an interest rate of 10 percent. The bonds would be callable after eight years at a price of $1,100 per $1,000 bond, declining to $1,000 by year 15. The indenture will not allow Fultex to issue any new debt with a higher priority, and Fultex is restricted from paying dividends in excess of 70 percent of net income. The debentures carry a modest sinking fund provision. Beginning at the end of year 5, 5 percent of the bonds would need to be retired each year. (*Note:* Fultex would have a balloon payment equal to 50 percent of the issue at the end of year 15.)

Combination Option. This is a 50-50 mix of the stock and bond options previously described.

Bethea and Gibbs then discuss future financing needs beyond those considered in Exhibit 5. Gibbs makes the point that industry production techniques are "ever changing" and that it is crucial that Fultex stay alert for the possibilities of innovation and efficiency if it is to flourish and not merely survive. It is quite difficult, however, to estimate the funds that would be required if Fultex suddenly had to alter its method of production. A "best guesstimate" is that $10 to $20 million would be necessary. Though Bethea would like to be able to finance this internally—and she believes that Fultex has roughly $5 million of excess liquidity at present—conversations with the firm's investment bankers indicate that this money could be raised externally, even if Fultex borrows the entire $81 million.

Bethea instructs Gibbs to make a detailed analysis of the three options and report back to her. "I, of course," Bethea emphasized, "will make the recommendation to the board. This is likely to be a sensitive matter given Harrof's memo and Barro's preferences. Your job is to be your usual thorough self. My job is to scrutinize the information you compile and make that recommendation."

QUESTIONS

1. (a) Calculate the following break-even sales volumes for Fultex at the present time (1995) assuming CGS is the only variable cost.

   i. EBT = 0. Use

   $$S^* = \frac{FC}{1 - VC/S}$$

   ii. Cash flow from operations; that is NI + Dep. = 0. Use

   $$S^* = \frac{FC - Dep.}{1 - VC/S}$$

   (b) Express your answers as a percentage of Fultex's sales. (These percentages are 69.8 and 59.4 for the seven competitors.)

   (c) What do your answers suggest about Fultex's risk?

2. Calculate Fultex's 1995 debt service coverage and capital service coverage ratios. The firm's lease payments total $3,360(000) and dividends equal $1,110(000). The firm's chief financial officer estimates that the ratios are 2.4 and 1.9 respectively for the firm's seven competitors.

   $$DSC = \frac{EBIT + Lease}{Int. + Lease + DD/(1 - t)} \quad \text{where } DD = \text{debt due}$$

   $$CSC = \frac{EBIT + Lease}{Int. + Lease + (DD + Div.)/(1 - t)}$$

3. (a) Calculate Fultex's 1995 DOL. The competitors' average is 3.0. Use DOL = 1 + FOC/EBIT.

   (b) Calculate its DFL (degree of financial leverage). The competitors' average is 1.1. Use DFL = 1 + INT/EBT.

   (c) Calculate its DTL (degree of total leverage). The competitors' average is 3.3. Use either DTL = 1 + FC/EBT or DTL = DOL × DFL.

   (d) Interpret your answers.

   (e) What do these figures suggest about Fultex's operating, financial, and overall risk?

4. In light of your previous answers, the information in Exhibit 3, and other information in the case, evaluate Harrof's argument that Fultex is overlevered at the present time (1995).

5. Complete the table in Exhibit 7. (Assume a dividend of $.10 per share on any new stock.)

6. (a) What is Fultex's 1996 and 1997 estimated earnings per share (EPS) if it uses the bond option? The stock option? The 1996 and 1997 estimated EPS are $2.53 and $3.22, respectively, if it uses the combination option.

   (b) What is the 1996 sales indifference point between the bond and stock options? Continue to assume that CGS is the only variable cost.

7. Complete the tables below showing selected financial ratios for Fultex in 1996 and 1997 for each financing option, assuming no external financing beyond the $81 million. These estimates are based in part on the best-guess (most likely) sales forecasts of Exhibit 5. Lease payments are $3,360(000) each year. See Exhibit 5 for yearly dividends and debt due without any new financing.

1996 Estimates

	Bond	Stock	Combination
Debt	.56	.36	.46
D/E	0.91	0.32	0.56
DSC	1.9		2.2
CSC	1.8	2.3	2.0
TIE	3.7	6.7	
FCC		5.3	4.0

1997 Estimates

	Bond	Stock	Combination
Debt	.51	.33	.43
D/E	0.72	0.25	0.45
DSC	2.3	3.0	
CSC	2.2		2.5
TIE		8.7	6.0
FCC	4.0		5.0

NOTE: DSC = debt service coverage (see question 2).
         CSC = capital service coverage (see question 2).
         FCC = fixed charge coverage
              = (EBIT + Lease)/(Interest + Lease)

8. With the stock option, the 1995 market value of Fultex is predicted to be $537.1 million, ignoring current liabilities. This estimate assumes the $95.5 million book value of long-term debt equals market value and the price per share is $32. Miller and Modigliani's equation, $V_L = V_U + (t \times D)$, implies that the value of the firm will *change* by t times the *change* in interest-bearing debt, where t is the corporate tax rate.

   (a) Assuming the bond option is chosen and using MM's equation, the value of Fultex's equity is predicted to be $393 million, with a price per share of $35.41. Show how these estimates were obtained.

   NOTE: Using the combination option and assuming 1.35 million new shares are issued, the price per share is predicted to be $33.52.

   (b) An estimate of value using MM's equation is usually considered to be an upper limit to the value of a levered firm in an efficient market. Why?

9. Use the worksheet in Exhibit 6 to develop a worst-case cash flow forecast. Note that the figures are in millions and the impact of the new financing is ignored.

10. Play the role of a consultant. Based on your previous answers, information in the case, and any other calculations you think are relevant, what option do you recommend? Defend your position.

SOFTWARE QUESTION

11. A few years ago, Fultex altered its production techniques in such a way that variable costs increased and fixed operating costs decreased. Management estimates that if the changes had not been made, 1995 variable costs would be 64 percent of sales and fixed cash operating costs ("operating expenses") would be $120 million.

   (a) Assume the production changes had never been made. Redo questions 1(b), 2, 3(a), 3(b), and 3(c).
   (b) What would Fultex's 1995 EBIT have been?
   (c) Do your answers to part (a) affect your answer to question 4? Explain.

SOFTWARE QUESTION

12. (a) A number of Fultex's top executives compiled the following worst-case scenario.

	$t + 1$ 1996	$t + 2$ 1997	$t + 3$ 1998	$t + 4$ 1999
Sales	$560.1	588.1	617.5	648.4
Operating margin	.125	.135	.135	.140
NWC/sales	.23	.23	.23	.23
DPS	.10	.10	.10	.10
Capital spending	$70	55	28	28

NOTE: DPS is dividend per share, NWC is net working capital.

Develop a cash flow forecast assuming the entire $81 million is borrowed. What are the implications of this forecast for the financing decision?

(b) When Elizabeth Bethea, the firm's CFO, was shown the above forecast, she thought the operating margin assumption was "too high" and NWC/sales was a "bit optimistic."

Redo the forecast assuming (1) a 12 percent operating margin in 1996 and 1997, a 13 percent operating margin in 1998 and 1999, and (2) NWC/sales is .24 each year.

(c) Assuming the same operating margin each year, how low can operating margin go before the cumulative cash flow in 1999 becomes zero? Use all the other assumptions in part (a). What is the implication of your answer for the financing choice? (You may want to consult Exhibit 2.)

EXHIBIT 1
Fultex's Current (1995) Income Statement and Balance Sheet

1995 Income Statement ($ Millions)

Sales	$560.1
Cost of goods sold	414.5
Gross margin	145.6
Operating expenses	63.9
Depreciation	19.0
EBIT	62.7
Interest	10.6
Earnings before taxes	52.1
Taxes (40%)	20.8
Net income	31.3
Earnings per share	$2.82
Dividends per share	$0.10

1995 Balance Sheet ($ Millions)

Assets		Liabilities and Equity	
Cash	$12.5	Accounts payable	$32.1
Accounts receivable	59.1	Debt due	10.9
Inventory	87.1	Other current	17.1
Current assets	158.7	Current liabilities	60.1
Net fixed	152.5	Bonds	95.5
Total assets	$311.2	Equity	155.6
		Total liabilities and equity	$311.2

EXHIBIT 2
Fultex's History of Sales, P–E, and Operating Margin*

Year	Sales (millions)	P–E Ratio	Operating Margin (%)
1978	$90.4	5.3	13.4
1979	106.9	2.4	12.3
1980	107.1	3.1	12.5
1981	124.7	5.5	12.2
1982	146.4	3.7	12.9
1983	176.5	5.6	13.3
1984	190.5	4.8	13.7
1985	238.4	4.6	14.1
1986	270.4	6.7	14.2
1987	275.3	8.9	13.2
1988	318.7	11.8	15.0
1989	353.0	9.7	14.8
1990	385.4	11.2	14.1

(continued)

EXHIBIT 2
(Continued)

Year	Sales (millions)	P–E Ratio	Operating margin (%)
1991	438.1	14.0	15.3
1992	459.1	14.2	15.1
1993	475.3	14.0	14.7
1994	505.8	13.5	15.0
1995 (present)	560.1	11.4	14.6

*Operating margin equals (EBIT + Dep.)/Sales.

EXHIBIT 3
Selected Financial Ratios, 1995 (Present Year)

	Fultex	Industry Average
Current	2.6	3.1
Quick	1.2	1.5
Debt	.50	.36
D/E[a]	0.61	0.24
Times interest earned	5.9	10.6
FCC[b]	4.7	7.3

[a]D/E is ratio of long-term debt to equity.

[b]FCC = fixed charge coverage = (EBIT + Lease)/(Interest + Lease)

	Normalized Income Statement	
	Fultex	Industry Average
Sales	100	100
Cost of goods sold	74	76
Gross margin	26	24
Operating expenses	11.4	13.5
Depreciation	3.4	2.5
EBIT	11.2	8.0
Interest	1.9	0.76
Earnings before taxes	9.3	7.24
Taxes (40%)	3.72	2.9
Net income	5.58	4.35

EXHIBIT 4
Fultex's Pro Forma 1996 and 1997 Income Statements ($ Millions)

	1996	1997
Sales	$640	$768
Cost of goods sold	473.6	568.3
Gross margin	166.4	199.7
Operating expenses	73.0	87.6
Depreciation	27.0	32
EBIT	66.4	80.1
Interest	9.9	9.2
Earnings before taxes	56.5	70.9
Taxes (40%)	22.6	28.4
Net income	$33.9	$42.5

NOTE: This forcast assumes that Fultex maintains its 1995 operating margin of 14.6 percent. Operating margin equals (EBIT + Dep)/Sales. The impact of the new financing is not considered.

EXHIBIT 5
Fultex's Best Guess (Most Likely) Sales and Cash Flow Forecast: 1996-1999 ($ Millions)

	$t = 0$ 1995	$t = 1$ 1996	$t = 2$ 1997	$t = 3$ 1998	$t = 4$ 1999
Sales	$560.1	$640	$768	$845	$890
Net income		33.9	42.5	48.2	51.0
Depreciation		27.0	32.0	34.4	36.9
Cash flow from operations		60.9	74.5	82.6	87.9
– Dividends		1.1	1.1	1.1	1.1
– Debt due		9	9	9	9
– Change in working capital		17.6	28.2	16.9	9.9
– Capital spending		70	60	30	30
Cash flow		($36.8)	($23.8)	$25.6	$37.9

NOTE: These estimates assume that the change in net working capital equals 22 percent of the change in sales. The figures do not, however, consider the impact of the new financing of $81 million. At the present time (1995) the firm has roughly $5 million of excess liquidity.

EXHIBIT 6
Worksheet for a Worst-Case Cash Flow Forecast: 1996-1999 ($ Millions)

	t = 0 1995	t = 1 1996	t = 2 1997	t = 3 1998	t = 4 1999
Sales	$560.1				
Operating profit					
Depreciation		27	31.6	34.0	36.5
EBIT					
Interest		9.9	9.2	8.6	8.0
EBT					
Taxes (40%)		___	___	___	___
Net income					
Depreciation		27	31.6	34.0	36.5
Cash flow from operations					
– Dividends		1.1	1.1	1.1	1.1
– Debt due		9	9	9	9
– Change in working capital					
– Capital spending		70	55	28	28
Cash flow[a]					

NOTE: Let the 1996 change in working capital equal 5 + .22 times the change in sales from 1995. For 1997 to 1999 let this change equal .22 times the yearly change in sales.

[a] At present (1995) the firm has approximately $5 million of excess liquidity. This forecast does not consider the impact of the new financing of $81 million.

EXHIBIT 7
Yearly Cash Outlays (Before Taxes) of Each Financing Option[a]: 1996-1997 ($ Millions)

	Bond Option		Stock Option		Combination	
Year	Int.	Div.	Int.	Div.	Int.	Div.
1996						
1997						

[a] Int. is the additional interest and Div. the extra dividends. There are no additional sinking fund payments during 1996 to 1997 with any of the financing options.

EXHIBIT 8
U.S. Recessions Since 1945

Recession Peak to Trough	Recession (Months)	Preceding Expansion (Monthly)
Feb. 1945–Oct. 1945	8	80
Nov. 1948–Oct. 1949	11	37
July 1953–May 1954	10	45
Aug. 1957–Apr. 1958	8	39
Apr. 1960–Feb. 1961	10	24
Dec. 1969–Nov. 1970	11	106
Nov. 1973–Mar. 1975	16	36
Jan. 1980–July 1980	6	58
July 1981–Dec. 1982	18	12
July 1990–Mar. 1991	7	91

Source: National Bureau of Economic Research.

NOTE: The National Bureau of Economic Research (NBER) identifies the beginning of a recession (when the economy peaks) and its end (when the economy hits its trough and begins to recover). The last U.S. recession (as of 1995) ended March 1991.

SHUCKERS
MILLER AND
MODIGLIANI

The results of the market test had surprised Rebecca Griffin, the general manager of the A.W. Shuckers Company. But the results of the meeting with the Taylor family, owners of over half of the firm's stock, surprised her even more.

EXTERNAL FINANCING

Shuckers is a maker of preserves, jams, and peanut butter, and also produces fruit juices, ice cream toppings, and low-sugar jellies. The firm is particularly well known in the Northeast though it has had some modest success in the potentially lucrative Midwest market. And about twelve months ago, management began to seriously consider entering the Midwest market "in a big way." Market research showed that Shuckers is definitely a recognizable name in that area, a result that surprised a number of Shuckers's executives, including Griffin. Encouraged by these results, management has decided to expand into selected areas of the Midwest, a decision that will require external financing.

THE MEETING

Griffin felt that the time was appropriate to meet with the Taylor family in part to discuss the expansion and in part to address the family's debt aversion. The company was founded 50 years ago by Roy Taylor, who had never borrowed a dime and had always insisted that Shuckers would "never a lender nor borrower be." For years Griffin has tried unsuccessfully to convince the family to use some debt financing, and at this meeting she decides to try once more.

At the meeting she explained that the company's expansion necessitated raising $22,000,000 of external funds. One option for raising this money, according to the firm's investment banker, is to sell new common stock at the current price of $13.50. Griffin emphasized, though, that if new shares were issued there was a real danger the Taylor family would own less than 50 percent of the company. Her suggestion was to raise any new funds by borrowing, which she felt very confident Shuckers could do at the choice rate of 8 percent. She underscored the fact that lenders would be "easy to find" given the company's strong financial position and the lack of any long-term debt in its capital structure. "Keep in mind," she told the group, "that this 8 percent rate is nearly one percent below the current home mortgage rate, and you know how safe a home mortgage loan is. The point is that if we can borrow at such a low rate, Shuckers *must* be a very safe company indeed!"

During her presentation none of the family seemed to show any interest. At the end of the talk she asked for any questions or comments. For half a minute, which seemed to her like half a day, no one said a word. Suddenly, Roy Taylor, Jr., stood up and declared, "I think the use of debt is the way to go. As a matter of fact, I think we should endorse even more borrowing in the future." Griffin was amazed not only because this was the first time a Taylor family member had proposed the use of debt, but also because of the force with which it was proposed. At this point a lengthy discussion followed on the use of debt financing, and the Taylor family divided into three camps: one group favored no debt, a second forcefully argued for its use, while the third worried about the impact on dividends.

Some felt Shuckers should maintain the family tradition, though they perceived that the growth of Shuckers necessitated external financing. This group, led by Barbara Taylor, said new shares would not reduce the Taylors' control if family members bought them (although none of them had the money) or if nonvoting shares were issued. Another faction, led by Roy Jr., stated that he did not want to "defile Dad's memory" but felt the company's policy was set in a depression mentality and during a period of little inflation when expansion could be financed internally. Roy also questioned the validity of the control issue. He pointed out that the family's ownership and interest in the company had been declining for many years; he also stated that most of the stock not controlled by the family was owned by corporate pension funds. And, it was likely that effective control of the company would remain with the family in any event since it was improbable that the managers of these funds would become "corporate busybodies." Further discussion indicated that only Barbara Taylor had any real interest in the company's operation and few cared about the degree of control the Taylor family would have. This surprised Griffin, who had thought the issue of family ownership would be an extremely important one.

IMPACT ON FIRM'S VALUE

The question of valuation was also addressed. Roy Taylor III, an economics graduate student, pointed out that a "levered firm is worth more than an unlevered firm." Pressed on what he meant, he said, "If we borrow, the price of Shuckers stock should rise." Shuckers has been publicly traded for the last three years, and his statement stirred the interest of those who admitted they were considering selling their shares. Griffin, for her part, said executive talent would be easier to obtain since stock options were likely to become more valuable through the "judicious use of debt." Barbara said she had trouble understanding why using debt would increase the stock's price. "People borrow money to buy stocks all the time, right? If investors are unhappy in some mysterious sense with our all-equity policy, why can't they simply create their own debt policies? I mean, I really don't see what difference it makes whether Shuckers borrows or an investor borrows and uses this money to buy our stock. I must admit, however, that no one here would be able to borrow money at 8 percent on their own."

A third faction was puzzled by all the debt controversy. These individuals didn't like breaking with tradition but did like the idea that the value of their stock might rise. Most of this group were retired, in low tax brackets, and depended on Shuckers' dividends for income. They were very concerned that any borrowing would jeopardize the current dividend of $1 per share in the event sales decreased. Some even questioned the ability of Shuckers to repay the debt, let alone pay dividends. One elderly gentleman did emphasize, however, that Roy Sr. never literally followed the maxim he was so fond of: "Never a lender. . ." He pointed out that Shuckers always extended credit to its customers and received credit from its suppliers, and that "old Roy never minded taking out a short-term note if he had to."

The discussion was getting extremely unwieldy. It was agreed, however, that Griffin should prepare a report on the whole issue for another meeting next month. She was instructed to include "everything relevant" but to make sure the following questions were addressed. Would debt increase the value of the firm? If so, by how much? Is there some optimal amount of debt the firm should shoot for? How risky would the use of debt make the firm?

REFLECTIONS

Back at her office Griffin brewed some coffee and pondered the issues raised. She feels confident, though not certain, that all the new money should be borrowed. But is it wise to use even more debt and retire stock? She never expected that possibility would even be brought up let alone seriously discussed.

All debt would be raised as debentures that would mature in 12 to 15 years. There would be no sinking fund, which means that Shuckers would not have to pay any of the principal until the bonds mature. The interest rate on the debt would be 8 percent. Fortunately, the firm's business risk is low, and in the last 30 years sales and EBIT have never declined, even in the recessions of 1974, 1981 to 1982, and 1990. Griffin is very much aware that the firm can't take on so much debt that its commercial strategy is neglected. A key point, therefore, is the possible financial needs of Shuckers in coming years, especially in bad times.

FORECASTING CONSIDERATIONS

Though no new expansion projects are planned, Griffin would like to budget $750,000 each year for capital spending, including replacement projects. And receivables can be a problem for Shuckers. At times the average collection period has increased 10 days more than expected. The composition of this increase is relevant to the firm's financial situation. Roughly seven days of the rise in the ACP is relatively transitory and lasts anywhere from one to three months. The remaining portion is relatively permanent and lasts between 12 and 24 months. The transitional component can be easily financed from the firm's cash account and by a modest increase in accounts payable. The three-day "permanent" component has typically been financed from operating profit. Griffin recognizes that this may not be possible should Shucker decide to borrow.

There is talk that the industry's production techniques may change somewhat in the future. The impact is hard to gauge, though it is probably at least three to five years away, assuming it even occurs. Griffin had no good idea how much money this would require, though she "guesstimated" a total of $3 million with $8 million the upper limit.

She then decided that a worst-case, five-year cash flow forecast should be based on the following:

1. Sales each year will be $192,000(000) and EBIT $19,808(000), amounts found in Exhibit 2.
2. The firm's present working capital situation is adequate; that is, receivables, inventory, accounts payable, and accruals are normal.
3. If Shuckers borrows, then its cash position by the end of year 1 should be sufficient to finance a five-day "permanent" increase in the ACP. (This represents an amount over and above any cash the company has presently.)
4. Dividends are $1 per share.
5. Yearly depreciation will be $900(000).
6. Shuckers will need the ability to raise $4 million in years 3 and 5 (a total of $8 million) for new capital equipment if industry production techniques change.
7. Equipment replacement will require $1,100(000) a year.

QUESTIONS

1. Exhibits 1 and 2 present the firm's balance sheet and income statement under different assumptions about the firm's borrowing.

   (a) Calculate the times interest earned and debt ratios under each capital structure.

(b) Assuming CGS is the only variable cost, calculate the break-even sales volumes

$$S^* = \frac{FC}{1 - VC/S}$$

(c) What do your answers suggest about the ability of Shuckers to meet its debt obligation?

2. (a) Estimate the value of Shuckers under each alternative using $V_L = V_U + (t \times D)$. (Ignore current liabilities in these calculations since they do not include any interest-bearing debt, and the current price of a share of Shuckers stock is $13.50.)

(b) Estimate the market price of a share of Shuckers under each capital structure.

(c) Calculate the MV/BV and the P-E ratios.

3. (a) Use the format of Exhibit 4 to develop a worst-case cash flow forecast using Griffin's assumptions and assuming capital structure C is selected. What implications, if any, does this forecast have for the capital structure choice?

(b) Do her assumptions seem reasonable? Justify your choice.

4. Miller and Modigliani's value equation implies the firm's value will change by t × ΔD. This is usually considered an inflated estimate of the increase. However, based on the information provided in the case and your previous calculations, the equation may well apply for Shuckers. Why?

5. What do you think is the capital structure that maximizes the value of Shuckers? Justify your answer.

6. Exhibit 1 assumes the firm can sell new stock at a (gross) price of $13.50 per share. If Shuckers votes to change its capital structure to, say, 50 percent debt and decides to repurchase some of its stock, is the price likely to remain at $13.50?

7. What recommendation regarding Shuckers's capital structure would you advise Rebecca Griffin to make? Defend your advice.

EXHIBIT 1
Balance Sheet Projections for Shuckers ($000s)*

Assets	A	B	C
Current assets	51,360	51,360	51,360
Net fixed	38,400	38,400	38,400
Total assets	89,760	89,760	89,760

(continued)

EXHIBIT 1
(Continued)

Liabilities and Equity	A	B	C
Current liabilities	16,960	16, 960	16,960
Bonds	0	22,000	27,920
Equity	72,800	50,800	44,880
Total liabilities and equity	89,760	89,760	89,760

NOTE: A = 5,003 shares, B = 3,200 shares, C = 2,762 shares.

*A = Balance sheet with no borrowing.

B = Balance sheet with only the new funds ($22,000) raised by borrowing.

C = Balance sheet if company achieves a 50 percent debt ratio, which is the industry average. (All figures are book value.)

EXHIBIT 2
Income Statement Projections for Shuckers ($000s)

	A	B	C
Net sales	192,000	192,000	192,000
Cost of goods sold	153,600	153,600	153,600
Operating costs	18,592	18,592	18,592
EBIT	19,808	19,808	19,808
Interest	0	1,760	2,234
Earnings before taxes	19,808	18,048	17,574
Taxes (50%)	9,904	9,024	8,787
Net income	9,904	9,024	8,787
Earnings per share	1.98	2.82	3.18

EXHIBIT 3
Selected Averages of Comparable Firms

Times interest earned	6.0
Debt ratio (%)	50
Breakeven sales volume (% of sales)	59.5
Market to book ratio (MV/BV)	1.2
Net income to net worth (%)	20
Price-to-earnings ratio (P–E)	6.0

EXHIBIT 4
Worksheet for a Worst-Case Cash Flow Forecast

	Year				
	$t + 1$	$t + 2$	$t + 3$	$t + 4$	$t + 5$
EBIT	_____	_____	_____	_____	_____
Interest	_____	_____	_____	_____	_____
EBT	_____	_____	_____	_____	_____
Taxes (50%)	_____	_____	_____	_____	_____
Net income	_____	_____	_____	_____	_____
+ Depreciation	_____	_____	_____	_____	_____
Cash flow Operations	_____	_____	_____	_____	_____
− Cash for ACP	_____	_____	_____	_____	_____
− Capital spending	_____	_____	_____	_____	_____
− Dividends	_____	_____	_____	_____	_____
Cash flow	_____	_____	_____	_____	_____
Cumulative cash flow	_____	_____	_____	_____	_____

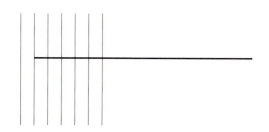

PART VII

VALUATION

L.A. CAFE VALUATION

Pat Thompson was stunned by the estimate of his partner, Craig Moore. "How can a business," Thompson asked Moore, "with sales of less than $800 thousand be worth nearly $5 million?" Moore calmly replied that he had "merely used a formula recommended by experts" to obtain the estimate.

For nearly twelve years Moore and Thompson have been owners of the L.A. Cafe. The restaurant has always been successful, which is not surprising given Moore's extraordinary culinary talents, Thompson's exceptional administrative expertise, and their prior experience as maitre d's at two leading area restaurants. Until six months ago, their relationship was extremely harmonious; the men were equal partners in both time and money. Recently, however, Moore has been spending less time at the restaurant and generally seems disinterested in the whole business. Questioned by Thompson, Moore admitted that he has tired of the restaurant and would like to sell his interest, move to New York and work as a maitre d'.

Thompson likes the idea of being L.A.'s sole owner and asked Moore what he thought L.A. was worth. Moore's response of $4.8 million left Thompson shocked, and he became extremely aggravated when Moore refused to divulge the mysterious formula he used to make the estimate "until the time was right." Further discussion lead nowhere until Thompson persuaded Moore to meet with Nathan Rogers, their accountant and financial advisor for the last five years. Both trusted Rogers and felt he had a good understanding of the restaurant business.

THE MEETING WITH ROGERS

At their meeting Moore revealed the formula that he had used. He had gone to the library and consulted a leading financial textbook where he found the following equation.

$$P_0 = \frac{D_1}{i - g}$$

D_1 was the company's earnings before interest and taxes (EBIT) from the current year ($96,000); g was the yearly growth in EBIT over the past seven years, 10 percent; and i was the rate at which he thought money would be borrowed, 12 percent. Thompson was quick to point out that the restaurant business is highly competitive and risky; therefore it is unlikely past growth rates can be maintained. As evidence he cited the 4 percent per year growth of the last two years, which is far below the yearly increases during the previous five years.

Thompson also asked Moore if he considered the $40,000 after-tax cost of remodeling, or that most area restaurants last about 15 to 20 years before going out of business and that he would have to assume the outstanding debt of the restaurant. Moore admitted he wasn't sure "the formula has considered all this," and then dryly mentioned that he might insist on dividing the restaurant's liquid assets. Rogers also pointed out that both of them have been taking minimum salaries out of the corporation. That is, they have been taking about $25,000 each in salaries (a total of $50,000). But experienced restaurant managerial help would be 50 percent more than this. Rogers then attempted to calm an obviously emotional Thompson and soften Moore's firm position by pointing out as tactfully as possible that he is confident the restaurant is worth "somewhat less" than what Moore estimates. "One rule of thumb," Rogers continued, "that is sometimes used by business brokers in pricing restaurants is fair market value for assets plus 20 percent for a goodwill factor, less the amount of any interest-bearing debt." He quickly pointed out, however, that any rule of thumb is at best only an approximation. It can't be expected to apply to a wide range of situations, each involving different conditions and circumstances. "In other words," he summed up, "the restaurant could be worth more or less than this." Finally, he emphasized that there is no magic number of value that "we are searching for. It is best to think of a range of values; that is, the business is worth between A and B . . . I see my job as trying to narrow that range as much as possible." After further discussion, Moore and Thompson agreed that more analysis is called for and asked Rogers for a detailed report.

POSTMORTEM

After they left, Rogers talked about the case with his partner, Edwin Daugherty, for nearly an hour. Daugherty said it was a good idea for Rogers to have mentioned that there is no magic number for the value of the business. "This gets them in the right frame of mind for the inevitable bargaining later on. I mean, all we can really do is narrow the discussion to a range of reasonable values. Negotiation and personality are likely to determine the final price." Rogers agreed and decided to make estimates under three different scenarios. (See Exhibit 2.)

There were a number of points that Daugherty and Rogers agreed were common to all three scenarios.

1. An estimate should discount the future yearly after-tax cash flow a buyer can expect to receive.

2. The restaurant's present working capital and equipment situation is adequate.

3. The amount of yearly depreciation will be about equal to the yearly principal repayment on the debt.

4. No cash will be necessary to support any future increases in working capital. This occurs because changes in receivables and inventory will be offset by the changes in accounts payable and other current liabilities.

5. Any growth in earnings before taxes (EBT) will be used to purchase or maintain equipment.

NOTE: Assumptions 3, 4, and 5 imply that the after-tax cash flow a buyer will receive each year equals the net income or earnings after taxes (EAT) estimate of each scenario.

6. The valuation estimate should consider a competitive wage and the renovation cost.

7. The appropriate after-tax discount rate is 20 percent.

8. The relevant tax rate is 35 percent.

Exhibit 2 presents the assumptions that are specific to each scenario.

QUESTIONS

1. Give as many reasons as you can why Moore's initial estimate of the value of the restaurant was inappropriate.

2. Calculate the current liquidation value of the business assuming the assets can be sold at 75 percent of book and all debt is paid off at 100 percent of book.

3. Daugherty and Rogers believe that their valuation estimate should reflect competitive managerial wages. Do you agree that this adjustment to an EBT (earnings before taxes) estimate should be made? Why or why not?

4. Estimate the value of the restaurant in each of the three scenarios.

5. Using the business brokers' rule of thumb, estimate the value of the restaurant.

6. If Moore insists on dividing up the cash and marketable securities, what would happen to your estimates in question 4? (Assume the restaurant currently has the optimal amount of these assets.)

7. How important are the liquidation value estimates in Exhibit 2 to the analysis? Explain.

8. Suppose Moore insists the value of the business is equal to the estimate obtained under "optimistic" assumptions. Should Thompson buy the restaurant? Suppose he feels an identical restaurant could be established for (equity of) $150,000. How would this affect your answer?

9. Suppose Rogers obtains information on three other restaurants that were sold in the last year, and their market to book (MV/BV) ratios were 1, 0.85, and 0.75. How would this information affect the negotiations?

SOFTWARE QUESTION

10. Rogers has decided that the valuation estimates need to be redone in view of new information gathered by his partner, Daugherty.

First, it now seems that the $40,000 after-tax remodeling estimate is a "lower limit" and could run as high as $65,000. Second, the EBT and liquidation value estimates in Exhibit 2 need to be raised since it appears that the restaurant can be run a bit more efficiently than Rogers initially assumed. Third, Daugherty has convinced Rogers that the appropriate discount rate "could be as low as 15 percent."

After some thought, Daugherty and Rogers have modified the scenarios in Exhibit 2 as follows.

	Scenario		
	Pessimistic	*Moderate*	*Optimistic*
EBT/year	$60,000	$65,000	$70,000
Life of business	7 years	10 years	15 years
Terminal value	$40,000	$60,000	$130,000
Discount rate	.21	.18	.15
Remodeling costs	$65,000	$50,000	$40,000

Further, Daugherty's research uncovered information on two other restaurants that sold in the last year (this is in addition to the three mentioned in question 9). The market to book (MV/BV) ratios were 1.1 and 1.0, respectively.

Finally, Rogers wants to estimate the restaurant's current liquidation value "more precisely." He thinks that it is reasonable to assume that receivables can be converted into cash at 80 percent of book value, inventory at 70 percent and buildings/equipment at 60 percent. These figures are all net of any liquidation expenses. He will also assume that all debt is paid off at 100 percent of book value.

Redo your answers to questions 2, 4, 5, 8, and 9 in light of this new information.

EXHIBIT 1
Current Year Balance Sheet and Income Statement

1. Balance Sheet

Assets		Liabilities and Equity	
Cash	$ 46,500	Notes payable	$ 22,500
Accounts receivable	28,500	Accounts payable	34,500
Inventory	24,000	Other current	25,500
Building &		Bonds	88,500
equipment	186,000	Equity	114,000
		Total liabilities and	
Total assets	$285,000	equity	285,000

2. Income Statement

Sales	$765,000
Cost of goods sold	337,500
Operating expenses	331,500
EBIT	96,000
Interest	13,500
Earnings before taxes	$ 82,500

EXHIBIT 2
Assumptions Specific to Each Scenario

	Pessimistic	Moderate	Optimistic
EBT	$75,000/yr	$82,500/yr	$90,000/yr
Life of Business	7 yrs	10 yrs	15 yrs
Liquidation value at end of period (after-tax)	$40,000	$70,000	$140,000

OT SNACK COMPANY VALUATION

James Fussell had a lifelong dream of owning and running his own business. After losing his job as controller of a medium-sized corporation for the second time in three years, he began giving it even more thought. In both cases the firm Fussell was working for had been purchased by another firm and most of the acquired firm's top managers had been let go. Owning his own firm was one way to avoid being subjected to the decisions of others that could change his life so quickly. With this goal firmly in mind, Fussell simultaneously started looking for a job to pay his present bills and for a company to own that would give him the sense of control and satisfaction he had dreamed about.

James Fussell

James Fussell was born and raised in Florida. He graduated with a degree in management from the University of South Florida in 1971. After college he accepted a job with the accounting firm D. E. Gatewood, certified public accountant. To improve his accounting skills he completed 36 additional hours of accounting courses. After taking these courses, Fussell took and passed the certified public accountant (CPA) exam. "I felt an accounting background was needed for running my own business in the future, and that by working with a certified public accounting firm I would strengthen that skill and learn about many different types of firms." After five years, Fussell took a job with Blue Bell, Inc. In Greensboro, North Carolina. Blue Bell, Inc. was a publicly owned corporation in the very competitive textile business, and although profitable, its return on investment was not as high as some stockholders of the company desired. The decision was made to take the company private, and a group of Blue Bell executives made an offer that was accepted by a majority of the stockholders. To reduce expenses and help pay off the debt incurred in purchasing Blue Bell, the new owners drastically reduced the scope of operations and eliminated many middle- and upper-level management positions. Fussell was among those who were forced out.

Fussell was fortunate and quickly found a job with Thomasville Furniture Company. He started in March, but by October, that company had been purchased by Weyerhauser, Inc., a much larger multidivision corporation, and Fussell was once again looking for a job. This time he was determined to locate a job that would be temporary until he could find a firm to own and run. With his accounting skills and past background, he quickly found a position with Old Salem, a historical preservation foundation, as controller. At the same time he contacted several business brokers about helping him locate a firm for sale. He also enlisted the help of literally dozens of friends and acquaintances. Fussell considered several businesses but rejected them as not the type he wanted. In October 1993, his broker asked him to look at OT Snack Company, which he described as a bakery. Fussell thought it was a bakery in a shopping center and was not enthusiastic, but after visiting the business he became very excited.

OT SNACK COMPANY

OT Snack Company was formed by Alton Bodenheimer and Grady Griffin, Jr., in 1949. The fried pie has been the firm's only basic product; although at one time it produced a honeybun, production of that item was discontinued in 1977. The company slowly built up its business by selling to vending machine companies and through distributors who sold the pies as a desert to the lunch counter trade. The owners concentrated on quality and service and expanded sales throughout the Carolinas, Virginia, Tennessee, and Georgia. By the end of 1993, OT Snack employed 52 people and produced between 400,000 and 500,000 dozen pies a year. These pies were produced with six different fillings—apple, cherry, peach, raisin, chocolate, and lemon.

Production

A fried pie is as simple a bakery product as can be imagined. A fruit or pie filling is wrapped in pie dough, and it is deep-fried in fat. The actual production at OT was in four basic steps. First, the pie filling was cooked and then cooled. The fruit fillings were made from dried fruit, water, and sugar plus ingredients to retard spoilage. The mixture was stirred and cooked for about an hour and then cooled for 48 hours.

In the second step, the dough was prepared and cut into sections. These sections contained enough dough to make six dozen pies. Women, who worked on a piece rate, rolled out the individual pie shells with a metal rolling pin, placed the filling in the shell, and formed the shell around the filling. This finished product was then placed on a screen to be deep-fried in fat.

Next the pies were deep-fried in fat for three minutes, put on cooling racks, and moved into a holding room. In the final step, the pie was wrapped in a glassine wrapper and placed into a tray for shipping. There was virtually no excess inventory kept at the plant as all production was made to fill current orders.

The trays were stacked according to customer orders and were usually picked up the same day they were produced.

Personnel

OT employed 46 people in production and the average pay was about $5.50 per hour. Turnover was very low, and 31 of the employees had been given gifts of stock in the firm. This stock amounted to 10 percent of all the outstanding shares. OT also had a very good benefit program. The production operation was managed by John Davis, who had worked for OT since mid-1964. John had worked in all phases of plant operations and knew the production operation and the cycle of the business as well as anyone. Although turnover was very low, production efficiency was also low. Sales had been declining since 1987 (see Exhibit 1), and on days when orders were low, employees not on piecework were in the habit of staying at work and on the payroll, although not doing any work.

Part of this casual attitude was due to the fact that the city of Winston-Salem had not issued any building permits since 1984 in the South Marshall Street Redevelopment area where OT was located. The city planned on redeveloping the area with upscale condominiums. OT's current sole owner, Alton Bodenheimer, was too near retirement to plan for a move to a new location. With the future of the present location in limbo, he had allowed the business to decline. All of the production equipment was old and outdated, for there certainly was no incentive to replace equipment if the plant was going to be relocated in the near future. The equipment, however, had no salvage value and was in dire need of immediate replacement.

In addition, no new customers had been added in several years and the business served a static customer base. Evidence of the lack of current marketing was that none of OT's products were sold in local grocery stores. An indication of Bodenheimer's attitude was shown in early 1992 when he asked if he was looking forward to retirement. His reply was: "Hell, I've been retired for 10 years!" One employee said that a typical day for Bodenheimer was to come into the plant in the morning and see what orders they had; go to a local coffee shop for about an hour and a half; come back to the plant until lunchtime; and then, shortly after lunch, go play golf. The redevelopment project and the thought of having to move had simply taken away his desire to plan for the future of the company.

Financial Information

In late 1993 OT Snack Company was a profitable firm producing a good product with a loyal customer base. Production was about 400 dozen pies per hour. Rather than move the business, the owner, Alton Bodenheimer, had decided to sell the company. What James Fussell saw when a business broker showed him the financial statements (see Exhibit 2) and when he subsequently toured the plant was a product with tremendous potential. The owner was asking $1.2 million for a business that had $450,000 in cash and marketable securities and almost no liabilities. The property, which Fussell had appraised by an independent appraiser at $297,000, would be purchased by the city of Winston-Salem in early 1994 at the appraised priced.

Although the plant's capacity was 12,000 dozen pies per week, its current weekly production was about 9,000 dozen pies, which were sold at $2.70 a dozen. (The pies were sold in vending machines for 45 to 50 cents each.) Fussell believed that the market for these pies could easily be doubled without having to hire another salesperson. With that in mind, and knowing that the plant had to be moved, Fussell began looking for a new home for OT Snack and for ways to both produce and sell more pies.

Automated Equipment

Through a friend Fussell learned about an automated equipment line that would produce fried pies. He flew to Duluth, Minnesota, to see the equipment in operation. The production line was produced by the Moline Corporation and cost $497,000 to purchase and install. The equipment produced pies on a continuous conveyor. At one end, the dough was produced and extruded onto a sheet and rolled to the appropriate thickness, trimmed, and cut into strips. The filling was deposited into the stirps, which were folded, and the pie was cut out, with the scrap dough recycled back to the beginning. The pie was then fed into the fryer, which was maintained at a constant temperature, and the pies were cooked for exactly three minutes. The pies were then moved onto a cooling conveyor.

This equipment would reduce the number of people required for production by almost 65 percent. In fact, only 17 people would be needed to operate the entire process, and the equipment was capable of producing 24,000 dozen pies per week (double the present capacity). For planning purposes, Fussell assumed that the economic life of the equipment and its depreciable life would be the same.

A building suitable for production was located on the north side of Winston-Salem in Northridge Business Park. The annual lease on this building was $75,000. At about the same time, Fussell found that he could lease the automated equipment for $8,000 per month from the leasing department of a local bank, Central Carolina Bank, if OT would put down a deposit of $200,000.

Marketing

Before finally deciding on whether to purchase OT Snack Company, Fussell did a quick marketing survey. The firm had about 15 current customers who ordered once or twice a week. In addition, he found that several potential customers had contacted OT in the recent past. These customers included Vendors Supply of North Carolina, Waldensian Bakeries, and Fox Bakeries, all located in North Carolina; Palmetto Bakeries in South Carolina; and Vending Services of America, located in Georgia. Several of these firms were primarily bread and bakery goods distributors who were looking for additional products to sell to their customers—supermarkets, convenience stores, service stations, etc.

DECISION TIME

Fussell went over all the facts to make sure that he had thoroughly investigated the firm and its potential. He then made two income projections for 1994 sales based on the assumption that OT would operate in its new location in 1994. The salaries, shown in Exhibit 3, were based on what Fussell expected to pay the two managers who were presently on salary; the management fee was what he hoped to earn. The first income projection was based on sales of $1.2 million and assumed that the pie operation would operate with the automated production line. The second projection assumed a sales level of about $2.7 million. (See Exhibit 4.)

James Fussell thinks he has done a very exhaustive study of OT Snack and the potential of the fried pies market in the region presently served by OT. Although sales have declined in the last few years, Fussell believes that the company still produces a quality product and gives excellent service to its current group of customers. The potential for the firm seems outstanding. After checking with his banker, Fussell knows he can purchase the business based on a loan on the assets of the firm, cash from his savings and investments, and a mortgage on his home and all his personal assets.

Fussell faces two very important decisions. Should he take the plunge and buy this firm? Given an affirmative answer to the first decision, he must then determine what price he would be willing to pay for OT Snack Company. He actually would be purchasing 90 percent of the stock, since the employees own 10 percent). The second decision is based on the first; that is, if he buys OT Snack Company, should he automate the production process?

QUESTIONS

1. Assuming Fussell wishes to buy the firm, what should he pay for it?

2. How should Fussell pay for the firm?

3. If Fussell buys the firm, should he automate? (Calculate both the net present value and the internal rate of return.)

4. What is the dollar break-even point before and after automation?

5. Assuming an average rate of inflation of 7 percent between 1987 and 1993, what was the actual sales decline in constant dollars?

6. Given your answers above, would you advise Fussell to buy OT Snack Company? Why or why not?

EXHIBIT 1
OT Snack Company Sales: 1984–1993

1984	$801,828
1985	1,043,478
1986	1,387,024
1987	1,553,755
1988	1,506,317
1989	1,488,852
1990	1,246,352
1991	1,039,402
1992	1,116,108
1993	1,098,236

EXHIBIT 2

Form **1120**	**U.S. Corporation Income Tax Return**	OMB No. 1545 0123
Department of the Treasury Internal Revenue Service	For calendar year 1993 or tax year beginning .... , 1993, ending .... , 19 ... ▶ Instructions are separate. See page 1 for Paperwork Reduction Act Notice.	19**93**

A Check if a:	Use IRS label. Otherwise, please print or type.	Name	B Employer Identification number
1 Consolidated return (attach Form 851) ☐		OT Snack Company Inc	56 0712408
2 Personal holding co. (attach Sch. PH) ☐		Number, street, and room or suite no. (If a P.O. box, see page 7 of instructions.)	C Date incorporated
3 Personal service corp. (as defined in Temporary Regs. sec. 1.441 4T— see instructions) ☐		434 Marshall St.	1-1-60
		City or town, state, and ZIP code	D Total assets (see Specific Instructions)
		Winston-Salem, NC 27101	$ 678049 42

E Check applicable boxes: (1) ☐ Initial return (2) ☐ Final return (3) ☐ Change of address

Income

1a	Gross receipts or sales |1098 236 01| b Less returns and allowances	0| c Bal ▶	1c	1098236 01
2	Cost of goods sold (Schedule A, line 8)		2	722414 28
3	Gross profit. Subtract line 2 from line 1c		3	375821 73
4	Dividends (Schedule C, line 19)		4	10663 21
5	Interest		5	17981 50
6	Gross rents		6	
7	Gross royalties		7	
8	Capital gain net income (attach Schedule D (Form 1120))		8	
9	Net gain or (loss) from Form 4797, Part II, line 20 (attach Form 4797)		9	3220 35
10	Other income (see instructions—attach schedule)		10	
11	**Total income.** Add lines 3 through 10 ▶		11	407186 76

Deductions (See instructions for limitations on deductions.)

12	Compensation of officers (Schedule E, line 4)		12	100 000
13a	Salaries and wages	33,519 47	b Less employment credits	0| c Bal ▶	13c	33519 47
14	Repairs and maintenance		14	5503 77
15	Bad debts		15	222 32
16	Rents		16	
17	Taxes and licenses		17	41257 49
18	Interest		18	344 05
19	Charitable contributions (see instructions for 10% limitation)		19	715 00
20	Depreciation (attach Form 4562)	20	13056 89		
21	Less depreciation claimed on Schedule A and elsewhere on return	21a		21b	13056 89
22	Depletion		22	
23	Advertising		23	3285 19
24	Pension, profit-sharing, etc., plans		24	155715 02
25	Employee benefit programs		25	28290 85
26	Other deductions (attach schedule)		26	54724 78
27	**Total deductions.** Add lines 12 through 26 ▶		27	436634 83
28	Taxable income before net operating loss deduction and special deductions. Subtract line 27 from line 11		28	10551 96
29	Less: a Net operating loss deduction (see instructions)	29a			
	b Special deductions (Schedule C, line 20)	29b	9063 72	29c	9063 72
30	**Taxable income.** Subtract line 29c from line 28		30	61488 23
31	**Total tax** (Schedule J, line 10)		31	11490 28

Tax and Payments

32	Payments: a 1992 overpayment credited to 1993	32a			
b	1993 estimated tax payments	32b	5800 00		
c	Less 1993 refund applied for on Form 4466	32c ( )	d Bal ▶	32d	5800 00	
e	Tax deposited with Form 7004	32e			
f	Credit from regulated investment companies (attach Form 2439)	32f			
g	Credit for Federal tax on fuels (attach Form 4136). See instructions	32g		32h	5800 00
33	Estimated tax penalty (see instructions). Check if Form 2220 is attached ▶ ☐		33	
34	**Tax due.** If line 32h is smaller than the total of lines 31 and 33, enter amount owed		34	5690 28
35	**Overpayment.** If line 32h is larger than the total of lines 31 and 33, enter amount overpaid		35	
36	Enter amount of line 35 you want: Credited to 1994 estimated tax ▶ Refunded ▶		36	

Please Sign Here

Under penalties of perjury, I declare that I have examined this return, including accompanying schedules and statements, and to the best of my knowledge and belief, it is true, correct, and complete. Declaration of preparer (other than taxpayer) is based on all information of which preparer has any knowledge.

▶ Signature of officer	Date	▶ Title

Paid Preparer's Use Only

Preparer's signature ▶ Robert Baker	Date	Check if self-employed ☐	Preparer's social security number 240 48 3108
Firm's name (or yours if self-employed) and address ▶ Robert W. Baker, CPA 3378 Nottingham Rd, Salem NC		E.I. No. ▶ 56 0794 4950	ZIP code ▶ 27104

(continued)

EXHIBIT 2
(Continued)

Form 1120 (1993)   Page **4**

Schedule L	Balance Sheets	Beginning of tax year		End of tax year	
	Assets	(a)	(b)	(c)	(d)
1	Cash		109 517.45		106 125.13
2a	Trade notes and accounts receivable	58 422.30		63 207.55	
b	Less allowance for bad debts	( )	58 422.30	( )	63 207.55
3	Inventories		48 272.71		45 485.77
4	U.S. government obligations				
5	Tax-exempt securities (see instructions)				
6	Other current assets (attach schedule)		289 368.17		353 913.39
7	Loans to stockholders				
8	Mortgage and real estate loans				
9	Other investments (attach schedule)				
10a	Buildings and other depreciable assets	264 054.25		259 816.45	
b	Less accumulated depreciation	(181 620.09)	82 434.16	(188 541.45)	71 275.00
11a	Depletable assets				
b	Less accumulated depletion	( )		( )	
12	Land (net of any amortization)		17 597.44		17 597.44
13a	Intangible assets (amortizable only)				
b	Less accumulated amortization	( )		( )	
14	Other assets (attach schedule)		18 567.48		20 445.14
15	Total assets		624 179.71		678 049.42
	Liabilities and Stockholders' Equity				
16	Accounts payable		14 564.53		10 731.43
17	Mortgages, notes, bonds payable in less than 1 year		1 200.00		
18	Other current liabilities (attach schedule)		40 100.25		43 241.33
19	Loans from stockholders				
20	Mortgages, notes, bonds payable in 1 year or more		3 900.00		
21	Other liabilities (attach schedule)				
22	Capital stock: a Preferred stock				
	b Common stock	46 550.00	46 550.00		46 550.00
23	Paid-in or capital surplus				
24	Retained earnings—Appropriated (attach schedule)				
25	Retained earnings—Unappropriated		517 864.93		577 526.66
26	Less cost of treasury stock		( )		( )
27	Total liabilities and stockholders' equity		624 179.71		678 049.42

Note: You are not required to complete Schedules M-1 and M-2 below if the total assets on line 15, column (d) of Schedule L are less than $25,000.

Schedule M-1	Reconciliation of Income (Loss) per Books With Income per Return (See instructions.)				
1	Net income (loss) per books	59 661.73	7	Income recorded on books this year not included on this return (itemize):	
2	Federal income tax	11 490.28			
3	Excess of capital losses over capital gains			Tax-exempt interest $	
4	Income subject to tax not recorded on books this year (itemize):			Increase C.V. Life Ins. in excess of prem. paid	600.89
5	Expenses recorded on books this year not deducted on this return (itemize):		8	Deductions on this return not charged against book income this year (itemize):	
a	Depreciation . . . $		a	Depreciation . . . $	
b	Contributions carryover $		b	Contributions carryover $	
c	Travel and entertainment $			....	
	penalty 84			....	
	....	.84	9	Add lines 7 and 8	
6	Add lines 1 through 5	71 152.85	10	Income (line 28, page 1)—line 6 less line 9	

Schedule M-2	Analysis of Unappropriated Retained Earnings per Books (Line 25, Schedule L)				
1	Balance at beginning of year	517 864.43	5	Distributions: a Cash	
2	Net income (loss) per books	59 661.73		b Stock	
3	Other increases (itemize):			c Property	
	....		6	Other decreases (itemize):	
	....			....	
	....		7	Add lines 5 and 6	
4	Add lines 1, 2, and 3	577 526.66	8	Balance at end of year (line 4 less line 7)	577 526.66

EXHIBIT 3
OT Snack Company Income Statement (Projections)

Sales	$1,200,000
Cost of materials	
Raw materials	418,800
Supplies/mfg.	18,480
Freight	1,320
	$438,600
Direct labor	142,500
FICA	10,189
NCUC taxes	428
Utilities	20,040
Sick pay	3,400
Employee benefits	21,375
Laundry	3,000
Repairs and maintenance	3,600
Sanitation	1,800
Depreciation	73,000
Property taxes	14,300
	$293,632
Gross profit	$467,768
Sales administration	
Salaries	62,000
FICA	4,433
Professional fee	10,000
Travel	3,000
Rent	75,000
Insurance	23,720
Management fee	71,500
Telephone	4,000
Employee benefits	9,300
Equipment-lease	96,000
	$358,653
Income before taxes	$109,115
Income taxes	
Federal	35,896
State	6,546
	42,442
Net income	$66,673

EXHIBIT 4
OT Snack Company Income Statement (Projections)

Sales	$2,756,000
Cost of materials	
Raw materials	961,844
Supplies/mfg.	42,442
Freight	3,032
	$1,007,318
Direct labor	253,300
FICA	18,111
NCUC taxes	760
Utilities	46,025
Sick pay	3,400
Employee benefits	37,995
Laundry	3,000
Repairs and maintenance	3,600
Sanitation	1,800
Depreciation	73,000
Property taxes	14,300
	455,291
Gross profit	$1,293,391
Sales & administrative	
Salaries	62,000
FICA	4,453
Professional fee	10,000
Rent	75,000
Insurance	23,700
Management fee	354,900
Travel	3,000
Telephone	4,000
Employee benefits	9,300
Equipment-lease	96,000
	642,353
Income before taxes	651,038
Income taxes	
Federal	214,191
State	39,062
	253,245
Net income	$397,785

CASE 36

FABRICARE, INC. VALUATION

In early 1986, Roy Tyson purchased Professional Building Maintenance, Inc. (PBM), a building maintenance and cleaning firm located and operating in the Danville, Virginia area. The firm specialized in providing cleaning services in commercial and professional offices, such as banks, law offices, and medical practices. Over the next 5 years, revenues increased more than 400 percent, from $212,100 to $851,430 in 1991 (see Exhibit 1 and 2). The revenue growth rate slowed in 1991 as PBM's market share (currently 40 percent) in the area expanded and the potential new prospect pool declined. Roy was confident that the expertise he had gained while operating PBM could be applied successfully to similar firms in other geographical markets that possessed greater growth potential than Danville.

In 1992, he learned that a building maintenance firm, Fabricare, Inc., located in Lynchburg, Virginia, was for sale. Fabricare's most recent (year-end 1991) revenues were less than one-half of those of PBM, but Roy believed the growth potential to be much greater because Fabricare had only a small share (approximately 10 percent) of the Lynchburg market. As he looked over the 1991 income statement and balance sheet for Fabricare, Roy was trying to decide (1) if he should purchase the company and (2) if so, at what price.

Fabricare, like PBM, was in the building maintenance business, but approximately one-half of its revenues came from commercial establishment carpet cleaning. The owner of Fabricare was approaching retirement age and no preparation had been made for management succession in the small firm. On investigation, Roy learned that Fabricare had about $384,000 in revenues in 1991, a figure that had grown only modestly over the previous three years. (Exhibit 3 is a 1991 income statement, derived from Fabricare's 1991 tax return. Exhibit 4 is an unaudited 1991 balance sheet for Fabricare). Fabricare's current owners were not much on keeping careful records. Past income records were not reliable in Roy's judgment. Hence, the decision regarding acquisition of Fabricare had to be based primarily on Roy's own projections of cash flows from Fabricare and on an appraisal of the quality of the assets that would be acquired.

In assessing Fabricare's market position, Roy visited the competitors' premises noting, in particular, the number of service vehicles that each business had available. Although a relatively crude method of measuring the business activity level of each firm and relative market shares, he had found this to be a fairly accurate indicator in the Danville area. From these observations, Roy believed that Fabricare had only a 10 percent share of the building maintenance business in Lynchburg. In addition, Roy learned from some of the local firms that made use of building maintenance services in Lynchburg that the bidding techniques and performance standards were similar to those he had experienced from his competitors in Danville.

Lynchburg had a larger business and professional community than Danville and offered greater immediate growth potential than existed in the saturated Danville market. Upon a closer examination of Fabricare, Roy saw a firm whose business could be expanded from its current customer base into a more successful, full-service building maintenance firm like PBM. Roy felt strongly that he could capture about the same market share (40 percent) in Lynchburg as he had in Danville. Beyond that level, Roy found additional market share difficult to obtain from customers who often were more concerned about cost considerations than quality of performance.

Roy also considered a startup operation, but he concluded that the purchase of an existing firm would give him quicker access to the market. In addition to the current customer base, he would also obtain employees who were familiar with the business and the area. Based on an estimate of the current and future total market for building maintenance services in Lynchburg and a projection of Fabricare's market penetration that matched the historical performance of PBM, Roy estimated that sales revenues under his management could be:

1993: $400,000
1994: $600,000
1995: $900,000
1996: $1,200,000
1997: $1,500,000
1998 and beyond: $1,600,000

To develop pro forma statements that could assist in the valuation of the firm, Roy made the following assumptions, based on his experience at PBM:

1. Pretax operating profit equals 13.5 percent of sales.
2. Taxes computed using 30 percent combined (state and federal) tax rate.
3. Additional net working capital investment equal to $8,450 in 1993 and thereafter 16.9 percent of incremental sales.

4. Capital investment requirements equal to $25,000 in 1993, $30,000 in 1994, $40,000 in 1995, $60,000 both in 1996 and 1997, and $70,000 per year thereafter. These capital outlays are needed to replace and recondition vehicles, sweepers, carpet cleaning equipment, and equipment and furnishings used in the main company office.

5. Annual depreciation was expected to total $5,000 in 1993, $11,000 in 1994, $20,000 in 1995, $45,000 in 1996, and $70,000 per year thereafter.

6. If the acquisition is completed, the effective date will be January 1, 1993.

Under its present management, sales and profit growth was expected to be substantially less than under Roy's management and ownership. Based on what he knew about the past performance of Fabricare, Roy felt that the current managers would be lucky if they could grow their 1991 yearly after-tax cash flows of $30,654 ($28,615 net income after tax plus depreciation of $2,039) by 5 percent per year.

As a starting point in estimating a required return on equity, Roy used data from publicly held building maintenance and cleaning firms. This analysis led Roy to conclude that a 15 percent return on equity was suitable for firms in that industry. However, because PBM and Fabricare were privately held and suffered from a lack of liquidity for their owners, because of the increased risk associated with locationally nondiversified firms, and because the owners were not well-diversified with respect to their own portfolio of assets, Roy concluded that a 20 percent return on equity was appropriate for valuing both PBM and any potential acquisition in the industry.

A similar analysis of publicly held firms and data from Robert Morris Associates for smaller firms in the industry indicated that a 20 percent return requirement was reasonable and achievable. This analysis also led Roy to conclude that a capital structure containing up to 30 percent debt was typical. However, Roy did not wish to assume any liabilities associated with the Fabricare operation, because he was unsure of the business reputation of the current owners and did not want to have to deal with any outstanding claims against the current owners. Hence, he planned only to acquire the assets of Fabricare and to negotiate a "noncompete" agreement with the current owners. The assets to be acquired included fixed assets (trucks and equipment), leased property improvements, and working capital, including cash, inventories, and accounts receivable. These assets had a current book value of $154,088, but Roy felt a more reasonable liquidation value was $140,000. Roy and the Fabricare owners agreed that if an agreement to purchase was completed, the final sales price would be adjusted to reflect changes in the working capital accounts, from the amounts outstanding at year-end 1991, as shown in Exhibit 4.

Roy's first problem was a valuation of Fabricare. If he sought to acquire the firm, he did not want to overpay. Fabricare did have some good contracts on which Roy felt his firm could build. These contracts, although not long-term, were with customers who had used Fabricare for several years and were thought to be loyal customers. The owners of Fabricare were asking a price of $275,000. Roy's intuition told him that this asking price was too high, given the performance of Fabricare and Roy's own experience at PBM. Publicly traded building maintenance service firms were currently selling at a multiple of 65 percent of sales, and 8 times current earnings. Roy had recently learned about the concept of free cash flows and wanted to apply this valuation technique as well.

Roy knew that he wanted to purchase Fabricare as an entry into the Lynchburg market. The basic questions were (1) to determine a valuation for Fabricare; (2) to determine a valuation for the combined firms; and (3) to decide how to finance the purchase of Fabricare. After these questions were answered, Roy still had to negotiate a price with the current owners of Fabricare. With these thoughts in mind, Roy got out his calculator and began his analysis.

QUESTIONS

1. If Roy Tyson were to acquire Fabricare, what is the maximum amount that he could pay for the firm, assuming that the acquisition is effective at the beginning of 1993?

2. In the valuation of Fabricare, Roy is trying to decide the price he is willing to pay for the firm. In a proper valuation of Fabricare, what role should (1) the book value of the assets to be acquired from Fabricare, (2) price-to-earnings ratios for publicly traded building maintenance firms, (3) market value as a percentage of sales analysis for publicly traded firms, and (4) an estimate of the value of Fabricare under current management play in the analysis? Are there any factors that might lead you to recommend that Tyson pay less for Fabricare than the amount computed in question 1?

3. What value would you recommend as a starting point for negotiations?

EXHIBIT 1
PBM, Inc. Statement of Income

	1991	1990	1989
Sales	$851,430	$748,880	$550,140
Operating expenses:			
Salaries*	497,674	453,072	341,543
Payroll taxes	35,579	32,673	27,577
Supplies	42,371	34,024	28,716
Subcontractor fees	13,008	11,814	10,181
Repairs/maintenance	6,643	5,862	5,322
Uniform expense	2,721	1,924	1,297
Vehicle expense	7,529	7,289	11,180
Travel	4,925	4,612	4,585
Depreciation	24,882	20,042	25,101
Total operating expenses	$635,332	$571,312	$455,502
Gross margin on sales	$216,098	$177,568	$94,638

(continued)

EXHIBIT 1
(Continued)

	1991	1990	1989
General and administrative expenses:			
Accounting/professional	$12,704	10,180	9,328
Advertising	1,571	1,410	1,270
Bank charges	3,705	2,948	2,312
Conventions/meetings	1,521	1,865	1,771
Contributions	2,500	2,115	1,810
Insurance	35,700	20,684	18,449
Office supplies	8,574	7,112	6,579
Rent	10,500	9,008	8,283
Retirement	10,325	9,717	9,412
Taxes/licenses	2,110	1,962	3,545
Utilities	8,443	7,653	6,412
Total general and administrative expenses	$97,653	$74,654	$69,171
Income before taxes	$118,445	102,914	$25,467
Income taxes	31,438	30,777	5,632
Net income after taxes	$87,007	$72,137	$19,835

*In 1991, salaries include $92,450 compensation to officers of PBM, Inc. (Roy and his wife).

EXHIBIT 2
PBM, Inc. Balance Sheet

	December 31, 1991	December 31, 1990
Current assets:		
Cash	$47,632	$25,666
Inventory	3,446	2,997
Note receivable	102,820	79,651
Accounts receivable	102,594	65,420
Total current assets	$256,492	$173,734
Fixed assets:		
Building	$28,286	$28,286
Furniture and fixtures	99,741	72,978
Equipment	1,984	1,514
Automobiles and trucks	39,666	39,666
Less: Accumulated depreciation	(116,353)	(91,471)
Net fixed assets	53,324	50,973
Goodwill	31,787	32,337
Total assets	$341,603	$257,044

(continued)

EXHIBIT 2
(Continued)

	December 31, 1991	December 31, 1990
Current liabilities:		
SUTA payable	$1,063	$1,570
FUTA payable	(487)	3,008
State withholding	1,640	580
Federal withholding	32,468	25,127
FICA withheld—employee	34,040	27,899
FICA accrued—employer	33,611	30,802
Payroll tax deposits	(104,281)	(92,334)
Miscellaneous deductions	15,467	5,296
Accrued wages payable	16,922	19,179
Income tax provision	(5,580)	(1,428)
Total current liabilities	$24,863	$19,699
Long-term debt:		
Note payable—CFB	$230	$743
Note payable—First Virginia	2,803	9,902
Total long-term debt	3,033	$10,645
Total liabilities	$27,896	$30,344
Shareholders' equity:		
Common stock	$38,400	$38,400
Retained earnings	275,307	$188,300
Total shareholders' equity	$313,707	$226,700
Total liabilities and shareholders' equity	$341,603	257,044

EXHIBIT 3
Fabricare, Inc. Statement of Income, 1991 *(unaudited)*

Sales	$384,385
Operating, general, and administrative expenses:	
Salaries and wages	$172,816
Rent	3,498
Payroll taxes	54,763
Interest	2,885
Depreciation	2,039
Advertising	8,856
Supplies	54,525
Office expense	10,732
Other expenses	38,502
Total operating, general, and administrative expenses:	$348,616
Income before taxes	$35,769
Income taxes	7,154
Net income after taxes	$28,615

EXHIBIT 4
Fabricare, Inc. Balance Sheet, December 31, 1991 *(unaudited)*

Current assets:	
Cash	$29,052
Accounts receivable	56,167
Inventory	8,584
Total current assets	$93,803
Fixed assets:	
Furniture, fixtures and equipment	$49,651
Automobiles and trucks	39,522
Less: Accumulated depreciation	(28,888)
Net fixed assets	$60,285
Total assets	$154,088
Current liabilities:	
SUTA payable	$855
FUTA payable	247
State withholding	995
Federal withholding	20,006
FICA withheld—employee	21,771
FICA accrued—employer	18,643
Payroll tax deposits	(51,587)
Miscellaneous deductions	11,242
Accrued wages payable	9,918
Income tax provision	(3,342)
Total current liabilities	$28,748
Long-term debt:	
Note payable	$12,500
Total liabilities	$41,248
Shareholders' equity:	
Common stock	$25,000
Retained earnings	87,840
Total shareholders' equity	$112,840
Total liabilities and shareholders' equity	$154,088

NARRAGANSETT PRODUCTS
ACQUISITION: MULTIPLE OPTIONS

Narragansett Products is a regional producer of soft drinks and sells mainly in the states of New Hampshire, Massachusetts and Rhode Island. Three years ago, in 1993, it made the decision to diversify into the bottled water industry, whose market enjoys a good reputation in a health-conscious America and is especially popular in areas where the quality of municipally provided water is suspect. Firms cater to businesses and homes, obtaining income mainly from the delivery of bottled water and the rental of water coolers. The market Narragansett entered has one highly successful firm, Mineral Springs, which is family owned with yearly sales of about $6 million. The next largest firm is Beaumont Water, and there are 10 extremely small companies with one or two trucks, six of which have appeared in the last two years.

When the decision was made to produce bottled water, nearly all of Narragansett's executives were extremely confident that the venture would be highly profitable. This optimism was based on (1) projections showing the bottled water market was growing; (2) cost estimates implying that Narragansett could undersell its competitors by 10 percent; and (3) Narragansett's ability to pick "winners" in the soft drink market. Unfortunately, there was a barrier to entry that few realized: businesses were not buying a product so much as a service, and the marketing strategies of mass advertising (newspaper, radio, etc.) and price discounts simply did not work. Mass advertising was ineffective because consumers believed correctly that all bottled water was really the same thing. Therefore, it is hard for a company to differentiate its product, unlike firms in the soft drink industry. Price discounts failed for two reasons. First, a company's expenditure on bottled water is a very small proportion of its expenses. Thus, managers were not especially attracted by price discounts. More important, however, businesses were not buying a product so much as a service—a visit and chat with the delivery person. All in all it was hard to convince firms to switch bottled water companies. As one manager put it: "So we save a few bucks. But that means we won't see Fred every week. And—my goodness— Fred's like family! It wouldn't be right to switch."

THE CURRENT SITUATION

At this point Narragansett's bottled water business has shown operating losses of nearly $300,000, which does not include the initial investment of more than $800,000. Management is now taking a critical look at the decision made nearly three years ago and must decide between one of four options. It can continue as is; abandon the project completely; stop producing bottled water but retain ownership of the land and lease the building; or go after the bottled water market by acquiring Beaumont Water. The "as is" alternative does not require any additional expenditure and is expected to generate the situation shown in Exhibit 1. No one finds this option especially appealing. Management's thinking is, "If we stay in this market, let's do it right or give the project its pink slip."

Abandoning the project has at least one vocal supporter, Clifton Willard, a plant manager, who argues that this strategy will give Narragansett "immediate benefit." The land that Narragansett paid $200,000 for 10 years ago has a market value of $380,000 and is not presently needed. The factory would, of course, be sold with the land and is worth about $90,000. He admits that the trucks Narragansett purchased have relatively little market value since they are highly specialized; that is, they were built to carry the 5-gallon jars of water and are not especially suitable for other purposes. A reasonable estimate is that they could be sold for 50 percent of their book value. The remaining equipment can also be sold at 50 percent of book. The receivables are generally of good quality, and Narragansett should obtain $72,000 when they are collected. "And, of course," notes Willard, "we could liquidate at 100 percent of book, our inventory of bottled water."

Stan Covington, the company president, also favors abandoning the project, though his proposal is not quite as drastic as Willard's. He suggests keeping the land and renting the building, though the trucks and equipment would be sold, the receivables collected, and the inventory liquidated. Leasing the building would be a "simple matter" and would net $40,000 a year, a figure that includes all yearly expenses but not taxes. He agrees with Willard that the land is not needed by Narragansett now, but in three to five years it might be since Narragansett's soft drink sales have been growing, and it is very likely that the company will need additional area for expansion. The location of the current bottled water plant is considered ideal for growth. "At a minimum," argues Covington, "if we keep the land it can always be sold in the future. The current market value is nearly 100 percent more than we paid for it and should continue to appreciate this way." He also points out that the factories could be used for the production of soft drinks.

BEAUMONT WATER

Beaumont Water has been in business nearly 100 years, has always been owned by the McGeary family, and is the second largest bottled water firm in the area in terms of annual sales. To help evaluate the feasibility of acquiring Beaumont, Narragansett hired Fraley and Associates, a respected consulting firm, which has a bit of a national reputation. The first step in the acquisition process was to accurately determine Beaumont's most recent income statement. Unbelievably, this was a very difficult and time-consuming task because the current owner, Tom McGeary, simply never appreciated or liked the idea of keeping accurate records. All sales were made in cash and then deposited. In order to estimate last year's sales, Fraley and Associates had to examine deposit records, being careful not to count cash resulting from the sale of assets like machinery and water coolers. Expenses were estimated using canceled checks, and an on-site verification of Beaumont's assets was made. (See Exhibit 3 for the balance sheet estimate. Exhibit 4 presents Beaumont's current income statement as well as a consolidated pro forma income statement of the two firms, and Exhibit 5 provides excerpts from the report of Fraley and Associates.)

Narragansett's executives feel quite confident that these estimates are accurate, and are pleased with the thoroughness of Fraley and Associates. Narragansett is also confident that the bottled water market is expanding. The area's economy is projected to grow sharply in the next five years and this means more businesses to serve (and households as well should Narragansett decide to enter that market). And then there is the result of a survey done by Elizabeth Lonon, the director of marketing. At the end of each business day for three full months, Lonon faithfully queried the cooler installation man at Beaumont and determined that, based on the number of new coolers they installed, Beaumont's sales should have doubled. The problem, Lonon was astonished to learn, was that they removed as many old coolers as they installed. The service of Beaumont was the major problem. Apparently some new orders were never processed, others were processed literally months after they were initially placed, and missed deliveries were common.

"Refresh my mind," Willard says, somewhat sarcastically. "Exactly why are we interested in buying this company? Certainly not for its bookkeeping system or its management policies. And certainly not for its assets. I mean, the market value of all it owns is only about $800,000, and we're considering paying $2 million for the firm. It all sounds crazy to me. The difference of 1.2 million represents goodwill, which we can't even depreciate."

Lindsay Carter, the chief finance officer, then proceeds to address this question at some length.

Our original idea that the industry is growing wasn't wrong, only our ideas about marketing the product. Believe it or not, we're buying Beaumont's name and loyal customers. After all, it has been around for nearly a century and only recently has it gone downhill. Acquiring Beaumont will give us a toehold in the market.

We know how to deliver a product and provide quality service. I believe that Beaumont has been a victim of its inability to serve all its new customers of the last few years. If you think about it, you'll notice that based on Elizabeth's research, Beaumont apparently had *new* sales of well over $2 million in the last two years. How much new business did we get during the same period with our heavy advertising and lower prices? About $800,000, that's all! And keep in mind the area's expansion will bring in new business and may well strain local water supplies and cause a reduction in water quality.

Lonon agrees that Willard has raised a good question but tends to side with Carter. "We can't look at what Beaumont *is*," she says, "we have to look at what it *can be*." She also points out that the acquisition contains an "attractive financing package." McGeary wants $2 million for Beaumont but only $1 million up front. McGeary would finance the remainder with a 7-percent, 5-year loan, though the current market rate of interest on this type of debt is 12 percent. The terms of the loan allow Narragansett to pay only the interest each year and the entire principal can be deferred for five years; that is, a balloon payment of $1 million would be due in five years.

At this point discussion returns to other issues in the investigation of Fraley and Associates. Their report indicates that a consolidation of the companies will result in an increase in profitability even if there is no change in the sales of each firm from the acquisition. (See Exhibits 4 and 5.) And the report also suggests one reason that the firm has been losing customers. Beaumont's delivery men were actually responsible for loading their own trucks. Many would frequently not begin deliveries until 11 or 11:30 in the morning and exhausted at that. The result was that many customers were not served or received late deliveries. A consolidation would easily correct this. Idle equipment of Narragansett's could be moved to Beaumont's plant to automate the loading. Only one night shift operator-loader need be hired and the trucks could be ready to go by 8 A.M. (*Note:* The cost of this extra person has already been considered in Exhibit 4.)

It also is obvious to Narragansett's management that the actual cost of Beaumont could differ, and perhaps substantially, from the asking price of $2 million. There is, of course, the attractive financing arrangements surrounding the purchase. On the other hand, it is clear that Beaumont's (net) working capital policy has hurt sales, and this will require funding to change. In addition, Narragansett will need $100,000 to buy equipment that Beaumont is currently leasing.

After further discussion a consensus is reached on a number of issues relevant to the choice.

1 The projections shown in Exhibit 1 should continue indefinitely.

2. The consolidated pro forma income statement in Exhibit 4 is quite reasonable; the net income projection is relatively low risk because it depends mainly on the merger, which management believes would easily bring about greater efficiency.

3. If Beaumont is acquired, annual sales could easily reach $4 million during year 3 and might top $5 million in four to five years.

4. Cost of goods sold will be 25 percent of sales; selling expenses will change by 20 percent of sales exceeding $2.8 million; and general and administrative and miscellaneous fixed expenses will both change by 5 percent of sales exceeding $2.8 million.

5. Narragansett's current net working capital situation (CA-CL) is reasonable.

6. The appropriate tax rate is 40 percent.

7. The acquisition would enable Narragansett to handle annual sales of $5 million to $6 million without any increase in fixed assets.

8. Any lease would last five years and could be renewed indefinitely.

9. The yearly cash flow with each option will equal EBIT adjusted for taxes less any change in working capital requirements. (Any cash flow resulting from depreciation is assumed to be used to maintain existing equipment.)

A final problem involves the appropriate discount rate. The lease option is considered a lower risk than either the "as is" or acquisition options. The yearly cash flows from the "as is" option should be discounted at 13 percent and those from the lease at 10 percent. With the acquisition alternative, management has identified three distinct cash flow streams. Management will use a 13 percent rate on the cash flow generated by sales of $2.8 million or less. It feels 16 percent is the appropriate cost of capital (required return) for the incremental cash flow on sales between $2.8 million and $4 million. Finally, a 22 percent rate will be used on the incremental cash flow generated by sales above $4 million. (*Note:* All rates are on an after-tax basis.)

QUESTIONS

1. How relevant to the decision are the $800,000 initial cost of the project and the operating losses of $300,000?

2. (a) Calculate the incremental cash flows for the "abandon completely" alternative. (Be sure to consider the tax effects from the sale of the land, trucks, equipment, and factory. Use the cash flows from the "as is" option as the base position to calculate these incremental amounts.)

   (b) What would the incremental cash flows be from the "abandon-but-lease" alternative? (Use the "as is" option as the base position.)

   (c) Calculate the NPV's of these options.

   (d) Based on these calculations and other information in the case, are these alternatives superior to the "as is" position? Which of the two is more consistent with the objective of value maximization? Explain.

3. What will be the cost of Beaumont after considering the financing surrounding the purchase, Beaumont's (net) working capital situation, and the additional equipment that would be purchased?

4. Fraley and Associates estimated that net income after the merger will exceed the sum of the net incomes both firms achieved individually. Does this seem reasonable? Explain.

5. (a) Develop pro forma (consolidated) income statements for annual sales of $4 million and $5 million.
   (b) Calculate the relevant incremental cash flows. (Use the "as is" cash flows as the base position to calculate these incremental amounts.)
   (c) What is your estimate of Beaumont's value? Explain.

6. Does it make sense for Narragansett's management to use so many discount rates in its evaluation? Explain.

7. Based on your previous answers, any other calculations you feel are relevant, and information provided in the case, which alternative do you recommend? Fully support your position.

8. What additional information would you like to have to make a more informed decision?

 SOFTWARE QUESTION

9. Some of Narragansett's managers are having second thoughts on a number of estimates relevant to the Beaumont acquisition. For example, Lindsay Carter, the CFO, thinks that the discount rates used are too high. And Clifford Willard, a plant manager, believes the cost estimates are too low.

   After some discussion, the following scenarios were generated. Each represents the personal favorite of a Narragansett executive.

   Perform the appropriate analysis. Based on these results, do you recommend that Narragansett Products purchase Beaumont Water?

	S − 1	S − 2	S − 3	S − 4
A. Sales ($000)				
year 1	2,800	2,800	2,800	2,800
year 2	2,800	2,800	2,800	2,800
year 3	3,500	3,100	3,500	3,500
year 4	3,500	3,300	3,500	4,000
year 5 & beyond	4,200	3,600	3,800	4,500
B. Discount rates[†]	.12/.15/.20	.12/.15/.20	.10/.13/.17	.10/.16/.22
C. CGS/sales	.25	.25	.28	.29
D. Adm. expenses[*]	.05	.08	.07	.08
E. Selling expense[*]	.20	.22	.22	.22
F. Misc. fixed exp[*]	.05	.05	.05	.05
G. NWC/sales	.13	.12	.12	.15

[*] Items D, E and F apply to annual sales above $2.8 million, and are expressed as a proportion of sales.

[†] Each set of three refers to the appropriate discount rate to use on the increment of cash flows resulting from (1) sales less than $2.8M, (2) sales between $2.8M and $4M and (3) sales above $4M.

EXHIBIT 1
Pro Forma "As Is" Income Statement for Narragansett's Bottled Water Division ($000s)*

Sales	$800
Cost of goods sold	200
Gross margin	600
General administrative expenses	150
Selling expenses	290
Miscellaneous fixed	10
Depreciation	100
EBIT	50
Taxes (40%)	20
Net income	$30

*Management feels this situation could persist indefinitely.

EXHIBIT 2
Narragansett's Bottled Water Division Balance Sheet (1996): Book Value ($000s)*

Assets		Liabilities and Equity	
Cash	$8		
Accounts receivable	80	Accounts payable	$28
Inventory	50	Accruals	16
Current assets	138	Current liabilities	44
Factory	100		
Equipment	50	Equity	564
Trucks	120		
Land	200		
Total assets	$608	Total liabilities and equity	$608

*The net working capital situation assumes annual sales are $800,000.

EXHIBIT 3
Beaumont Water's Current Balance Sheet (1996): Market Values in ($000s)
(Prepared by Fraley and Associates)

Assets		Liabilities and Equity	
Cash	$5	Accounts payable	$13
Accounts receivable	0	Accruals	11
Inventory	100	Current liabilities	24
Current assets	105	Equity	741
Factory	190		
Equipment	90		
Trucks	80		
Land	300		
Total assets	$765	Total liabilities and equity	$765

EXHIBIT 4
Fraley and Associate's Estimate of Consolidated Income Statement ($000s)[*]

	Narragansett	Beaumont Water	Consolidated
Sales	$800	$2,000	$2,800
Cost of goods sold	200	580	700
Gross profit	600	1,420	2,100
General & administrative expenses	150	380	440
Selling expenses	290	600	800
Miscellaneous fixed	10	240	160
Depreciation	100	110	235
EBIT	50	90	465
Taxes (40%)	20	36	186
Net income	$30	$64	$279

[*]The figures on Narragansett are the projection of its "as is" position, and those on Beaumont represent Fraley's estimate of Beaumont's situation for the previous year. All estimates assume a reasonable working capital policy.

EXHIBIT 5
Excerpts of Fraley and Associate's Study on Beaumont Water

- Enclosed you will find our estimate of Beaumont's most recent income statement and its current balance sheet. Please note that the asset values are estimated market values.

- There is little doubt that Beaumont has been poorly run. Here are a few examples: failure to require a deposit on the water coolers has resulted in the company absorbing the full cost of all breakage on the part of the customers; leasing costs are excessive; Beaumont rents a number of trucks each year for what it would cost to buy them new. The same is true of its leased computer. Our consolidated income statement assumes you discontinue leasing and purchase this equipment at an estimated cost of $100,000.

- Consolidation will most definitely reduce costs. Distribution will be more efficient, and more effective use will be made of plant, equipment, and trucks.

- See our estimate of a consolidated income statement in Exhibit 4. The Narragansett numbers are the figures you supplied us. The Beaumont numbers represent our estimate of this firm's most recent income statement. It is our opinion that the consolidated figures could persist indefinitely, assuming reasonable service of Beaumont's present customers and a reasonable credit policy.

- Beaumont has no receivables because all sales were in cash. This undoubtedly has hurt sales. Its abnormally low amount of accounts payable and accruals reflects its policy of paying its suppliers very promptly and its employees once a week. We judge your net working capital situation (CA-CL) to be typical of a firm in this industry.

UNITED HOUSEWARES DIVESTITURE

Sales of United Housewares have increased nearly 8 percent per year over the last four years, yet the firm's operating profit has failed to keep pace. "The problem," Alvin Adamson—the firm's president and chief executive officer—emphatically stated at a recent board meeting, "is the anemic performance of the Food and Beverage (F&B) division."

United has four divisions, organized by product lines. The Soap and Detergent and Toiletries divisions are the two largest, with annual sales of nearly $400 million each. F&B accounts for about $300 million of annual sales, and the Housewares division for around $100 million.

AN ACQUISITION

The F&B division was created six years ago when United acquired McGuire, a firm with a number of brand-name coffees and juices. United decided to expand into the food and beverage market in part because these products are not especially sensitive to the economy. Management also felt that food and beverage products were consistent with the company's stated policy of delivering quality household items. And finally, McGuire—a firm with many products that are household names in many parts of the country—was for sale at a price United's management labeled a "bargain."

Unfortunately, the acquisition has been nothing but a headache for United with one mistake following another. There have been, for example, a number of run-ins with the Food and Drug Administration (FDA). The FDA actually seized a shipment of orange juice because of misleading claims about freshness. And management initiated a price war with Folger's in order to increase the market share of one of its coffees. The strategy failed.

Perhaps the biggest problem has been management structure. United's structure gives heavy responsibility to division managers, unlike McGuire's hierarchy where decisions are passed down from the top. In effect, McGuire's management had to learn a new corporate culture. They were given more freedom but were asked to make more decisions and accept more responsibilities. The result, apparently, is that some decisions were not made and others were made too late. Adamson even tried changing the division manager three times, but to no avail.

A few months ago Adamson formed a committee to recommend whether McGuire should be sold or whether it should continue to be operated by United. The committee, after extensive analysis, concluded that it is in the best interest of United's stockholders to sell McGuire and, thus, dismantle the F&B division. A number of companies have shown interest in McGuire, and the committee concluded that it is clear that United is not able to manage the firm efficiently.

MANAGEMENT'S REACTION

This recommendation was not easy for Adamson to accept. He is a competitive type who doesn't like to get beat at anything, and it was he who led United into food and beverages. He recognizes, however, that the recommendation is sound, and there is even one argument for divestiture that the committee didn't consider.

Marketing estimates that the future of the Toiletries division is "extremely bright," and the division is ripe for expansion. However, there is an industry labor shortage and skilled technicians and managers are tough to find. This means that the expansion must be internally staffed, which would be difficult to do if United keeps McGuire. According to Adamson, "The Food and Beverage division has been chewing up executive time and will continue to do so if we keep it."

All things considered, Adamson realizes that United isn't much of a food company and should concentrate on areas that it knows best.

Not all of United's managers favor the divestiture, however. Some argue that the divestiture will reduce the firm's product diversification and thus raise the risk of the firm to investors. Others believe that United is not likely to receive a decent price for McGuire, given its sorry financial history. They are especially concerned that McGuire might be sold for less than its book value. They find this possibility "alarming" and predict that "investors would react unfavorably."

Adamson isn't taking these objections too seriously mainly because he thinks that McGuire has considerable value. He argues that

> the reasons we bought McGuire are still sound. It has an established customer base and many well-known products. Numerous marketing surveys have shown that its products rate very high in customer loyalty and name recognition. The value of McGuire isn't determined by its performance under our management—which quite frankly wasn't and isn't very good. No, its value is determined by what it *can* and *will* be if it is managed effectively.

HOLLY GRETHER

Though United will hire outside consultants to estimate the value of McGuire, Adamson thinks that it is a good idea to develop an in-house estimate, and Holly Grether—an executive in the finance department—volunteers to make it.

Grether thinks that the starting point for the analysis should be McGuire's liquidation value. The inventory can be sold to net 70 percent after taxes, and this same percentage can be applied to the firm's receivables. McGuire's plant and equipment is adequate to support inflationary increases in sales. Most of it is state-of-the-art, and a reasonable estimate of its after-tax market value is $14 million. Liquidation will, of course, involve legal and administrative fees and Grether estimates that these will run $750,000.

Grether—like Adamson—is confident that McGuire is "worth more alive than dead" and one way she will estimate this value is by using a "comparables" approach. The idea is to develop price-earnings (P-E) and market-to-book (MV/BV) multiples using information on firms comparable to McGuire. However, she realizes that finding such firms is hard to do since companies differ so much in terms of size, product lines, markets, and so on.

After much thought and discussions with other managers, Grether compiled the information shown in Exhibit 3. These are firms that have two important characteristics: They manufacture products similar to those of McGuire and they are companies that may well be interested in an acquisition. Still, she is not comfortable with the list because these companies are at best only "sort of like" McGuire. It isn't clear, though, if a more appropriate set of firms exist.

Grether will also use a discounted cash flow (DCF) framework to estimate McGuire's value. Her approach will be to estimate the expected cash flows assuming no interest expense, discount these cash flows at the appropriate cost of capital, and then adjust for financial leverage. But developing an estimate using a DCF model is not especially easy either. Grether knows that DCF estimates are frequently sensitive to assumptions made about growth, profit margins, the cost of capital, and the terminal value.

Grether strongly feels that using McGuire's past profit margins is inappropriate. It is a virtual certainty that the firm's operating margin, that is (EBIT + Depreciation)/sales, would increase substantially if it were run by people who know the food and beverage business. After all, the problem is not that McGuire lacks attractive and brand-name products. The problem has been improper pricing, production inefficiencies, and poor marketing decisions which, quite frankly, could have been avoided.

She also decides to make the conservative assumption that sales and operating costs will grow with inflation at about 3 percent a year given the Federal Reserve's apparent commitment to anti-inflationary policies. Thus she will ignore the possibility of any "real growth" in sales.

At first she was going to use a five-year time horizon. That is, she was going to estimate the cash flows for five years and then develop an estimate of McGuire's terminal value at the end of year 5. At the suggestion of Theodore

Seitz, the firm's comptroller, however, she decides to assume that the firm will last "indefinitely," but assume a no-growth scenario after year 5. Thus her DCF model will be a perpetuity with 3 percent growth in years 1 through 5 (1996–2000) and zero thereafter. The advantage of this approach according to Seitz is that "you avoid the difficulty of estimating a terminal value."

The firm's current (1995) working capital situation is considered "efficient and appropriate." Depreciation should be 2.2 percent of sales and, in order to maintain plant and equipment, capital expenditures will run 3 percent of sales each year. The relevant tax rate is 30 percent.

Perhaps the trickiest part of the analysis is to estimate the appropriate cost of capital. The long-term government bond rate is 8 percent and Grether thinks that it is reasonable to assume that debt used to finance McGuire would run 100 basis points more than this. The risk-premium on an investment of average market risk is about 7 percentage points above the risk-free rate, and Grether estimates that a beta of .9 is appropriate for McGuire's unlevered cash flows. Finally, she will assume a capital structure (using market values) of 20 percent long-term debt and 80 percent equity.

QUESTIONS

1. Evaluate the argument that the divestiture is not in the stockholders' interests because it would reduce United's product diversification and thus increase United's risk.

2. Evaluate the argument that the divestiture is not in the stockholders' interest because United is "not likely to receive a decent price due to the division's sorry financial history."

3. Evaluate the prediction by some of United's managers that "investors will react unfavorably if McGuire is sold for less than the book value of equity."

4. Estimate the liquidation value of McGuire.

5. What are the strengths and weaknesses of each of the following valuation methods:

   (a) A discounted cash flow (DCF) approach.

   (b) The price-earnings (P-E) and market-to-book (MV/BV) methods.

6. Estimate McGuire's unlevered cost of capital.

7. It is common when using a DCF approach to use a finite number of years, say five to seven, and then estimate a terminal value for the firm at the end of this time. This terminal value estimate is difficult to make, and apparently some of United's managers think that the problem can be avoided by assuming a perpetuity and assigning no-growth to the cash flows occurring after the initial growth period. Does this approach really avoid the problem of estimating a terminal value? Explain.

8. Use a DCF methodology to estimate the value of McGuire assuming that United continues to operate it. You may assume a perpetuity using a no-growth scenario after five years.

9. Use a DCF methodology to estimate the value of McGuire assuming that it is run efficiently. You may assume a perpetuity using a no-growth scenario after five years.

10. (a) Estimate the value of McGuire using a price-earnings (P-E) approach.

   (b) Estimate its value using a market-to-book (MV/BV) approach.

11. Based on your previous answers, information in the case, and financial theory, how much is McGuire worth? Defend your estimate.

SOFTWARE QUESTION

12. You have been hired as a consultant in order to help United estimate McGuire's market value.

   (a) You have reviewed the assumptions used to estimate McGuire's value if United continues to operate it (see question 8).

   Based on conversations with a number of United's executives and your own expertise, you decide that the following assumptions are more appropriate.

	New Estimate	Base-case
Sales growth	.03	.03
Operating margin	.06	.04
Working capital/sales	.11	.10
Cap spending/sales	.025	.03
Depreciation/sales	.022	.022
Unlevered cost of capital	.143	.143
Debt-equity ratio	.25	.25

   Perform the appropriate analysis. Does your analysis affect your answer to question 11? Explain.

   (b) You have also reviewed the assumptions of the DCF method for estimating McGuire's value if it is run efficiently (see question 9). Discussions with managers in the food and beverage industry suggest that the original assumptions—and hence the value estimate based on these assumptions—are "pretty reasonable but can be improved."

   You think that it is a good idea to determine which of these assumptions are most important to the value estimated in question 9. Your goal is to concentrate on "firming up" the estimates on the most important variables, though first, of course, you need to "identify" these variables.

   You decide to investigate the impact that each of the following changes has on the value estimate.

	New Estimate	Base-case
Sales growth	.04	.03
Operating margin	.11	.10
Working capital/sales	.08	.10
Cap spending/sales	.025	.03
Unlevered cost of capital	.13	.143
Debt-equity ratio	.30	.25

Perform the appropriate analysis. Which changes seem to be most important? Defend your choices.

EXHIBIT 1
McGuire's Income Statements: 1992–1995 ($ Millions)

	1992	1993	1994	1995
Sales	$241.9	$261.3	$287.4	$304.6
Cost of goods	164.5	175.0	201.2	210.2
Gross margin	77.4	86.3	86.2	94.4
Administrative	61.7	69.7	77.4	82.8
Depreciation	7.7	8.4	9.2	9.7
EBIT	8.0	8.2	(0.4)	1.9
Interest	1.2	1.2	1.4	1.7
Earnings before taxes	6.8	7.0	(1.8)	0.2
Taxes (30%)	2.0	2.1	(0.5)	0.1
Net Income	$4.8	$4.9	($1.3)	$0.1

EXHIBIT 2
McGuire's Balance Sheets: 1992-1995 ($ Millions)

	1992	1993	1994	1995
Assets				
Cash	$6.0	$7.6	$6.7	$6.4
Receivables	20.1	23.9	23.9	29.7
Inventory	19.6	21.6	23.1	25.0
Other current	1.5	1.6	1.7	1.8
Current assets	47.2	54.7	55.4	62.9
Gross fixed	36.2	45.7	55.7	67.0
(Depreciation)	12.0	20.4	29.6	39.3
Net fixed	24.2	25.4	26.1	27.7
Total assets	$71.4	$80.1	$81.5	$90.6

(continued)

EXHIBIT 2
(Continued)

	1992	1993	1994	1995
Liabilities and equity				
Accounts payable	$13.6	$15.6	$16.7	$22.3
Debt due	1.7	1.7	2.0	2.4
Accruals	7.3	9.1	8.6	9.1
Current liabilities	22.6	26.4	27.3	33.8
Long-term debt	10.0	10.0	11.7	14.2
Common stock	25.0	25.0	25.0	25.0
Retained earnings	13.8	18.7	17.5	17.6
Total liabilities and equity	$71.4	$80.1	$81.5	$90.6

EXHIBIT 3
Financial Information on Firms Selected by Holly Grether

	1995 Sales[a]	1995 P-E	1995 MV/BV	1993	OM[b] 1994	1995
Church & Dwight	389.6	14.7	1.41	.092	.115	.11
Kimberly-Clark	6300.5	12.3	1.66	.154	.158	.16
Lancaster	492.2	7.6	0.70	.125	.131	.123
Newell	1165.0	13.0	1.39	.162	.186	.203
Oneida	410.0	8.8	0.58	.107	.105	.109

[a] In $ millions.

[b] OM = Operating Margin = (EBIT + Dep.)/Sales

PART VIII

INTERNATIONAL FINANCE

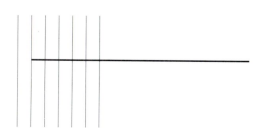

GENERAL MOTORS— EUROPE THE REGIONAL TREASURY CENTER INTERNATIONAL FINANCE

In the fall of 1994, Ellen Stanley transferred to the Regional Treasury Center (RTC) of General Motors—Europe in Belgium after a two-year stint in the Treasury Department of General Motors in Detroit. She was generally well versed in the responsibilities of the treasurer of a large domestic industrial firm, but this assignment was her first in dealing with the international and foreign exchange issues of her firm.

Stanley was spending about four months in the various areas of the RTC in Brussels to familiarize herself with its primary responsibilities. By the time she completed her rotation, she would cover the three areas within the RTC: financing and investment, trading, and accounting.

In the current portion of her training she was trying to quantify the exposure of GM to the currencies of the various countries in which GM operates throughout Western Europe. Second, she needed to assess how the firm had lessened or should attempt to lessen its exposure to these major currencies.

DEVELOPMENT OF GENERAL MOTORS' RTC

During her training, Stanley learned that General Motors was but one of 200 companies that had set up regional coordinating centers within the small Western European country of Belgium. The king of Belgium in 1982 made a conscious decision to provide substantial tax breaks to multinational corporations that set up coordination centers within his country. These tax benefits included exemption from corporate taxes for 10 years. In addition, the centers were exempt from withholding taxes (currently 25 percent) on all payments of dividends, interest, and royalties. Also, the centers were provided a tax credit of 25 percent for interest paid by the centers. The idea behind this credit was to enable banks to finance investment projects through the centers at a much lower rate than would be available in other European countries. Likewise, the coordination centers were permitted to receive leasing income free of income taxes.

Other tax benefits included the absence of a registration tax on capital and a tax on real estate by the coordination center; exemption from foreign exchange regulations; and tax concessions for expatriate employees. In brief, Belgium created an excellent environment for General Motors, Levi Strauss, Phillips Petroleum, Dow Corning, and many other businesses to carry out the treasury function of their organizations, including their foreign exchange activities.

CURRENT SITUATION FOR GENERAL MOTORS IN EUROPE

Although the General Motors' RTC could be instrumental in helping the firm acquire funds at a reasonable cost as well as managing its foreign exchange exposure, the firm's major task was building automobiles within the highly competitive European market. Volume leaders in Europe were as follows:

Manufacturer	Home Country
Volkswagen/Audi	Germany
Fiat	Italy
Peugeot/Citroen	France
Ford	U.K.
Opel/Vauxhall (GM)	Germany
Renault	France

The market shares for these six producers ranged from 10.1 percent to 14.6 percent. As the value of each country's currency changed, the competitive position of each manufacturer was helped or hurt. Depreciation in currencies improved the competitiveness of the domestic producer(s) within those countries. Appreciation in currencies impaired competitiveness by raising costs and prices relative to other nondomestic producers. At the present time the Italian lira, the British pound, and the German mark have been relatively strong. Most of General Motors' assembly operations are done in Germany.

In order to cope with the strong currencies in their home countries, both Ford and General Motors adopted a similar strategy. First, to balance their foreign exchange exposure, they diversified their production locations. However, because of economics of scale, the carmakers eventually found it prohibitively expensive to have multiple assembly locations. Instead of multiple assembly plants, the firms relocated the plants that produced such components as brakes, radiators, and transmissions. As Stanley learned, with these relocations the firms were able to benefit from lower wage scales as well as the weaker currency environments. However, it was important for both firms to balance higher shipping costs against gain that might be realized from lower wage rates and weaker currencies than the pound or mark.

A second strategy for both General Motors and Ford was the diversification of their supplier bases into weak-currency and low-wage countries. This end was accomplished by purchasing tires, plastics, and glass in France and Italy, the home of some of their major competitors. Some of their government-owned competitors, like Volkswagen and Renault, had a difficult time employing this multicountry supplier diversification because of political resistance to foreign purchases by government corporations. The situation provided Ford and General Motors with a significant competitive advantage over Volkswagen and Renault.

THE FOREIGN CURRENCY SITUATION FOR GM—EUROPE

Even with all of General Motors' attempts to balance and diversify its foreign exchange, Stanley was amazed to find that the company still had significant imbalances in its relationship between purchases and sales.

Stanley's main assignment for this phase of her training rotation was to identify the magnitude of the firm's exposures in the various key currencies. In addition, since she was new on the job, she was asked to suggest strategies that the firm might use to soften the effect to these exposures. For a veteran in the RTC this assignment could have been done almost intuitively, but for a rookie there were some serious questions that needed to be answered.

QUESTIONS

1. What is the magnitude of the foreign exchange exposure for each of the currencies in Exhibit 1?

2. Does the exposure to the German mark help or hinder the competitive performance of General Motors?

3. How would the parent company in Detroit view the situation if the gross buys and gross sales in Germany were reversed?

4. The data in the case address the currency flows for General Motors—Europe that are tracked by the Regional Treasury Center in Brussels. However, another issue involves the stock of assets that the firm has in Europe. Speculate on what you think might be happening to the value of GM's investment in

Europe in light of the various currency appreciations and depreciations, especially the German mark.

5. What techniques and financial instruments might the RTC employ to control its currency exposure? Explain these techniques in light of the French currency situation.

6. What financial benefits, if any, does General Motors have from locating its treasury function in Belgium? What benefits, if any, accrue to Belgium?

7. What parties, if any, might be harmed by the existence of regional treasury function like GM's?

EXHIBIT 1
Estimated Annual Currency Flows ($ Millions): 1994

Country	Gross Buys	Gross Sales
Germany	$ 5,845	$ 2,400
U.K.	440	2,245
Spain	1,395	1,340
France	380	920
Holland	55	750
Belgium	705	560
Italy	180	530
Austria	485	465
Sweden	0	255
U.S.	255	140
Japan	455	0
Australia	195	0
Other	0	785
	$10,390	$10,390

TOLLISON INTERNATIONAL FINANCE

"I haven't seen the numbers for this project," admitted Rick Gunter, the chief financial officer of Tollison, Inc., to Roberta Gates, a company vice president, "but the thought of opening a new plant in a foreign country scares me. I mean, what do any of us know about Germany and German culture anyway? We could easily screw up not because we don't understand the auto parts business but because we don't understand Germans!"

GENERAL MOTORS

It is easy to find evidence that General Motor's (GM) North American operation has been in decline for many years. Its market share in the United States was an impressive 52 percent in the early 1960s and is down to about 33 percent in 1994. And in 1992 the red ink reached an astonishing $22.5 billion, the largest loss in corporate history. Nor does the future look especially promising. GM has decided to close 21 of its 120 North American plants and eliminate 75,000 of its 370,000 employees over the next three years.

GM's European division stands in remarkable contrast to this bleak scenario. Profits in 1992 were nearly $2 billion, sales have increased for seven consecutive years, and the Opel—a GM car—has actually surpassed the Volkswagen as the most popular car in eastern Germany.

TOLLISON, INC.

Tollison, Inc., headquartered in Darien, Connecticut, has annual sales of $62 million, employs 420 workers, and manufactures parts used by a variety of domestic and foreign companies. For example, it produces components used in electrical, ignition, fuel, and brake systems in cars of General Motors, Ford and Porsche. It also manufactures parts for Honda lawnmowers and John Deere construction equipment. Sales to domestic firms account for over 90 percent of Tollison's revenue and the firm has no overseas plants. Instead, parts for foreign clients are manufactured in the United States and shipped to their ultimate destination, usually Germany and Japan. This may be changing, however.

GM is eager to maintain its European dominance and thinks that one key is to thoroughly modernize a number of its less efficient plants. One such facility is located in Frankfurt, Germany, where GM will install state-of-the-art robotics in an effort to hold unit costs down. It also plans to open a new facility at Eisenbach, Germany in order to keep up with expanding demand.

At first glance all this would appear to be good news for a parts manufacturer like Tollison that has dealt with GM for years. The rub is that GM will require suppliers to offer just-in-time components delivery in order to secure a contract. When Vaughn Westall, Tollison's CEO, learned of this requirement he immediately saw the problem: Either Tollison opens a facility convenient to GM's European operations or it loses GM's European business. And—as Carol Finley, the firm's general manager, pointed out—if GM feels this way, can other car manufacturers like Porsche be far behind?

TOLLISON'S GERMAN PROJECT

Westall quickly formed a committee headed by Finley to investigate possible European locations. With the help of an international consulting firm, the committee recommended that Tollison consider building a plant in Wurzburg, Germany, a location convenient to all the German automakers, which means that the firm would be able to supply components on an as-needed basis. In addition, the facility would be near a rather highly skilled labor pool, an important consideration because Tollison's production methods require a large degree of technical expertise.

The up-front (1994) cost is estimated to be 7.5 million marks, and Tollison believes that it can borrow 40 percent of this from a German bank. Though Tollison is not well known in Germany, management thinks that the loan can be obtained if the bank is convinced that Tollison is serious about the project and provided the loan is adequately secured. In fact, Westall and two other top executives went to Germany a week ago in part to investigate the Wurzburg site and in part to make contact with German banks. Another visit with German banks is planned if Tollison decides to go ahead with the project.

Exhibit 1 shows the incremental cash flow projections for the project. The estimates are made in marks because all sales and expenses will be transacted in the German currency.

These projections are considered to be conservative since they do not consider either the possibility that Tollison may be able to secure contracts with other German car manufacturers like Volkswagen, or that it could supply parts for GM's new Eisenbach plant. And the proposed Wurzburg facility would be large enough to accommodate much of this potential demand. In addition, the cash flows have been adjusted downward to consider the (admittedly small) political risk of the project.

Tollison will convert these estimates into dollars and this requires projections of the future exchange rate between the mark and the dollar. Most international experts think that neither the U.S. nor the German government are interested in entering the foreign exchange market. Nor is it clear that they have the financial clout necessary to influence exchange rates even if they wished. Thus Tollison's management believes that the mark-to-dollar exchange rate will be "market determined" over the period. That is, they think that it is reasonable to assume a floating exchange rate between these currencies. Exhibit 2 shows the mark-to-dollar exchange rate and the inflation history of Germany and the United States for the past ten years.

EXECUTIVE OPINION

The majority of the company's top management favor the project. Indeed, a number of Tollison's executives consider the decision a no-brainer. Finley, for example, argues that if the plant is not built then the firm will lose GM's European business and, quite possibly, Porsche's. Thus she sees the plant as an "absolutely essential defensive move." In addition she cites the "likely possibility" of stiff European trade barriers that would make exports to Europe "very expensive." A plant in Germany would circumvent these barriers.

Finley also thinks that the plant "will undoubtedly help us make inroads in the European market." She is especially optimistic about securing a contract with Volkswagen.

Westall wants to "carefully examine the project's financials" but he is obviously eager to enter the European market. "We make quality parts at a competitive price," he notes. "And we've sold to GM and Porsche *despite* the fact that we've not been a convenient supplier. I agree with Finley; we could hit it big in Europe if we can promise prompt delivery of needed parts. Look, we've discussed building a German facility before but never really pursued the idea. Maybe GM's ultimatum is the kick-in-the-pants we need."

CONCERNS

Some executives led by Harold Baines, the company's treasurer, are worried that this project is much riskier than Tollison's typical projects. Baines notes, "We rarely have to deal with sales estimates of the magnitude of this project." Another problem, as he sees it, is that Tollison not only has to estimate sales and costs for the German facility, but it also has to forecast future exchange rates. Thus, Baines argues, there are "more ways to be wrong on this project." He believes that it needs to be cautiously approached and thoroughly analyzed and, at a minimum, the discount rate should be raised above the customary 12 percent.

Gunter, the CFO, worries that Tollison's lack of familiarity with the German culture could hurt in "unanticipated ways." He's heard, for example, that Germans tend to be much more direct and straightforward in their social and business dealings. Consequently, behavior that would be rude and abrasive by American standards would be perfectly reasonable and acceptable to a German. And any hint or suggestion that it is otherwise would risk alienating the Germans.

Westall thinks that the point is well made. "If you want to do business with people they have to like you, at least a little. And this won't happen unless our executives understand German culture." At the same time he also believes that this is not an issue of "real concern" since the facility would use a number of German executives plus Tollison's American managers would be thoroughly trained in the German culture before they went abroad. Westall emphasizes, however, that "cultural differences do exist and this is easy to forget when dealing with people who not only look like we do, but many of whom also speak fluent English."

Baines also wonders about the desirability of using a German rather than an American bank. Any borrowing is likely to be a five-year term loan and he notes that German rates are about three hundred basis points higher than the rate available at United States financial institutions. In addition, there is considerably more hassle involved in obtaining a German loan since Tollison is not well known abroad. All things considered, Baines concludes that "it makes more sense to borrow locally."

QUESTIONS

1. GM will make any payments for parts at its German plants in marks. In fact, GM informed Tollison that any contract must be in marks. How do you explain GM's insistence?

2. (a) Tollison could borrow in the United States with a lot less hassle and bother than Germany. What advantages, if any, are there to securing a loan from a German bank?

   (b) One Tollison executive wonders why the company doesn't borrow in the United States because "the rate we'd get at a German bank is about three hundred basis points above a comparable loan in the states." Evaluate this argument.

3. Consider the following parity.

$$E_t/E_o = [(1 + rf_G)/(1 + rf_{US})]^t$$

where E_t = mark/$ exchange rate in t years
E_o = this exchange rate at present ($t = 0$)
rf_G = risk-free interest rate in Germany for an investment of t years
rf_{US} = this rate for the United States

The firm's financial manager will use the above parity to estimate the mark-to-dollar exchange rate for each year of the project. Though technical accuracy requires separate estimates of rf_G and rf_{US} for each year, in the interest of simplicity the firm will assume that one risk-free rate is appropriate for each country over the life of the project.

Using the above parity and assuming rf_G = .10 and rf_{US} = .07, complete the table below.

Year	Exchange Rate: Marks/$
1994 ($t = 0$)	1.50
1995 ($t + 1$)	
1996 ($t + 2$)	1.59
1997 ($t + 3$)	1.63
1998 ($t + 4$)	1.68
1999 ($t + 5$)	1.72
2000 ($t + 6$)	
2001 ($t + 7$)	

4. Tollison uses a 12 percent hurdle rate for its "typical" projects. Do you think a higher rate should be used for this project? Defend your position.

5. (a) Calculate the NPV of the project (use a discount rate consistent with your answer to question 4).

   (b) Based on your previous answer and other information in the case, what do you recommend the firm do? Defend your advice.

6. (a) An international consulting firm believes that Germany's inflation relative to that in the United States will be "much larger than investors think." If the firm is right, would the estimates of E_t in question 3 have to be adjusted? If so, explain the direction of the adjustment and the theoretical rationale for the adjustment.

   (b) For the purpose of analyzing this project, would you recommend that the estimates in question 3 be used, or would you recommend a new set of estimates incorporating the view of the international consulting firm? Explain your reasoning.

7. Suppose that the current mark-to-dollar exchange rate, that is, E_o, is being pegged by the German authorities. Specifically, suppose that the mark-to-dollar exchange rate is too low, that is, it takes too few marks to buy a dollar relative to the market-determined rate. How, if at all, would this affect your exchange rate forecasts? Explain.

8. The conventional wisdom is that a prudent current ratio (CA/CL) for firms in the auto parts industry is 2. Tollison's financial manager is recommending, however, that Tollison use a current ratio of 1 for the German facility. Does this make financial sense? Explain.

9. (a) Consider the information in Exhibit 2. Is the general downward trend in the mark-to-dollar exchange rate consistent with the inflation rates in the two countries? Explain.

   (b) Note the upward trend in the mark-to-dollar exchange rate in question 3. Assuming flexible exchange rates, what implicit assumption is being made about future rates of inflation in Germany and the United States?

EXHIBIT 1
Cash Flow Estimates in Marks of German Project (000s)

			Year				
$t = 0$	$t + 1$	$t + 2$	$t + 3$	$t + 4$	$t + 5$	$t + 6$	$t + 7$
1994	1995	1996	1997	1998	1999	2000	2001
(7,500)	2,500	2,700	2,900	3,000	3,100	3,100	3,500

EXHIBIT 2
Exchange Rates and Inflation for Germany and the United States: 1983–1993

	Exchange Rate		Inflation	
Year	Marks/$	%Change	U.S.	Germany
1983	2.55	NA	3.2	3.3
1984	2.85	11.8	4.3	2.4
1985	2.46	−13.7	3.6	2.2
1986	2.17	−11.8	1.9	−.1
1987	1.80	−17.1	3.7	.2
1988	1.76	−2.3	4.0	1.3
1989	1.88	6.8	4.8	2.8
1990	1.62	−13.9	5.4	2.7
1991	1.66	2.4	5.2	3.5
1992	1.55	−6.7	2.9	3.2
1993	1.54	−0.1	2.7	2.9

C A S E 4 1

SLOVO WOOD PRODUCTS VALUATION

Natural Toys (NT) is a successful manufacturer of wooden toys and wood furniture for children. Though it has some overseas markets, all of its production facilities are in the United States, and its market is overwhelmingly in the United States. It is therefore ironic that it is considering the purchase of Slovo Wood Products, a government-owned company located in Lithuania.

Lithuania declared independence from the Soviet Union on March 11, 1990, and the last Soviet troops left in 1993. Lithuania is now a democratic nation which embraces private property and free enterprise. The transition was not without pain—the industrial output of state enterprises fell an estimated 60 percent—but the privatized companies are now expanding.

The government has not been able to sell every company: Slovo Wood Products is one of the remaining firms. When Slovo's customers got a chance to buy relatively cheap, high-quality competing foreign products, they turned away from Slovo in droves. Slovo has struggled to stay alive, and its current existence can best be described as zombie-like. The company made no profits in 1995, though they were able to cover their cash costs. The operating rate has been deteriorating as the old machinery breaks down more and more often, and the plant now runs only a third of the time because of frequent breakdowns.

The government is anxious to get rid of this facility; it has offered to sell the company for $1 million which will go directly into the company to purchase new equipment and increase working capital. Slovo, however, will come encumbered with $10 million in 20-year debt which bears an 8 percent rate of interest. This is not a market-determined rate, but rather represents special concessionary financing which is offered as part of the deal. Basically, the government has been loaning Slovo money for years, and this is a "work out" to them. That is, the government gives a lower-than-market interest rate and generous repayment terms. There is no sinking fund required on the debt. The annual interest payment is 8 percent and NT's management estimates that the market rate on this debt is 12 percent. Interest payments are due at the end of each of the next twenty years.

NT will buy the firm through a shell subsidiary so that the parent corporation will not be responsible for the firm if default occurs. In other words, NT will set up a separate subsidiary, Natural Toys/Lithuania. NT will own all the stock of Natural Toys/Lithuania, but it will not be responsible for any of their debts. They are in the same position and enjoy the same protection as any other shareholder—if Natural Toys/Lithuania goes belly up, NT will not be responsible for any of their subsidiary's debts.

Slovo Wood is a very attractive prospective to NT. First, Slovo produces a number of products which, with some modifications, can supply the NT plants in the United States. Slovo has the advantages of abundant supplies of raw materials as well as relatively low-cost labor (wages average about $100 per month). The production facilities are, to be sure, out of date and use too much labor by American standards. However, the lower cost of labor in Lithuania makes this much less of a problem. Also, the government will allow NT to fire up to half the employees if it takes over the firm.

While mass firing may seem like pretty stern medicine, it is probably necessary; Slovo Wood has far too many people and cannot continue losing money at the present rate. With fewer employees, more effective equipment, and NT's technical expertise, Slovo will quickly become a low-cost—and profitable—producer.

Management expects that sales will be $20 million a year for the next twenty years. Slovo's operating margin, that is, (EBIT + Dep.)/sales, is estimated to be 6.5 percent, and capital spending to replace equipment will run 1 percent of sales per year. Principal on the 8-percent $10 million loan from the Lithuanian government is not due until the end of year 20, and at that time Slovo's terminal value is estimated to equal the debt due.

Taxes are not a consideration. In the 1980s, NT made a number of ill-fated attempts to diversify, and the resulting losses earned NT such a large tax carry-over that NT can ignore taxes.

NT figures that its own cost of capital is about 11 percent, comprised of 25 percent debt at an 8 percent cost and 75 percent equity with a cost of 12 percent. Despite the fact that Slovo is located in a different country, NT will use it as a parts supplier to its own operations, so it feels that the business risk is about the same. And though there is some currency exposure and potential losses on currency fluctuations, these risks are likely to be small because the government has adopted a policy of tying the currency (called the litas) to the dollar. In any case, if the litas depreciates, NT will just get its supplies at a cheaper price in dollars. And while Lithuania's currency *might* appreciate, it is not likely; Lithuania's economy is pretty much flat on its back and economic progress will be slow for quite a while. On balance, NT is willing to ignore the currency risk.

NT realizes that Slovo may be risky but it figures that even if Slovo goes belly up, they will have all their cash back in a little over three years, and they can just walk away from the project. Of course, if Slovo turns out well, then management knows that it will probably put in more investment and expand output. For the time being, however, they like the idea of making this wager.

QUESTIONS

1. Estimate the market value of Slovo's debt.

2. (a) How would Slovo's unlevered cost of capital compare to that of Natural Toys? Explain.

   (b) According to Miller and Modigliani (MM), what is NT's unlevered cost of capital? (Note that NT exists in a no-tax world.)

3. Given their current capital structure, do Slovo and Natural Toys have the same cost of capital? Explain.

4. It is not clear from the case if the debt is transferable. That is, since the debt was offered on a concessionary basis, it may contain a "due on sale" clause so that if Natural Toys sold Slovo, it would have to pay off the debt. Would that affect your recommendation on what Natural Toys should do? If so, why and in what way?

5. Do you recommend that NT use debt or equity to raise the $1 million necessary to purchase Slovo? Defend your choice.

6. The purchase of Slovo can be likened to the purchase of an option. Discuss.

7. (a) Based on the information in the case, Slovo will generate a cash flow of $300,000 per year for the stockholders of Natural Toys. Explain how this was derived.

   (b) What is the appropriate discount rate to use when calculating the present value of these cash flows? What is the present value at that interest rate?

8. Should Natural Toys make the purchase? Defend your recommendation.

EXHIBIT 1
The 1995 Income Statement of Slovo Wood Products ($ Millions)

Sales	$ 15.0
Cost of goods sold	10.5
Gross margin	4.5
Operating expenses	4.5
Depreciation	0.2
EBIT	(0.2)
Interest	0.8
Earnings before taxes	(1.0)
Taxes	0.0
Net income	($1.0)

EXHIBIT 2
The 1995 Balance Sheet of Slovo Wood Products ($ Millions)

Assets	
Cash	$0.1
Accounts receivable	1.2
Inventory	1.8
Current assets	3.1
Net fixed	10.0
Total assets	$13.1
Liabilities and Equity	
Accounts payable	$1.3
Other current	1.7
Current liabilities	3.0
Bank loans	10.0
Equity	0.1
Total liabilities & equity	$13.1

PART IX

MISCELLANEOUS TOPICS

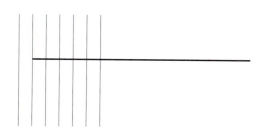

C A S E 4 2

LA POSTA MEXICAN RESTAURANTS, INC.
FINANCIAL ANALYSIS AND BUSINESS ETHICS

Cindy Garcia was putting the finishing touches on her financial analysis for La Posta Mexican Restaurants for the 1994 Annual Institutional Investment Conference at the Four Seasons Hotel in Dallas. The conference was sponsored by her employer, Dillon Sutton and Company, a Dallas-based regional investment banking firm. Cindy was not entirely satisfied with the outcome of her analysis, and she knew that her boss, Lazar Freed, the director of institutional research, was even less satisfied with the results of her analysis. He told her that the people on the corporate finance side of the firm would be furious about her analysis and proposed recommendation.

CINDY GARCIA'S BACKGROUND

Cindy was a senior analyst in the research department specializing in retail industries including food retailing. She has a B.S. degree in accounting from the University of Texas at Austin. Upon graduation, she spent two years in public accounting with Peat Marwick, during which time she earned the CPA designation. She then completed her MBA at the Wharton School of the University of Pennsylvania at which time she joined her current employer, Dillon Sutton and Company. During her three years with the firm, she completed her Certified Financial Analyst (CFA) designation and received her first promotion from financial analyst to senior financial analyst. Last year, she was named to the second team of a prestigious national magazine's All-Star Analyst Team.

Her current position required her to write research reports on retail companies which have ties to Dillon Sutton and/or retail firms which are especially important players in the Texas marketplace. She loved her work, and she was

highly regarded by institutional money managers. They especially respected her work on the companies for which Dillon Sutton acted as the lead underwriter on Initial Public Offerings (IPOs). In addition to those IPO companies, she followed such companies as Lone Star Steak House, Brinker International, Perkins Family Restaurants, Neiman Marcus, McDonalds, and seven or eight other firms including La Posta.

LA POSTA MEXICAN RESTAURANTS

The research report she would be making tomorrow emphasizes the expected performance of the chain over the next eighteen months. Her findings and recommendations would be a significant input into the investment decisions of portfolio managers who didn't follow La Posta very closely but respected Dillon Sutton and Cindy's information on this attractive high-growth company.

La Posta Mexican Restaurants was founded in the late 1970s but didn't go public until May 1992 with Dillon Sutton acting as the lead underwriter in the syndicate. The initial price was $12 per share. Between May 1992 and today (May 1994) the stock rose quickly to $22 per share and then in recent months has dropped back to a range of $12 to $14 per share. The founders of the company, Tom Pearson and Ben Sanchez, still own 48 percent of the outstanding shares, but have expressed an interest in reducing their ownership position. The precipitous drop in share price has the two owners upset because they can't understand the market's treatment of the company in light of the brilliant growth record and potential for continued growth.

Sales and profits have more than doubled since the IPO and the owners expect sales and profits to double again between 1994 and 1996. The company currently has a little over 100 restaurants concentrated in the largest cities in Texas (Houston, Dallas, Austin, San Antonio, and El Paso). In addition to rapid internal growth, the company has accelerated its growth by the recent acquisition of a small chain of Mexican restaurants called Taco Amigo, which has twenty stores in the same large Texas cities.

THE PROBLEM FACING CINDY GARCIA

Cindy Garcia is very bullish on the management of La Posta as well as the firm's long-term growth and profits prospects. However, her pro forma financial analysis indicates that La Posta is having some difficulty "digesting" the recent purchase of the twenty Taco Amigo restaurants. Her estimates indicate that EPS growth would be slowed by a combination of higher training costs to integrate the new employees of Taco Amigo and slower than expected sales at existing Taco Amigo locations—at least relative to La Posta stores. She estimates that these factors would slow La Posta's earning growth for the next three quarters.

As a result of these factors she thought she should lower her estimated EPS figures by $.03 for 1994 and $.04 for 1995 compared to her earlier estimates, which she released in January 1994. Her forecast EPS for 1994 and 1995 was $.71 and $.91, respectively. Her estimates were approximately $.03 lower for both years than the consensus of the four other analysts who follow the company for other investment banking firms. Her data was based in part on information which she generated through her contacts in the Texas fast-food industry. This information would not be readily available to all analysts, but she has developed a strong information network in the industry, and it had helped her in the past to provide remarkably accurate forecasts.

Even without her downward revision in EPS forecasts, the stock has fallen dramatically over the past nine months, from $22 per share to $12.75 per share today. Restaurant stocks have not done well lately after the end of the euphoria surrounding fast-food companies such as Boston Chicken and Lone Star Steak House.

Cindy had been rating La Posta both a strong short-term and long-term buy. Based on her latest pro forma analysis she thought her short-term recommendation should be lowered to a neutral rating while maintaining a strong long-term buy recommendation. When she discussed her pro forma analysis and proposed lower rating with her boss, Lazar Freed, he expressed a combination of dismay and deep concern. There were even some veiled statements that such a report would not sit well with some influential senior people in the corporate finance department.

It was well known in Dillon Sutton that La Posta would probably be interested in an additional stock offering in the near future to finance the aggressive growth plans of the firm. Freed pointed out that her adverse review could have a detrimental impact on the price of La Posta stock since she was such a respected analyst of the restaurant firm. And everyone at Dillon Sutton knew that Pearson and Sanchez were already upset about the recent large drop in the price of the stock.

Given that the investment banking business had slowed in recent months as a result of fewer IPOs, Freed and others in Dillon Sutton didn't want to risk losing an important client. Freed was not very subtle in pointing out that Cindy's bonus was closely linked to overall company profits. He also made some oblique statement about the importance of being a team player when times get tough.

CINDY'S DECISION

It is 1:15 A.M., ten hours before her presentation to the institutional investors conference. She has to make some decision on how to describe her view on La Posta growth prospects. She knows that her report will be distributed to the firm's small retail customers after the conference is over. She ponders how they will react to her report.

QUESTIONS

1. How important do you think Cindy's information and rating would be for institutional investors? What would be its impact on stock price?

2. Who are the stakeholders of Cindy's information?

3. What obligation should Cindy feel toward the institutional investors? Retail customers?

4. Should Cindy write her report to reflect the wishes of her boss and the other executives in Dillon Sutton?

5. How would you handle this situation if you were Cindy?

EXHIBIT 1
Pro Forma Income Statement: 1994 and 1995 (Millions)

	Actual 1993	(1994: est.)	(1995: est.)
Revenues	$82.4	$93.0	$107.4
Expenses	57.0	63.1	71.3
Income from operations	25.4	30.1	36.1
Interest expense	2.1	1.1	1.2
Income before taxes	23.3	29.0	34.9
Taxes	(10.3)	(13.1)	(14.5)
Net income	13.0	15.9	20.4
EPS	$.58	$.71	$.91
Analyst consensus		$.74	$.94

BOE OF COLOMBIA BUSINESS ETHICS

Boe Chemical is one of the largest chemical companies in the world, and annual sales in its most recent (1996) fiscal year exceeded $10 billion. Products include natural gas, coal, agricultural and industrial chemicals, nylon, polyester and other fibers, adhesives, and even pharmaceuticals. Boe has plants in more than two dozen countries, and foreign sales account for nearly 40 percent of total sales.

The firm has a plant in a suburb of Bogota, Colombia, that employs over 2,000 people. The plant accounts for about $400 million in sales of polyester, a fiber used in clothing, industrial products, carpet, and tires. The complex is situated on 25 acres and, at first sight, resembles a penitentiary. Security is quite tight, largely because of the constant presence of Colombian bandits.

Ryan Dansforth and Kyle Manning are the firm's plant manager and purchasing agent, respectively. Both are Americans, which is a bit unusual since it is the policy of most companies operating in a foreign country to use a significant amount of local labor. The plant manager is usually a local, trained by the firm, who is likely to hire relatives for many administrative positions, including the job of purchasing agent. In fact, Boe had a Colombian plant manager until he left a few months ago, apparently to take a prestigious government position, and took his relatives with him. Dansforth and Manning are therefore merely "temporary help" until suitable local replacements can be found and trained.

Boe operates in industries where long-term agreements with suppliers are not unusual. For example, it is common to have a 10-year contract with a clause that the vendor can match any lower price that Boe might be offered during the contract period. The firm's purchasing agent negotiates these contracts and, as might be expected, is the target of many a salesperson.

Manning seems to relish the attention he receives from the vendors. He frequently has a business lunch with a salesperson and never has had to pay the bill. An avid golfer, he is often invited to play at the one course in the area. And one ethylene glycol salesperson even presented Manning with a $1,200 set of clubs on the purchasing agent's birthday. Perhaps the biggest perk came in January.

When one vendor learned that Manning was a big football fan, he arranged tickets and travel and provided accommodations to the 1996 Super Bowl.

Dansforth has observed all the attention Manning receives and how Manning actively encourages this attention. He sincerely believes that all of this is not in the best interest of the company and calls Manning into his office one Tuesday morning.

DANSFORTH Kyle, we both know that a purchasing agent attracts salespeople like cookies attract children. Some attention is normal, but I think you're overdoing it. I'd go so far as to say that you almost tease those guys. The fact is that these salespeople are trying to bribe you because you're the purchasing agent. You can accept the small stuff—the lunches, the golf, that sort of thing. But the big items—the golf clubs, the trips—have got to stop.

Manning realizes that Dansforth could fire him immediately if he shows any sign of disagreement. Still, Manning feels that his personal integrity and business judgment are being questioned, and he feels a strong need to respond.

MANNING In my opinion, nothing in my dealings with salespeople has been illegal or unethical. Cite me even one example where I cost the company money in my position as purchasing agent. I do my job. And maybe I do create the expectation that I'll favor one salesperson over another. But that's their problem, not mine. Anyway, a lot of these salespeople are just nice and thoughtful. I like to socialize, so it's natural to be friendly. Besides, believe it or not, a lot of business gets discussed at lunch, on the golf course, and, yes, even on the Super Bowl trip.

Dansforth is surprised at Manning's response and is tempted to simply make it clear that he is ordering and not requesting that Manning change his behavior.

DANSFORTH Maybe you haven't cost the company any money to this point. But it is inevitable that a person's business judgment will be affected, though in your case I'm sure it wouldn't be consciously. As I see it, driving a car too fast is wrong even if the speeder hasn't been in an accident. And I'm concerned that you're not presenting the proper Boe image. Look, like I said, take the lunches and the golf. These are normal business items. But the big stuff has got to stop.

Manning senses that he'd better not press the issue and agrees to comply. Still, he feels that he's being treated unfairly, especially since he thinks the company has been inconsistent in what it considers appropriate professional behavior.

A recent example involved the plant's compressor. A few months ago it broke down, nearly halting daily production. Colombia has a law that does not allow a firm to import any product until the government has determined it is not available from a Colombian manufacturer. And such approval can literally take many months as the government "investigates" the situation. Boe's CEO hired the wife of Colombia's chief of customs for $15,000 to act as an "agent" for Boe.

The objective, of course, was to get the Colombian government to look the other way regarding enforcement of the law. In fact, approval was obtained overnight to import a new compressor.

Nor is this an isolated example. It is a way of life in many foreign countries to hire agents whose sole purpose is to allow a firm to circumvent local laws.

In addition, Manning doesn't have to look far to find examples of Boe's top executives accepting perks. One senior manager, an avid fisherman, went on a costly fishing trip with the mayor of Bogota. Manning doesn't know who paid for the trip, but he knows it wasn't Boe's manager. The trip was justified on the grounds that it is vital to cultivate a good relationship with local government officials. Had the manager not gone on the trip—or so it was argued—the mayor would have been insulted.

Back at his Colombian apartment that evening, Dansforth reflects on the meeting with Manning, and he is having second thoughts on his handling of the situation. Dansforth admits that Manning did not spend company funds for his own benefit. He recalls one of Boe's CEOs who uses company funds to maintain three country club memberships and to purchase his own plane. These items are justified on the grounds that they are necessary to develop and maintain important business contacts and present the proper corporate image.

Further, Dansforth randomly pulled a dozen of Manning's purchases and concluded that all the sampled items were indeed bought at highly competitive prices. Thus, while Dansforth can't be absolutely sure, it does appear that Manning tries to get the best possible deal from sales representatives.

QUESTIONS

1. (a) If Manning weren't the purchasing agent, do you think the attention he receives from salespeople would stop?

   (b) Dansforth labels the lunches, the golf, the golf clubs, and the Super Bowl trip as "bribes." Do you agree? Why or why not?

2. Do you think it is unethical for Manning to accept the items listed in question 1(b)? Defend your answer.

3. (a) Under what circumstances, if any, is it proper for a firm to hire an "agent" to circumvent local laws?

   (b) Consider the compressor example cited in the case. Was it ethical for the company to hire the wife of the chief of customs as an agent? Explain your position.

4. As stated in the case, in order to locate in a foreign country, an outside firm must often hire locals for important supervisory positions. These supervisors commonly practice nepotism, hiring relatives to fill managerial and

administrative jobs. This practice does not always result in employing the most capable individuals; nonetheless, the top management rarely interferes in the hiring practices of these supervisors. Do you think it is fair that management allows this nepotism to continue? Defend your answer.

5. Executives in many firms use company money to purchase such items as tickets to the World Series, country club memberships, even airplanes. Under what circumstances, if any, do you think such purchases are appropriate? Fully explain your position.

6. Was Dansforth's order to Manning appropriate? That is, is it appropriate for Manning to accept from salespeople the small items like a lunch and not the big items like a set of golf clubs? Defend your answer.

7. What differences, if any, are there between personal ethics and business ethics?

MORROW CONSTRUCTION FINANCIAL LEASE

During the past six months, William "Billy" Morrow has been recovering from a serious illness while his son, Bill Jr., has run the family's company, Morrow Construction (MC). It is now Billy's first day back and he is fuming. Three months ago his son purchased four pavers at a cost of $600,000. Now MC needs asphalt equipment costing $580,000 and there is no available cash.

Morrow Construction decided to manufacture its own asphalt after Ted Sebrof, an MC manager, realized the company could save in two ways by doing so. First, it was 25 percent cheaper for MC to produce its own asphalt rather than buy it directly. Second, making it would reduce labor costs, since workers waited an average of four hours for purchased asphalt to arrive at the construction site. "Manufacturing our own asphalt lets us get the asphalt where we want it, when we want it," Sebrof pointed out. The equipment was extremely profitable, and according to Billy, there was "no way" its purchase would be postponed.

The problem was financing. Billy was upset that the pavers had been bought. Their purchase wasn't critical, and more important, the firm had exhausted its borrowing limit with the bank and used virtually all its cash. "You know a bank won't accept asphalt equipment as collateral on a loan!" Billy screamed at his son. "You mortgaged the family's real estate to get the pavers and there's nothing left to pledge! Poor planning, that's what I'd call it! We could have borrowed the funds at 10 percent. Now we're stuck with leasing, and you know how expensive that can be! If we lease, the yearly depreciation charge is lost, and that's a lot of tax savings since we pay taxes at a 30 percent rate."

Billy then asked his accountant, Myra Cunningham, to evaluate the two leasing proposals the company had received. One is from the Bradford Equipment Corporation, the other is from Leasing Unlimited. The proposals are similar in many respects. First, MC would lose the yearly depreciation in either case. Second, each leasing firm would be responsible for any insurance and property taxes. These items would total $5,000 a year if MC purchased the asphalt equipment. Third, both leases are noncancellable; that is, MC would be legally obligated for all payments even if it stops using the equipment, a possibility that is extremely remote. Consequently, MC cannot cancel the lease except by paying off the entire contract, and should it default MC could be forced into bankruptcy. Finally, both leases permit MC to purchase the equipment at fair market value at the end of the leasing period, an option that the firm is very likely to exercise.

The two proposals, however, are quite different in their treatment of the investment tax credit the equipment qualifies for, in the timing and amount of the lease payments, and in the provision of maintenance. Bradford Equipment's proposal is a five-year lease with six yearly payments of $100,000 each, and the first payment would be due immediately. Bradford Equipment would receive the 10 percent investment tax credit, and MC would be responsible for all maintenance of the asphalt equipment. Leasing Unlimited's proposal is also a five-year lease with five yearly payments of $153,000, but the first payment would not be due until the end of year 1. Leasing Unlimited will allow MC to keep the 10 percent investment tax credit and will provide up to $10,000 a year in maintenance.

Leasing Unlimited emphasized that their proposal provides some maintenance and gives MC more "up front" money since MC could keep the ITC and there is no immediate leasing payment. Bradford Equipment said it keeps the ITC and does not provide maintenance in order to keep the lease payments down. As evidence it pointed out that their lease requires a total of $600,000 (= $100,000 × 6), while Leasing Unlimited's requires $765,000 (= $153,000 × 5).

Billy said he found the issue "a bit confusing." He also admitted he favored the Leasing Unlimited proposal because of the maintenance arrangement. Cunningham said she would try to "make some sense out of the information" and pointed out that MC did, in fact, have an alternative to leasing. She knows private investors who would be willing to accept third mortgages on properties the Morrow family owns. In addition, loans could be obtained from the companies that hold Morrow's tax-sheltered investments. "Of course, this money won't be cheap," she was quick to note. "I estimate we could raise the money we need at a rate of 11 percent after taxes."

As Cunningham reviewed the proposals of the leasing companies she noticed that neither discussed the residual value of the asphalt equipment at the end of the leasing period. It was Billy's best guess that the equipment would have an after-tax market value of $200,000 in five years, and he feels a conservative or minimum estimate is $130,000 (also after taxes). It is clear that the lost residual value represents an opportunity cost of leasing, but Cunningham is unsure whether to use Billy's best guess or minimum estimate. She also thinks it is a good idea to carefully check her estimate on the after-tax rate at which MC could borrow.

QUESTIONS

Assume if MC buys the equipment that depreciation is straight line over five years on the cost of the equipment less the investment tax credit. The relevant tax rate is 30 percent.

1. Which of the two residual value estimates should Cunningham use when evaluating the leasing proposals? Justify your choice.

2. (a) How much up-front financing does each proposal give MC?

   (b) Estimate the yearly cost (years 1–5) of each proposal.

3. (a) Morrow Construction could have borrowed the money to purchase the asphalt equipment at a before-tax rate of 10 percent. Evaluate each lease assuming this option exists.

   (b) Evaluate each lease against the borrowing option MC actually has, the 11-percent after-tax rate estimated by Myra Cunningham.

4. Complete the table below.

The NPV of Each Proposal at Various After-Tax Interest Rates

After-Tax Rate	Leasing Unlimited ($)	Bradford Equipment ($)
0.07	−37,200	−41,800
0.09	−2,100	−13,000
0.10	+14,400	—
0.11	+30,000	+13,300
0.12	—	+25,600

5. Use the completed table in question 4 to calculate the equivalent interest charge (EIC) of each proposal. That is, determine the interest rate that equates the amount of financing each leasing alternative provides with the present value of future cash outflows.

6. What do your answers in 3(b) and 5 suggest is the cheaper leasing alternative? The cheapest way to finance the equipment? Explain your choices.

7. How much more financing does the Leasing Unlimited proposal give MC? What is the *incremental* EIC of this money?

8. Suppose that Myra Cunningham is wrong and MC does not have the option to borrow money to buy the equipment. Suppose also that the only way that MC would be able to use the equipment is to lease it. Explain a technique for evaluating the two leasing proposals in this situation.

STINSON PAVING FINANCIAL LEASE

Stinson Paving, specializing in the development and construction of private roads, was started in 1951 by Tim Stinson. His younger brother, Jeff, became a partner in 1960, and the firm grew despite the fact that neither brother was especially ambitious or aggressive in seeking new business.

By 1990 annual sales totaled nearly $3 million when the brothers sold the business to Phillip Hartman. Hartman proceeded to diversify the firm's construction business and actively sought state, local, and federal contracts on roads and bridges. And Hartman has been successful. Sales in 1996 exceeded $8 million, primarily because of the firm's extensive government highway contracts.

BONDING

One key to obtaining government contracts has been Stinson's bonding capacity, that is, its ability to obtain surety bonds. These bonds are issued by surety companies (often a large insurance company like Aetna) and are a guarantee that the contractor has sufficient funds to complete any project the firm is bidding on. A surety bond is therefore a form of insurance and in essence is protection against frivolous bidding by contractors.

The ability of a firm like Stinson to obtain such bonds is a prerequisite to doing any significant construction project. Indeed, the Miller Act of 1933 makes it mandatory for firms to have a surety bond to obtain federal contracts, and most state and local government projects require one as well. It is easy to see that a firm's bonding capacity (the maximum value of the bonds a surety company will extend to a contractor) sets a clear limit on the contractor's business. It is also easy to see why surety bonds have frequently been called "the lifeline of the construction industry."

Obtaining such bonds is becoming more difficult, however. Many surety companies incurred significant losses in the mid to late eighties and some even left the bonding business entirely. With the survivors nervous about possible losses, bonding costs are likely to rise sharply and bonding requirements will surely stiffen.

Hartman is very protective of the firm's bondability and realizes that a surety company looks carefully at a contractor's balance sheet as well as its technical expertise and reputation. He has always been eager to maintain as low a debt ratio as possible in order to present a strong balance sheet. This debt-ratio concern is especially troublesome to Hartman given the tightening of bonding standards and is something of an issue regarding two new scrapers the company needs.

A scraper is used in road construction and essentially moves dirt from one spot to another. The firm has decided that it wants two Caterpillar 627 scrapers, which have a "cut to fill" range of nearly 6,000 yards. That is, the scrapers can remove dirt and transport it to another area up to 6,000 yards away, quite a large distance for this type of equipment.

These scrapers cost $300,000 each and Hartman is not clear how they should be financed. His first reaction was to use all equity, which would lower the firm's debt-to-equity ratio. A conversation with the firm's banker, however, made it quite tempting to borrow the needed funds. The bank is willing to lend at 10 percent, a rate Hartman finds a bit tempting. He believes that inflationary expectations are rising, which should result in higher interest rates.

A LEASING PROPOSAL

The financing waters were further muddied when Hartman received a leasing proposal from WTE Capital, one of the nation's largest and most reputable leasing companies. The lease would run five years and include six yearly payments of $108,000 each, with the first payment due immediately. The lease is noncancellable and Stinson Paving must pay off the entire contract if it wants an "early out." Stinson Paving would also be responsible for the annual insurance and maintenance expenses of $1,000 and $25,000 respectively. In addition, the trucks could be purchased at fair market value at the end of the leasing term.

What Hartman finds attractive, however, is the fact that WTE claims the lease can be structured to keep it off the balance sheet. If so, Hartman reasons, he can present a stronger balance sheet to surety companies than if he borrowed the funds. His initial reaction to the lease is quite favorable. It seems to involve the advantage of debt, a fixed and presumably "low" borrowing cost, without the balance sheet disadvantage of debt.

Hartman has reviewed the financing possibilities with Tina Montieth, the firm's accountant. Montieth said she will evaluate the lease but needs to know how Hartman intends to finance the scrapers if the lease is not selected. When Hartman asked why this was necessary, Montieth said this dictates the interest rate she will use in the evaluation.

If the funds were borrowed, she explained, the after-tax borrowing rate would be appropriate. If all equity were used, then a 16 percent after-tax rate, the firm's cost of equity, is the correct discount factor. If Hartman were to use a combination of debt and equity, she would then evaluate the lease using the firm's weighted average cost of capital (WACC) of 14 percent. She will also assume, for the purpose of analysis, straight line depreciation over five years on the full cost of the scrapers. The relevant tax rate is 40 percent.

A BETTER DEAL?

Montieth also said it may be possible to bargain for a better leasing payment from WTE. An important factor in setting these payments is the residual value assumption used by the lessor, that is, the assumed market value of the scrapers at the end of the contract. A low residual value implies high annual payments. If she could convince WTE that its residual value was too conservative, she believes she could obtain a lower annual payment. One difficulty, though, is that the lessor's residual value estimate is considered confidential information and is not readily available. Montieth, however, believes she can deduce the figure WTE is using.

Hartman feels that the scrapers, given proper maintenance and normal use, have an economic life of 10 to 15 years. And he thinks that a "very reasonable" estimate is that in five years the scrapers will be worth 40 percent of their original cost. He believes that an independent and objective appraisal would reach the same figure. He admits, however, that this estimate is about as precise as any other business forecast the firm makes. A "quite conservative and probably lower limit" prediction would be 25 percent. That is, Hartman believes it is unlikely that the residual value of the scrapers in five years will be less than 25 percent of their original cost.

QUESTIONS

1. Evaluate Montieth's argument that the interest rate used to evaluate the lease depends on how the scrapers would be financed if the lease is not selected.

2. What is the appropriate residual value estimate to use in the lease evaluation? Explain.

3. Calculate the NPV of the lease.

4. (a) By accounting conventions, if a lease meets any of the following conditions it is classified as a capital lease and must be shown directly on the balance sheet.

   i. The lease transfers ownership of the asset to the lessee before the lease expires.

   ii. The lease allows the lessee to purchase the asset at a bargain price.

    iii. The term of the lease is equal to, or greater than, 75 percent of the asset's estimated useful life.

    iv. The present value of the lease payments is equal to, or greater than, 90 percent of the asset's market value.

    Will the lease Hartman is considering appear directly on the balance sheet? Explain.

  (b) One factor that surety companies look at is a firm's debt ratio. Bondability is enhanced with a low debt ratio. If this lease is selected, how will the debt ratio look compared to a loan? All equity? Explain your answer.

5. Based on your previous answers and other information in the case, how do you think the scrapers should be financed? Justify your choice.

6. Montieth thinks she may be able to negotiate a better lease payment in part because she believes the leasing company is using a residual value estimate that is too low.

  (a) Why would a low residual value assumption result in a high lease payment?

  (b) The pre-tax return and residual value assumption used by the lessor are considered to be confidential information. Fortunately for Montieth, a confidant has informed her that the leasing company strives for a 12-percent before-tax return. Armed with this information, what residual value estimate is the leasing company using?

7. (a) Assume the leasing company wants a 12 percent before-tax return. If Montieth can convince WTE that a $120,000 per scraper residual value is appropriate, what annual leasing payment would WTE give Stinson Paving?

  (b) Does this affect your answer to question 5? Explain.

AT&T
DIVIDEND POLICY

On January 9, 1982, AT&T signed a consent decree with the U.S. Justice Department, which had argued that AT&T was making it tough for people to buy equipment and services from competing companies. The proposed remedy was to have AT&T spin off the companies that provide local telephone service. These companies—commonly called "Baby Bells"—still enjoy a monopoly over substantial portions of their slow-growing but stable markets. In contrast, AT&T was to provide high-tech equipment and services in fast-growing areas. As a result, when the breakup finally happened in 1984, AT&T was transformed from a company with extremely stable earnings into a multibillion-dollar start-up operation with uncertain earning potential. The new AT&T had to decide on a dividend policy. The following case uses fictitious characters and conversations, but the issues discussed were very real.

The AT&T board of directors set up a committee to study and recommend how much to pay out as dividends. The committee has four members: Jerry Cunningham, chief financial officer, who has the responsibility to keep the company financially sound; Joan Sheehan, investor relations manager, whose function is to provide a conduit for information to investors and to keep investors as happy as possible; Brian Kennedy, an outside director who heads a high-tech company; and Bill Larson, another outside director, who heads a mature, highly successful auto manufacturing firm. The following is a transcript of their meeting.

SHEEHAN Up until divestiture, AT&T followed the same approach as most other utilities—we paid stable, generous dividends. By that, I mean the dividend was 70–80 percent of the earnings in a normal year. Since earnings grew steadily with only occasional, small declines, the dividend rate could be periodically increased. Of course, the dividend was never cut, even in bad years, because shareholders depended on the dividend. Widows and orphans could buy the stock, secure in the knowledge that there would be no surprises. There were many other owners too—stable dividends have a lot of devotees. Naturally, over the years, we acquired a set of stockholders who liked that dividend policy. Our first option is to keep these shareholders happy and continue the same pattern: pay out a large percentage of normal earnings.

LARSON I'm afraid you'll find that policy is no longer practical. Look at the businesses you're in today. You have long-distance calling, where MCI, Sprint, and other people are trying to eat your lunch. You manufacture telephone equipment, but you have no track record as an independent company on which to base sales forecasts. You have a new line of PCs—just like every other high-tech company. And you've got whatever gadgets are developed by the research group, which will probably entail substantial start-up costs. There's lots of promise here, but there's also lots of risk and variability. If you try to pay out a high percentage of your normal earnings, you'll find that you'll earn less than dividends in some years. That means you'd have to draw down your capital reserves to pay dividends! Shareholders don't like that kind of thing.

CUNNINGHAM Some chief financial officers don't like that kind of thing, either! This corporation is constrained by the amount of cash flow it has. We have good investment opportunities for every bit of cash flow we're expected to make. I don't want to go out and borrow money when earnings are down—or worse yet, try to sell additional shares—to raise money to pay dividends!

LARSON At U.S. Motors, we solve the problem by keeping the dividend at a low percentage of normal earnings and then paying extra dividends once a year when earnings are high enough to warrant it. That way, we are able to pay shareholders a nice yield, but we don't have to cut dividends in bad years—we just stop paying the extra dividend.

CUNNINGHAM That's not a bad way to go, but I think it will be some time before we make enough to warrant extra payments.

KENNEDY Why don't you do what my corporation does: Don't pay dividends. You plow every bit of money back into the business. I might point out that it has some tax advantages, too. Shareholders have to pay taxes on dividends but they don't have to pay taxes on the higher share price until they sell the stock.

SHEEHAN You're absolutely right, of course. And your shareholders would probably support you in that policy since it is the one you have followed consistently. However, we have a clientele of shareholders who bought AT&T shares thinking they were going to get income. And if we don't pay a dividend, they will be extremely unhappy. Many of them would sell the stock. Unless we found enough people who liked the new dividend policy to replace them, it would depress the share price.

KENNEDY It wouldn't hurt the share price in the long run.

SHEEHAN True, but I'm sure the price of the stock would drop on the day we announced the change, and my telephone rings in the short run! I think you'd find that yours would too, Jerry.

CUNNINGHAM I have no doubt you're right. Unfortunately, that doesn't leave us with many options. We have to start out paying a high percentage of the earnings we expect to make. How about giving a stock dividend instead of cash during the fourth quarter? That way, it would look like we were doing something for the shareholders, and yet it wouldn't cost us any cash. How would that go down?

SHEEHAN It would not be well received by several thousand shareholders who were going to use the dividend for Christmas gifts.

KENNEDY The shareholders could always sell a few percent of their shares to raise money.

SHEEHAN It can be very expensive to sell just a few shares. For some of our smaller shareholders, their stockbrokers would get more money than they did! And it would certainly be much less convenient.

CUNNINGHAM So what options are left?

SHEEHAN Essentially, given the constraints, there is only one that is attractive from a shareholder relations viewpoint: Pay a dividend based on the old dividend policy and announce that it won't be raised until the dividend is only 40 percent of normal earnings, which is more typical of a large manufacturing company. That way, people who really want a dividend will have a long time to sell their stock and there won't be any rush to do so.

I might point out that it would be a good idea to keep the dividend reinvestment program. Shareholders who subscribe to the program allow us to use their dividend to purchase new shares either from the company or on the open market, at our discretion. It has been a very popular program with shareholders and it is also a good source of new capital.

CUNNINGHAM I'm in favor of raising all the new capital we can. In fact, how about issuing stock?

LARSON Won't that reduce earnings per share?

CUNNINGHAM It will actually help earnings per share in the long run, because any additional money we get can be invested in projects that earn more than the equity cost of capital.

LARSON I hope you're right, Jerry, but, as you know, projects don't always earn as much as managers expect them to earn.

SHEEHAN The stock analysts that cover our stock wouldn't like a stock issue. We're a new company without a proven track record. I think a new stock issue would hurt investor confidence.

KENNEDY If you're really so hard up, you can always go to your friendly banker or float more debt.

CUNNINGHAM The credit-rating companies tell us that we have as much debt as we can handle if we want to keep our debt rating.

I'm afraid we are pretty well boxed in. This is very frustrating. We can't issue debt, and we can't issue stock, and now I'm finding that we can't get any money by changing dividend policy.

LARSON It is an interesting situation. At my company and at many others, we estimate how much money we'll need to reinvest in the business, and we pay out the remainder as dividends. You don't have that option. For the time being, I'll go along with Joan's suggestion.

KENNEDY I still don't understand why shareholders are so anxious to pay taxes, but I'm willing to accept the fact that your shareholders are. I'll go along with Joan's proposal too.

CUNNINGHAM I concur. Joan, please write up a summary of the meeting and a proposal that we can bring to the next board of directors meeting. Thank you, gentlemen.

LARSON Brian, let's have lunch and you can try to convince me to cut the dividend at U.S. Motors.

KENNEDY Fine. Let's go.

Lunch with Larson and Kennedy

KENNEDY My firm is growing very rapidly, and we have plenty of investment opportunities for the funds. It makes sense for us to hold on to every dollar, because we can make more for our shareholders than they can.

LARSON U.S. Motors is not in that position. During recessions or sales declines we may be a little tight on cash, but most of the time we have plenty. Why shouldn't we pay it to the shareholders?

KENNEDY Because shareholders will have to pay taxes on the income. If you reinvest it, and make more money, the price of your shares will rise, and the shareholders won't have to pay taxes on the increase in value until they sell the shares. If you don't have any investment opportunities that look good, you can always purchase shares of your company's stock on the open market.

LARSON I have two objections to your suggestion. First, many of our shareholders are pension funds, college endowment funds, and institutions that don't pay taxes. Obviously our dividends don't increase their tax burden. Second, if we did as you suggested and routinely bought shares in the open market rather than paying dividends, our shareholders, as a whole, probably would pay less taxes. But the IRS knows that too, and they aren't happy about the idea of losing the tax revenue.

KENNEDY I admit the IRS can make waves, but there are lots of good business reasons you can give them for buying the shares. For example, you can always say you want to purchase the shares so that you have stock you can use to buy another corporation.

LARSON That position is easier to justify for a company like yours than a company like mine, which has an enormous free cash flow. No, Brian, I see your point but I'm afraid that my company does not have the kind of investment opportunities that let us use your strategy safely. I'd be willing to go along with your idea if you had some real evidence of your theory or could prove that it made a big difference, but I haven't heard any facts from you, just theories. Am I right?

KENNEDY I'm afraid you are right. My argument makes sense to me, but I must admit that financial experts haven't come up with conclusive proof.

LARSON In fact, I seem to remember some young MBA telling me that firms that pay no dividend have a slightly lower share price than you'd otherwise expect. You could probably cite an expert who took a different view. Let's just agree to disagree and get on with lunch.

QUESTIONS

1. (a) Are stockholders likely to view a stock dividend as an acceptable sub-stitute for a cash dividend? Defend your answer.
   (b) Why do you think corporations issue stock dividends?

2. Under what circumstances, if any, does it make sense to forego positive NPV projects in order to avoid a cut in DPS? Explain.

3. (a) What is the short-run residual theory of dividends? The long-run resid-ual theory?
   (b) Of the two theories, do you advise using the short-run or the long-run theory?
   (c) Which, if any, of the residual theories does AT&T appear to be follow-ing? Explain.

4. Do dividends matter? Would the firm be able to raise the price of its shares by adopting one dividend policy, and depress it by adopting a different one? Why or why not?

5. Should management care if shareholders are replaced by a different share-holder group? How upset could shareholders be?

6. Some theories of finance say that managers of companies do not manage companies in order to maximize profits, but to make their own life easier. Make a case that Jerry Cunningham is just trying to make his own job eas-ier. Then defend him against those charges.

7. How could dividend policy affect Cunningham's own financial interests?

8. Is a dividend reinvestment program a good idea? Is it a good substitute for a low dividend payout ratio?

9. Is Sheehan right when she says that issuing more stock will "not be well re-ceived" by stock analysts, thereby implying that the price of the stock will be depressed?

10. Based on information in the case and financial theory, what dividend pol-icy do you recommend that AT&T pursue? Defend your recommendation.

A N D E R S O N
A U T O P A R T S
D I V I D E N D   P O L I C Y

"In a way, this is a pleasant problem to have," remarked Harry Gidwitz, the CEO of Anderson Autoparts, to Ian Lyle, director of marketing, as they entered the company's boardroom. "I suspect we wouldn't have to deal with it if our future didn't look so good."

ANDERSON

Anderson is a relatively small auto parts producer with annual sales of $150 million. Despite a reputation for low cost and above average quality products, Anderson's sales history is not especially impressive. There have been a number of problems that have plagued the firm. Though automakers are not able to manufacture parts as cheaply as outside suppliers (due largely to higher wage differentials), the practice of relying on outside suppliers runs the disastrous production risk that the supply of parts will be interrupted. For this reason and because automakers want to minimize inventory costs, auto parts suppliers must be able to provide "just-in-time" delivery (parts arrive when needed) and equipment of exceptional quality. Until recently, Anderson could do neither. But an improved quality control system and a more efficient distribution network now enables the firm to deliver products "as needed" with a very low failure rate.

Anderson historically has also had difficulty in developing the innovative products in demand by automakers. This too has changed. The firm has a number of new auto parts that are quite useful to car manufacturers. For example, it developed a new stainless-steel exhaust system that is much lighter than the traditional cast-iron system.

The result of all these changes is that in 1996 (present year) Anderson's sales increased by 20 percent and its earnings per share by 73 percent. And the future looks bright. Anderson has obtained its first-ever multiyear contract with a car manufacturer and more are expected. (See Exhibit 2 for the best-guess or most likely five-year sales forecast.) The anticipated growth, however, will require considerable capital to finance. Harry Gidwitz believes this is a good time to take a critical look at Anderson's dividend policy, which he has characterized as "historically generous but probably appropriate." Exhibit 1 shows the firm's dividend history, which has resulted from a policy of level dividends with increases only when management felt the increase was sustainable.

DIVIDEND DISCUSSION

There is no shortage of opinions among Anderson's directors about what should be done. John Forsyth, an outside director and president of Northeastern Power & Light, believes that to lower the dividend per share (DPS) would be a sign of weakness and would lower the share price. "In fact," argues Forsyth, "we are poised for our largest growth in sales and EPS in the history of the company. If we lower DPS we will send the financial markets a wrong signal about our future prospects."

"I agree with John," says Ian Lyle, director of marketing. "A dividend decision has aspects of a marketing decision. Appearances count. If we lower DPS we run the risk of transmitting a wrong message." Lyle then hands out a memo containing two pieces of evidence—one theoretical and one empirical—to support his view. He refers to the equation $P_0 = D_1/(K - g)$, which he feels is an indication that an increase in DPS will raise the price of Anderson's stock. He then cites the experience of Hawkins-Elgin, another industry firm, which eliminated dividends in 1991 and promptly saw the price of its stock drop 20 percent in 10 days. Lyle believes the firm should strongly consider making the yearly dividend a constant percentage of EPS in order to keep the growth of DPS in line with the growth of EPS. "That way," he argues, "we send the right signal to the financial markets about our earnings prospects." His specific proposal is to make DPS 50 percent of EPS, a percentage that he notes is low by historical standards.

Jean Bloomingdale, Anderson's treasurer, is sympathetic to the view that dividends should not be cut. She knows, however, that the firm will have substantial capital requirements over the next three to five years. Bloomingdale refers the group to the five-year sales and cash flow forecast that she made a few weeks ago. (See Exhibit 2.) In her view, the most sensible dividend policy is to determine each year how much cash the firm internally generates, implement all attractive investment projects, and pay any leftover cash as dividends. "This way," she observes, "we might be able to avoid external funds and minimize the hassle and flotation costs of raising the capital we need."

Jesse Bergenfeld, an outside director and chief financial officer of the nation's largest toy manufacturer, seems amused by what he has heard to this point. "Everything said so far ignores the risk of the industry you're in. Sales and EPS projections don't always work out, you know, especially in an industry heavily dependent on automobile sales." He cites the "erratic" sales history of Anderson over the last 15 years. (See Exhibit 1.) Moving quickly to the chalkboard, he scribbles what he thinks future sales could be (see Exhibit 2(a)) and notes that these estimates are consistent with the expectation of higher sales yet take into account the fluctuations of Anderson's past sales. "And," Bergenfeld points out, "your firm needs financial flexibility to handle sudden shifts in production technique and your product mix. All of this," he concludes, "argues for a conservative DPS."

Helen Carrol, a senior vice president, can see merit to all the arguments. She wonders, though, if dividends shouldn't be eliminated entirely until the firm's financial situation becomes more stable. Carrol then presents data (see Exhibit 3) that seem to contradict Lyle's evidence. "Within each industry there is an inverse relationship between payout and the price to earnings (P/E) ratio. Note especially the automobile manufacturers where the two foreign producers have lower payouts and higher P/E's than the three American firms."

THE CEO'S VIEW

Gidwitz wonders how much all of this matters anyway. He's sure that Anderson will be able to raise money from external sources if necessary. "The important thing this company faces is the successful implementation of the commercial strategy we've begun in the last year or so. This is where we'll be judged by investors." Still, he thinks it might be embarrassing for Anderson if it had to tap external sources when, say, the share price was unusually low. And he admits he likes the idea of avoiding external financing if possible in order to minimize the hassle and cost of raising the needed capital. At the same time, he believes the firm's stockholders "expect DPS to increase, especially in light of our bright future." He then refers to a company survey showing the vast majority of the stockholders are happy with the firm's present dividend policy. "Perhaps a reasonable compromise is an increase in DPS to $1.10, keeping it there until our growth levels and avoiding any new stock issues. That way, we keep our stockholders happy and avoid the amusing situation of simultaneously paying dividends and selling new shares. If we need external funds, we borrow. Flotation costs are lower with a bond issue than a stock issue anyway." Discussion then centers on other points that are seen as relevant to the decision. At book values, the firm currently has $15 million of long-term debt and $60 million of equity. This is a debt/equity ratio of .25, which the firm feels is optimal.

No one feels it is a good idea to pay any dividend if to do so means the firm would have to forego any of its planned investments, especially given the substantial publicity surrounding Anderson's present situation.

QUESTIONS

1. Evaluate John Forsyth's argument that a cut in dividends will cause the price of Anderson's stock to decline.

2. Evaluate the theoretical and empirical evidence presented by Ian Lyle.

3. How do the following factors affect the dividend decision: the business risk of the industry? the possibility that there may be a sudden change in production techniques or in the firm's product mix?

4. Evaluate the evidence presented by Helen Carrol in Exhibit 3. Specifically, is it reasonable to conclude that a low payout has caused a high P/E? Defend your answer.

5. Suppose the position of Jean Bloomingdale is adopted. That is, each year the firm determines the cash it has generated internally, implements all attractive investment projects, and pays out any remaining funds in dividends. Using the information in Exhibit 2, calculate the expected annual amount of dividends. Discuss the desirability of such a policy, making sure you consider the impact on the firm's debt/equity mix and assuming any funds needed are borrowed.

6. Evaluate Ian Lyle's suggestion to make DPS 50 percent of EPS each year. The format of Exhibit 4 should be useful in the analysis.

7. Evaluate the following points made by Harry Gidwitz.

   (a) The firm's dividend decision is relatively unimportant and is unlikely to affect the price of the firm's stock one way or another.

   (b) It would be "amusing" to simultaneously pay dividends and sell stock, perhaps to the same stockholders. (Can you think of any reasons why it might be in the interest of existing stockholders for the firm to do this?)

8. Suppose Harry Gidwitz's position is adopted; that is, the firm implements all attractive investments, DPS is $1.10, and no new common stock is issued. Compute the firm's debt/equity ratio in each of the next five years. Discuss the desirability of such a policy. The format of Exhibit 4 can be used in the analysis.

9. What DPS do you recommend if the dividends are treated as a long-run residual? The format of Exhibit 4 should be useful, and you may assume that any necessary borrowing occurs in year 1 (1997).

10. Play the role of a consultant. Based on your previous answers and other information in the case, what dividend policy do you recommend? Defend your recommendation.

11. What additional information would you like to have to make a more informed decision in question 10?

EXHIBIT 1
Selected Financial History of Anderson Autoparts[*]

	($ Millions) Sales	P/E ratio	EPS	DPS
1982	$80.6	5	$0.80	$0.50
1983	82.8	5.1	0.87	0.50
1984	88.3	4.6	0.89	0.50
1985	76.5	7	0.72	0.50
1986	90.1	6.2	0.88	0.60
1987	95.3	6.6	0.90	0.60
1988	78.4	35	0.10	0.60
1989	100.1	7.1	0.84	0.60
1990	106.2	6.7	0.90	0.60
1991	107.3	10	0.89	0.70
1992	100.7	11	0.46	0.70
1993	115.6	7.7	0.98	0.70
1994	122.4	8.3	1.12	0.80
1995	125.6	8.2	1.10	0.90
1996 (present)	150.1	13	1.90	1.00

[*]The firm presently has 4 million shares of common stock outstanding.

EXHIBIT 2 (a)
Best-Guess (Most Likely) Sales and Financial Forecast of Anderson: 1997–2001 ($ Millions)

	$t = 0$ 1996	$t = 1$ 1997	$t = 2$ 1998	$t = 3$ 1999	$t = 4$ 2000	$t = 5$ 2001
Sales	$150	$173	$198	$228	$262	$302
Net income		8.7	9.9	11.4	13.1	15.1
Change in working capital		4.6	5	6	6.8	8
Capital spending[a]	_____	10	7	3	8	2
Funds needed		$14.6	$12	$9	$14.8	$10

[a]Amount is over and above depreciation charges. The firm's DPS is presently $1 with 4 million shares outstanding.

EXHIBIT 2(b)
Bergenfeld's Future Sales Scenario: 1997–2001 ($ Millions)

	$t = 0$ 1996	$t = 1$ 1997	$t = 2$ 1998	$t = 3$ 1999	$t = 4$ 2000	$t = 5$ 2001
Sales	$150	$170	$185	$170	$250	$230

EXHIBIT 3
Financial Information Compiled by Helen Carrol

Industry	Firm	P/E	Payout (%)[a]
Retail	Wal-Mart	26	14
Retail	Sears	14	45
Retail	Kmart	13	60
Brewing	Coors	20	25
Brewing	Anheuser-Busch	16	34
Auto	Honda	18	10
Auto	Volvo	8	20
Auto	GM	6	34
Auto	Chrysler	5	25
Auto	Ford	5	30

[a]Payout = (DPS/EPS) $\times$ 100.

EXHIBIT 4
Worksheet to Analyze Anderson's Future Financial Position $ Millions)

	$t = 0$ 1996	$t = 1$ 1997	$t = 2$ 1998	$t = 3$ 1999	$t = 4$ 2000	$t = 5$ 2001
Net income		8.7	9.9	11.4	13.1	15.1
(Dividends)		___	___	___	___	___
To retained earnings						
Funds needed		14.6	12	9	14.8	10
(Deficit)						
Debt	15					
Equity	60	___	___	___	___	___
D/E	0.25					

ALTMAN ENTERPRISES BANKRUPTCY

Jim Altman started Altman Enterprises in 1951 in Columbus. Altman Enterprises is a chain of discount retail stores located in the Midwest that specializes in the sale of nationally advertised, brand-name consumer electronics, small appliances, photographic equipment, sporting goods, toys, silver, crystal, and miscellaneous products. At first the business grew slowly through the expansion of the existing store space and by keeping the expansion costs within his ability to pay for the expansion out of current earnings. The store proved profitable as customers liked the discount prices that were usually lower than the better-known national chain stores located in the same area. In 1975 Jim decided to expand to a second store, in a new shopping mall in Columbus, and this required borrowing capital in the form of a term loan from his bank. Until this point, Jim had borrowed only to finance his inventory and these loans were short-term ones that were paid down each year.

Both stores grew in sales and profits over the next five years when Jim then decided to expand to two different cities in the same state. The expansion was again financed with a term loan, but Jim found that paying off this loan was not as easy as the first one had been. Still, sales and profits were almost the same as for the original two stores of approximately the same square footage. Altman used some of his top employees as managers for the new stores and they had done a very fine job of managing the stores in a way that was consistent with Jim's philosophy. With the success of these stores, Altman expanded rapidly, increasing to 45 stores in a four-state area over the next fifteen years. This expansion was financed through the sales of both mortgage bonds and subordinated debentures.

Starting in about 1986, Altman found that his stores were starting to lose market share due to increasing competition from larger national chain discount stores like Wal-Mart. Jim reacted by remodeling some of his stores and cutting prices.

This helped stem the loss of market share but, more importantly, left Altman with shrinking profit margins. The recession that hit the Midwest in 1991 saw a further reduction in revenues and several of the stores were no longer profitable. After careful study of the profitability of each store and its prospects for the future, and considering the competition in each area, Jim closed almost a dozen stores. Unfortunately, the cash flow hemorrhaging continued and Altman Enterprises continued to lose market share and revenues, and was not profitable in 1992 and 1993. In fact in 1993, Altman Enterprises lost over $28 million. Jim hoped to make it through the 1994 Christmas season, a time when the stores made more than 42 percent of their annual profits, with enough cash to pay his creditors.

The Christmas season was not good and Altman missed the payments on several outstanding obligations, including the interest payments on the mortgage bonds. At this point his creditors were putting tremendous pressure on Altman to come up with a plan that would put the company back on course and able to resume payments on its current debts. By the end of January, Jim realized that he would be unable even to make the payroll. Attempts to borrow additional money, to make payments on current obligations, were not successful. After several long meetings with his largest creditors, Jim realized that he had no plan that offered a reasonable chance of turning Altman Enterprises around.

After consultations with his top financial people and his lawyers, Altman decided, with the approval of his Board of Directors, to declare the firm bankrupt and filed for bankruptcy under Chapter 7 of the bankruptcy laws. Although filing for Chapter 11 had been considered, Altman's creditors never could even come close to agreeing to any of the suggested changes that Jim proposed. To them, the value of the firm's assets would only deteriorate further the longer the firm continued operating, leaving them with even greater losses.

The balance sheet at the time bankruptcy was declared, January 30, 1995, is shown in Exhibit 1. The sale of Altman Enterprises' assets yielded the following:

Sale of fixed assets which were pledged as security for the mortgage bonds	$9,540,000
Sale of inventory, furniture, fixtures, etc.	60,032,000
Collection of receivables	1,860,000
Total proceeds	$71,432,000

The amounts due and the priority for the distribution of assets in a liquidation under Chapter 7 of the Bankruptcy Act can be summarized for the assets involved in this case as follows:

1. Secured creditors (mortgage bond holders) are entitled to the proceeds from the sale of the specific assets that were pledged. In this case assume that the $9,540,000 proceeds from the sale of fixed assets were those that were pledged as security for the mortgage bonds.
2. Trustees' costs have been estimated to be $11,420,000.

3. Although there is a per-person limit on the amount of wages paid employees in a bankruptcy, in this case $2,680,000 is due the employees and this amount is under the limit specified by law.

4. Federal, state, and local taxes due were $1,925,000.

5. If a pension plan is unfunded, it has a claim above that of general creditors for an amount up to 30 percent of equity. In this case the pension plan was underfunded by $1,842,000.

6. All other creditors, including the holders of trade credit (accounts payable), unsecured loans, debentures, and any unsatisfied portion of secured loans are considered general creditors.

7. Preferred stockholders can receive an amount up to the par value of the issue after general creditors are satisfied.

8. Common stockholders have a claim on any remaining funds.

QUESTIONS

1. Determine the distribution of the proceeds among the claimants.

2. Who are the stakeholders in this case?

3. What is the difference between a firm that is technically insolvent, one that is legally insolvent, and one that is bankrupt?

4. What is the difference between a claim filed in bankruptcy court as a voluntary petition and an involuntary petition?

5. Firms in financial distress may file under either Chapter 7 or Chapter 11 of the current bankruptcy proceedings. What is the difference between these two? Which route did Altman take?

6. Explain how a firm that has failed can be reorganized to operate successfully.

7. What factors determine whether a bankrupt firm is reorganized or liquidated?

8. As a business begins to experience problems with cash flows, what are some typical actions it might take?

EXHIBIT 1
Altman Enterprises Balance Sheet (just before liquidation): January 30, 1995

Assets		Liabilities	
Cash	$935	Accounts payable	$26,393
Accounts receivable	2,690	Notes payable	18,000
Inventory	103,503	Accrued wages	2,680
Total current assets	107,128	Accrued taxes	1,925
		Total current liab.	48,998
Net fixed assets	40,304	First mortgage bond	6,000
Total assets	$147,432	Subordinated deb.[1]	2,375
		Other liabilities	65,021
		Total long-term	73,396
		Preferred stock	1,000
		Common stock	8,054
		Paid-in capital	17,618
		Retained earnings	−1,634
		Total equity	25,038
		Total liabilities	$147,432

[1] Subordinated to notes payable.

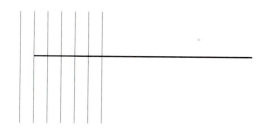

PART X

COMPREHENSIVE CASES

A NOTE ON SOLVING COMPREHENSIVE CASES

The cases in this section are unstructured; that is, they contain no end-of-case questions to guide the analysis. In a sense they are truly "real world," since actual problems rarely come with a set of questions to answer. These cases, therefore, present an opportunity to analyze situations exactly as they occurred. And that can be an exciting and educational experience. At the same time, however, unstructured cases are potentially frustrating. "Where do I begin?" and "What am I supposed to do?" are quite reasonable questions for a student to ask.

The purpose of this note is to provide a framework—tips, if you will—to help you solve relatively comprehensive cases. Before proceeding, though, a word of caution is appropriate.

It is tempting to believe that complicated, real-world problems can be reduced to some type of "cookbook" approach. Such is not the case. Therefore, do not view the steps we present as a set of rules to be followed slavishly. Instead, they are best viewed as a framework to organize and direct your thinking.

A Framework for Approaching Comprehensive Cases

1. What is the problem (or problems) that must be dealt with?
2. What options are there for dealing with the problem?
3. (a) What information do I have to evaluate these options?
   (b) Filter this information. Some of it may be irrelevant to the problem, and some estimates may be of better quality than others.
4. What models are appropriate for analyzing the options?

NOTE: Points 3 and 4 may feed back on each other. That is, the available information may affect the choice of models, and the models you use will affect the information selected.

5. What assumptions must be made to use the model? Defend these assumptions as well as possible.
6. (a) Evaluate the model.
   (b) Discuss the implications of the model and, where possible, bring in qualitative factors surrounding the decision.
7. Time permitting, see how sensitive the results are to different assumptions.
8. Based on 6 and 7, state your conclusions and recommendations.

Elaboration of Selected Points:

Point 2. A very important real-world step is to determine what options management has to address any problem it faces. Here are some examples. A bank officer who is evaluating a loan request from a firm may have a number of options to consider, including (1) not granting the loan; (2) granting some proportion; and (3) granting the full amount but with various maturities. Or consider a firm that is deciding whether to replace a piece of equipment. Options include (1) not replacing it; (2) buying various newer models; (3) buying various rebuilt, older models; and (4) leasing or renting new equipment.

In the interest of time, of course, a case will frequently limit the available choices. Still, it is a good practice to ask what other options management might have and why it is reasonable to rule them out. And it is possible that management is not considering an alternative that seems reasonable to you. While you may not have enough information to evaluate this option, it is perfectly appropriate at some point in your analysis to raise the question, "Why doesn't management consider . . . ?"

Points 3 and 4. The models you want to use are simply the financial tools you've been exposed to in previous finance courses. These include ratios, cash flow forecasts, discounted cash flow (DCF) techniques like the NPV, and the economic order quantity (inventory decision). Sometimes there may be insufficient information to apply a financial technique. Maybe you would like to develop a worst-case cash flow forecast but lack a worst-case sales estimate (though it is possible—based on information in the case—that you can develop your own).

The reliability of information given in the case, especially any future projection, should be carefully considered. For example, a manager who sponsors a new project is likely to have a tendency to be overly optimistic about the future cash flows of the project. Nor can it be assumed that managers faithfully pursue an objective of maximizing stockholders' value. A so-called agency problem may well exist. An executive worried about the impact of a project failure on his professional reputation may be unduly concerned with risk from the standpoint of value maximization, especially if stockholders have diversified portfolios.

Point 5. An analyst almost surely will have to make assumptions. A project's NPV, for example, depends on some assumption about future cash flows. There are three possible situations you may find yourself in.

1. The case states the assumptions that management intends to use, but there is little basis in the case to determine how reasonable they are.
2. The case states assumptions that management intends to use, but there is information in the case to judge their reasonableness.
3. No clear-cut assumptions are stated and you have to formulate your own.

In the first instance, it is best to simply incorporate these assumptions in your analysis. It is good practice, however, at some point in your analysis to note that "the validity of my numbers and recommendations depends in part on the reliability of the information used." In the second instance, there may be reasons in the case to believe that certain assumptions are inappropriate. Perhaps you detect some sort of agency problem and you suspect that the assumptions are unduly pessimistic. Or maybe the assumptions presented have ignored relevant information. Consider, for instance, an estimate of future labor costs that ignored the fact that the local labor market was tightening. In each of these situations it would be appropriate to adjust any estimates.

In the third situation you may find that there are competing sets of assumptions, perhaps two different sales forecasts. Or maybe no assumptions are presented. In these cases, you will have to decide—based on the information in the case—which ones are appropriate.

Finally, note that in the last two instances we are dealing with a situation where there is information in the case that allows us to scrutinize a set of assumptions. Now strictly speaking, we are not talking about assumptions, which are statements accepted without proof. Instead, we are dealing with hypotheses; that is, beliefs we can analyze to gauge their reasonableness.

Point 6. This involves the evaluation of any financial statistics we've compiled. It is an analysis of any numbers we've compiled. What do these ratios suggest? What do these NPVs imply? But a thorough analysis will consider more than all the quantifiable information. There may well be nonquantifiable or intangible factors surrounding the choice. For example, suppose a firm will be forced to lay off workers if a project is not undertaken. "Intangibles" include the effect of the layoff on the morale of the remaining employees and any possible "bad press" the firm might receive. Or suppose the owner of a company derives personal satisfaction from having the largest sales volume of any firm in the market. It would be perfectly appropriate from a value maximization standpoint to consider this in an evaluation.

Point 8. Your recommendation will be based primarily on the analysis of the financial statistics you calculate and any intangibles surrounding the case. It is a good practice, however, to make sure that any suggestions are feasible and realistic. For example, an elaborate procedure for determining a firm's cost of capital or required return may not be feasible if management lacks sufficient financial expertise. And a recommendation to undertake a DCF analysis for *all* equipment replacement decisions may be impractical if "hassle and bother" are considered.

And, finally, your recommendation might include the suggestion that management explore some option or options that it is not presently considering. (See point 2.)

A L P I N E   P R E S S

"There are 8,264 different types of errors you can make in a printing job," Jim Crandall has been heard to say. "And over the years I guess I've made nearly every one twice over."

Crandall is the owner of Alpine Press, a company with annual sales of nearly $8 million. The firm does a wide range of printing, including annual reports, organizational brochures, even wedding invitations. He purchased the firm in 1976 when there were 16 employees and the business occupied 10,000 square feet. Now, 20 years later, there are 65 employees, and the business occupies 35,000 square feet.

Crandall has always stressed quality printing and has even been known to redo projects that customers were perfectly satisfied with. He feels strongly that "if it's not as good as we can do, we redo it."

THE PROBLEM

Crandall now faces a decision about replacing a printing press, the Miller, named after its manufacturer. Though the machine is 15 years old, this is not necessarily "ancient" for equipment of this sort. Still, the Miller has been "chewing up" maintenance time the last few years. As a result, not only have maintenance costs been increasing, but the machine's down time has been increasing as well. Though the Miller has been able to achieve its production target of $500,000 of sales per year, Crandall is certain this volume will not be maintained. Exhibit 1 shows estimates of the annual sales he expects from the Miller over the next seven years. After reviewing these figures, he even wonders if they aren't a bit generous, especially in the later years.

Crandall is "nearly certain" the machine should be replaced and has narrowed the choice to two models: the Akiyama, which is made in Japan, and the German-manufactured Heidelberg. With a decision like this there are often factors other than cost that influence the choice. Will the machine be expertly installed? It is vital that a press be firmly level because the error tolerance in a typical job is in thousandths of an inch. Does a manufacturer offer professional assistance in press operation? A new piece of equipment requires employee re-training, and it is necessary that a producer offer operator assistance during the first few weeks after a sale. Does a manufacturer offer prompt and reliable maintenance support? The equipment must be examined twice a year to minimize the chance that problems will arise, and if a malfunction does occur, Crandall wants the machine repaired as quickly as possible.

However, the technical support of each firm is excellent and Crandall feels these factors are "a wash." Nor is there much to choose from on the basis of annual operating costs. (See Exhibit 2.) For example, two workers are required to run either press. An operator feeds the ink and paper into the machine, while a pressman adjusts the equipment for the type of printing being done. The Heidelberg, though, because it is a bit bigger and more expensive, will require more space, increase the firm's annual insurance premium, and cost somewhat more to maintain. These increases, however, are relatively small.

The real differences involve each machine's contribution to annual sales and purchase price. The Akiyama is essentially a modern replacement of the Miller. Purchase of the Akiyama in effect allows Alpine to maintain sales at current levels. Looked at from a different angle, Crandall realizes that his predictions on the Miller imply a reduction in sales, and it is possible that if the Miller is kept he would be unable to fill orders from existing customers.

THE HEIDELBERG'S SUPERIORITY

The Heidelberg does everything that the Akiyama can do and more. The most significant difference is that the Heidelberg can be run at a much faster speed than the Akiyama. This is important because customers frequently want their orders filled very quickly. Virtually all presses can be run at faster rates, but the Heidelberg's speed is legendary in the graphics business. At present Alpine's capacity to fill quick orders in-house is limited relative to the number of requests received. Orders are often farmed out to another graphics company, mainly as a service to Alpine's customers, and Alpine only breaks even on this type of business.

If the Heidelberg is purchased, all work of this sort could be done in-house. In addition, Crandall would promote more heavily the firm's ability to take quick orders, and that service should increase annual sales. The Heidelberg's sales figures in Exhibit 1 include estimates of annual quick-order sales. Crandall is less confident about these predictions, however, since they involve estimates of future sales increases.

The cost of the Akiyama is $400,000, which includes installation. The base price of the Heidelberg is $880,000 and also includes installation. Both manufacturers provide the same guarantee and offer free operator assistance during the first four weeks after the sale.

As Crandall reflects on the choice, a number of difficulties come to mind. If he stays with the Miller he will likely use it for the remainder of its economic life, seven years. He is also likely to keep the Akiyama that long as well, at which time he would replace it. The Heidelberg is a different story, however. If purchased, Alpine would probably use this press for its entire useful life, estimated to be 25 years. And Crandall is unclear whether or how to incorporate this longer period into the analysis.

Crandall thinks it is reasonable, based on conversations with used-equipment brokers and his own expertise, that the current after-tax market value of the Miller is $45,000, and that the Akiyama's after-tax market value in seven years will be $120,000. He is unsure, though, what the value of the Heidelberg will be at that time. This press has only been manufactured for three years and there is virtually no data on its resale value. Crandall believes, however, that the cost of this machine new will rise by 4 percent a year.

ANOTHER PROBLEM

The second problem involves Alpine's project evaluation technique. For all equipment decisions, both large and small, Alpine has used the payback method. Crandall likes the payback for two reasons. First, it is simple and easy to use. Alpine's management must make numerous equipment-related decisions during the course of a year, and convenience is an important factor. Crandall also views a project's payback as a measure of the project's risk. He views a short payback as an indication of relatively low risk.

Crandall has asked Denise Molton to help him in the evaluation. Molton has an undergraduate degree in marketing and an MBA in finance. A recent hire, she divides her time between sales and finance, and she has already contributed important ideas to the firm's marketing and finance policies.

When they meet, Crandall hands Molton a list of questions he wants answered.

1. Is the payback an appropriate evaluation tool for all projects?
2. Should the same technique be used to evaluate low-cost and "big-ticket" items?
3. (a) Is it necessary to estimate the market value of the Heidelberg in seven years given that it would probably be used for 25 years?
   (b) If "yes" is given to the preceding question, how can a reasonable estimate of market value be obtained?
4. Use whatever financial techniques are appropriate to evaluate which, if either, of the two printing presses should be purchased.

Back at her office, Molton reflects on some issues she thinks are relevant to her assignment. She decides that a 40 percent tax rate is appropriate, but she is a bit unclear on what discount rates to use. Molton is comfortable using a 10 percent after-tax rate to evaluate a simple cost-reduction project. She realizes that the printing presses involve sales projections and, thus, are projects of higher risk. She also thinks that the Heidelberg is a riskier investment than the Akiyama. Her first reaction is to use a 12 percent after-tax rate on the Akiyama and a 14 percent rate on the Heidelberg. She believes, however, that rates of 14 and 16 percent respectively could also be right and secretly hopes that her choice of discount rates will not affect any recommendation on the printing presses.

EXHIBIT 1
Annual Sales Estimates for Each Press

	Year						
	$t + 1$ 1997	$t + 2$ 1998	$t + 3$ 1999	$t + 4$ 2000	$t + 5$ 2001	$t + 6$ 2002	$t + 7$ 2003
Miller	$450,000	450,000	400,000	400,000	400,000	400,000	400,000
Akiyama	$500,000	500,000	500,000	500,000	500,000	500,000	500,000
Heidelberg	$600,000	600,000	600,000	600,000	600,000	600,000	600,000

EXHIBIT 2
Estimated Annual Cash Operating Costs of Each Press*

	Miller	Akiyama	Heidelberg
Labor[a]	$65,511	$65,511	$65,511
Pension fund[b]	3,276	3,276	3,276
Welfare benefits[c]	4,160	4,160	4,160
Payroll taxes[d]	6,551	6,551	6,551
Utilities	1,842	1,142	1,932
Maintenance	38,500	9,000	14,600
Fire & sprinkler insurance	1,760	1,760	2,870
Rent[e]	2,000	2,000	2,500
	$123,600	$93,400	$101,400

[a]One operator at $29,984 per year plus one pressman at $35,527.

[b]Five percent of labor.

[c]Health, disability, and life insurance premiums.

[d]Social Security and unemployment insurance.

[e]Charge for space occupied by each machine.

*These figures do not include material costs, which run 10 percent of sales.

ROSLYN

Billion-dollar apparel companies such as Calvin Klein and Liz Claiborne are unusual in the garment industry, which consists primarily of dozens of much smaller apparel makers. One such firm is Roslyn Manufacturing, a producer of women's apparel, located in Bedford, New York. The firm was started 14 years ago by Justin Rose and Brett Lynn, who between them had nearly 25 years of experience with a major garment manufacturer. And the partnership initially blended very well. Rose, reserved and introspective, is extremely creative with a real flair for merchandising and trend spotting. Mainly as a result of his genius, the Roslyn label is synonymous with quality and "in" fashions. Lynn, outgoing and forceful, has contributed important merchandising and marketing ideas, but has mainly assumed the duties of the firm's chief operating officer.

THOUGHTS ON SELLING OUT

Rose, however, is seriously considering the sale of his 50 percent interest. Though he still enjoys the creative side of the business, he is tired of the cash crunches that the firm has faced over the years. Periodically the retailers Roslyn deals with have encountered financial difficulties and have strung out their payments. For example, at one point nearly 40 percent of Roslyn's receivables were more than 90 days overdue. And in situations like this, factoring companies (firms that buy the receivables of apparel companies) would cut back on the credit they advance on orders to the more unstable retailers. A firm like Rosyln faced a most unpleasant choice: Either ship to these retailers (which often meant a mad scramble for cash) or risk losing sales. Fearful of the second possibility, at Lynn's insistence Rosyln would continue to supply all but the most unreasonable orders. And Lynn is quick to point out that, despite this decision, the company's average collection period of 62 days is not terribly different from the industry median of 50 days.

Another reason that Rose wants to sell his interest is that he is losing confidence in Lynn's managerial expertise. When the firm was small Rose felt that

Lynn did a fine job, but he now wonders whether Lynn is capable of efficiently running a firm as large as Roslyn. He questions, for example, the firm's inventory procedures and Lynn's decision three years ago to retire all long-term debt. The latter move was predicated by Lynn's fear that Roslyn's business risk was increasing. He cited the difficulties of seemingly rock-solid retailers like Bloomingdale's and Campeau to support his claim. Lynn also pointed out that the company's stock represents an extremely large proportion of the personal wealth of both him and Rose. "It's true," he told Rose, "that we could borrow at 9.5 percent, which is only two percentage points above the long-term government bond rate. But given our personal investment situation, I hesitate to add any financial risk to the high business risk we're exposed to."

THE CONSULTANT'S RECOMMENDATIONS

Although Rose owns half of the company, Lynn's personality is such that he has effectively seized control of the firm, and no major decision that he opposed has ever been approved. An important recent example of this was Lynn's reaction eight months ago to the report of a consulting firm. The consultants recommended that Rosyln implement more sophisticated accounting procedures and make greater use of the computer. They also suggested that Rosyln "very seriously" consider building a state-of-the-art distribution center that would allow the firm to handle big orders from retailers such as K Mart and Wal-Mart. Lynn read the report thoroughly and said he would explore further computerization and alternative accounting procedures. However, he rejected the distribution center because he considered the estimated $5-million to $8-million cost "excessive." He felt that "sizeable" capital budgeting projects should be avoided until he was confident that the firm was on a solid financial base. In fact, Roslyn's capital budget over the last three years has equalled the money necessary to maintain the firm's plant and equipment, an average of $124(000) a year. Lynn admits, though—and Rose agrees—that without large orders from the major retailers, sales growth should only be in line with inflation, about 4 percent per year.

Rose wondered whether Lynn was really concerned that implementation of these proposals would necessitate bringing in outside capital, given his debt policy. If so, Lynn would own less than half of Rosyln, a scenario that might eventually lead to his ouster.

In fairness, however, the relationship between the two partners has been relatively smooth over the years. And Rose admits that he may be unduly critical of Lynn's managerial decisions. "After all," he concedes, "the man seems to have reasons for what he does, and we have been in the black every year since we started, including the last one, which was especially difficult for a firm in our business." Nonetheless, at present (late 1995), Rose has decided to seriously pursue the sale of his interest, and believes he has two options: sell to Lynn or to a major apparel maker.

POSSIBLE SUITORS

Rose knows that there are a number of much larger apparel manufacturers who are shopping around for additional acquisitions. The company's banker gave Rose a list of big apparel makers that might be interested in purchasing Rosyln (see Exhibit 6), but cautioned that these firms were looking for companies with specific characteristics. Most important, the firm would need to have established brand names. In addition, current management must be the people who developed the firm's corporate culture, they must still be capable of performing, and they must be willing to remain. Rosyln undoubtedly has the reputation, and Rose is more than willing—even eager—to stay on.

Still, he fears that these major firms may simply be bargain hunting. It is no secret that the misfortunes of many big retailers have made the operation of a company like Rosyln more difficult. Rose thinks there will be no shortage of apparel firms wanting to acquire Rosyln.

And he wonders how a potential buyer would react to Lynn's presence. After all, a new owner would not have absolute control over Roslyn's operation, and Lynn is likely to be a hard person to deal with.

When Rose informed Lynn of his desire to sell, Lynn said that he was not surprised and wanted the chance to make an offer. Lynn thought he could find backers but made it clear that any agreement would require Rose to stay with Rosyln for at least three years, a condition Rose feels he "can live with."

Rose thinks that the starting point for the analysis should be the liquidation value of the firm. The inventory, though excessive in his view, contains fashionable items in good condition and probably can be sold to net 70 percent of book value after taxes. Rose believes this same percentage is appropriate for the firm's receivables. Most of Roslyn's plant and equipment is state-of-the-art, and a reasonable estimate is that the after-tax market value is $400,000. Liquidation has a cost, of course, since there would be legal and administrative fees. Rose has no good idea what they would run and decides to assume $300,000.

He is confident, however, that Rosyln is "worth more alive than dead" and wonders if a comparables approach wouldn't be useful. The problem, of course, is to find firms that are really comparable. Companies differ so much in size, product line, markets, etc., that true comparables are hard to find. And ideally such firms should be publicly traded.

Rose concludes that he "most certainly" needs outside help to decide what price to accept and is sure Lynn will do the same.

EXHIBIT 1
Roslyn's Sales and Operating Margin: 1986–1995*

Year	Sales ($000s)	OM
1995	$22,900	.062
1994	22,100	.066
1993	21,000	.061
1992	19,700	.057
1991	16,700	.078
1990	15,600	.082
1989	14,300	.081
1988	11,100	.073
1987	9,100	.054
1986	8,300	.042

*Operating margin = (EBIT + Dep.)/Sales

EXHIBIT 2
Roslyn's Income Statements: 1993–1995 ($000s)

	1993	1994	1995
Sales	$21,000	$22,100	$22,900
Cost of goods sold	16,130	16,530	17,180
Gross margin	4,870	5,570	5,720
General & administrative expenses	3,590	4,110	4,300
Depreciation	100	92	90
EBIT	1,180	1,368	1,330
Interest	140	120	96
Earnings before taxes	1,040	1,248	1,234
Taxes (35%)	364	437	432
Net income	$676	$811	$802

EXHIBIT 3
Roslyn's Balance Sheets: 1993–1995 ($000s)

	1993	1994	1995
Assets			
Cash	$740	$341	$453
Receivables	3,210	3,130	3,940
Inventory	2,520	3,450	3,440
Current assets	6,470	6,921	7,833
Net fixed	580	610	650
Total assets	$7,050	$7,531	$8,483
Liabilities and equity			
Debt due	$210	$200	$160
Accounts payable	1,030	830	950
Accruals	1,010	1,090	1,370
Current liabilities	2,250	2,120	2,480
Term loans	1,210	1,010	800
Equity	3,590	4,401	5,203
Total liabilities and equity	$7,050	$7,531	$8,483

EXHIBIT 4
Roslyn's Cash Flow Situation: 1993–1995 ($000s)

	1993	1994	1995
Net income	$676	$811	$802
Depreciation	100	92	90
Cash flow operations	776	903	892
— Adjusted working capital needs	141	970	400
— Capital spending	120	122	130
— Dividends	0	0	0
Cash flow	$515	($189)	$362

Adjusted Working Capital

	1992	1993	1994	1995
Accounts receivable		$3,210	$3,130	$3,940
Inventory		2,520	3,450	3,440
— Accounts payable		1,030	830	950
— Accruals		1,010	1,090	1,370
Adjusted working capital	$3,549	$3,690	$4,660	$5,060
Change adjusted working capital		141	970	400

EXHIBIT 5
Selected Ratios for Apparel Manufacturers, Annual Sales of $10–50 Million: 1993–1995

	Median[a]	Lower/Upper Quartiles[b]
Current	1.7	1.3/2.6
Quick	0.8	0.6/1.6
Average collection period	50	41/68
Fixed asset turnover[c]	25	12/40
Inventory turnover (CGS)[d]	6	3.5/8.1
Total asset turnover	2.8	2.0/3.5
Debt[e]	.57	.41/.71
Days purchases outstanding[f]	25	18/32
Operating margin[g]	.08	.039/.107

[a]The median is the middle value of the industry statistic. For example, half the industry firms had a current ratio above 1.7 and half had a current raio below 1.7.

[b]The left or lower number shows the cutoff for the bottom 25 percent. The right or higher number shows the cutoff for the top 25 percent. For example, 25 percent of the industry firms had a current raio below 1.3, and 25 percent had a current ratio above 2.6. By implication, 50 percent of these ratios fell between 1.3 and 2.6.

[c]Sales/Net Fixed

[d]CGS/Inventory

[e]Debt/Assets

[f]This shows the average length of time that trade debit is outstanding. Also called the average payment period. Calculated as $A/P \div (CGS/360)$.

[g]Operating margin = (EBIT + Dep.)/Sales.

EXHIBIT 6
Financial Information on Large Apparel Manufacturers Seeking Acquisitions

Firm	Sales[a]	OM[b]	Beta	D/E[c]	P–E
Crystal Brands	$857	.125	1.2	0.18	9.6
Garan	137	.108	0.85	0.17	7.9
Hartmax	1,297	.072	1.2	0.14	29
Kellwood	760	.090	1.4	0.23	8.6
Osh Kosh	315	.151	1.1	0.03	13.2
Russell	688	.230	1.1	0.13	15.1

[a]In $ millions

[b]OM = Operating Margin = (EBIT + Dep.)/Sales.

[c]Long-term debt divided by equity, market values.

RANDALL INDUSTRIES

A classic caricature involves a highly scientific and technically minded individual who is seemingly oblivious to the details of everyday life. With shoes unlaced—if they are worn at all—and hair uncombed, our "hero" is constantly thinking about how things work and ways to perform tasks differently and better. Richard Randall doesn't fit this caricature perfectly, but he's close. He is 68 years old, completely self-taught, and has a scientific imagination described as "immense" by one of his business associates. Randall formed Randall Industries (RI) 30 years ago in 1965 when he found that there was quite a demand for a company that could help solve the technical problems of other companies.

RANDALL INDUSTRIES

According to Randall, RI is best described as "a firm that makes gadgets that other firms want." Though Randall has never pursued an especially aggressive sales strategy, customers range from small regional businesses to Fortune 100 companies. RI will design and produce products especially tailored to a client's situation, and it enjoys a certain amount of monopoly power since its services are highly unusual. Over the years the firm has developed 15 patented products. However, it is especially well known for its hydraulic presses, which can be used in a variety of industries, including tobacco and textile. And while it is a bit of an exaggeration to claim its products are recession proof, orders have never been particularly sensitive to the state of the economy.

While Randall's technical expertise is unquestioned, his business sense is virtually nonexistent. To him, "cost of goods" is simply a number on an accounting statement that is usually less than sales. And "loans" are what you get when you need money. Yet somehow he has muddled through. The firm has been in the black most years and has never been short of orders to fill. And Randall is especially proud of the fact that his three sons chose to enter the firm.

The company, however, presently faces its most serious financial crisis. The Bank of Ohio has informed Randall that the company's credit line will not be renewed and the $200,000 note must be paid in full when it becomes due in early October, three months hence. According to bank officials, an extension is simply out of the question.

Even worse is the company's status with its suppliers. June orders were quite large and July promises to be nearly as good, yet RI may be unable to get the materials and parts it needs. Accounts payable total about $600,000 and almost 75% are more than 100 days overdue. As one purveyor succinctly put it in a recent phone call, "I love you to death, Richard, but enough is enough! I've got bills to pay, too."

THE BROTHERS REACT

The situation is so bad that Marvin Randall, the oldest of Richard's three sons, did the unthinkable. He called a meeting with his two brothers and did not invite his dad. Marvin knows that the firm needs cash to stay afloat but isn't sure how much. And he knows that the family's financial situation is such that the ability to supply equity is simply not there.

At the meeting Robert, the youngest son, suggested they approach another bank, one much smaller than the Bank of Ohio. He pointed out that the Bank of Ohio is one of the largest in the country, and its credit standards are set "from high above in another city." Local bank executives, therefore, will not have much discretion in approving a loan. "What we need," Robert said, "is a local bank that is familiar with our services and our family." Thomas, the middle son, thought this was an excellent idea but cautioned that "we'll have to develop a *very* strong case. *Any* bank needs to feel, first, that the loan can be paid off and second, that it's adequately secured."

After further discussion, each brother chose a task. Thomas would look critically at the firm's costs and decide what expenses could be cut or eliminated. Marvin agreed to approach each of the firm's suppliers and see if he could work out a suitable repayment schedule with them. Robert's task was to approach Ligonier Savings and Loan and Arden Bank and Trust, two locally owned financial institutions, and determine if they would be receptive to a "sales pitch" by RI. With time critical, the brothers agreed to meet in 72 hours, again without their father.

THE NEXT MEETING

At this meeting Robert was the first to speak. He said both financial institutions were "willing to listen." Yes, they were familiar with the firm, its products, and the family. And, yes, they would carefully consider any loan request. As one of the bankers said, "If I weren't convinced that your technical skills are top notch and unique, and your family's character impeccable, I'd tell you that you're wasting your time."

Thomas said that "at first, a close look at our expenses was painful." But it quickly became evident that numerous items were unnecessary and others were excessive. "It really hurt," Thomas sadly stated, "to see what Dad has been spending money on. There was $20,000 of unneeded materials he bought from a young salesman just to help the guy out. He subcontracted $50,000 worth of jobs that we could do for half that in-house. I could go on, but you get the idea." The brothers agreed that costs could be cut sharply, but they also thought the next four to six months could be a bit difficult while all the cost-cutting changes were implemented.

Marvin's report was the least encouraging. Some of RI's suppliers were quite understanding of what the brothers were trying to do and agreed to cooperate as much as their situations allowed. Others, though, insisted that their accounts be paid in full if RI wanted to continue its relationship with them. And, Marvin admits, this reaction is understandable given that many of RI's bills are six months past due.

THE BROTHERS DECIDE

After considerable discussion, the brothers decided to request a term loan of $575,000. The loan, if granted, would be "interest only" in 1995, payable in equal amounts over a five-year period, 1996–2000, and would carry a rate of 12 percent. While the brothers would like to request a longer term, it is clear that anything beyond five years is not feasible.

The loan would be used to pay the note due of $200,000, pay off the bills of the angrier suppliers, and maintain a minimum cash balance of $75,000.

The brothers also agreed that any forecasts should make the following assumptions.

1. Sales will grow at 5 percent per year.
2. Cost of goods sold will equal 75 percent of sales.
3. Operating expenses will total 15.5 percent of sales in 1996 and 14 percent thereafter.
4. Depreciation will be $90,000 a year
   (Exhibit 3 shows EBIT projections incorporating assumptions 1–4.)
5. Annual purchases of new equipment will be $100,000.
6. Inventory turnover (sales) will be 8.
7. Accruals will total 3 percent of sales and "other current assets" 0.6 percent of sales.
8. Accounts payable is estimated to be 13.5 days of sales.
9. Accounts receivable is predicted to be 20 days of sales.
10. Customer deposits are forecast to be 22.5 days of sales.

NOTE: Assumptions 6–10 are in terms of total sales.

Assumption 1 allows for no inflation-adjusted sales growth and reflects the inflation forecasts of a number of economists.

Assumption 8 results from assumption 2, and the facts that purchases are predicted to be 60 percent of cost of goods sold and RI's terms of credit are typically net 30.

Assumptions 9 and 10 reflect the brothers' decision to firm up RI's collection procedures. Because every sale is literally a special order, a customer deposit is typically required with payment made according to RI's "25/25/50" plan. It takes about 90 days from the time an order is received until the product is made and delivered. At that point a sale is recorded. At the time of the order, RI's policy is to request a deposit equal to 25 percent of the order. Another 25 percent is due when the product is delivered, that is, at the time a sale is recorded. The remaining 50 percent is due after the sale on terms of net 30.

Though this is the stated policy, it has usually not been enforced. Regarding deposits, the elder Randall would simply request that a client "give us what you can." He had a similar attitude regarding collections: "Pay us when you can."

Assumption 9 allows for overdue credit sales. Robert thinks 80 percent of the credit sales will be paid on day 30, with the remaining 20 percent paid late.

Actually, Marvin believes that the firm's "25/25/50" plan is too generous. He argues that "a 50/50 split makes better business sense, would be viewed as fair by our clients, and would not hurt sales." He proposes that RI require a 50 percent deposit when the order is made, with the remaining 50 percent payable on terms of net 30. Though there is some support for this idea, the brothers agree to stay with the firm's present credit policy.

THE BIGGEST PROBLEM

In addition to RI's financial difficulties, there is another problem—perhaps the biggest problem of all. Every brother thinks that any business plan to rescue the company cannot involve their father. Good business sense dictates that the three sons remove him from any contact with the firm.

At the same time, however, they know that the company has been and remains their dad's whole life. Although he is not in the best of health anyway, the decision to oust Randall would surely subject him to great emotional and physical stress. This is especially likely given that part of the financial plan is to eliminate positions that Randall created to accommodate three of his lifetime friends. Still, if the firm continues the way it's been going, there is the very real possibility that there will be no Randall Industries for Randall to be part of.

This is the hardest thing for the brothers to face: the realization that whether or not they remove their father, he could die from losing his beloved company.

EXHIBIT 1
Randall Industries Income Statements: 1991–1995 ($000s)

	1991	1992	1993	1994	1995[a]
Sales	$3,591.1	$3,127.8	$3,390.7	$3,739.5	$3,811.0
Cost of goods sold	2,825.0	2,410.2	2,868.0	2,916.8	2,934.5
Gross margin	766.1	717.6	522.7	822.7	876.5
Operating expenses	646.6	606.0	691.3	643.0	590.7
Depreciation	65.0	70.0	100.0	117.0	120.0
EBIT	54.5	41.6	(268.6)	62.7	165.8
Interest	65.6	54.6	40.7	45.3	72.3
Earnings before taxes	(11.1)	(13)	(309.3)	17.4	93.5
Taxes[b]	0	0	0	7.0	37.4
Earnings after taxes	($11.1)	($13)	($309.3)	$10.4	$56.1

[a]Projection based on the first six months. Also assumes some improvement in the firm's costs during the last six months. Includes interest on a new $575,000 loan.

[b]The relevant tax rate is 40 percent.

EXHIBIT 2
Randall Industries Balance Sheets: 1991–1995 ($000s)

	1991	1992	1993	1994	1995[a]
Assets					
Cash	$ 16.4	$ 8.8	$ 41.2	$ 36.6	$ 76.2
Accounts receivable	635.4	424.8	528.2	487.0	370.5
Inventory	431.1	475.8	396.0	450.1	476.4
Other current	21.7	24.3	20.5	12.9	22.9
Current assets	$1,104.6	$ 933.7	$ 985.9	$ 986.6	$ 946.0
Net P+E	759.0	731.0	701.0	726.0	750.0
Total assets	$1,863.6	$1,664.7	$1,686.9	$1,712.6	$1,696.0

(continued)

EXHIBIT 2
(Continued)

	1991	1992	1993	1994	1995[a]
Liabilities and equity					
LT debt due[b]	$ 95.0	$ 108.0	$ 54.8	$ 62.4	$ 60.0
Note payable	204.5	208.1	200.0	200.0	0
Accounts payable	411.7	374.8	508.0	600.0	244.5
Customers' deposits	90.8	26.8	266.0	154.9	158.8
Accruals	70.6	77.0	152.2	148.1	114.3
Current liabilities	$ 872.6	$ 794.7	$1,181.0	$1,165.4	$ 577.7
LT debt[c]	247.0	139.0	84.2	115.1	630.1
Common stock	96.0	96.0	96.0	96.0	96.0
Retained earnings	648.0	635.0	325.7	336.1	392.2
Total liabilities and equity	$1,863.6	$1,664.7	$1,686.9	$1,712.6	$1,696.0

[a]Projection based on the first six months, assumes that the changes described in the case are implemented, and that the $575(000) term loan is granted. All interest-bearing debt borrowed at 12 percent.

[b]All the 1995 total of $60(000) is due in 1996.

[c]The 1995 total includes the $575(000) term loan, and $55.1(000) of an equipment loan payable as follows: $25.1(000) in 1997 and $30(000) in 1998.

EXHIBIT 3
EBIT Projections: 1996–2000 ($000s)*

	1995	1996	1997	1998	1999	2000
Sales	$3,811	$4,001.6	$4,201.6	$4,411.7	$4,632.3	$4,863.9
Cost of goods sold		3,001.2	3,151.2	3,308.8	3,474.2	3,647.9
Gross margin		1,000.4	1,050.4	1,102.9	1,158.1	1,216.0
Operating expenses		620.3	588.2	617.6	648.5	681.0
Depreciation		90.0	90.0	90.0	90.0	90.0
EBIT		$290.1	$372.2	$395.3	$419.6	$445.0

*The forecast assumes annual sales growth of 5 percent, CGS will equal 75 percent of sales, and OE will equal 15.5 percent of sales in 1996 and 14 percent thereafter.

C A S E 5 2

VIDEO STATION

When Mike Gibbons picked up the morning newspaper, one headline got his immediate attention: "Blockbuster Video to Open in September 1995." As he read the article under the headline, he learned that Blockbuster Video was planning to open a 6,500-square-foot videotape rental store within 50 yards of his own 5,000-square-foot video rental store. Although he heard that Blockbuster had done a market survey in early spring and that it had inquired about leasing two different pieces of commercial property, Mike had not expected them to come to a town as small as Lumberton.

As he finished the article he started making notes on the possible consequences of the arrival of Blockbuster on his business and to map a strategy for the four-month period before the proposed opening. Since Mike had visited Blockbuster stores to learn as much about their operation as possible, he felt like he knew the volume of sales they needed to be profitable and that it would be very hard for both him and Blockbuster to be profitable in the limited Lumberton market, whose population is 26,000.

BACKGROUND

Mike Gibbons and a partner started Video Station three years ago when Mike was 21 with $22,000 in start-up capital. The basic concept was to deliver rental videos to customers' homes just like pizza. Customers could order from a video library of just over 500 tapes, and for $2.99, Video Station would deliver the requested tape to a customer's home. The next day the tape could be dropped in one of four drop boxes located throughout Lumberton. Since opening the store, Mike had lowered the price to $1.99 for one night. The business quickly outgrew the original 143-square-foot room, and Video Station expanded into an adjacent room that was remodeled to handle walk-in business. During the first year of business, Mike's partner ran the day-to-day operations while Mike finished his last year of college and worked at Video Station on the weekends. Revenues that first year were $64,000 with all surplus cash flows used to purchase additional tapes.

During the second year, Mike's partner, who had finished college the previous year, decided to enter law school, so Mike bought him out. Video Station expanded to a second store located in a small shopping mall. The 1,200-square-foot store contained about 1,500 videotapes. To finance this expansion required additional capital that was obtained by a $100,000 loan based on Mike's personal assets. The money was used to remodel the second store, purchase the initial inventory for the second store, increase the inventory in the first store, and purchase a general-purpose vehicle for deliveries. Revenues during the second year were $173,000. Mike received an annual salary of $12,000, and all other profits were used to purchase additional tapes.

During the third year, Video Station opened a third store that had 5,000 square feet of retail floor space plus additional space for offices. This store contained more than 12,000 tapes and required an additional $200,000 loan for the remodeling and the purchase of tapes. Revenues grew each month and the total revenue for the year was $278,000. Video Station was just beginning its fourth year when Mike read the announcement of the planned arrival of Blockbuster Video.

PRESENT POSITION

The growth of Video Station had come partly at the expense of some of the smaller video rental stores, and over the past two years, 10 of them had gone out of business, leaving 9 smaller competitors. Mike estimated that his remaining competitors had an average of less than 1,000 videotapes each and combined had less than half the total video rental business in Lumberton. He also estimated that the present annual revenues from video rentals in Lumberton were about $600,000. To Mike, this did not seem to be enough business for both big stores (Video Station and Blockbuster) to be profitable.

Although the growth of Video Station has been phenomenal, the business has not been profitable. The sales mix has been 90 percent in-store rentals and 10 percent delivery. The cost of furnishing the last two stores plus the cost of purchasing a large inventory of tapes required Mike to borrow almost $300,000. The growth of revenues, however, has been up to Mike's forecasts, and he expects Video Station to become profitable this year. The income statement for the first six months indicate that his estimates are on target. (See Exhibit 1.)

Although the income statement indicated a healthy firm, Mike knew that what would be important in the next few months would be cash flows. Cash would be needed to keep the business afloat during the time after Blockbuster opened, when sales could be greatly reduced by the promotional campaign that Blockbuster normally used to open new stores. His cash flows for the past three months were positive (see Exhibit 2), although he had purchased slightly more videotapes than usual. Finally, he looked at his most recent balance sheet to see what his financial position was while going into a period of tough competition. (See Exhibit 3.) Two items looked ominous: notes payable and retained earnings.

The notes payable, which had been used to purchase the tape inventory, make leasehold improvements, and buy fixtures and office furniture for the last two stores, required only interest payments for the next three years. The other item, retained earnings, was negative because during the first three years of operation, Video Station had large depreciation expenses. Before Blockbuster had announced its opening Mike felt that Video Station had gone through its growth period satisfactorily and was finally poised to become a profitable operation. That time now seemed far away.

BLOCKBUSTER VIDEO

Blockbuster Entertainment Corporation operates and licenses Blockbuster Video stores that rent videotapes. The firm has grown from 19 stores in 1986 to 3,593 stores (2,698 company-owned and 895 franchises) in 43 states, Canada, the United Kingdom, and Guam by the end of 1994. The typical Blockbuster store carries 7,000 to 13,000 tapes and the stores range in size from 4,000 to 10,000 square feet. In 1994 the 2,109 company-owned stores that had been in operation for more than one year were averaging monthly revenues of $71,842.

Although the growth in the United States in consumer spending on video rentals seems to have slowed, Blockbuster Video believes it has the opportunity to take market share away from smaller competitors through its strategy of building large stores with a greater selection of tapes than most of its competitors. As the largest video chain in the United States, Blockbuster Video also has advantages in marketing and in the purchase of inventory. Blockbuster Video's pricing is $3.50 per tape for two nights. However, there apparently has been some discussion within the organization to give local stores some pricing discretion.

According to a prospectus, Blockbuster plans to purchase a vacant lot in Lumberton for about $310,000 and move into a 6,400-square-foot building that would be built to its specifications. The company would lease the building under a long-term agreement for $8.50 per square foot per year for the first three years. The cost of completely furnishing the building, including the videotapes, will be approximately $375,000, and Blockbuster plans to spend more than $150,000 on the grand-opening promotions. Blockbuster's operating costs are very close to Video Station's since their computer checkout equipment is similar and both firms have about the same personnel costs. Both companies depreciate their tapes over 12 months.

Efforts to Negotiate

After analyzing Blockbuster's plans, Mike called George Atkins, president of SEC Video, who had the Blockbuster Video licensee agreement for Virginia and North and South Carolina. Mike thought a meeting with Atkins could help him learn more about Blockbuster's plans in Lumberton; he also wondered if Blockbuster was interested in purchasing Video Station. Video Station has about the same size store that Blockbuster is planning to build, uses the same type of computer checkout system and many of the same fixtures, and has the same open-store layout. Mike's thinking was simple: there was not enough business for both stores to be profitable. Blockbuster would save a lot of money by moving into his store and needed only to make minor change to have a store that looked just like all other Blockbuster stores. Mike had not thought about owning a video store all his life, and he had been thinking of returning to graduate school even before the Blockbuster announcement.

Atkins seemed very happy to meet with Mike and invited him to his office in Sumter, S.C. During the meeting Atkins made a tentative offer to purchase Video Station for 40 percent of current sales plus the value of the existing tapes, and he seemed willing to purchase the leases on Mike's two stores. He did state that he would not consider a move into Mike's store because there was not enough parking area. In addition, all Blockbuster stores were to be new and the company had a policy against moving into existing stores. Interestingly, during the meeting, in which Atkins tried very hard to learn what Video Station's revenues were, he stated that he thought the potential video rental market in Lumberton was about $1 million per year. Mike thanked Atkins for his time and agreed to think about his offer.

After calculating what he thought was a reasonable point to start negotiating, Mike met with Atkins about a month later. Mike opened the meeting with a brief statement of what had happened in their last meeting and again asked if Blockbuster would not consider using Video Station's existing building, as the cost saving to Blockbuster would be enormous. Atkins again stated Blockbuster's new-store policy, which the company felt was necessary for the image it wished to maintain. He then reminded Mike that Video Station was worth more right now than it ever would be again, about how large Blockbuster was compared to Video Station, and how they would soon be able to take Mike's customers through promotions like giving away a Bronco or similar popular car each month until they had the market share they wanted.

Atkins then offered to purchase Video Station for 40 percent of his last 12 months' sales. This figure included all of Video Station's assets but none of its liabilities. This offer was so far from the previous offer that Mike did not attempt to negotiate, but he did leave open the possibility of future talks. Atkins stated this was his final offer, and he told Mike that "I will not call you again." He then hurried off to his private plane to fly to a similar-sized town about 40 miles away to discuss the purchase of that town's largest video store. As the plane taxied from the control tower, Mike began mentally analyzing his options and wondering about the future of Video Station when Blockbuster Video opened its store in less than three months.

EXHIBIT 1
Video Station, Inc., Income Statement
Six Months Ending June 30, 1995

Revenues		$167,842
Expenses		
Salaries	$41,743	
Payroll taxes	3,848	
Depreciation	46,102	
Utilities	7,301	
Rent	11,514	
Misc. taxes	8,873	
Office expenses	12,661	
Maintenance	838	
Interest expense	14,588	
Total expenses		$147,438
Income before taxes		$20,404

EXHIBIT 2
Video Station, Inc., Cash Flow, April–June 1995

Cash received		$85,774
Cash expenditures		
Purchases	$26,308	
Salaries	22,768	
Payroll taxes	2,391	
Utilities	3,614	
Rent	5,754	
Maintenance	395	
Other taxes	4,353	
Office expenses	7,876	
Interest expense	7,279	
Total cash expenditures		$80,738
Net cash inflows		$5,036

EXHIBIT 3
Video Station, Inc., Balance Sheet
June 30, 1995

Cash	$5,264
Inventory	3,700
Prepaid expenses	1,390
Total current assets	$10,354
Office equipment	$48,409
Furniture & fixtures	53,400
Videotapes	223,068
Leasehold improvements	39,800
Accumulated/depreciation	(114,823)
Total assets	$260,208
Accounts payable	$15,429
Withholding/FICA payable	2,270
Notes payable	257,518
Total current liabilities	$275,217
Common stock	$10,400
Retained earnings	(25,409)
Total liabilities and equity	$260,208

HENDERSON RADIO

"One thing is certain," said Roberta Flannagan with a smile to her husband, Robert, over breakfast on Monday. "I'll get a number of views on what our required return on equity is. I'm sure I'll get a rather detailed memo from TH, and Fred and I seem to differ on the company's future prospects." Flannagan is the chief finance officer of Henderson Radio, and until her arrival six years ago there was no formal evaluation of the company's required return or cost of capital, and no systematic procedure for evaluating capital budgeting proposals. Investment selections were frequently made on "feel" and the opinion of Fred Millner, the firm's talented general manager. Fortunately, his sense of what would sell was uncanny and Henderson grew rapidly.

THE FIRM

Henderson, like many firms in the electrical equipment industry, is well diversified in terms of products and markets and obtains a healthy percentage of its sales from government contracts. Unlike most of the other companies, however, it has not been especially aggressive in seeking government defense business. Management's thinking is that the political winds surrounding defense spending can abruptly change direction, so it is best to stay out. Henderson is also unusual in that it has made no effort to move outside the electrical equipment industry. In recent years companies like American Electric and Westinghome have entered such areas as financial services and cable TV. Millner has always resisted this type of diversification, which he believes would overextend the company. And precisely that has happened to some of the firms that tried.

Six years ago Millner worried that the industry was becoming "too darn competitive" and felt Henderson would have to improve in all areas to continue to grow. At his request the finance department was strengthened and Flannagan was hired as a result. Currently it is time to review the hurdle rate the firm uses in its capital budgeting. The final decision is made from Flannagan's office, but suggestions are always received from Millner and Thomas Henderson, a major stockholder and son of the company's founder.

TWO MEMORANDA

When Flannagan arrived at her office on Monday she found memos from both of them and a letter from the firm's investment bankers. Millner suggested using a lower proportion of debt to finance projects. Although he feels the firm's debt-equity mix has been optimal, he believes "increasing industry competition coupled with uncertainty surrounding the world economy" dictate a more conservative financing mix in the future. Millner also notes that production techniques within the industry are changing. Specifically, production processes will likely involve a larger amount of fixed costs and a smaller amount of variable costs. This will raise the degree of operating leverage and, consequently, increase the volatility of corporate earnings. "The tea leaves are small," he wrote, "but if you look carefully you can read them." He recommended that "any cost-of-equity estimate assume a 4 percent per year increase in dividends into the foreseeable future." But Millner, who was still not comfortable with the concept of a required return, wondered why the estimation was necessary. He pointed to an in-house study showing the company earned 21.3 percent on the investments it had made over the last decade. "Why not use the return we have actually achieved as the hurdle rate instead of speculating on what we think the rate is? Please give this idea consideration," he wrote in his memo.

Thomas Henderson's opinions were quite different. "If it were my decision I would use 10 percent equity and 90 percent debt. It makes no sense to use as much equity as we do considering debt is so much cheaper." (See his argument in Exhibit 1.) He then stated that if his suggested financing mix was considered too radical he felt the company could safely increase its debt proportion to 30 percent, which he thought was the upper range of the industry average. Finally, he predicted a "rosy future" for earnings and believed yearly dividends should increase by 16 percent per year.

FLANNAGAN'S VIEW

Flannagan was certainly not in accord with Millner. She agreed there was more competition but felt the market would be larger, too. For example, she believed a strong demand for personal computers would lead to a much greater demand for semiconductors, an important product of Henderson. Flannagan's view was that dividends and earning would grow indefinitely at a rate of 9–11 percent per year. Nonetheless, she has much respect for Millner, who she thinks is the top GM in the industry. Flannagan, however, does agree with Millner regarding the technological changes that will alter the industry's production techniques and cause an increase in operating leverage. She also believes that this fact is not fully appreciated by industry analysts and the GMs of other firms.

The letter from the investment bankers contained no surprises. It pointed out that the industry debt percentage ranged from 15 percent to 25 percent, where the amounts of debt and equity were measured at book values and not market values, and when accruals and accounts payable (so-called free capital) were excluded. The bankers recommended no increase in Henderson's present debt percentage because of uncertainty about how the financial markets would react and because there was some possibility Henderson's bond rating would fall. They also felt the company could issue bonds at 12 percent and notes at 10 percent and pointed out that one prestigious investment advisory service was predicting annual earnings and dividend growth for Henderson of 11 percent over the next four years and 6 percent per year after that.

After reading all the correspondence Flannagan then reviewed some other information she had gathered, including the firm's current financing mix. (See Exhibit 2.) Over the past year Henderson's stock ranged in price from $45 to $64 a share, and it is now at $50. The current dividend is $4 per share, and the firm's relevant tax rate is 40 percent. Beta estimates for the company's stock ranged from 1.3 to 1.7. These figures suggested Henderson was above average in risk, a view she knew few of the company's executives would argue with. After surveying a number of studies, she concluded investors must expect a risk premium of 8 percent above the risk-free return to buy the stock of an average risk company, and a 17 percent premium if the company was considered extremely risky. Finally, she noted the current rate on long-term government bonds was 9 percent.

As Flannagan began to prepare an estimate of the required return she thought, "I wish someone would invent a method that takes the judgment out of the evaluation. It may be true that the study of the required return is a science, but the application of the theory is a real art."

EXHIBIT 1
Thomas Henderson's Argument for Using More Debt

"The name of the game is to get our required return or hurdle rate as low as possible. I mean, if we can achieve a low hurdle rate we'll have more projects whose IRR exceeds this low rate. And what will happen to the value of our stock if we consistently implement projects whose return exceeds this hurdle rate? It will go up, of course, thereby benefiting our stockholders. Now suppose the cost of debt is 10 percent and the required return on equity is 20 percent. If (as an example) we use half debt and half equity, the hurdle rate would be 15 percent. But suppose we go easy on the equity and heavy on the debt; say we use 10 percent equity and 90 percent debt. If my arithmetic is correct the hurdle rate is 11 percent. The logic of this argument is overwhelming! Let's use as large a proportion of debt as possible."

EXHIBIT 2
Henderson Radio's Liabilities and Net Worth (Book Value) ($000s)

Accounts payable	$20,068
Notes payable	7,266
Other current	14,186
Bonds	55,360
Common stock	102,598
Retained earnings	94,602
Total liabilities and equity	$294,080

BAXTER PAVING

Baxter Oil refines and markets petroleum products, mainly in the Northeast and Midwest. Annual sales total more than $11 billion with nearly 20 percent from areas outside its energy operations. Most of the nonenergy income comes from Baxter Highway Construction, its engineering and construction operation, which paves highways for federal, state, and local governments. Revenue is obtained by bidding on highway contracts, and because government demand for this type of construction is relatively assured, income from this area is decidedly more stable than the sales of petroleum products.

Baxter Paving (BP), a subsidiary of Baxter Highway Construction, is incorporated in 19 states, primarily in the Midwest, and is the largest paving contractor in the United States with sales in 1996 of over $1 billion. BP is presently very interested in the lucrative Ohio market, where the state legislature has appropriated $5 billion for road construction over the next 10 years.

THE CONSTRUCTION PROCESS

Highway construction involves three distinct phases. First, the road site is graded or smoothed by cutting the hills and filling the valleys. The second stage requires base preparation, in which some type of foundation is laid, and in the final phase the road is paved with 5 to 12 inches of asphalt. The process typically involves two separate firms. The initial phase is done by a separate grading company, and then a firm like BP steps in and does the base preparation and paving. During the entire construction process, government inspectors periodically check the site to ensure that the state's specifications are being met.

Dr. Jailan Pak is the director of pavement design for Ohio's Department of Transportation and has convinced the DOT to alter the state's requirements for the base preparation phase of road construction. In the past, in order to meet state specifications, a contractor merely needed to compact and pave the soil after it had been graded. This method frequently left the road's base unstable and resulted in unsightly and costly potholes. Maintenance costs were extremely high and the highways would wear out rather quickly.

Dr. Pak successfully argued that the highways need a more stable foundation. Ohio's DOT now requires that the road's base be prepared by mixing cement—and occasionally lime—with crushed stone into the soil. The result is a solid foundation that will substantially reduce maintenance costs.

BP's management believes that for the next few years a bid price of $1.90 per square yard plus materials would win much of this base preparation work. If successful, therefore, BP would receive $1.90 for each square yard of road base, plus the cost of all materials. (See Exhibit 2.) Though the changes in the DOT specifications are potentially lucrative, they have caused a problem for BP. What's the best way to meet these specifications and become a successful bidder?

TWO OPTIONS

For the firm to do all road work in house requires the use of one machine to mix the crushed stone and cement into the soil and a second machine to fine-grade the surface after the mixing is completed. A mixing machine would cost $240,000 and the fine-grade equipment $260,000. Each machine has a useful life of 15 years, and yearly maintenance (overhaul) costs would total $20,000.

BP could also subcontract the mixing and fine-grading required in the base preparation. The subcontracting price would run $1.20 per square yard for the required mixing and fine-grading. In addition, BP would provide all the necessary materials. Should BP sub this work, it would do nothing during the base preparation phase except assume full responsibility for any cost overruns and for meeting the state's requirements. Note that BP would pocket the difference between the bid price on the base preparation and the amount paid the subcontractors except for monitoring and administrative costs of $90,000 per year. And of course it would still perform the necessary paving.

MANAGEMENT REACTION

There is considerable discussion about how BP should respond to the DOT specifications. John Haney, executive vice president, believes that all the necessary work should be done in house. He argues that this "almost surely" is the most profitable way to go, "considering how expensive subcontractors are."

Bart Hahn was BP's senior vice president and second-in-command for more than 15 years. Ten months ago he was made president. And Hahn is very apprehensive about BP performing all the base preparation work. First, he notes that the firm is presently operating at capacity, and additional work would require an increase in supervisory and technical support. Second, BP has never prepared a road base in the manner now required by the state. "We could easily screw up," he argues, "with cost overruns, that type of thing." Third, he isn't sure the new DOT requirements will last and believes that a subtle political risk is involved. He points out that these new specifications increase the cost of a road to the state, adding, "I can certainly see the possibility that some politician or politicians—eager to reduce expenses in the short run—will have these new requirements voted out." In short, he sees little point in BP "gearing up" to meet the new DOT regulations in house. All things considered, Hahn believes BP should subcontract all the required base preparation work.

Ron Farr, a company vice president, thinks Hahn's last point is well made. "The political winds can change abruptly," he notes. "If so, and if we buy the equipment to do the work, where are we? Pretty much stuck with equipment we don't need, that's where. And don't forget that the DOT's road expenditures depend on the state's tax revenue, which is heavily influenced by the state of the economy. Sure, Ohio's legislature has appropriated $5 billion for highway construction. But what the legislature votes in can also be voted out."

Rebecca Morgan, comptroller, believes that Hahn is overreacting and points out that BP's parent company, Baxter Highway Construction, has a very capable technical staff in Chicago. It would be a "simple matter" to obtain their help, and they would also assist in recruiting and training any necessary personnel. Further, she notes that the state has inspectors who check the work at various stages. Thus, in her view, the possibility of a major problem is actually rather small.

Hahn, obviously unimpressed with all this, responds quickly. "There are a number of problems with your arguments. Sure, we could get technical help from the Chicago office. But every time we do this we give up a little bit of control. We risk losing our autonomy, not controlling our destiny. Let's keep Chicago out of this . . . unless you don't mind outsiders meddling in our affairs. And although the state has inspectors, you know how much trouble and expense we incur when they detect a construction flaw. The cost overruns can be substantial, as I said before."

Elenore Mosely, chief construction engineer, isn't sure what to do but doesn't like the prospect of BP losing more control to its parent company. She believes, however, that the new DOT specs are permanent, pointing out that the savings in yearly maintenance costs are "enormous over the long run." Responding to a point raised by Farr, she explains that the equipment does have alternative uses should the state's new road requirements change. "We can, for example, use a mixing machine to recycle asphalt. And keep in mind that the market price of old and new asphalt is about the same." The yearly after-tax cash flows would be $120(000), assuming the new equipment is used in its best alternative use. (Mosely calls this "the cash flows of the fallback position.")

Mosely also has mixed feelings about whether BP has the expertise to successfully meet the new specs. She concedes that BP doesn't have experience in this technology at present, but believes that the process isn't terribly difficult. She does worry, though, that the firm's technical and supervisory staff is currently "overextended to a degree" and that qualified personnel may be difficult to get.

ANOTHER OPTION

Haney thinks there is another option that has not been discussed. He suggests that BP rent or lease the necessary equipment, making sure that any lease has a cancellation clause. "That way," he argues, "we don't have to worry about the political risk involved. If the DOT's requirements change suddenly, we can simply return the machines to the leasing firm." Farr sees a number of disadvantages to this. First, he feels it is likely to be "very expensive" to obtain some type of cancellation clause. Second, it doesn't overcome the expertise problem. Still, he thinks the option is worth pursuing. He wonders, though, if it wouldn't be more "financially prudent" to obtain some type of relatively short-term (two- to five-year), noncancellable financial lease, which he feels certain would be cheaper than either renting or obtaining an operating lease that would have a cancellation clause.

POSSIBLE COMPETITION

One concern shared by all the managers is that new competitors will enter the market if BP doesn't respond appropriately to the new requirements. At present BP is the only paving contractor within a 100-mile radius, primarily because this market is not large enough to support more than one firm. The new state requirements, however, effectively increase the demand for paving and construction and raise the likelihood that new firms will want to enter the geographical area served by BP. Management would very much like to deter new entry if possible. Everyone believes that the key is to charge a price that is unlikely to attract the attention of possible competitors. The price of $1.90 per square yard plus materials is probably high but can be expected to persist for the next three years. That is, management believes that for the next three years BP can successfully bid at this price for the state's jobs without attracting new firms to the market. Beginning in year 4, however, it is considered essential that BP's bid should be low enough to deter entry.

A task force has estimated that this price is $1.40 a square yard plus all materials. The assumptions used to obtain this estimate are listed in Exhibit 3.

At a subsequent meeting and after considerable discussion, a consensus is reached on a number of points thought to be relevant to the decision.

1. The appropriate time frame for planning purposes is 10 years.
2. (a) Performing all work in house would require additional office and storage space costing $300(000).
   (b) Ninety percent of this cost is depreciable; the remainder is not depreciable because it is for additional land.
3. The value (after taxes) of the new building and extra land will be $150(000) after 10 years.
4. (a) For purpose of analysis, straight line depreciation will be used.
   (b) All equipment will be depreciated over 5 years, all structures over 10.
5. BP expects the annual volume of new base preparation work to equal 1,000(000) square yards in years 1–4, and 1,500(000) square yards in years 5–10. These figures assume BP has successfully deterred new entrants.

6. The relevant (marginal) tax rate is 40 percent.
7. Due to BP's lack of expertise in this type of work, supervisory and administrative costs will be higher in years 1 to 3 than 4 to 10. Cash overhead expense is therefore predicted as follows: year 1, $400(000); year 2, $350(000); year 3, $300(000); years 4 to 10, $285(000).
8. Working capital requirements total 20 percent of dollar sales.
9. Because of the political and technical risks associated with undertaking the base preparation work in house, the appropriate after-tax discount rate is 20 percent, which is 5 percentage points above the usual rate. However, management will use the 15 percent rate to evaluate the possibility of hiring subcontractors.

There is some disagreement on the probability that the new state requirements will exist in any year. For purposes of analysis, a 70 percent probability, the majority view, will be used. There is a vocal minority, however, that feels this is too low. This group notes that a number of other states have had similar requirements for many years because of the savings in road maintenance and repair. Consequently, they believe that it is a "virtual certainty" the new specifications will last.

As this meeting adjourns, Hahn says that he has heard no convincing arguments for performing all the work in house. And unless he receives "compelling evidence to the contrary," he favors the use of subcontractors.

EXHIBIT 1
Production and Cost Requirements of Preparing Road Base to Meet New Specifications

---

1. *Mobilization and "Teeth" Costs.* These involve transporting the equipment and materials to the job site and changing the "teeth" on the machines, 6 cents per square yard.
2. *Mixing Costs.* This involves mixing the crushed stone and concrete into the soil. These costs run 19 cents per square yard and include direct labor, routine maintenance, and fuel.
3. *Fine-Grade Costs.* This expense is for fine-grading the road's base and runs 15 cents per square yard. It includes direct labor, routine maintenance, and fuel.
4. *Machine Overhaul Costs.* Two machines, $20(000) annually (i.e., $10(000) per machine).
5. *Cash Overhead Expense.* This item includes supervisory and administrative salaries plus miscellaneous fixed expenses: year 1, $400(000); year 2, $350(000); year 3, $300(000); years 4 to 10, $285(000).

EXHIBIT 2
Material Costs

Crushed stone is $4 per ton (1 ton = 2,000 pounds) and 800 pounds of stone per square yard of road base are required. Concrete is $67 per ton and 50 pounds of concrete per square yard of road base are required.

EXHIBIT 3
Assumptions Used to Estimate Bid Price Necessary to Deter Competition Beginning in Year 4

1. A potential entrant will assume that 400(000) square yards per year of base preparation work can be obtained.
2. The relevant time period is 10 years.
3. The tax rate is .40.
4. The up-front cost is $700(000), which includes working capital requirements and is net of the present value of the project's terminal value.
5. Annual unit variable costs are 44 cents per square yard.
6. Annual fixed cash expenses are $200(000).
7. Annual depreciation is $70(000).
8. The required return (cost of capital) is .15.

CASE 55

MEREDITH CORPORATION

The Meredith Corporation is a major producer of rotary power lawn mowers, including walk-behinds and riding mowers. Secondary products include lawn and garden tools such as tillers, cultivators, and snow throwers. The firm has two major manufacturing plants—one in Greenspan, California, and one in Lynchburg, Georgia—with a total of 2.5 million square feet. Over 30 percent of its sales are to Spears and Kalmart. Though sales have increased nearly threefold in the last 15 years (see Exhibit 2), they have fallen three times over the same period. The 1980 sales drop was due to a recession and because Spears—upset at a price increase it considered inappropriate and excessive—reduced its purchases. Sales also fell in 1982, a recession year, and in 1991 due to a fire at the Georgia plant. Fortunately, Meredith's net income has been in the black for the last 25 years, though it fell to 2 percent of sales in 1980, 1982, and 1991.

Four years ago the company hired Stuart Handelman as CEO. One of Handelman's objectives was to diversify Meredith's customer base because he felt the company was too heavily dependent on major retailers. He cited the incident with Spears as an example of the problems such a dependency can cause. Before Handelman was CEO about 50 percent of Meredith's sales were to two major wholesalers. Today it is slightly more than 30 percent. Handelman was also concerned with Meredith's relatively low profit margin, which he concluded was the result of cost inefficiencies rather than improper pricing of the firm's products. Finding and correcting these inefficiencies, however, have proven more elusive than he first thought. Though the gross margin has risen in each of the last two years, it still remains below industry standards. (See Exhibit 3.)

A major decision that Meredith must currently make is how to raise $50 million. These funds would be used to modernize the two plants and expand the Lynchburg facility in order to accommodate the expected sales increases in Meredith's mower business in the important southeastern market. The modernization is considered necessary for both offensive and defensive reasons.

Offensively, this should reduce the firm's costs, and, it is hoped, enable Meredith to achieve competitive profit margins. Defensively, Meredith needs some new equipment simply to remain competitive with other producers.

Management is considering three possible financing alternatives to raise the needed $50 million.

Stock Option. This involves the sale of new common stock at a price of $27 per share. Meredith would net $25 after the $2 per share flotation cost.

Bond Option. The bonds would be 15-year debentures bearing an interest rate of 10 percent. The bonds would be callable after seven years at a price of $1,100 per $1,000 bond, declining to 1,000 by year 15. The indenture requires that Meredith's current ratio can't fall below 2, the debt ratio can't exceed 0.54, and yearly dividends are limited to 60 percent of net income. The bond agreement also requires a sinking fund whereby 5 percent of the bonds would be retired in years 1 through 14. (Note that Meredith would have a balloon payment equal to 30 percent of the issue due at the end of year 15.) Meredith could satisfy the sinking fund provision in one of two ways. It could purchase the required amount of bonds in the open market and deliver them to the trustee, American Bank and Trust. It could also simply give American Bank and Trust sufficient cash to purchase the bonds at par value. The trustee would then retire the required amount by a lottery method.

Combination Option. This is a 50–50 mix of the stock and debenture options previously described.

Meredith's board of directors is clearly split on which alternative to choose. A summary of a recent board meeting shows the various positions.

PRO DEBT

Dr. Theodore Burgmeister, marketing professor. Believes the firm is underlevered. Points out that the current and quick ratios are above industry norms, as are the coverage ratios: the times interest earned and fixed charge coverage. In his judgment the debt and D/E (long-term debt divided by equity) ratios are "well below" average. (See Exhibit 3.)

John Shreiner, treasurer. Agrees with Burgmeister that Meredith is underlevered. Also believes that the firm's stock is "unappreciated" by investors. Feels that the sales estimates in Exhibit 4 are too low. Wants EPS up and feels debt will do this. Wonders if this isn't an appropriate time to evaluate the firm's dividend policy.

Tyler Cogburn, chief financial officer. Favors debt for three reasons. First, in his view, inflation will escalate so any money borrowed now can be repaid with "cheaper" dollars. Second, the covenants on the bonds aren't very restrictive. Third—and this he gives the most emphasis—he feels that Meredith's profits will soar and it would be "unfair" to existing stockholders to sell new stock at this time. Like Shreiner, believes the sales estimates of Exhibit 4 are low. Admits, though, that the new projects do involve risk.

PRO EQUITY

Preston Hunter, retired CEO of New England Life and Casualty. Worried about Meredith's ability to repay debt. Believes the analysis of Burgmeister may be "incomplete." Cites Meredith's relatively poor profitability. Notes that a number of highly uccessful firms in the industry have relatively low debt ratios. Urges a debt moratorium until profitability improves.

Cynthia Palmer, senior vice president. Concerned about the firm's business risk. Feels it must be higher than the industry average because Meredith produces a relatively large proportion of durable goods. Notes that durable-goods purchases are likely to be postponed if a recession hits.

Gordon Greenwood, director of marketing. Agrees with Palmer and worries about Meredith's ability to pay more debt. Cites the three sales decreases in the last 15 years. Believes Meredith was "lucky" that sales didn't fall when a drought hit much of the South in the late 1980s. Admits, however, that the firm's net income has not been in the red in 25 years.

Katherine Devlin-Cutter, chief operating officer. Sees merit to all the arguments. Wonders if the combination bond/stock option or some type of preferred stock offering would be an acceptable compromise. Feels that, in a pinch, dividends could be reduced or eliminated.

Stuart Handelman, current chairman and CEO. "Personal bias" is to use the option—most likely debt—that increases Meredith's EPS the most since EPS is such a "closely watched indicator of performance." Also is worried about future financing. Doesn't want to limit Meredith's financing flexibility.

Beverly Davis, economist. Strongly thinks that the Federal Reserve will fight any inflationary pressure even at the risk of a recession. Believes, though, that the Fed will probably be able to engineer a "soft landing," that is, eliminate inflationary tendencies without precipitating a recession. Thinks Palmer's observations about durable goods are well made.

Exhibit 5 shows the consensus "best-guess" sales and cash flow estimates for the next four years, 1996 to 1999. These estimates assume:

1. The firm is able to get its operating margin, i.e., (EBIT + Dep.)/Sales, to the industry average by 1997.
2. The change in net working capital (i.e., cash + receivables + inventory − accounts payable − accruals) equals 22 percent of the change in sales.
3. Dividends are $.50 per share each year.

The forecast also assumes that all the proposed capital budgeting projects are implemented. Thus the sales projections assume that Meredith increases sales in the southeastern market. These estimates also include the additional depreciation on the new plant and equipment. They do *not*, however, consider the impact of any new debt nor the additional dividends of a stock issue.

EXHIBIT 1
Meredith's Current (1995) Income Statement and Balance Sheet

1995 Income Statement ($000s)

Sales	$500,000
Cost of goods sold	355,000
Gross margin	$145,000
Operating expenses	108,000
Depreciation	7,000
EBIT	$30,000
Interest	3,050
Earnings before taxes	$26,950
Taxes (40%)	10,780
Net income	$16,170
Earnings per share	$1.97
Dividends per share	0.50

1995 Balance Sheet ($000s)

Assets		*Liabilities and Equity*	
Cash	$12,500	Accounts payable	$31,800
Accounts receivable	65,900	Debt due	5,000
Inventory	98,850	Other current	27,250
Current assets	$177,250	Current liabilities	$64,050
Net fixed	50,000	Bonds	29,000
Total assets	$227,250	Equity	134,200
		Total liabilities and equity	$227,250

EXHIBIT 2
Meredith's History of Sales, P–E, and Operating Margin[a]

Year	Sales (millions)	P–E Ratio	Operating Margin (%)
1979	$189.4	7.8	8.8
1980 (recession)	150.6	13.2	7.9
1981	225.9	10.6	8.3
1982 (recession)	200.6	11.4	6.6
1983	250.4	8.1	7.7
1984	261.6	9.9	9.0
1985	285.5	12.4	7.7

(continued)

EXHIBIT 2
(Continued)

Year	Sales (millions)	P–E Ratio	Operating Margin (%)
1986	308.7	10.6	6.9
1987	360.9	11.4	7.5
1988	400.0	15.1	7.2
1989	418.1	12.6	8.1
1990 (recession)	420.6	10.1	6.1
1991	395.8	12.4	7.1
1992	441.6	12.2	6.0
1993	447.2	11.6	6.2
1994	485.3	13.1	6.8
1995 (present)	500.0	13.7	7.4

[a]Operating margin equals (EBIT + Dep.)/Sales.

EXHIBIT 3
Selected Financial Ratios, 1995 (Present Year)

	Meredith	Industry Average
Current	2.77	2.39
Quick	1.22	1.02
Debt	.41	.51
D/E[a]	0.22	0.38
TIE	9.84	7.88
FCC[b]	8.15	6.34

[a]D/E is the ratio of long-term debt to equity.

[b]FCC = Fixed Charge Coverage = (EBIT + Lease)/(Interest + Lease)

Normalized Income Statement

	Meredith	Industry Average
Sales	100.00	100.00
Cost of goods sold	71.00	70.00
Gross margin	29.00	30.00
Operating expenses	21.60	20.10
Depreciation	1.40	1.70
EBIT	6.00	8.20
Interest	0.61	1.04
EBT	5.39	7.16
Taxes (40%)	2.16	2.86
Net Income	3.23	4.30

EXHIBIT 4
Meredith's Pro Forma 1996 and 1997 Income Statements ($000s)

	1996	1997
Sales	$525,000	$600,000
Cost of goods sold	370,125	420,000
Gross margin	$154,875	$180,000
Operating expenses	110,250	120,600
Depreciation	10,500	13,000
EBIT	$34,125	$46,400
Interest	2,800	2,400
Earnings before tax	$31,325	$44,000
Taxes (40%)	12,530	17,600
Net income	$18,795	$26,400

NOTE: The 1996 forecast assumes a gross margin of 29.5 percent and that operating expenses will be 21 percent of sales. The 1997 forecast assumes a gross margin of 30 percent and that operating expenses will be 20.1 percent of sales. Neither forecast considers the impact of the new financing.

EXHIBIT 5
Meredith's Best Guess (Most Likely) Sales and Cash Flow Forecast: 1996–1999 ($ Millions)

	$t = 0$ 1995	$t + 1$ 1996	$t + 2$ 1997	$t + 3$ 1998	$t + 4$ 1999
Sales	$500	$525	$600	$680	$690
Net income		18.8	26.4	30.7	31.4
Depreciation		10.5	13.0	14.0	14.1
Cash flow from operations		$29.3	$39.4	$44.7	$45.5
— Dividends		4.1	4.1	4.1	4.1
— Debt due		5.0	5.0	5.0	5.0
— Change in working capital		5.5	16.5	17.6	2.2
— Capital spending		35.0	28.0	17.0	15.0
Cash flow		($20.3)	($14.2)	$1.0	$19.2

NOTE: These estimates assume that the change in net working capital equals 22 percent of the change in sales. The figures do not, however, consider the impact of the new financing of $50 million. At the present time (1995) the firm has neither a cash surplus nor deficit.

EXHIBIT 6
Meredith's Worst-Case Cash Flow Forecast: 1996–1999 ($ Millions)

	$t = 0$ 1995	$t + 1$ 1996	$t + 2$ 1997	$t + 3$ 1998	$t + 4$ 1999
Sales	$500	$500	$520	$530	$540
Net income		14.5	15.0	17.0	19.6
Depreciation		10.5	13.0	14.0	14.1
Cash flow from operations		$25.0	$28.0	$31.0	$33.7
— Dividends		4.1	4.1	4.1	4.1
— Debt due		5.0	5.0	5.0	5.0
— Change in working capital		8.0	6.0	4.0	3.0
— Capital spending		34.0	27.0	17.0	15.0
Cash flow		($26.1)	($14.1)	$0.9	$6.6

NOTE: The impact of the $50 million of the new funds is ignored. This forecast assumes that the new projects do not increase sales as much as expected and allows for a recession in 1996. Sales are not predicted to decrease in 1996 because management feels that the sales-enhancing effect of the new projects will offset any tendency for sales to decrease as they did in the 1980 and 1982 recessions. Operating margin is forecast to be 7.5 percent in 1996, 8 percent in 1997, 8.5 percent in 1998, and 9 percent in 1999. These are all above the 1995 level of 7.4 percent but below those used in Exhibits 4 and 5. Management's rationale is that some improvement is a virtual certainty given the new projects and the emphasis on cost effectiveness. The forecast allows for working capital difficulties and assumes that $1 million of capital spending can be eliminated in 1996 and 1997 without seriously disrupting the firm's commercial strategy.

EXHIBIT 7
Yearly Cash Outlays (Before Taxes) of Each Financing Option ($ Millions)

	Bond Option			Stock Option			Combination		
Year	Int.	SF	Div.	Int.	SF	Div.	Int.	SF	Div.
1996	$5	2.5	0	0	0				
1997		2.5	0	0	0				

NOTE: Int. is the additional interest, SF is the extra sinking fund payment, and Div. is the extra dividends.

SMITHFIELD DRUG

The earnings of drugstore companies are not especially sensitive to the state of the economy. This is mainly because about 70 percent of a drugstore's merchandise mix is composed of prescriptions, toiletries, tobacco and cosmetics. And these items are minimally related to economic conditions.

Smithfield Drug operates a chain of drugstores and is virtually a household name in much of the Northeast. On the one hand Smithfield is quite a dull company. Sales growth has been steady but unspectacular for nearly two decades. On the other hand its readily identifiable name and product mix mean that sales are virtually "recession-proof." "We're dull but reliable," its chief financial officer once remarked at a board of directors meeting.

LBO

What constitutes a highly leveraged firm seems to be a relative concept. When J. P. Morgan created U.S. Steel in 1901 with a financing package resulting in a 35 percent debt ratio, his deal was considered to be highly leveraged. The Federal Reserve has used a 75 percent debt figure as part of its definition of a leveraged buyout (LBO). And considering that the average debt-to-asset ratio of U.S. firms is roughly 55 percent, a company whose ratio is above the Fed's guideline would indeed seem to be highly leveraged. Still, it is not unusual for the debt proportion of Japanese firms to exceed 80 percent.

By either the Federal Reserve or Japanese standard, however, the proposed acquisition of Smithfield by three of its top managers would appear to be highly levered. If successful, John Lewis, Isao Ozaki, and Andrew Weisenberger would control a firm with a debt ratio of around 90 percent.

Lewis, Ozaki, and Weisenberger are eager to acquire the firm using as much debt as possible; they would take the company private, run it for five years, then go public. They want to purchase Smithfield primarily because they believe the firm is not being run very efficiently. They can cite numerous examples of unnecessary corporate perks, bloated divisional budgets, and haphazard supervisory procedures. They feel strongly that profit margins will increase if they can take the firm private and avoid costs like registration and listing fees that are incurred with outside ownership. In short, the trio feels that with their ownership and direction, Smithfield will become a "leaner and meaner" organization. They are also quite frank to acknowledge their need of a professional challenge. All are highly successful corporate managers in their mid-fifties with lots of energy.

TBE

The managers have enlisted the investment banking firm of Thornton, Brock and Edwards (TBE) to assist and advise them. And while there are rumors circulating that Smithfield is a takeover target, at this point the details of any possible offer are far from complete. The firm's present (1996) stock price is $31 a share, and at a recent meeting Laura Osborne, a TBE representative, thought that a bid of at least $34 would be necessary. She recommended that the trio consider an offer of $36, with $31 in cash and $5 in pay-in-kind (PIK) preferred stock. Since there are 7.4 million shares of common stock and TBE's fee is $3 million, the offer requires $269.4 million. (Note that the new owners would also assume $4 million of long-term debt that Smithfield presently has. See Exhibit 1). As a starting point, Osborne suggested the following financial package.

$35 million in equity, to be provided by Lewis, Ozaki, and Weisenberger.
$133.2 million in secured debt.
$64.2 million in debentures.
$37 million in PIK preferred stock.

Osborne pointed out that the equity and bonds were the sources of cash to be given Smithfield's stockholders. It is important, therefore, that the debt yield a competitive return so that both securities can be sold at par.

The PIK preferred stock would be given directly to Smithfield's stockholders to sell or keep as they see fit. This preferred stock works as follows. For the first three years, a holder will not be entitled to any cash dividends but would receive more preferred stock. Starting at the end of year 4, cash dividends would be paid on the full amount of preferred stock accumulated over the first three years.

At the same meeting, the following estimates were made.

1. (a) The management group feels it is a "virtual certainty" that annual sales will increase.
   (b) They believe some reduction in the firm's costs are "inevitable assuming reasonable management."
   (c) The best-guess (most likely) projections are shown in Exhibit 2.
   (d) They also feel that cost savings greater than those implied by Exhibit 2 could be achieved.

2. Smithfield's present working capital situation is adequate to support the sales growth projected in Exhibit 2, and could possibly be a source of cash at these sales volumes.

3. Capital spending should run between $7 and $11 million a year, with a best guess of $9 million.

4. The secured debt could be sold at par if it yielded 10 percent.

5. The debentures would be considered junk bonds by investors and would have to yield 13 percent to sell at par.

6. None of the debt would carry sinking fund provisions.

7. The pay-in-kind preferred stock would carry a coupon of 15 percent and would pay no cash dividends for the first three years. Thus, the number of shares of this security would increase by 15 percent a year during the first three years. Cash dividends would start at the end of year 4 and equal 15 percent of the total amount of preferred stock outstanding.

8. TBE will make an estimate of Smithfield's $t = 5$ market value. The management group thinks that after their planned changes, Smithfield's risk can best be evaluated using the firms listed in Exhibit 3.

OTHER CONSIDERATIONS

Unfortunately for the trio, they may not be the only suitors of Smithfield. It is believed that another group led by the firm of Katcavage and Roberts, famous for its LBO's, is also interested. Osborne said that Smithfield's board of directors would "be very thorough in analyzing any and all bids" and "most certainly will pursue an objective of maximizing shareholder value. This means, of course, that the key factor will be the highest bid in terms of present value." She then explained that the "highest" bid is not necessarily the one the board will take, however. The firm's directors will also want to know where the money will come from ("Can a bidder deliver?") and whether antitrust problems would exist (the government could disallow an acquisition). Osborne doesn't think any of these secondary issues are likely to matter and that the offer with the highest present value will be accepted.

When a bid is all in cash, the board will obviously have no problem in deciding its present worth. But if part of the offer is in securities, a board must evaluate what the securities could sell for. In other words, their cash value could be more or less than their par value. With the financing package outlined above, the market value of the 15 percent PIK preferred stock is unclear. Osborne thinks that investors will evaluate this with a capitalization rate of 13 to 17 percent.

And she emphasized that the rate estimates on the secured and unsecured debt were just that—estimates. Market conditions could well change by the time these securities are sold. Further, "One never knows exactly how the financial community will react. In order for these bonds to sell at par, rates higher or lower than those discussed might have to be offered." Finally, Osborne said that neither the bid price nor the financing package are "etched in stone."

Lewis, Ozaki, and Weisenberger have spent much time listening to the advice of TBE. And while they will continue to listen carefully, it is clear that they will make up their own minds about what to do. At this point, they have many questions, but the two most important are:

1. How risky is the bid and financial package proposed by TBE?
2. If all goes as planned, what return on equity can they expect?

EXHIBIT 1

Smithfield's Current (1996) Balance Sheet and Income Statement ($ Million)

Assets		Liabilities and Equity	
Current	$98	Current	$40
Fixed	82	Bonds	4
		Equity	136
Total	$180	Total	$180

Income Statement

Sales	$293.3
Cost of goods sold	176.0
Gross margin	117.3
FOC	94.0
EBIT	23.3
Interest	0.4
Earnings before taxes	22.9
Taxes (40%)	9.2
Earnings after taxes	$13.7

EXHIBIT 2
Management Group's Pro Forma Income Statements ($ Million)*

	1997 t + 1	1998 t + 2	1999 t + 3	2000 t + 4	2001 t + 5
Sales	$305.0	$317.2	$329.9	$343.1	$356.8
Cost of goods sold	176.9	180.8	184.7	192.1	199.8
Gross margin	128.1	136.4	145.2	151.0	157.0
FOC[a]	90.0	88.0	91.5	95.2	99.0
EBIT	38.1	48.4	53.7	55.8	58.0
Interest	22.1	22.1	22.1	22.1	22.1
Earnings before taxes	16.0	26.3	31.6	33.7	35.9
Taxes (40%)	6.4	10.5	12.6	13.5	14.4
Earnings after taxes	$9.6	$15.8	$19.0	$20.2	$21.5

[a]Includes annual depreciation of $7 million.

*This forecast assumes (1) sales growth of 4 percent per year; (2) cost of goods will be 58 percent of sales in year 1, 57 percent in year 2 and 56 percent in years 3–5; (3) FOC can be cut to $88 million in two years and at that point rises with sales growth.

EXHIBIT 3
Comparables Chosen for TBE's Value Estimate ($ Million)

Firm	Sales	Beta	Debt[a]	Equity[a]
Anchor Drugs	$255	0.85	$40	$120
Babcock	520	1.2	195	150

[a]Market value.

E V E R L A S T

Everlast is a well-known battery manufacturer headquartered in the United States. It is holding a meeting to review plans for a new plant in Arabia, a small country on the Persian Gulf. At the meeting is Ed Phillips, the CEO; Robert Strauss, treasurer and CFO; and Susan Altman, head of the international division. Susan Altman is making the presentation.

ALTMAN Today we're here to discuss a proposal to build a battery manufacturing plant in Arabia. The plant will cost $10 million and generate a rate of return of 18.4 percent and an NPV of $945,800. Our share of the cost is $7.5 million, with the remainder provided by our prospective partner in Arabia, Mr. Mohammed Jeddah. Mr. Jeddah owns a facility in Arabia that was previously used by a firm that went bankrupt. The plant is in good condition, and all necessary facilities such as railroad sidings, electricity, water, and telephone service are already in place. Mr. Jeddah has agreed to transfer ownership to our new subsidiary, Everlast Arabia, in return for a 25 percent interest in the new company. We will provide working capital, machinery, technical expertise, and sales outlets. The machinery for the plant can be built in our plant in Houston and shipped to Arabia. Based on our experience at opening other plants, we expect minimal start-up problems.

Unlike many countries, the rulers in Arabia are very probusiness. There is little threat of expropriation, and the tax code and investment code are reasonable. There's no difficulty in repatriating profits. As is common in the Gulf countries, there is a requirement that locals own 25 percent of the enterprise. That reduces our profits, but it's better than some other countries in the area that require local control of a majority of the shares. Also, unlike many other countries, the regulations and tax rates are the same for foreigners and nationals. Finally, there are no local currency controls. As overseas projects go, this one is a piece of cake.

PHILLIPS Can you step us through the financials?

ALTMAN Certainly. As you can see from your handout, Exhibit 1 shows annual sales of 20 million units. Given the current forecasts of prices in the European market, this generates revenues in the first year of $10 million. Our equipment is expected to last seven years, at which point it is likely to be technologically obsolete. Consequently, I've assumed this is a seven-year project and we will withdraw at the end of that time. Obviously, if conditions warrant, we can stay longer.

STRAUSS You should be aware, Ed, that the tax component here represents port taxes, tariffs, employment taxes, and some miscellaneous taxes but no income taxes.

ALTMAN No income taxes!

STRAUSS That's right. The Arabian government has given us a 10-year income tax holiday, so we pay no Arabian taxes. Normally, we would pay U.S. taxes on the profits. But, as you know, our plant in Letho lost money for several years. The tax law allows us to offset our profits in Arabia with our losses in Letho, so we pay no U.S. taxes either.

PHILLIPS By the way, you've been talking about dollar figures. Shouldn't we be talking in terms of the local currency, Arabian pounds?

ALTMAN The numbers in the handout are in Arabian pounds, but since the Arabian pound is pegged, one-to-one, to the U.S. dollar, we can use our currency. As you can see from Exhibit 1, I have one line at the bottom where I translate Everlast's share of the cash flow into dollars.

PHILLIPS Is there a risk of devaluation?

ALTMAN Yes, in fact there's a fairly high probability that the pound will be devaluated. The currency is overvalued by 20 percent. However, the government has enough reserves to sustain an overvalued currency for a long time.

PHILLIPS What happens to the financials if there is a devaluation?

ALTMAN I don't have numbers on that case, but I don't think it will make much difference because neither our revenue nor most of our costs are in Arabian pounds. For example, our sales are all in Europe, and we assume European currencies will, on average, remain stable vis-a-vis the dollar. So the revenues, measured in dollars, would not be affected by the devaluation. Materials (which are entirely imported) would cost the same in dollar terms. Even labor would probably cost about the same, because most of our workers would be expatriates, and we'd probably have to pay them in dollar terms.

To the extent we employ Arabians, labor costs might be lower because—at least initially—we'd pay them the same number of Arabian pounds per week, but it would cost us fewer dollars to buy those pounds. It's hard to tell about labor cost because we don't know the mix of employees yet. Frankly, we may not be hiring very many Arabians.

PHILLIPS I've heard that the government gives them so much—free medical services, cheap fuel, electricity, and so on—that it's hard to motivate them.

ALTMAN That's often the case. But more important, most of the jobs we have will be on a production line or on the maintenance crew or the loading docks.

Those are definitely not the jobs that Arabians want. We'll train some for the front office and sales, but I doubt they will make up more than 10 percent of the labor force.

STRAUSS On the other hand, the value of our plant would drop. If it were worth £3.4 million before and the pound drops by 20 percent, then the value of our investment drops 20 percent, too.

ALTMAN The plant is going to be more profitable than ever after devaluation since labor costs may drop slightly, and so other costs like taxes may decrease in dollar terms, too. So it seems to me that the plant must be more valuable, not less.

STRAUSS How much would it sell for?

ALTMAN I don't know. I'll have to look into that.

PHILLIPS Let's talk a little more about the rate of return. Your NPV estimate assumes a required return of 15 percent, which is the hurdle rate for our U.S. projects. Shouldn't we use a higher rate for a foreign investment?

ALTMAN As a general rule, I agree. All of the other foreign projects I've presented to the board have had rates of return in excess of 20 percent. But this project is much safer than the typical foreign investment. The infrastructure is built and in excellent condition, taxes are no problem, shipping costs to our markets are modest, the government is stable, and the life of the project is only seven years—we get our money out pretty quickly.

PHILLIPS True, but this project does not make it if the tax law changes. We don't usually approve projects that are so close to the hurdle rate that a tax advantage would make a difference.

STRAUSS In this case, though, there is a time limit on using the losses. If we don't use them up soon, they'll pass the time limit and we can't use them at all.

PHILLIPS Why can't we build the same plant in Europe? Then the transportation costs would be even lower, and we could avoid some tariffs.

STRAUSS True, but then we wouldn't be able to use the tax credits.

ALTMAN The costs of building and operating a plant in Europe are higher, too.

PHILLIPS Why don't you look at some of the issues we've discussed and we'll meet again Monday morning.

EXHIBIT 1
Battery Plant Projections (Base Case)[e]

	t + 1	t + 2	t + 3	t + 4	t + 5	t + 6	t + 7
Unit Sales	20,000	20,000	20,000	20,000	20,000	20,000	20,000
Sales	10,000	10,500	11,000	11,600	12,200	12,800	13,500
Wages	3,000	3,000	3,100	3,200	3,300	3,400	3,600
Shipping	800	850	900	950	1,000	1,050	1,100
Material	2,400	2,550	2,800	2,950	3,050	3,200	3,400
Taxes[a]	1,000	1,050	1,100	1,150	1,200	1,250	1,300
Overhead	800	850	900	950	950	1,000	1,000
Depreciation	700	700	700	700	700	700	700
EBIT	1,300	1,500	1,500	1,700	2,000	2,200	2,400
Income Taxes	0	0	0	0	0	0	0
EAT = NI	1,300	1,500	1,500	1,700	2,000	2,200	2,400
+ Depreciation	700	700	700	700	700	700	700
Cash Flows[b]	2,000	2,200	2,200	2,400	2,700	2,900	6,500
Everlast's CF[c]	1,500	1,650	1,650	1,800	2,025	2,175	4,875
Exchange Rate[d]	1	1	1	1	1	1	1
Everlast's CF[c]							
Cash flow ($ U.S.)	1,500	1,650	1,650	1,800	2,025	2,175	4,875

[a]Considers port taxes, tariffs, employment taxes, and some miscellaneous taxes.

[b]Note that the cash flow for year 7 considers the value of the plant, estimated to be 3.4 million Arabian pounds.

[c]75 percent of CF (25 percent goes to Everlast's Arabian partner).

[d]Arabian pounds/U.S. dollars.

[e]All items except unit sales in thousands of Arabian pounds. Everlast's up-front cost is $7.5 million, and the estimated NPV and IRR are $945.8(000) and 18.4 percent, respectively.